Rethinking Ibn 'Arabi

RETHINKING IBN 'ARABI

GREGORY A. LIPTON

OXFORD
UNIVERSITY PRESS

OXFORD
UNIVERSITY PRESS

Oxford University Press is a department of the University of Oxford. It furthers the University's objective of excellence in research, scholarship, and education by publishing worldwide. Oxford is a registered trade mark of Oxford University Press in the UK and certain other countries.

Published in the United States of America by Oxford University Press
198 Madison Avenue, New York, NY 10016, United States of America.

CIP data is on file at the Library of Congress
ISBN 978-0-19-068450-1

1 3 5 7 9 8 6 4 2

Printed by Sheridan Books, Inc., United States of America

For Manzar

Contents

Acknowledgments ix

Prologue xi

Introduction: Ibn 'Arabi and the Cartography of Universalism 1

1. Tracking the Camels of Love 24

2. Return of the Solar King 55

3. Competing Fields of Universal Validity 84

4. Ibn 'Arabi and the Metaphysics of Race 120

Conclusion: Mapping Ibn 'Arabi at Zero Degrees 151

Notes 183

Index 269

Acknowledgments

THIS BOOK OWES its existence above all to my many mentors and teachers, whom I cannot thank enough or adequately. I must begin by expressing my gratitude to Carl Ernst, who served as my advisor throughout my graduate studies at the University of North Carolina at Chapel Hill. He has been my principal mentor in both the academic study of religion and Islamic studies; without his perceptive guidance, kind patience, and remarkable character, I could not have begun this work. Second, I must thank Omid Safi for his many years of generous support, laser-beam insight, and stunning example of walking with love in academia. Thank you as well to Tony Stewart, who tutored me in the nuances of theoretical writing as a beginning graduate student and has offered constant support ever since. I must also thank Juliane Hammer and Cemil Aydin, who, along with Professors Ernst, Safi, and Stewart, served on my dissertation committee at UNC and provided critical feedback while this book was still in its initial phases.

With respect to the study of Ibn 'Arabi in particular, which is what originally drove me to graduate school, I must first and foremost thank my longtime friend and mentor Bilal Hyde for introducing me to Ibn 'Arabi's thought more than twenty years ago. In the same breath, I must also extend special gratitude to my beloved friend and teacher Manzarul Islam, whose patient guidance over the past decade in both the study of Ibn 'Arabi and the Arabic language is a gift beyond price. My deep gratitude also goes to my dear friend and colleague Cyrus Zargar. In addition to his critical insight regarding my engagement with Ibn 'Arabi's thought in general, his more than generous help in reading through and commenting on the majority of the translations in this book has been invaluable. Here, I must also express my heartfelt gratitude to Gary Edwards and Adel Gamar for their many years of scholarly advice and encouragement.

Since I began work on this book, there have been many beloved colleagues who have read through chapters and given essential feedback. Peter Wright—my boon companion and intellectual confidant since the start of my graduate training—has over the years read various parts of this material and provided instrumental critique; his style of inquiry and philosophical approach to Islamic studies (and being human) have been formative to my own thinking and work. Ilyse Morgenstein Fuerst read the majority of the chapters of this book when it was in its initial stages and has provided an enormous amount of insightful advice; she is one of the wisest humans I know, and I am truly grateful to consider her a beloved sister, friend, and mentor.

I owe my wonderful colleagues at Macalester College special thanks for their generous help in the middle and final stages of this project. Brett Wilson, Erik Davis, Susanna Drake, William Hart, and Matthew Rahaim (at the University of Minnesota) all read chapters of this book and provided indispensable feedback as well as support. Here, I must also extend particular gratitude to my colleague Samuel Asarnow in the Department of Philosophy who has been a crucial, if often critical, conversation partner. He has taken valuable time to entertain my many philosophical queries, and my critique of Kant in the concluding chapter owes much to his close reading and subsequent challenges. Any philosophical infelicities found there, and throughout this book, remain my own.

Special thanks must also go to my primary mentor at Macalester, James Laine, who encouraged me to apply for the Berg Postdoctoral Faculty Fellowship, without which I would not have been able to have completed this project. I am therefore especially grateful to Charles and Kathleen Berg for the tremendous blessing of the Berg Fellowship, which provided the financial support needed to work on this book with a reduced teaching load while at Macalester from 2015 to 2017. I would also like to thank Gregory Alles who, as the managing editor at the journal *Numen*, shepherded to publication my article "De-Semitizing Ibn 'Arabī: Aryanism and the Schuonian Discourse of Religious Authenticity," in volume 64 in 2017 (pp. 258–93). I am grateful to Brill for their permission to republish parts of this article in the expanded essay that comprises chapter 4.

Finally, I turn to my family, and offer my deepest gratitude to my loving father, Jeffrey—the consummate *mensch*—whose unremitting support, encouragement, and optimism are worth a price far beyond rubies. Last, but certainly not least, I wish to thank my beloved wife Connie—without whose sanity, wisdom, humor, beauty, support, and self-sacrifice I could never have completed this book.

Prologue

> In time, those Unconscionable Maps no longer satisfied, and the Cartographers Guilds struck a Map of the Empire whose size was that of the Empire, and which coincided point for point with it. The following Generations, who were not so fond of the Study of Cartography as their Forebears had been, saw that that vast Map was Useless, and not without some Pitilessness was it, that they delivered it up to the Inclemencies of Sun and Winters. In the Deserts of the West, still today, there are Tattered Ruins of that Map.
>
> JORGE LUIS BORGES, "On Exactitude in Science."[1]

WHILE MY OSTENSIVE concern in this book is to analyze how particular ideas of the medieval Muslim mystic Ibn 'Arabi have been translated within a contemporary field of interpretation, the meta-subject that frames this analysis is the larger issue of religious universalism. And while my approach is necessarily critical, I am not overly concerned to weigh in on the ongoing debate regarding the ontology of religion itself—that is, whether or not religion *is* "of its own kind" (*sui generis*).[2] Yet, it seems fairly clear to me that the related, and likewise ongoing, scholarly struggle to find a universal definition of religion is well-nigh impossible. This is so, as Talal Asad has persuasively argued, "not only because its constituent elements and relationships are historically specific, but because that definition is itself the historical product of discursive processes."[3] For the methodological purposes of this study, I thus profess a type of philosophical quietism where my general aim, in Wittgensteinian fashion, is to take account of "language-games, describe them, *and sometimes wonder at them*."[4] In the following chapters, I therefore attempt to remain at the level of discourse by asking *how* those ideas and ideals we privilege *as* religious are conceived, received, and ultimately naturalized. More specifically, I seek to show how the speculative metaphysical ideas of Ibn 'Arabi have been read, appropriated, and universalized within the discursive context of Traditionalism or the Perennial Philosophy (*philosophia perennis*)[5] with a primary focus on the interpretive field of Perennialism associated with the *sui generis*, or "nonreductive," tradition of religious universalism connected to Frithjof Schuon.[6]

Thus, even though this book takes seriously claims of religious *terra firma*—that is, religion "as such"—its analytical concern revolves around the discursive "maps" that chart such claims. Of course, the metaphor of mapmaking in the field of religious studies is well worn, made famous many years ago by J. Z. Smith's seminal essay "Map Is Not Territory."[7] Smith's essay ends with his oft-quoted rejoinder to the mathematician Alfred Korzybski's famous dictum, "'Map is not territory'—*but maps are all we possess*."[8] Yet, Smith's cartographic metaphor is equally applicable to the religious practitioner in the so-called real world as it is for the scholar of religion in the academy. In performing what he calls a "deep"—and indeed "transgressive"[9]—reading of Smith's essay, Peter Wright has recently emphasized this essential point:

> The student of religions . . . is not all that different from the practitioner of a religion. The practices of reading and writing, interpretation and criticism—i.e., the practices that . . . constitute for Smith the study of religions as a humanistic adventure among texts—belong to the same family of activities that constitute ordinary religious practice. The scholar of religions and the adherent of a particular religious tradition are both engaged in a quest romance that produces a species of "cartography."[10]

Thus, while there may be what scholars like to think of as a "critical distance" between the academic discipline of religious studies and the object of their study—the religious themselves—it nevertheless appears to be a difference of degree rather than of kind.[11]

One of the ways that the differences among such maps have been categorized is by orders of abstraction away from the original "insider map of believers."[12] Yet, when dealing with contemporary scholars of religion who consider their own scholarship a vehicle for spiritual gnosis, as was famously the case with the comparativist Mircea Eliade, then any supposed distance between the academic study of religion and asserting religious truth rapidly vanishes into the thin air of theory itself.[13] As Steven Wasserstrom observes, "Eliade's Historian of Religions himself somehow recapitulated the paradigmatic experience of the traditional believer; only thus could he *see* the real forms, and therefore only in this way could then *show* them to the reader."[14] Similarly, in his introduction to *The Essential Writings of Frithjof Schuon*, religious studies scholar and Perennialist Seyyed Hossein Nasr claims that "ideally speaking, *only saintly men and women* possessing wisdom should and can engage in a serious manner in that enterprise which has come to be known as comparative religion."[15]

To be sure, the art of mapmaking is an elitist enterprise. As cosmographical projections, maps assert particular correspondences to reality, able to be read and followed by anyone with skill enough to do so. As such, all maps inevitably claim, to one degree or another, *the universal* through their ability to offer privileged access to truth. In its most unassuming form, such universalism is based on the assertion that territory can be abstracted outside of time and culture—a particular locality can be reified and placed within a less complicated dimension, represented by semiotic simplifications. The usefulness of cartography in the history of humanity is of course beyond question. The notion, however, that maps are reliable representations of reality is more complicated. Indeed, the full quote of Korzybski's popular maxim referred to above reads: "A map *is not* the territory it represents, but, if correct, it has a *similar structure* to the territory, which accounts for its usefulness."[16] One of the best ways of articulating the problematics underlying Korzybski's deceptively simple insight has been dubbed Bonini's paradox by William Starbuck: "As a model grows more realistic it also becomes just as difficult to understand as the real-world processes it represents."[17] This paradox has numerous ramifications in many fields, but for my purposes here it is useful to consider what it brings to bear on the concept of the universal. The closer we approach any notion of "reality," the more complex such ideas are, and increasingly less useful. The idea of the universal, like a map, is only of use when it simplifies reality; yet, when reality is simplified, there is always a choice involved—something *must always* be left out. Thus, the paradox of religious universalism is that all such discourse simultaneously reveals and conceals: the more it shines light upon a claimed universal perspective, the more it occludes others. As Milton Sernett observes:

> Perhaps psychohistorians will someday explain for us why the archives of the past overflow with examples of how religion has, on the one hand, served as a cross-cultural unifying principle while, on the other hand, it has been a means by which insiders define themselves over against outsiders.[18]

Even though universal perspectives are useful as models of unification, they are also necessarily divisive as discourses through which specific communities operating within particular times and places stake out their claims. In this sense, as Ernesto Laclau put it, "the universal is no more than a particular that has become dominant."[19] Yet, from a metaphysical perspective, the fact that universals are derived from so-called particulars does not necessarily diminish their universal status. In the case of universalizing religions such as Christianity or Islam, historical particulars constitute much of revelation itself. But to argue that such particulars can become universally applicable *is not necessarily* to argue that they transcend their particularity. Rather, part of the paradox of universalism is an inherent confusion between the universal and the particular, as Laclau observes: "Is it universal or particular? If the latter, universality can only be a particularity that defines itself in terms of a limitless exclusion; if the former, the particular itself becomes part of the universal, and the dividing line is again blurred."[20]

The concern that fuels the theoretical impetus behind this book thus focuses on universalist mapping practices that tend to lose sight of—or simply disregard—the inherent, dialectical tension between the universal and the particular as conceived within all religious discourse. As a pertinent example of this, and one that I revisit in chapter 4, the Perennialist scholar James Cutsinger recently asserted that to be objective, scholars of religious studies "must entertain the possibility" that Frithjof Schuon was able to directly access "the Truth—with that capital 'T'" in ways that are not explicable through "*sheerly natural causes or purely human phenomena.*"[21] Cutsinger goes on to make the even bolder claim (coming as it does from a professor in a religious studies department at a public research university) that such a gnostic "power of immediate or intuitive discernment [is] unobstructed by the boundaries of physical objects and *unaffected by the limitations of historical circumstance.*"[22] Taking Cutsinger's definition of gnostic power at face value,[23] it stands to reason that if "limitations of historical circumstance" could indeed be shown as constitutive for any given transcendent claim to universal knowledge, then such a claim would necessarily be called into question. Thus, setting aside the thorny question of ontology, and in response to Cutsinger, the contention that threads together the various arguments throughout this book is simply this: all universal claims *inevitably* carry the burden of their own socio-historical genealogies. That is to say, every map bears the situated perspective of its cartographer.

In regards to my personal cartographic perspective, one final note is in order. In terms of the field of Ibn 'Arabi studies, the insights contained in this book are critically indebted to two of the most formidable, contemporary scholars who write on Ibn 'Arabi in European languages: Michel Chodkiewicz and William Chittick. In the last several decades, their immeasurable contribution has enriched and transformed how Ibn 'Arabi is read and understood. Both scholars are at pains to articulate the importance of sacred law for Ibn 'Arabi—a point I revisit from different perspectives throughout this work. No doubt, they would also agree that Ibn 'Arabi's discourse would qualify as universalist in some fashion. Yet in terms of critically inspiring my particular theoretical interposition, Chodkiewicz has importantly, *albeit discretely*, brought to light the absolutist and exclusivist nature of Ibn 'Arabi's particular brand of universalism in opposition to

Chittick's more inclusivist interpretive framework. In the first half of this book, I spend significant time fleshing out this particular aspect of Chodkiewicz's wide-ranging insight, while critiquing the aspect of Chittick's work that has seemingly attempted to attenuate what I refer to as Ibn 'Arabi's political metaphysics and its embedded supersessionism. Yet, any critique of Chittick I proffer here must be understood as situated within a larger indebtedness owed to his prolific and careful expositions of the Andalusian Sufi's corpus. Without having encountered and benefited from Chittick's extraordinary erudition, I could never have begun my ongoing journey of understanding and appreciation of Ibn 'Arabi's work and thought. I thus offer the interventions of this book not in the spirit of opposition, but as additional vantage points to a necessary and ongoing conversation.

Introduction

IBN ʿARABI AND THE CARTOGRAPHY OF UNIVERSALISM

What we normally call universalism is a particularism thinking itself as universalism, and it is worthwhile doubting whether universalism could ever exist otherwise.

NAOKI SAKAI, "Modernity and Its Critique: The Problem of Universalism and Particularism."[1]

REVERED BY COUNTLESS followers and admirers spanning over seven centuries and nearly as many continents, the Andalusian Sufi Muḥyī al-Dīn Ibn al-ʿArabī (d. 1240), or more popularly Ibn ʿArabi, is commonly referred to as "the Greatest Master" (*al-shaykh al-akbar*)—or as Bulent Rauf, one of his most seminal New Age commentators, once called him: "the universal Doctor Maximus."[2] In the chapters that follow, I will show how Ibn ʿArabi imperially mapped the religious Other, while simultaneously exploring the ways in which his ideas have been mapped and universalized within the interpretative field of the prolific Swiss-German esotericist Frithjof Schuon (d. 1998). This book is thus an attempt to theorize Ibn ʿArabi's own conception of universalist metaphysics in juxtaposition to his contemporary universalist reception—a reception that I argue projects European concepts of religion upon the Andalusian Sufi's discourse in the guise of transhistorical and transcultural continuity. I hold such a theoretical lens essential in the study of Ibn ʿArabi, and Sufism more broadly, for without it scholars run the risk of unwittingly perpetuating and further naturalizing long-standing European orders of religious authenticity.[3] As such, I approach my subject first and foremost from the framework of religious studies, in the sense that I am preoccupied with how various discursive communities employ the protean and situated category of "religion."[4]

In this introduction, I broadly chart the theoretical and discursive waters through which this book attempts to navigate. Beginning with an overview of my analytical trajectory, I problematize the notion of the universal in both the discourse of Ibn 'Arabi and the interpretive field of contemporary Perennialism. In addition to establishing a framework for how Ibn 'Arabi's socio-political life-world can be read within an absolutist cosmology of a so-called perennial religion or *religio perennis*, I introduce the racio-spiritual grammar of Schuonian Perennialism and the orders of exclusion it harbors. I conclude with a chapter overview.

Mapping the Double Bind of Universality

In his groundbreaking work on European imperialism, *The Darker Side of the Renaissance*, Walter Mignolo asserts that "maps *are* and *are not* territory."[5] Here, Mignolo alludes to Alfred Korzybski's famous claim, which I have already referred to in the prologue—that is, "a map *is not* the territory it represents."[6] Yet, Mignolo goes on to argue that nevertheless, maps *are* territory "because, once they are accepted, they become a powerful tool for controlling territories, colonizing the mind and imposing themselves on the members of the community using the map as the real territory."[7] Here, Mignolo echoes Jean Baudrillard's assertion that today it is the map "that engenders the territory."[8] It is through careful attention to this dual sense of cartography, and the controlling power of its universal pretensions, that I approach the subject matter of this book.

Within the contemporary study of religion, the term "universalism" presents a double bind, since it is used to represent both exclusivist and inclusivist perspectives. Premodern proselytizing religious traditions—what the nineteenth-century French scholar of religion Léon Marillier aptly dubbed "universalizing religions"[9]—were framed within supersessionist doctrines of *universal* validity. Based on the original Latin *universus*, "all together, all taken collectively, whole, entire,"[10] the term "universalism" as applied to such religions refers to how their truth claims are interpreted from within as valid for all people and all times.[11] Yet the term "universalism" is also commonly employed to articulate a meaning that focuses on the essential unity of various religions as a *plurality* rather than on the universal nature of one particular tradition. This usage denotes various types of inclusivist and pluralist perspectives that recognize broader sets of valid doctrines or religious formations, typically understood as united within an underlying or transcendent universal truth or *ur-religion*—what Schuon has defined as "the underlying universality in every great spiritual patrimony of humanity, or what may be called the *religio perennis*; this is the religion to which the sages adhere, one which is always and necessarily founded upon formal elements of divine institution."[12]

Yet, a closer look at such apparently tolerant, pluralistic modalities of universalism in comparison with the seemingly coercive triumphalism of their proselytizing cousins reveals a disturbing paradox. Because maps purport intelligibility no matter who reads them or from what perspective, every map inherently claims an inclusive, universal validity. But like all ontological truth claims, maps can only offer a simplified perspective—a perspective that is, in keeping with the traditional metaphor, only two-dimensional. This two-dimensionality is thus an imposition upon the reader that reduces him or her to its flattened horizon. Such a coercive flattening can be likened to the anxiety articulated by the philosophy of Emmanuel Levinas in the face of the horrors of the Shoah as "the tyranny of the universal and of the impersonal," where the "irreducible singularity" of the individual is threatened by theorizations of ontic totality.[13] Here, Levinas pushes back against the political ramifications of Western metaphysics as traditionally plotted at the cost of the Other subsumed within an egoistic whole—what Levinas similarly refers to as the "imperialism of the same."[14] In such an endeavor, ontology can be likened to an enchanted looking glass of great power within which situated ideals of the self are perceived at the level of a transcendence that claims to encompass the Other.[15] In other words, every recourse to universalism, whether inclusive or exclusive, is an imposition of a particular homogenous perspective—a sameness ultimately based on exclusion. As the sociologist Ulrich Beck observes:

> In any form of universalism, all forms of human life are located within a single order of civilization, with the result that cultural differences are either transcended or excluded. In this sense, the project is hegemonic: the other's voice is permitted entry only as the voice of sameness, as a confirmation of oneself, contemplation of oneself, dialogue with oneself.[16]

While premodern forms of universal religious discourse—such as the medieval supersessionism of Christianity and Islam—are seemingly self-aware of their own hegemonic exclusivism, it is only in modernity where discourses of religious universalism claim to variously include all worldviews equally. Yet, just below the surface of modern universalist schemes of religious inclusivism lie orders of exclusivism that are seldom acknowledged, since any such acknowledgment would throw into question their entire raison d'être. From this perspective, cosmological maps should be understood as hegemonic projections of absolute knowledge. Indeed, the core argument of this book is that all modalities of universalism—both premodern, overtly imperial forms and modern, ostensibly tolerant forms—are particular instantiations of power. Thus, "the moment you embrace universality and the idea of truth *you are entangled in a struggle* with the partisans of particularity and of alternative versions of universal truth."[17]

While I read the cosmological maps of Ibn 'Arabi as naturally inscribed by medieval Islamic imperialism, I locate Schuonian Perennialism as similarly inscribed by European imperialism and its attendant colonization of knowledge under the auspices of a civilizing mission. In the conceptual spaces constructed within both of these mapping strategies, in the words of Mignolo, "a universal knowing subject is presupposed."[18] Moreover, there is a correspondence between universal knowledge and an assumed (in Ibn 'Arabi's case) or unspoken (in Schuon's) cache of power. How cosmic space is mapped in each of these two discursive regimes has a direct bearing on how religion itself is imagined. Yet with all of their obvious differences, their maps yield surprisingly similar enunciations of universal validity founded on premises of specific localities.

Charting the Discursive Trajectory

Echoing self-critical discussions in the field of religious studies that began over fifty years ago,[19] Tomoko Masuzawa observes that "the idea of the fundamental unity of religions—or what may be reasonably termed liberal universalism—has been in evidence in much of the comparative enterprise since the nineteenth century."[20] Yet, Masuzawa submits that "many of today's scholars would likely contest, rather than accept, this presumption that the unity of 'religious experience' should be the basis of religion as an academic discipline."[21] While such a position may be less common in religious studies today, it still plays a critical role in the academic study of Islamic mysticism, or Sufism, with scholars who are sympathetic to the particular philosophical and theological orientation of Perennialism.[22] Indeed, Seyyed Hossein Nasr has described Schuon as a "master of the discipline of comparative religion," asserting that "from the point of view of sheer scholarly knowledge combined with metaphysical penetrations, *it is hardly possible to find a contemporary corpus of writings with the same all-embracing and comprehensive nature combined with incredible depth*."[23] Although Schuon's large corpus of over thirty works remains relatively obscure, his philosophical framework commands one of the most dominant knowledge regimes in the contemporary "Western"[24] reception of Ibn 'Arabi. Indeed, James Morris, a leading expert on Ibn 'Arabi, has acknowledged Schuon's ubiquitous influence in interpreting and transmitting Ibn 'Arabi's thought to "academic specialists in the spiritual dimensions of religious studies."[25]

Ibn 'Arabi's monistic-leaning mysticism has a long-standing and popular correlation with the Islamic metaphysical axiom known as "the Unity of Being" (*waḥdat al-wujūd*). Although this particular terminology was never explicitly used by Ibn 'Arabi himself, it has indeed come to emblematically represent his unitive metaphysics that professes God as the ontological reality of all things.[26]

Through his correlation with the doctrine of the Unity of Being, Ibn 'Arabi is often associated in the West with Schuon's thought and his ostensibly similar concept of "the Transcendent Unity of Religions"—the title of his first major work.[27] In the second half of the twentieth century, Schuon not only served as the leader of the first organized traditionalist European Sufi order (*ṭarīqa*)[28] but also, upon the death of the French Traditionalist René Guénon in 1951, became the foremost proponent of the Perennial Philosophy.[29] *The Transcendent Unity of Religions* (*De l'Unité transcendante des Religions*, 1948) argues that a transhistorical religious essence unifies all religious traditions beyond the limits of exoteric absolutism, thus embracing all normative religious traditions as universally valid means to the divine. According to Perennialist thought, such religious universalism forms the basis of the most ancient wisdom and is the sacred inheritance of all great mystics from every religious tradition.

Indeed, Ibn 'Arabi himself is often alleged to have been a proto-Perennialist. For example, the Perennialist author and Schuonian William Stoddart has remarked that Ibn 'Arabi should be acknowledged as one of the main "forerunners of the perennial philosophy in the East" since he "explained with particular cogency how an 'essence' of necessity had many 'forms.' "[30] Stoddart's statement appears to be an allusion to Ibn 'Arabi's famous verses from his collection of poems, *The Interpreter of Desires* (*Tarjumān al-ashwāq*)—which I discuss in detail in chapter 1—that claim a heart "capable of every form" and profess "the religion of Love." Indeed, Schuon himself repeatedly mentions in his own writings these same lines of Ibn 'Arabi to help exposit the *religio perennis* as the underlying truth of all religions. In one such passage, he states:

> The *religio perennis* is fundamentally this: the Real entered into the illusory so that the illusory might be able to return into the Real. It is this mystery, together with the metaphysical discernment and contemplative concentration that are its complement, which alone is important in an absolute sense from the point of view of *gnosis*; for the gnostic—in the etymological and rightful sense of that word—there is in the last analysis no other "religion." It is what Ibn Arabi called the "religion of Love."[31]

As I will discuss momentarily, although Ibn 'Arabi's *ultimate* soteriological vision is famously informed by a radical hermeneutic of mercy acknowledging that even those in eternal damnation will eventually find contentment and bliss, throughout this book I demonstrate how close readings of his positions on the religious Other reveal a traditionally derived supersessionism based on the exclusive superiority of Islam and its abrogation of all previous religious dispensations. In direct opposition to prominent universalist and Perennialist readings, I throw into relief how Ibn ʿArabi's understanding of the religious Other is founded on a political metaphysics in which the Prophet Muhammad, and thus the religion of Islam, not only triumphs over but also *ultimately subsumes* all previous religions and their laws. While it is certainly true that Ibn ʿArabi's "theomonism"[32] is submersed within a unitive mysticism of love—a mysticism often taken in the West to be opposed to religious exclusivism—I argue that intertwined with this unitive love is a universal political metaphysics that discursively absorbs all religio-political competition.

Perennialism, Ibn ʿArabi, and the Universal

The idea of the universal has been directly associated with Perennialism since its early formation. While Guénon never used the term "perennial philosophy" (*philosophia perennis*) itself, preferring instead "the primordial tradition,"[33] the eminent historian and seminal Perennialist author Ananda K. Coomaraswamy did use it but with the additional term "universal"—that is, "*Philosophia Perennis et Universalis*"—noting that along with the idea of a perennial philosophy, "*Universalis* must be understood, for this 'philosophy' has been the common inheritance of all mankind without exception."[34] Moreover, in its direct connection with Perennialism, the idea of the universal is often imbricated with the thought of Ibn ʿArabi. For example, in his 1972 essay, "Islam and the Encounter of Religions," Nasr connects Ibn ʿArabi's aforementioned verses from *The Interpreter of Desires* with Schuonian Perennialism and the notion of the transcendent unity of religions. Not only is the Sufi "one who seeks to transcend the world of forms, to journey from multiplicity to Unity, from the particular *to the Universal*," but also Sufism itself "is *the most universal affirmation of that perennial wisdom* which stands at the heart of Islam and in fact of all religion as such."[35] Nasr goes on to state that "it is this supreme doctrine of Unity . . . to which Ibn ʿArabî refers in his well-known verses in the *Tarjumân al-ashwâq*. . . . It is a transcendent knowledge that reveals the inner unity of religions."[36] In his work *The Other in the Light of the One: The Universality of the Qur'ān and Interfaith Dialogue*, the Perennialist scholar Reza Shah-Kazemi similarly identifies his approach as both Schuonian[37] and "universalist,"[38] directly connecting it with Ibn ʿArabi and his doctrine of the "universal capacity of the heart," thus also referring to Ibn ʿArabi's famous lines from *The Interpreter*.[39]

Yet, here it is important to contextualize the often confusing, and confused, idea of the universal in relation to Ibn ʿArabi's metaphysics. In *Islam and the Fate of Others*, Mohammad Khalil categorizes Islamic universalism in a soteriological sense in relation to its supposed binary opposite of "damnationism." Here, these terms are used in the specific context of discourses having to do with the duration of Hell: universalists hold that all people will be granted eternal Paradise, while damnationists maintain that some will have to endure the Fire eternally. To complicate things even more, the category of universalism, for Khalil, includes the subgroups quasi- and ultimate universalism.[40] Somewhat ironically, Khalil is forced to classify Ibn ʿArabi as only a "quasi-universalist" since, according to Ibn ʿArabi's rather unique mixture of literalism and a hermeneutics of mercy, there will be people who will remain in Hell forever even though their punishment will cease and it will become blissful for them. As Khalil notes, the entire concept of "chastisement" for Ibn ʿArabi is "therapeutic"—that is, "it rectifies" because it is issued from God through the ruling property of divine mercy.[41] Thus, in one of his more well-known hermeneutical inversions, Ibn ʿArabi takes the rectification of divine chastisement to its logical conclusion where he claims that the punishment (*ʿadhāb*) of Hell ultimately transforms into a blissful "sweetness" (*ʿudhūba*) for its denizens.[42]

In addition to his binary universalism/damnationism, Khalil still further divides Muslim theological discourses into the now-standard threefold typology of inclusivism, exclusivism, and pluralism.[43] However, in Khalil's treatment he includes the additional subgroups of limited and liberal inclusivism.[44] Indeed, Khalil's proliferation of categories and final classification of Ibn ʿArabi as a "liberal inclusivist" over that of a pluralist—in addition to a quasi-universalist—quickly reaches a point of diminishing returns where such categories grouped together seem too complex to be overly useful.[45]

Yet, more important for the present discussion, Khalil jettisons the usual inclusion of truth claims within the standard threefold model mentioned above and situates his classifications from within a strictly soteriological basis.[46] As such, Khalil asserts that Ibn ʿArabi

> affirms the salvation of "sincere" non-Muslims, because of his belief that every single path we take is not only created by but leads to God—a God of mercy (*raḥma*) and nobility (*karam)*—he maintains that *all* of humanity, including even the most wicked, will ultimately arrive at bliss.[47]

Because his ultimate soteriology is informed by such a radical hermeneutic of mercy, Ibn ʿArabi holds that even those in eternal damnation will eventually experience eternal bliss. Yet, because Khalil does not address Ibn ʿArabi's views on the epistemological validity of other scriptural truth claims, the implications regarding a severe punishment for those in Hell during the interim period remain unarticulated.

Indeed, it is a popular contention, commonly encountered in Perennialist discourse, that Ibn ʿArabi's oft-mentioned notion of "the divinity of beliefs" (*al-ilāh fī al-iʿtiqādāt*)[48] is simply a doctrine on the universal divinity of religions or Schuon's transcendent unity of religions.[49] Yet, as I set forth in chapter 1, such assertions evince a reading of Ibn ʿArabi at once colored by contemporary universalist axioms and anachronistically embedded within the ubiquitous modern understanding of religions as "systems of belief." Even though Ibn ʿArabi held that every human being is engaged in worship—since the very essence of creation is precisely that—he asserted that "the one who associates partners with God" (*al-mushrik*) is "wretched" (*shaqī*) since he or she has discourteously gone against revelation.[50] And as I point out throughout the coming chapters of this book, there are multiple places where Ibn ʿArabi castigates the Jews and the Christians for their supposed blasphemy and unbelief.[51]

Khalil himself concedes that for Ibn ʿArabi, "although all will eventually attain felicity as they proceed toward God, the righteous will be spared the 'deserts, perils, vicious predators, and harmful serpents' found along the way."[52] Here Khalil quotes a larger discussion from Chittick (who, as I discuss in chapter 3, also writes within the Schuonian interpretative field) recounting Ibn ʿArabi's concept that all paths lead back to God. Chittick relates that for Ibn ʿArabi, perfect saints understand with the "eye of the heart" that all things, good and evil, exist through God's will and His "creative command" (*al-amr al-takwīnī*). However, Chittick immediately qualifies this statement by asserting the dialectical necessity of God's "prescriptive command" (*al-amr al-taklīfī*) in Ibn ʿArabi's thought, which is the origin of revealed law. Here, Chittick notes:

> In no way does their acceptance of all beliefs negate their acknowledgement that everyone is called to follow the prescriptive command, which sets down the immediate path to felicity. This is why Ibn al-ʿArabī writes, "It is incumbent upon you to practice the worship of God brought by the Shariah and tradition [*al-samʿ*]." He explains that the person who sees things as they truly are "travels on the path of felicity that is not preceded by any wretchedness, for this path is easy, bright, exemplary, pure, unstained, and without any crookedness or deviation. As for the other path, its final outcome is felicity, but along the way are found deserts, perils, vicious predators, and harmful serpents. *Hence no created thing reaches the end of this second path without suffering those terrors.*"[53]

Because Ibn ʿArabi holds "wrath" as an eternal divine attribute, its consequence of "chastisement" is *also* considered by him to be an eternal attribute.[54] It is therefore important to note that while Ibn ʿArabi held that "every single path we take is not only created by but leads to God," as Khalil does above, he *also* believed that the interim between any path and its destination of felicity is filled with either divine reward or chastisement. And as Chittick himself stresses in the passage above, the criteria that Ibn 'Arabi used for distinguishing between them was based on revealed law—that is, the sharia.

All of this is to say that even careful treatments of Ibn 'Arabi's thought can fail to distinguish between his clear notion of ultimate, universal salvation and the interim implications of his supersessionism.[55] As I argue in chapter 2 against the majority of Perennialist interpretations, including that of Chittick, Ibn 'Arabi is a staunch supersessionist, claiming that "the abrogation (*naskh*) of all of the (previously) revealed laws (*jamīʿ al-sharāʾiʿ*) by Muhammad's revealed law (*sharīʿa*)" is divinely decreed.[56] Although the sharia of Muhammad does permit the People of the Book to continue to follow their revealed laws, according to Ibn 'Arabi, it does so only if their adherents submit to the Qur'anic injunction of verse 9:29 and pay the "indemnity tax" (*jizya*) "*in a state of humiliation.*"[57] As I further show in chapter 3, Ibn 'Arabi clearly holds that the People of the Book are also guilty of "corruption of the text" (*taḥrīf al-naṣṣ*), having changed the actual words of their once-pure revelation. Thus, in sharp contrast to the Perennialist notion of the "universal validity" of religions, here the spiritual efficacy of Judaism and Christianity appears to be determined by *obedience* to the revelation of Muhammad rather than any particular validity that Ibn 'Arabi grants to the Torah or Gospel. While it may be initially comforting to hear that according to Ibn 'Arabi all Christians or Jews will ultimately be "saved," the implied potential for an untold number to suffer a prolonged period of "therapeutic" purification in Hell for following corrupted scriptures or abrogated dispensations without the salvific remuneration of an indemnity tax would seem to warrant pause for those who claim, like Sayafaatun Almirzanah, that Ibn 'Arabi's metaphysical approach "is very essential in enhancing interfaith dialogue and acceptance of different religious perspectives."[58]

Although exclusivist notions of religious supersessionism and socio-political authority in Ibn 'Arabi's thought remain largely unacknowledged or regularly relegated as accidental to his core metaphysics, his metaphysical cosmography was clearly formed within the medieval crucible of religious rivalry and absolutism. Thus, following Hugh Nicholson's recent disavowal of "*a nonrelational and nonpolitical core of religious experience*,"[59] I argue that the wider religio-political absolutism of Ibn 'Arabi's socio-historical location cannot be dissociated from his own metaphysical anthropology, cosmology, and cosmography. Ibn 'Arabi's monistic discourse purposefully blurs the dialectical boundaries between the human and the divine, thus marking modern attempts to decisively separate his mystical truth from his socio-political context as more reflective of longstanding

Euro-American discourses on religious authenticity than Ibn ʿArabi's own historically situated political metaphysics.

Mapping Ibn ʿArabi and the Political

Details of Ibn ʿArabi's life are strewn throughout the core texts of his vast corpus (currently estimated to comprise over 300 works of greatly differing lengths[60]). Gathered together, these details can be read as adumbrating something of an autohagiography.[61] Rather than rehash all of its contours, here I will briefly rehearse some of its more essential features and then discuss how they have been variously configured in contemporary universalist retellings.

Born in Murcia, Spain, in 1165 CE, Ibn ʿArabi's father most likely served its independent emir, Ibn Mardanīsh (r. 1147–1172), in some soldierly capacity. When Murcia fell in 1172 to the Almohads, Ibn ʿArabi's father moved his family to Seville, the provincial capital of the Almohad caliphate, where he pledged his allegiance and military service to the caliph Abū Yaʿqūb Yūsuf (r. 1163–1184). Coming from a military family, Ibn ʿArabi was himself trained as a soldier and was a member of the caliphal army.[62] When he was around fourteen or fifteen years old, he apparently experienced a formative spiritual awakening that would set the stage for a life filled with recurrent visions and claims of attaining the highest station of sainthood.[63] Soon after, he took up learning the traditional religious disciplines and devoted himself especially to the study of the Qur'an and hadith.[64] When he was nineteen years old, he definitively left the army, his wealth, and his intimate friends, dedicating his life to the mystical path.[65] It was during this time that he sat with and befriended mystics throughout Andalusia and Northwest Africa, whose stories he recorded in various places, but most famously in his hagiographical work *The Spirit of Holiness in the Counseling of the Soul* (*Rūḥ al-quds fī munāṣaḥat al-nafs*).

In the face of the steady progress made by Christian armies in the Iberian Peninsula and believing he had learned all he could from his teachers in the Islamic West, Ibn ʿArabi left Andalusia for good around the year 1200. This began a period of not only extensive traveling but also a prolific outpouring of writing, including his multivolume opus *The Meccan Openings* (*al-Futūḥāt al-makkiyya*), which he began in 1202—after encountering a theophanic youth (*fatā*) on the Hajj—and did not complete until 1238.[66] Besides Mecca, his eastward travels led him to Egypt, Palestine, Syria, Iraq, and Anatolia, where he spent various amounts of time and established several important relationships with powerful rulers. The most famous of these relationships, as I discuss in chapter 2, was his friendship with the Seljuk Sultan of Anatolia, ʿIzz al-Dīn Kaykāʾus I (r. 1211–1220), whom he advised to impose discriminatory regulations upon his "protected" (*dhimmī*) Christian subjects. In 1223, Ibn 'Arabi permanently settled in Damascus with the support and protection of the Banū Zakī, a prominent Damascene family of ulama.[67] There he spent the remaining seventeen years of his life transmitting his teachings to a small circle of intimate disciples and finishing his by now immense written corpus, including *The Ring Stones of Wisdom* (*Fuṣūṣ al-ḥikam*),[68] his *summa metaphysica*.[69]

Although the ostensible purpose for historical narratives, and especially biographies, is to accurately reproduce events they report, they too are maps. Such narratives offer, as Hayden White observes, "*a complex of symbols* which gives us directions for finding an *icon* of the structure of those events in our literary tradition."[70] Indeed, in Euro-American accounts, Ibn 'Arabi's life story has taken on the classical and Romantic mythos of an epic quest for illumination, more specifically, the journey "from the Occident to the Orient."[71] In his discussion of Ibn Sīnā's (d. 1037) famous "visionary recitals," Nasr notes that

> the Orient, being the place of the rising Sun, symbolizes the domain of pure forms, which is the domain of light, while the Occident, where the Sun sets, corresponds to the darkness of matter. . . . The gnostic's journey takes him from matter to pure form, from the Occident of darkness to the Orient of light.[72]

In a parallel construction, the distinguished Sorbonne Orientalist and esotericist Henry Corbin (d. 1978) imagined Ibn 'Arabi as a "pilgrim to the Orient," claiming that his turn eastward was an enlightened departure from a moribund Western legalism to an Oriental realm of spiritual enchantment. In Corbin's mapping of Ibn 'Arabi's heroic journey, the Andalusian Sufi leaves behind his "earthly homeland" in the Arab Occident and emerges in the Persian Orient as the spiritual equal of the celebrated Persian poet Jalāl al-Dīn Rūmī (d. 1273).[73] In so doing, according to Corbin, Ibn 'Arabi "attained to the esoteric Truth" and passed "*through and beyond the darkness of the Law and of the exoteric religion*."[74] Like Orientalist conceits about Rumi, Corbin held that Ibn 'Arabi eventually liberated himself from the restrictive and dogmatic shackles of exoteric Islam. Such assertions, similar to Schuon's own discursive practices, echo nineteenth-century European ideals of religious authenticity marked by a long-standing anti-Judaic tradition deprecating "legalism."[75]

While framing Ibn 'Arabi's life story as an epic quest for illumination in the Orient is perhaps the most common topos in his contemporary Euro-American reception, it is not the only one. For example, in *The Other Islam: Sufism and the Road to Global Harmony*, Stephen Schwartz takes an analogously Eurocentric, yet almost opposite approach. Here, Schwartz claims that it was Ibn 'Arabi's so-called Spanish Sufism itself that "inaugurated a truly European Islam, providing a model for moderate Muslims living in Christian Europe in the twenty-first century."[76] As such, Schwartz uncritically adopts a position that understands Sufism as an Islamic appropriation of Christian mystical and monastic traditions of a supposed European West.[77] Indeed, he refers to this "view of the historical relations between Islam and the West" as "a secret history of the interreligious linkage of Europe and Asia in the past thousand years."[78] The fruits of such a hidden past, according to Schwartz, have given rise to Sufism as an "alternative" to "the stagnation imposed in Islam today by radical ideology"—an alternative that reveals "tendencies toward an exalted spirituality, love of Jesus, and resistance to *Shariah*-centered literalism."[79]

Even though more nuanced than the two extremes of Corbin and Schwartz, Claude Addas—Ibn 'Arabi's most erudite contemporary biographer—also configures the topos of a journey to the Orient in a narrative that attempts to dissociate Ibn 'Arabi's original metaphysical purity from his own locality and later political engagement. Here, Addas claims that Ibn 'Arabi's Western abode afforded him a sanctified space "*resolutely aloof from political life*," while his Meccan investiture as "the Seal of the Saints" (*khātam al-awliyāʾ*), which I discuss more below, required that he enter the political sphere in "the role of 'advisor to princes' . . . among the Ayyūbids and the Seljuks."[80] Even so, Addas insists that Ibn 'Arabi still managed to ultimately distance himself from the politics of his day since such "circumstantial issues" had really nothing to do with his spiritual mission.[81]

Although all of the above narrative configurations are marked by different ways of interpreting Ibn 'Arabi's midlife sojourn eastward, they are at base universalist maps that attempt to show, in one way or another, the purity of Ibn 'Arabi's metaphysics as distinct from the corruptive particularism of time and place. In this book, I argue that such maps form part of a larger metaphysical tradition of cartography transmitted through a specific European intellectual and religious history. Indeed, since the theoretical intervention of the controversial German philosopher Carl Schmitt, the "depoliticization" of religious discourse in the modern West has become increasingly acknowledged and thus theorized in the field of religious studies. In his 1927 work, *The Concept of the Political*, Schmitt situates the modern privatization of religion as originating in the European reaction to the religious disputes of the sixteenth century when "theology, the former central domain, was abandoned because it was controversial, in favor of another—neutral—domain."[82] Schmitt therefore laments that "concepts elaborated over many centuries of theological reflection now became uninteresting and merely private matters."[83] Thus, as Grace Jantzen more recently observes, the Enlightenment impetus to quarantine religion (and its attendant threat of violence) to individual belief has played a central role in the modern Western concept of authentic religious experience

> as essentially a private, inner state, having nothing to do with outer, public realities. It was, instead, a strictly personal matter. It could, however, be cultivated; and could produce states of calm and tranquility which would enable return to those public realities with less anxiety and inner turmoil. Understood in these terms, *mysticism becomes domesticated, is rendered unthreatening to the public political realm.*[84]

Thus, the metaphysical category of mysticism as the universal core of exoteric religion emerges in secular modernity as a discursive site carrying with it an aura of authentic religiosity that is often called upon as a refuge from politics and the discord of religious rivalry and absolutism. Indeed, it is precisely the anachronistic imposition of the modern notion of "universality" upon Ibn 'Arabi that *depoliticizes* his discourse, thereby subtly associating his inward mystical quest with the transcendence of outward religious difference. For example, in a 1963 essay, the distinguished Islamicist and comparativist Wilfred Cantwell Smith situates Ibn 'Arabi's metaphysics (i.e., *waḥdat al-wujūd*) within a "universalist Ṣūfi interpretation of the Islamic order" in decided opposition to the "closed-system" of communal and "formalist" Islam.[85] Here, Smith depoliticizes Ibn 'Arabi's "metaphysical monism" by universalizing it, stating that "to believe in the ultimate unity of the world and the universe is to believe also in the unity of humankind."[86] Thus, according to Smith, any type of metaphysics that acknowledges a divine unity must also acknowledge the unity of all religions. In this book, I wish to unsettle such attempts to dissociate Ibn 'Arabi's unitive mysticism from what might be called his "political theology"[87]—a theology, I argue, that is constituted more by religious difference than by unity and forms an essential part of his own universalist tradition of metaphysical mapping.

The Perennial Religion in the Hierarchical Universe of Ibn 'Arabi

In the thirteenth-century Muslim world of cartography, the geographic system of Ptolemy was used to help place the Arabs within a universal context. In such maps, "the center of space and memory is the Arabic world."[88] Like their Christian counterparts in Europe who did not even acknowledge the Islamic world in their ethnocentric maps, Muslim cartographers like Muḥammad al-Idrīsī (d. 1166) similarly ignored the existence of Europe.[89] Just as medieval Muslim geography "took as its basic unit the Islamic Empire, the *Dar al-Islam*,"[90] so too did Muslim theo-cosmology. "The original Muslim universalizing impulse," as Amira Bennison notes, "rested on the idea, shared with Christianity, that the faith would ideally become the sole religion of mankind."[91]

Muslim universalism thus went hand in hand with the classical idea of the caliph, who "presided over a religion which was presented as the consummation of all previous divine revelation."[92] Indeed, as Peter Fibiger Bang observes, "At the heart of the notion of universal empire is a hierarchical conception of rulers and statehood."[93] And while Sufism is often imagined in the contemporary West as based on a type of inward "spirituality" that transcends all social and political divisions, medieval Sufism was in fact suffused with this type of imperial hierarchy. As Margaret Malamud notes:

> The [Sufi] model of dominance and submission that structured relations between masters and disciples replicated the way in which power was constructed and dispersed in medieval Islamic societies: namely, through multiple dyadic and hierarchical relationships of authority and dependence that were continuously dissolved and reformed. This pervasive pattern was operative in the spiritual, the political, and the familial realms.[94]

Malamud thus asserts that medieval Sufi discourse and practice affirmed and consecrated "hierarchy and inequality in the mundane world by connecting them to the divine will and order."[95] Yet, such hierarchical models within Sufism also played a critical role in the social cohesion of medieval Muslim societies, which "came to rely on authoritarian relationships grounded in esoteric doctrines to discipline and control the desires of its subjects."[96]

Though Ibn 'Arabi's thought was thoroughly inscribed by an Islamic imperial cosmology, his metaphysical vision did not simply promote the restoration of the original caliphal hierarchy. More radically, he envisioned himself as standing in for it altogether. As Marshall Hodgson perspicaciously observed, Ibn 'Arabi's own conception of spiritual hierarchy and the idea of a cosmic axial saint filled the political gap left by the disintegration of caliphal power beginning in the tenth century: "There might no longer be a caliph with power in the ordinary political sense. But there remained a true spiritual caliph, the immediate representative of God, who bore a far more basic sway than any outward caliph."[97]

Indeed, after claiming to attain to the Muhammadan Station and thereby inheriting "the comprehensiveness of Muhammad (*jam'iat muḥammad*),"[98] Ibn 'Arabi located his cosmic function at the very apex of the earthly hierarchy of saints: the Seal of the Saints, or more specifically, the Seal of Muhammadan

Sainthood (*khātam al-walāya al-muḥammadiyya*)—the historical manifestation of the Muhammadan Reality (*ḥaqīqa muḥammadiyya*) and thus the source of sainthood itself.[99] As I point out throughout the following chapters, although Ibn 'Arabi makes such extraordinary assertions regarding his own spiritual rank, his entire cartographic cosmology is nevertheless based on the hierarchical superiority of Muhammad as both "spiritual" exemplar *and* "prophetic" lawgiver. In a famous passage in *The Ring Stones of Wisdom*, Ibn 'Arabi compares himself as the Seal of the Saints to Muhammad as the Seal of the Prophets (*khātam al-nabiyyīn*), but qualifies this rather audacious correlation by asserting that his "inherited" perfection is only a single dimension of the comprehensive perfection of Muhammad.[100] In other words, Ibn 'Arabi continuously situates his own claims to spiritual perfection within the larger cosmology of the Prophet, who, regardless of anyone else's spiritual rank, remains God's ultimate caliph or "vicegerent" (*khalīfa*). Thus, Ibn 'Arabi never tires of asserting in various ways the primordial nature of Muhammad, who was given the station of "lordship (*siyāda*) . . . when Adam was between water and clay."[101] Indeed, according to Ibn 'Arabi, Muhammad was the very source of "spiritual support (*al-mumidd*) for every Perfect Human Being (*insān kāmil*)," beginning with Adam through "a continuous succession of vicegerents" until Muhammad's physical birth.[102]

If, then, we permit ourselves to speak of a so-called perennial religion or *religio perennis* according to Ibn 'Arabi, we can only do so within the hierarchical confines of his all-encompassing Muhammadan prophetology, where Muhammad—and the attendant idea of the *primordial* Muhammadan Reality—is projected as the alpha and omega of all historical prophets and their revealed laws. For example, in *The Meccan Openings*, Ibn 'Arabi discusses "the Religion" (*al-dīn*) in terms of the Qur'anic idea of the primordial "religion (*milla*) of Abraham":

> Consider God's statement "*follow the religion of Abraham*" [Qur'an 4:125],[103] which is the Religion (*al-dīn*). Here, Muhammad was commanded to follow the Religion, because the Religion is from God and no one else. Consider further Muhammad's statement, peace be upon him: "If Moses were alive it would be impossible for him not to follow me."[104] Here, following is attributed to Muhammad. Thus he, may God bless him and grant him peace, was commanded to follow the Religion and the guidance of the prophets, but not to follow them. For if the supreme leader (*al-imām al-a'ẓam*) is present, then no judicial authority (*ḥukm*) remains for any of his deputies except his authority. Only when he is absent do his deputies rule by his injunctions (*bi marāsimihi*). So, Muhammad is the ruler (*al-ḥākim*), both unseen (*ghayb*) and visible (*shahāda*).[105]

In this passage, Ibn 'Arabi begins by drawing on the robust Qur'anic notion of Abraham as a primordial monotheist (*ḥanīf*) who has come to the realization of God through contemplation of nature.[106] Yet, the very Qur'anic idea of "the religion of Abraham" is in itself adversarial, since the Qur'an stresses that Abraham was neither Jew, Christian, nor polytheist (*mushrik*).[107] As Uri Rubin notes, implicit in such Qur'anic usage "is the notion that polytheists as well as Jews and Christians have distorted the natural religion of God, which only Islam preserves."[108] As such, the Qur'anic notion of Abraham's primordial monotheism "retains this polemical context and is used to bring out the particularistic aspect of Islam as a religion set apart from Judaism and Christianity."[109]

In a sense that evokes the polemical Qur'anic notion of Abraham's pure monotheism—and in opposition to Perennialist convention—Michel Chodkiewicz has used the term *religio perennis* to describe Ibn 'Arabi's hierarchical notion of the successive manifestation of the Muhammadan Reality "from Adam to Muhammad."[110] According to Chodkiewicz, in Ibn 'Arabi's teleological map of cosmic history, "the *religio perennis* is periodically both restored and confirmed," and its "perfect and definitive expression" is the sharia of Muhammad, which "when it finally appears, *abrogates all earlier laws*."[111] As Chodkiewicz continues to note, and as I discuss in detail in chapters 2 and 3, the abrogation of the previous revelations by the Qur'an is qualified in Ibn 'Arabi's discourse by the aforementioned fact that the People of the Book who pay the indemnity tax (*jizya*)—and thus submit to the injunction of Qur'an 9:29—are subsumed within the prophetic hierarchy of Muhammad.[112]

Rather than the Perennialist universalist vision that all so-called orthodox religions are equally capable of guiding humanity because of an underlying perennial religion, Ibn 'Arabi's medieval universalism and its attendant traditional understanding of a so-called *religio perennis*, or primordial religion, appears to be much more exclusivist. As Jacques Waardenburg observes, the historical framework of medieval Islamic theology "is not one in which different religions succeed each other in a continuous history. It is, rather, the history of *the one religion* which has been revealed intermittently and which perpetuates itself through multiple histories."[113] Yet, such intermittent revelations

> were thought to be inherently true but to have been tainted by people in the course of history, resulting in a betrayal of the divine, revelatory, primordial religion (*Urreligion*) common to all. In order to restore and further this primordial, monotheistic religion, Muhammad was sent to bring a conclusive revelation. Once memorized and written down, the Quranic revelation channeled by Muhammed, unlike earlier prophecies, was held to have remained authentic and pure.[114]

Throughout the following chapters, I offer a reading of Ibn 'Arabi that—while acknowledging his particular mode of medieval universalism—refuses to transcendentalize his thought beyond his own historical locality. As a Muslim mystic living and writing at the height of the Islamic Middle Period, Ibn 'Arabi's cosmological maps are deeply inscribed by the normative and hierarchical categories of his day. In the idiom of Mignolo, Ibn 'Arabi *was where he thought*.[115]

Universalist Regimes of Particularism

Mystical texts that express authoritarian or exclusionary attitudes often challenge common presuppositions about what is thought to reside at the so-called core of religion—a "spirituality" that is private, psychological, experiential, noncoercive, nonpolitical, noninstitutional, and universally applicable. Yet, such presuppositions have more to do with the conceptual categories of religion produced within the socio-historical matrix of Western Christianity and the European Enlightenment than they do with the views and practice of premodern mystics themselves.

As Sherman Jackson notes, the "tradition of classical Islam" is often romanticized as being "pluralistic, egalitarian, [and] aesthetically vibrant" in opposition to modern discourses of religious absolutism.[116] Yet, this romantic idea "that 'extreme' or substantively repugnant views are the exclusive preserve of modern 'fundamentalist' interlopers who are insufficiently trained in or committed to the classical tradition *cannot sustain scrutiny*."[117] Of course, the Islamic tradition was not unique in producing discourses of so-called *unio mystica* that were also exclusivist. In the early and medieval Christian tradition, for example, Augustine (d. 430) believed that wars waged against heretics were charitable acts, and Bernard of Clairvaux (d. 1153) and Catherine of Siena (d. 1380) strongly supported the Crusades. Bernard himself is often considered to be the first inquisitor, and Teresa of Ávila (d. 1582) was an advocate of the Inquisition.[118]

Not only is the construction of *what* counts as mysticism reflective of "the institutions of power in which it occurs,"[119] as Jantzen has observed within the context of medieval Christianity, but also the conceptual history that informs *how* mysticism is interpreted and received is embedded within the regimes of knowledge through which it is (re)mapped.[120] This constructivist insight is critical to any contemporary study of mysticism; moreover, it is an insight that appears to cut two ways. Indeed, both Ibn 'Arabi's own mysticism and his Euro-American reception are products of particular knowledge regimes involved in the projection, universalization, and regulation of "truth."

While Ibn 'Arabi consistently enunciates Islamic absolutist frameworks, the Perennialist discourse that I analyze in this book variously denies or disregards them. As a result, a universalist ideal is imaginatively cast and historiographically instantiated, thus creating an iconic image of Ibn ʿArabi. Such anachronistic instantiation is what Wendy Brown has called a "buried order of politics"—a mode of "identity production and identity management in the context of orders of stratification or marginalization in which the production, the management, and the context themselves are disavowed."[121] In other words, constructions of Ibn ʿArabi's image as a universalist who accepted all religions as contemporaneously valid impose a religious ideal beyond the purview of their original intellectual context.[122] This type of ideological imposition on a historical figure has parallels with what has been called a "politics of nostalgia,"[123] where an imagined truth is projected back onto a romanticized past to instantiate, *and thus authorize*, a particular ideology or worldview.

As I bring to light in the latter part of this book and specifically argue in my conclusion, a corollary to this anachronistic portrayal is that such Perennialist discursive practices are inevitably traceable to historically situated, Eurocentric categories of religious authenticity made through a post-Kantian dichotomy between an imagined autonomous subject and its heteronomous Other. This dichotomy is readily apparent in a statement made by the Perennialist author Titus Burckhardt—a longtime friend and student of Schuon—in his now-classic work *Introduction to Sufi Doctrine*:

> For the most part Sufi masters have limited themselves to general indications of *the universality of the traditions. In this they respected the faith of simple folk*, for, if religious faith is a virtuality of knowledge (otherwise it would be merely opinion), *its light is none the less enclosed in an emotional realm attached to one particular translation of transcendent Truth.*[124]

Burckhardt's rehearsal of the Schuonian transcendent unity of religions (here, "*the universality of the traditions*") evinces a thinly veiled universalist elitism that presupposes a unified tradition underlying all religions. And yet, the faith of the "*simple folk . . . is none the less enclosed in an emotional realm*" that causes them to be attached, or limited, to only one "translation" or religion. As I discuss in the conclusion to this book, such Perennialist discourse strikingly echoes Kantian notions of *heteronomy*, which categorize particular religious forms as *accidental* and based on "sensible nature" in opposition to the universal essence of religion itself as philosophically realized.

Thus, while Burckhardt's Schuonian position may at first appear to acknowledge and celebrate diversity, on closer inspection it imposes what Mignolo has called a "monotopic hermeneutics" upon its objects of discourse. From within the myopia of such an interpretive framework, there is only one unified intellectual tradition through which all meanings must conform. In the history of modern Europe, this hermeneutic has "served to maintain the universality of European culture at the same time that it justified the tendency of its members to perceive themselves as the reference point to evaluate all other cultures."[125] Similarly, for the monotopic hermeneutics of Perennialism, of which the Schuonian interpretive field is the most prominent, religious people without the esoteric capacity for metaphysics are *devoid* of the true knowledge of religious unity. At the end of the same passage from which I quote above, Burckhardt goes on to precisely enunciate the "esoteric" axiom found within all modalities of Schuonian Perennialism: "those whose outlook is esoteric recognize the essential unity of all religions."[126] In his own work on Sufism, as I discuss at the close of chapter 4, Schuon asserts that "*esoterism alone* is absolutely monotheistic, *it alone* recognizing only one religion under diverse forms."[127] As the Perennialist scholar Patrick Laude notes (without irony), "Schuon went so far as to suggest that . . . religions are like 'heresies' in relation to *Religio Perennis*."[128]

Indeed, close readings of Schuon's writings reveal that the spiritual traditions facilitated by the various religions of the world are essentialized within a hierarchical spectrum according to their supposed capacity to enlighten—a capacity directly connected to a racial hierarchy.[129] For Schuon, this hierarchy ranges from the lowest mode of a passive Semitic theology that simply receives outward revelation to the highest mode of Aryan gnosis, which actively and directly *perceives* truth through esoteric realization. As such, Schuon criticizes Ibn 'Arabi himself for his mystical ambiguities, which he claims are due to "his at least partial solidarity with *ordinary theology*."[130] Schuon is similarly critical of Sufism for being "fundamentally more moral than intellectual"—a trait he attributes to "Arab or Muslim, *or Semitic*, sensibility."[131] As I demonstrate in chapter 4, the issue for Schuon is clearly racio-spiritual: the majority of Muslim mystics, including Ibn 'Arabi, succumbed to the so-called Semitic tendency for "inspirationism" that lacked the enlightened, Aryan "intellection" necessary to reliably discern the *religio perennis* from religious particularism.[132]

Thus, while I argue that Ibn 'Arabi's universalism is built upon and permeated by a politics of absolutism, I also contend that the Perennialist interpretive field is burdened with the pernicious prejudices of a Eurohegemonic intellectual tradition. By making religious universalism the apex of transcendent truth, Perennialist interpretive communities paradoxically repudiate religious particularism and its attendant discourses of situated morality as theologically or historically immature. As Olav Hammer remarks, "The price to be paid for such a universalising approach is of course that any true divergence between traditions must be silenced, and those faiths that are too different from the imagined 'perennial philosophy' are excluded."[133] In other words, the discursive practices of Perennialism promulgate a type of ideological exclusivism through a *universalization of sameness*. Mark Taylor has summarized a parallel poststructuralist insight: "When reason is *obsessed with unity . . . it tends to become as hegemonic* as political and economic orders constructed to regulate whatever does not fit into or agree with governing structures."[134]

In the chapters that follow, I aim to bring into perspective the paradoxical double bind that gives life to the idea of the universal—an intertwining double helix of exclusivity and inclusivity. In his provocative essay "Racism as Universalism," Etienne Balibar remarks on this double bind, noting that racism is particularism; the foundational notions of racism are always based on "divisions and hierarchies" that claim to be "natural." Yet, according to Balibar, the idea of racism is also, paradoxically, based on the production of "ideals of humanity, types of ideal humanity if you like, *which one cannot but call universal*."[135] While the need for religious tolerance in global modernity is a truism, the use of universalism to sanction Eurocentric and racialist categories of religious authenticity has become so naturalized within Euro-American history that it is often overlooked. It is precisely the aporia created by attempts to universalize religious truth, and the discursive politics attached to its cartography, that keeps the analysis throughout this book in play. Indeed, "the double-edged character of the 'universal,'" as Elizabeth Castelli warns, "needs to remain both fully in view and under continued interrogation."[136]

Chapter Overview

I have set out my subject in two overlapping parts of five chapters (including the conclusion). In the first part, I analyze Ibn 'Arabi's universalism by comparing his original textual discourse with regnant claims made by interpreters who work within (or on the margins of) the interpretive field of Schuonian Perennialism. Such claims may be said to form a tradition of "strong misreadings" of Ibn 'Arabi's original texts in the Bloomian sense, where innovative interpretations have been seminal in establishing a foundational universalist scaffolding for understanding Ibn 'Arabi and his perspective on the religious Other.[137] By thus offering revised readings that challenge this Perennialist canon of interpretation, I set out a new backdrop against which the practices of Ibn 'Arabi's contemporary interpreters are made to stand in sharp relief. In the second part, I flesh out the emergent contours and then track them to earlier discursive practices of European knowledge regimes and their attendant rules of subject formation.

Chapter 1, "Tracking the Camels of Love," is based on a revised reading of Ibn 'Arabi's most famous verses from *The Interpreter of Desires* (*Tarjumān al-ashwāq*), which begin by laying claim to a heart "capable of every form" and conclude by asserting to follow "the religion of Love."[138] Here, I contend that modern Euro-American presuppositions regarding the nature of "religion" as a "system of beliefs" inform how the celebrated verses are commonly received and interpreted. While Ibn 'Arabi's claim to a heart "capable of every form" is synonymous with a claim to be capable of every belief (*iʿtiqād*), it is not—as is often supposed—tantamount to accepting the validity of every religion. Rather, I argue that the celebrated verses of *The Interpreter* profess to inherit the comprehensive perfection of the Prophet Muhammad as God's beloved and, in so doing, reflect a discourse of religious absolutism and a subsumptive cosmology of power. It is precisely this cosmology of power that has been almost completely occluded by readings equating religion with belief.

In chapter 2, "Return of the Solar King," I challenge the widely held Perennialist view that Ibn 'Arabi rejected the supersessionist doctrine of abrogation (*naskh*), by demonstrating that his positions on the religious Other should be understood within a larger religio-political cosmology that envisions all religions and their laws as subject to the cosmic rule of Muhammad. Even though this chapter clearly shows that Ibn 'Arabi held Judaism and Christianity as abrogated by Islam, it nuances this assertion by showing that through obedience to the Qur'anic command requiring submission and the payment of the indemnity tax (*jizya*), the People of the Book are metaphysically subsumed within the broader cosmography of Ibn 'Arabi's conception of Islam and the absolute cosmological authority of the Prophet Muhammad.

In chapter 3, "Competing Fields of Universal Validity," I situate Schuonian Perennialism within the larger discursive tradition of essentialist, religious universalism through a comparison with the universalism of Friedrich Schleiermacher (d. 1834). In so doing, I throw into relief how Schuon, and those writing within the orbit of his interpretative field, make a Copernican turn away from Ibn 'Arabi's hierarchical Muhammadan cosmology to a multireligious model of cosmic pluralism united by a Schleiermacherian notion of a transcendent and universally valid religious a priori, or "religion as such." To clearly demonstrate this turn, I historicize Ibn 'Arabi's discourse on the religious Other in relation to his Andalusian home of Seville and show how it notably echoes the polemical style of Ibn Ḥazm (d. 1064) against Judaism and Christianity. Like Ibn Hazm, Ibn 'Arabi claims that the People of the Book were guilty of textual corruption (*taḥrīf al-naṣṣ*) and not simply a corruption of meaning (*taḥrīf al-maʿānī*) as implied in Perennialist discourse. Rather than due to any particular soteriological power of

Judaism or Christianity, or their respective symbolic systems, the salvation of the Protected People (*ahl al-dhimma*) appears to be metaphysically determined for Ibn 'Arabi by their submission to Islamic authority and their participation in its political sphere.

In chapter 4, "Ibn 'Arabi and the Metaphysics of Race," I reveal a buried order of politics underneath the Perennialist cosmology discussed in chapter 3 ironically constituted by and through long-held European discursive strategies of racial exclusion. Through a detailed comparison of Schuon's discursive practices with that of nineteenth-century Aryanist discourse, this chapter argues that although Schuon claims to recognize the universal validity of all religions beyond the limits of exoteric exclusivity, his work consistently presents as self-evident *the metaphysical superiority* of an Indo-European spiritual typology over that of the Semitic. Here, Ibn 'Arabi's "Semitic" propensity for subjectivism is understood as lacking the enlightened objectivity necessary to consistently discern the transcendent formlessness of essential truth from religious particularism. Thus, Ibn 'Arabi's own exclusive association with Islam and the Prophet Muhammad is rejected as an exoteric, and therefore *less authentic*, mode of spirituality in contrast to the more "essential" and autonomous religious truth of "pure metaphysics." The extent to which Ibn 'Arabi is thus decoupled from so-called Semitic subjectivism is the extent to which he is claimed to be an enlightened representative of Islam and authentic purveyor of the universal core of all religions—*the religio perennis*.

In the concluding chapter, "Mapping Ibn 'Arabi at Zero Degrees," I situate key discursive elements of Schuonian Perennialism within a genealogy of German idealism leading back to Kant (and ultimately Plato) to show metaphorical resonances with a Kantian metaphysics of autonomy and its attendant universalism. In contradistinction to Ibn 'Arabi's heteronomous absolutism explored in the first part of this study, here I track how Schuon's religious essentialism *functionally* echoes the discursive practices that mark Kant's "universal" religion as definitively defined against Semitic heteronomy. While both Kantian and Schuonian universalist cosmologies thus appear to reflect a similar Copernican turn where an autonomous, a priori universal perspective forms the essence of all religion, I argue that these respective discourses *also* metaphysically reflect the *imperial cartography* of the Copernican age itself and its attendant ideological conceit of a universal perspective that claims to transcend the confines of geocentric cosmology—that is, its own ethnocentric situatedness. I thus contend that it is precisely the discursive practices and grammar of this larger Eurohegemonic tradition of universalism—*along with its attendant religious, racial, and civilizational superiority*—that Schuonian Perennialism naturalizes within its interpretive field. I conclude by suggesting that the overlapping discursive formations of Kantian and Schuonian universalism conceal absolutist modalities of supersessionism that are ironically similar to those openly posited by Ibn 'Arabi. The exclusivism inherent within such discourse not only calls into question the Western ideal of religious universalism and the possibility of nonexclusivist religious identity but also throws into relief the historically constituted and situated nature of all discourse that aspires to transcendent truth.

1

Tracking the Camels of Love

We continue to speak of the "world view" of this or that religion, demonstrating that, even though we may no longer believe in God, we still believe in belief.

DONALD S. LOPEZ JR., "Belief."[1]

Our imagination tends to mold all concepts in its image.

ABRAHAM JOSHUA HESCHEL,
The Sabbath: Its Meaning for Modern Man.[2]

My heart has become capable of every form: it is a
  pasture for gazelles and a convent for Christian monks,
And a temple for idols and the pilgrim's Kaʿba and the
  Tables of the Tora and the book of the Koran.
I follow the religion of Love: whatever way Love's
  camels take, that is my religion and my faith.[3]

THESE CELEBRATED VERSES, as Michael Sells notes, "are among the more widely quoted passages in Sufi literature and have been used as an epitome of Muḥyī al-Dīn Ibn ʿArabī's thought in many modern accounts of Sufism."[4] They form a small part of Ibn 'Arabi's anthology of amorous poems called *The Interpreter of Desires* (*Tarjumān al-ashwāq*), which was first translated into English in 1911 by the British Orientalist Reynold Nicholson (d. 1945). Not only was *The Interpreter* the first full work of Ibn 'Arabi's to be translated into a Western language, but also the celebrated verses themselves remain a standard proof text for those who allege the existence of a premodern religious universalism. Indeed, Nicholson thought these lines so essential that he himself showcased them on the very first page of the preface to his original translation, noting that "they express the Ṣúfí doctrine that all ways lead to the One God."[5]

Only one year prior to Nicholson's English translation, the Hungarian Orientalist Ignaz Goldziher included these very same lines in his collection of essays originally written to be given as a series of lectures in America, but ultimately published as a book instead in their original German. Here, Goldziher too highlighted what he believed to be an articulation of religious universalism in stark opposition to the dogmatic assertions of organized religion. According to Goldziher, in such poetry "expression is given not only to a tendency toward the highest tolerance . . . but also to the recognition that it is the nature of denominations to disturb and retard. They are not sources of truth; truth is not to be ascertained through the strife of different creeds."[6]

In his 1914 work *The Mystics of Islam*, four years after his original translation of *The Interpreter of Desires*, Nicholson once again commented on these same lines, asserting that "*Love is the essence of all creeds*: the true mystic welcomes it whatever guise it may assume."[7] Such anodyne sentiments regarding Ibn 'Arabi's celebrated verses have continued to proliferate throughout the past hundred years and have become an emblem of Sufism itself.[8] A more recent example from popular literature is Chris Lowney's multiple-edition *A Vanished World: Muslims, Christians, and Jews in Medieval Spain*. Not only does Lowney devote his entire chapter on "Sufism" to Ibn 'Arabi as the "greatest mystical genius of Islam" (repeating, without citing, the famous claim made by British Orientalist A. J. Arberry),[9] but also here Lowney renders Ibn 'Arabi a synecdoche for the Spanish *convivencia*. Indeed, Lowney twice rehearses Nicholson's translation of Ibn 'Arabi's verses as quoted above—once in his chapter on Sufism and once in the epilogue. According to Lowney, these lines suggest how in Ibn 'Arabi's mysticism, and thus in the *convivencia* itself, "the polarizing distinctions that set Christian against Muslim against Jew faded into insignificance."[10]

Often garbed in language equating religion with belief, sentiments concerning the universality of Ibn 'Arabi's celebrated verses have continued to proliferate in both popular and scholarly treatments. One of only a few isolated voices in the crowd, the renowned scholar of Sufism Annemarie Schimmel would dispute this reading in several of her works, finding "not tolerance" (as Goldziher had claimed), but instead a "statement about the author's own lofty spiritual rank,"[11] as well as a "glowing tribute to Islam."[12] But in a 1984 article entitled "Ibn 'Arabī's Garden among the Flames: A Reevaluation," Michael Sells takes Schimmel to task for her apparent lack of faith, declaring that Ibn 'Arabi's claim to a heart "*capable of every form*" is indeed a "call for universality" that is "achieved not through political or social confrontation of the Islamic law but through the inner transformation of the individual's heart."[13] While Sells does not elaborate more on exactly what kind of "universality" is meant here, he continues to assert that Ibn 'Arabi's theory is an appeal for the "complete embracement of *all forms of belief*."[14] Although Sells's analysis revolves around Ibn 'Arabi's theory that human beings know God only through the projection of their own beliefs—a theory I will discuss in detail below—Sells's usage here of the term "belief" in the context of "universality" strongly evokes the synonymic association with the term "religion" itself.[15] More recently, Sells asserts that in Ibn ʿArabi's celebrated verses, "the heart open to every form is receptive to . . . the different *systems of belief*."[16] As if to confirm suspicions that the locution "systems of belief" might here allude to religion, Sells subsequently translates the twice-appearing Arabic word *dīn* in the celebrated verses as first "religion" and then again as "belief," *thus linking the two English terms.*[17]

Indeed, in the chapter that follows, I argue that modern presuppositions regarding world religions as "systems of belief" inform how the celebrated verses of *The Interpreter of Desires* are commonly read and received in the West. While Ibn ʿArabi's claim to a "heart capable of every form" is arguably synonymous with a claim to be capable of every "belief" (*iʿtiqād*), it is not tantamount—as is often interpreted—to accepting the Perennialist notion of the "universal validity" of *every religion*. Rather, I contend that the celebrated verses of *The Interpreter* profess to follow the comprehensive perfection of the Prophet Muhammad as God's beloved—the perfect expression of cosmic love itself. In so doing, Ibn ʿArabi's oft-quoted lines reflect a religious absolutism notable for a *subsumptive* cosmology of power. And it is precisely this cosmology of power that has been almost completely occluded by Euro-American readings equating religion with belief.[18]

"Religion" and the Discourse on Belief

Much has been written on how the grammar of "religion" in the contemporary West has shifted from a premodern modality of socio-political power involved with the production of disciplined knowledge to simply a form of personal belief in post-Enlightenment society.[19] This modern transition can be traced to the beginning of the seventeenth century with the thought of "the Father of Deism," Herbert of Cherbury (d. 1648), whose attempt to distill the universal features of Truth situated the notion of religion as merely "a mental phenomenon."[20] As Wilfred Cantwell Smith notes, it was this shift "that emphasized belief . . . as a basic religious category, and envisaged believing as what religious people primarily do."[21] Thus, the Euro-American notion of religion as distinct from disciplined forms of knowledge and power finds its bearings in what Talal Asad has called "a universal function in belief."[22] As Asad argues, what we might term "religion" in premodern contexts was primarily about knowledge production geared toward modalities of practice and discipline (both individual and societal)—modalities that were understood to *result* in personal belief as the outcome of such knowledge and not as its precondition.[23]

The English term "belief" is commonly deployed to represent the various derivations of the Arabic root *ʿ-q-d*, whose many meanings (such as to tie, knit, knot, conclude, settle, adhere to, oblige, or contract) relate to the general sense of "knotting" conveyed by the verbal noun *ʿaqd*.[24] It is thus reasonable, if not merely convenient, for Euro-American commentators to often equate (directly or by implication) religion's "universal function in belief" with what I call Ibn ʿArabi's discourse on belief—a discourse that he variously describes as "the god created in the beliefs" (*al-ḥaqq al-makhlūq fī al-iʿtiqādāt*) or "the divinity of beliefs" (*al-ilāh fī al-iʿtiqādāt*).[25] Thus, when "God lifts the veil from between Himself and His servant," Ibn ʿArabi claims, "the servant sees Him in the *form of his belief* (*ṣūrat muʿtaqadihi*)."[26]

For Ibn ʿArabi, when the heart is involved in such a knotting, then a "belief" (*ʿaqd/iʿtiqād/muʿtaqad/ʿaqīda*) is formed.[27] In his classic *Arabic-English Lexicon*, Edward Lane articulates this precise meaning of the first-form verb *ʿaqada* as "*he knit his heart to it*."[28] Ultimately, these knots, or beliefs, become various representations of God in the consciousness of believers. Thus, in his magnum opus, *The Meccan Openings* (*al-Futūḥāt al-makkiyya*), Ibn ʿArabi states: "The one who contemplates (*al-nāẓir*) God creates in himself, through his contemplation, what he believes (*yaʿtaqiduhu*). For he has only worshiped a god he created by his contemplation; he said to it 'Be!,' so it was."[29] In Ibn ʿArabi's most famous metaphysical work *The Ring Stones of Wisdom* (*Fuṣūṣ al-ḥikam*), he connects this to the *ḥadīth qudsī*: "I am as the thought My servant has of Me."[30] Ibn ʿArabi's celebrated contemporary Jalāl al-Dīn Rūmī (d. 1273) similarly expounds on this hadith via the voice of God:

> I have a form and image for each of My servants. Whatever each of them imagines Me to be, that I am. I am bound to images where God is; I am annoyed by any reality where God is not. O my servants, cleanse your thoughts, for they are my dwelling places.[31]

Yet, according to Ibn ʿArabi, this projected thought form of the believer onto God, although limited and incomplete, is not altogether unreal, for it is through the believer's particular conception of God that God self-discloses in the world—what Ibn ʿArabi calls "divine self-manifestation in the forms of beliefs" (*al-tajallī al-ilāhiyya fī ṣuwar al-iʿtiqādāt*)[32] or similarly "the divine transmutation in form" (*al-taḥawwul al-ilāhiyya fī al-ṣura*).[33]

The notion that Ibn ʿArabi's discourse on belief is somehow equated with "religion" was formally suggested by Nicholson himself in the preface of his original translation. Here, Nicholson notes that he wishes to "indicate in a few words some of the principal theories" contained in *The Interpreter of Desires*. Nicholson groups these so-called "principal theories" into three respective subheadings: (1) "*God and the World*," (2) "*God and Man*," and (3) "*Religion*." Under "*Religion*,"

Nicholson makes several comments supposedly reflective of Ibn 'Arabi's ideas followed by several (uncited) quotes from *The Ring Stones of Wisdom*. Thus, Nicholson asserts that for Ibn 'Arabi, "no form of positive religion contains more than a portion of the truth."[34] He then writes:

> "Do not attach yourself," Ibn al-ʿArabī says, "to any particular creed exclusively, so that you disbelieve in all the rest; otherwise you will lose much good, nay, you will fail to recognize the real truth of the matter. Let your soul be capable of *embracing all forms of belief*. God, the omnipresent and omnipotent, *is not limited by any one creed*."[35]

In the same section, Nicholson similarly comments (presumably in accordance with the opinion of Ibn 'Arabi): "It is vain to quarrel about religion."[36] He thus immediately quotes again from *The Ring Stones*: "Everyone praises what he believes; his god is his own creature, and in praising it he praises himself."[37]

Indeed, Nicholson's brief prefatory exegesis appears to have been formative for (or at least an early articulation of) a particular interpretive field in which there has been an increasing tendency to anachronistically read Ibn 'Arabi's notion of "the divinity of beliefs" as a doctrine on *the divinity of religions*. Such anachronistic slippage from *beliefs* to *religions* is thus easily projected onto Frithjof Schuon's iconic Perennialist conception of the "transcendent unity of religions."[38] For example, in 2010, the French Perennialist scholar of Sufism Éric Geoffroy noted that it was "Ibn 'Arabī who furnished a doctrinal framework for the concept of the 'transcendent unity of religions.' . . . To him, *all beliefs, and therefore all religions*, are true because each is a response to the manifestation of a divine Name."[39] Indeed, an earlier precedent for such a Perennialist association between *forms of belief* and *religious form* was set by the so-called father of modern Perennialism, René Guénon, who in 1945 noted that Ibn 'Arabi's heart "capable of every form" is an exemplary description of an adept who has "penetrated to the principal unity of all the traditions" and is "no longer tied to any particular *traditional form*."[40]

An important earlier instance of hermeneutical slippage between belief and religion regarding Ibn 'Arabi's discourse can be found in the seminal 1939 study *The Mystical Philosophy of Muḥyid Dīn-ibnul ʿArabī*, by Nicholson's very own doctoral student A. E. Affifi. Here, Affifi notes that Ibn 'Arabi's "universal religion" is inclusive of "all religions."[41] Affifi thus asserts that Ibn 'Arabi's "idealistic monism or pantheism," which he (mistakenly, as far as Affifi is concerned) "calls Islam," is "the embodiment of *all* religions and beliefs."[42] Affifi goes on to quote a line from *The Ring Stones of Wisdom*, "People have formed different beliefs about God, / And I *behold all* that they believe,"[43] which he thus claims "sums up" Ibn 'Arabi's "universal religion."[44]

Nearly twenty years later, the French esotericist Henry Corbin appears to make a similar conflation between Ibn 'Arabi's conception of belief and the modern idea of religion. In his now-classic treatise on Ibn 'Arabi, *Creative Imagination in the Sufism of Ibn 'Arabī* (*L'imagination créatrice dans le soufisme d'Ibn 'Arabî*), first published in 1958, Corbin translates *i'tiqādāt* as "croyances," which in his usage appears closer to denoting historical religions as "creeds" or "faiths" than simply conceptual "beliefs."[45] Thus, Corbin observes that "to the gnostic all faiths [*croyances*] are theophanic visions in which he contemplates the Divine Being; according to Ibn 'Arabī, a gnostic possesses a true sense of the 'science of religions' [*science des religions*]."[46] And likewise: "The vision of which the simple believer is capable still corresponds to the 'Form of God' which he sees along with those of the same religion and faith [*de même religion et de même confession*]: a 'God created in the faiths [*croyances*]' *according to the norms of a collective bond*."[47]

Yet it would be another twenty years until Corbin's implicit slide between belief and religion would be made explicit by the Japanese Islamicist and scholar of religion Toshihiko Izutsu in his influential work *Sufism and Taoism*. At the start of his concluding section entitled "Methodological Preliminaries," Izutsu transparently reveals an ideological debt to the universalism of Corbin informing his entire work:

> I started this study prompted by the conviction that what Professor Henry Corbin calls "un dialogue dans la métahistorire" is something urgently needed in the present world situation. For at no time in the history of humanity has the need for mutual understanding among the nations of the world been more keenly felt than in our days. . . . And meta-historical dialogues, conducted methodically, will, I believe, eventually be crystallised into a *philosophia perennis* in the fullest sense of the term. For the philosophical drive of the human Mind is, regardless of ages, places and nations, ultimately and fundamentally one.[48]

Although Izutsu's expressed intention for civilizational dialogue is obviously well meaning, we do not have to look far to see how his vision for a global perennial philosophy colors his interpretation of Ibn 'Arabi's universalism.[49] In *Sufism and Taoism*, Izutsu explores Ibn 'Arabi's recurring assertion that "it is only God who is worshipped in every worshiped object."[50] Such an idea is not so different than the oft-quoted assertion of the Protestant theologian Paul Tillich: "Faith is the state of being *ultimately concerned*."[51] From one perspective, Ibn 'Arabi is pointing to what Leonard Lewisohn has described in relation to the Persian poetry of Shabistarī (d. 1340) as "the *unity of devotional intention*, the 'doxological oneness', one might say, of both the polytheist's and monotheist's approach to the Absolute."[52] Yet like all of Ibn ʿArabi's metaphysics, any notion of a "doxological oneness" must also, and one could argue *primarily*, be understood from the perspective of an *ontological* oneness. For Ibn ʿArabi, such ontic unity within all "worship" is based on his oft-mentioned inspired reading of Qur'an 17:23—*Your Lord has decreed that you worship none but Him*—as God's predetermined will that is inherently obeyed by everyone regardless of their intention. As Ibn ʿArabi himself admits, this insight runs counter to its normative interpretation as a prescriptive command that must be heeded.[53] In other words, in Ibn ʿArabi's understanding, no matter who or what is "worshiped"—be it a person, idol, or one's own passions—that which is worshiped is ultimately an aspect of the Real (*al-ḥaqq*).[54] Since all of creation is ontologically contingent upon such "Truth," it spontaneously self-manifests within—*and according to*—the consciousness of the worshiper whenever and whatever he or she worships. As Ibn ʿArabi states in *The Ring Stones of Wisdom*:

> Every worshiper dubs their object of worship a "god," although its particular name might be "stone," "wood," "animal," "human," "star," or "angel." Thus, while the object of worship may have such a specific name, it is imagined by the worshiper to be at the (highest) level of Divinity (*al-ulūhiyya*).[55] Yet, in reality, it is only a particular self-manifestation of the Real (*al-ḥaqq*) to the consciousness of the worshiper in this specific place of worship and locus of manifestation.[56]

Like much of Ibn ʿArabi's thought, his metaphysical position here is perhaps best categorized as "theomonistic," which I define as the comprehension of the divine through the nondual prism of a universal being that is self-manifesting within both creation and human consciousness.[57] Yet in *Sufism and Taoism*, Izutsu takes this idea to a conclusion made possible only through a modern conception of religion. Here, Izutsu conflates Ibn ʿArabi's theomonistic understanding of God—which he essentializes as "the eternal Religion"—with the "various historical religions."[58] Izutsu thus states that

> it is [Ibn ʿArabi's] unshakeable conviction that *all religions are ultimately one because every religion worships the Absolute in a very particular and limited way*. Whatever one worships as God, one is worshipping through that particular form the Absolute itself, nothing else, because there is nothing in the whole world but particular self-manifestations of the Absolute.[59]

Such logic infers that God (as the single object of worship) and the various "religions" (as modalities of worshipping that object) are *necessarily* connected. As

I discussed in the introduction to this book, while Ibn 'Arabi may indeed have held that there is only one "eternal Religion"—or *religio perennis—it does not follow* that he held "all religions," as historically instantiated, to be constitutive of it. Indeed, as chapters 2 and 3 will show, this was decidedly not the case. *Nor does it follow* that Ibn 'Arabi equates God with "religion." Yet, Izutsu appears to arrive at these selfsame conclusions through his interpretation of Ibn 'Arabi's discourse on belief.

Just like Ibn 'Arabi's theomonistic idea that the ultimate object of all worship is God, so too is God the ultimate object of all beliefs. Likewise, just as every object of worship relates to a particular self-manifestation of God, each belief is a specific reflection of God. Yet, by translating several of the derivations of *ʿ-q-d* as "religion," rather than "belief," Izutsu smuggles in the modern idea that religion is primarily defined by privately held beliefs. Here, one example will suffice since I return to Izutsu in more detail below. In the following passage from *Sufism and Taoism*, Izutsu translates a statement from Ibn 'Arabi's *The Ring Stones of Wisdom*:

> Generally speaking each man . . . necessarily sticks to a particular religion (*ʿaqīdah*, i.e., religion as a system of dogmas) concerning his Lord. . . . God in all particular religions (*iʿtiqādāt*) is dependent upon the subjective act of positing (*jaʿl*) on the part of the believers.[60]

Izutsu here openly acknowledges the strain he imposes upon the Arabic term *ʿaqīda*, which normally denotes the idea of "a doctrine," "a belief," or a "religious tenet."[61] Instead, Izutsu justifies his choice of "religion" by parenthetically adding "religion as a system of dogmas." Further on in the passage above, Izutsu translates *iʿtiqādāt*—a term that *always* denotes "beliefs" in Ibn 'Arabi's discourse—as "religions."

While there are notable exceptions such as Schimmel's aforementioned reading, and a more recent interpretation by William Chittick,[62] which I discuss briefly below, the lexical choices in translation made by formidable scholars like Affifi, Corbin, and Izutsu have arguably been formative for an entire interpretive field—an interpretive field that has not only influenced later hermeneutical perspectives but also (and perhaps more important from an analytical standpoint) one that casts into relief how modern ideas about "religion" are ubiquitously embedded within contemporary Western scholarship. Although more recent translations have improved upon such earlier choices, Euro-American presuppositions about what constitutes "religion" continue to dictate how Ibn 'Arabi is understood regardless of the details of how he is translated.

Dīn, Obedience, Law, and the Religious Other

To categorize Ibn 'Arabi's discourse in such contemporary universalist terms presupposes that he defines "religion" in the same way that it has come to be construed in the modern West, that is, as "a set of beliefs to be confessed."[63] Yet, Ibn 'Arabi's discourse does not present the Arabic term *dīn*, which is closest to the modern concept of "religion," as a set of beliefs; rather, he defines the term more in alignment with premodern conceptions of religion as "obedience" (*inqiyād*).[64] At the start of the chapter on the prophet Jacob in *The Ring Stones of Wisdom*, Ibn 'Arabi states:

> Religion (*al-dīn*) is equivalent to your obedience (*inqiyādika*), and that which is from God, Most High, is the revealed law (*al-shar*ʿ) to which you are obedient. So religion is obedience (*al-inqiyād*), and the Law (*al-nāmūs*) is the revealed way (*al-shar*ʿ)[65] that God, Most High, has prescribed (*shar*ʿ*a*).[66]

Although the definition of *dīn* as "obedience" is a normative denotation in classical Islamic theology,[67] Ibn 'Arabi's interpretation of the ontological nature of obedience is decidedly less so. In *The Ring Stones*, Ibn 'Arabi categorically states: "The divine command (*al-amr*) demands obedience."[68] This is a comprehensive statement that summarizes the divine–human relationship, much like Ibn 'Arabi's aforementioned ontological interpretation of Qur'an 17:23 as a divine command that all beings "worship" God. Because Ibn 'Arabi assumes that the command of God is absolute, regardless of whether the human being obeys or transgresses, both responses entail *islām*—that is, submission to God. Such submission, according to Ibn 'Arabi, is analogous to "obedience"[69]—either in what pleases or in what displeases God as necessarily determined by God's "rulings" (*al-aḥkām*) in the sacred law or sharia.[70] On the outward (*ẓāhir*) level, if a person "submits" to God in what is not pleasing, then God responds by either pardoning or punishing them. Thus, in all cases, God "obeys" the actions of the person by rewarding, pardoning, or punishing.[71] On a deeper level—that is, the "secret" (*sirr*) or "inner" (*bāṭin*) perspective—Ibn 'Arabi states that it is the essences (*dhawāt*) of human beings that determine whether they obey or transgress, not God.[72] From such a theodicean viewpoint, God is entirely passive. In his typical discursive style, Ibn 'Arabi takes this theomonistic path to its logical extreme and "the secret that is even beyond this": since contingent beings originate from nonexistence (*al-*ʿ*adam*), "there is no existence except the existence of the Real (*al-ḥaqq*)."[73] In other words, it is only God who obeys, transgresses, rewards, pardons, and punishes.

For Ibn 'Arabi, the lynchpin that keeps all of these shifting relationships in play within the context of earthly existence is the sharia where the nexus of divine rulings is located for each prophetic dispensation. As Ibn 'Arabi specifically states in the same chapter in *The Ring Stones*: "The servant institutes religion (*al-dīn*), while the Real (*al-ḥaqq*) establishes the rulings (*al-aḥkām*)."[74] He goes on to assert that "religion is recompense (*al-jazāʾ*), just as religion is submission (*al-islām*), and submission is identical with obedience (*inqiyād*)—obedience to that which brings happiness, as well as that which does not bring happiness—and that is recompense."[75]

Thus, while it is certainly the case that Ibn 'Arabi's idea of "religion" (*dīn*) is theomonistic in the sense that all beings "worship" and "obey" God whether they intend to or not, *it does not follow* that for Ibn 'Arabi all formal means of worship or obedience are the same or equally valid. According to Ibn 'Arabi's notion that "religion is recompense," some forms of "religion" or "obedience" bring the reward of happiness and some do not. Thus, for Ibn 'Arabi, only those paths of worship that have been "prescribed" by God through revelation are salvific.[76] For example, Ibn 'Arabi states in *The Meccan Openings*:

> "*Your Lord has decreed that you worship none but Him*" [Qur'an 17:23]—that is, He has "determined." Thus, on account of God, the gods are worshiped. Yet, the only aim of every worshiper is God; therefore, the only worshiped thing in itself is God. The one who associates partners with God (*al-mushrik*) is only mistaken because he has set up for himself a particular way that was not prescribed to him from a revealed portion of the Divine Truth (*al-ḥaqq*). So, he is wretched (*shaqī*) on account of that.[77]

Indeed, this same idea can also be found in Ibn 'Arabi's commentary of *The Interpreter of Desires* itself, where he states:

> We know that every soul and each religious community (*milla*) seeks salvation (*najāh*), which is loved by everyone. Yet, since they do not know it, they are ignorant of the way that leads to salvation. Even so, every sect and religious community imagines that they are on the correct path. Indeed, all condemnation that occurs between different religious communities and sects is because of the way that leads to salvation but not regarding it itself. And if someone knew he was on the wrong way, surely he would not persist on it.[78]

Thus, according to Ibn 'Arabi, "the way that leads to salvation" is not guaranteed to every religious community even though each community thinks its particular way is correct. While the various religious communities are not necessarily to blame for being on the wrong path, since their so-called deviance is caused by (a predetermined) ignorance, at the same time religious paths should in no way be considered equally valid means to the divine.

In light of this, the idea of religion in terms of Ibn 'Arabi's discourse seems to have very little to do with "belief" and much more to do with law.[79] This explains why Ibn 'Arabi prefers to refer to religion in the plural as "revealed laws" (*sharāʾiʿ*), as opposed to "religions" (*adyān*), since it is the actual set of rulings that change with each prophetic dispensation that serves as the criteria from which "obedience" can be assessed within any given community.[80] As we will see in chapter 2, because Ibn 'Arabi views the messengership of Muhammad as "universal," he holds his attendant divine law to be abrogative and thus controlling in a totalizing manner.[81]

Although Affifi, Corbin, Izutsu, Sells, and others have chosen to read Ibn 'Arabi's discourse on belief as, at base, a kind of proto-pluralist discourse on "religion" and religious unity, Ibn 'Arabi himself does not include specific, non-Muslim religious communities in his expositions of this idea. He does, however, repeatedly mention scholastic theological positions—like those of the Ashʿarīs and Muʿtazilīs—as competing, rational discourses that limit a limitless God.[82] Ibn 'Arabi's discourse on belief thus appears to be primarily an *intra*religious critique on speculative theology (*kalām*) and the metaphysical hazards of rational conceptions of the divine more broadly. The basis of this idea, like much of Ibn 'Arabi's thought, seems to have been prefigured by Abū Ḥāmid al-Ghazālī (d. 1111), who referred to untying "the knot of beliefs" (*ʿuqdat al-iʿtiqādāt*) as a means to attaining a deeper experiential knowledge (*maʿrifa*) of the outward tenets of Islamic faith.[83]

Indeed, one of the foundational sources for Ibn 'Arabi's ideas about religious belief stems from a text that is anything but inclusive of the religious Other. As mentioned above, Ibn 'Arabi refers to the "divinity of beliefs" as the "*divine self-manifestation in the forms of beliefs*" or similarly "*the divine transmutation in form.*" He repeatedly locates the scriptural proof text for this phenomenon through various, mostly partial, narrations of a single hadith contained in the canonical collection of *Ṣaḥīḥ Muslim*.[84] In the most often repeated portion of this hadith, God manifests Himself on the Day of Resurrection to those who used to worship Him in a form they do not recognize. As such, they deny Him until "He has transmuted into His form within which they saw Him the first time,"[85] at which time they affirm Him. Ibn 'Arabi uses this hadith as evidence that God is only acknowledged in the particular forms of belief that people hold of Him and denied in unfamiliar ones. While there are two main narrations in *Ṣaḥīḥ Muslim* of this hadith, one by Abū Hurayra and one by Abū Saʿīd al-Khudrī, the oft-quoted phrase claiming that God was not recognized until He "transmuted" (*taḥawwala*) back into His original form is only contained in the narration of al-Khudri.

What is conspicuously left out of every discussion that I have ever run across on Ibn 'Arabi's use of the al-Khudri narration of this hadith is the fact that it specifically begins by recapitulating Qur'an 9:30 and thus narrates that both "the Jews" and "the Christians" are summoned before God and asked what it was that they had worshiped, in which they respond "'Uzayr" and "the Messiah," respectively, both groups claiming each as the "son of God."[86] In the hadith narration, they are then branded liars and thus fall into the fire of Hell. Indeed, it is only those who "worshiped God, the righteous and the wicked" who remain to witness the various theophanies of God, thus either accepting or denying them.[87]

After a detailed discussion on divine self-manifestation (*al-tajallī al-ilāhiyya*) in *The Meccan Openings*, Ibn 'Arabi quotes the aforementioned "hadith of theophany" (*ḥadīth al-tajallī*) narrated by al-Khudri *as described above* without any comment or qualification regarding its reference to Qur'an 9:30 and its subsequent consignment of the People of the Book to Hell.[88] Even though "the Jews" and "the Christians" are presumably a synecdoche in this hadith for those particular groups from among the People of the Book supposedly guilty of worshipping false gods, Ibn 'Arabi's tacit acceptance of its polemic with no further interpretation evinces how his discourse is here comfortably circumscribed within the theological boundaries of its foundational tradition.

Indeed, it is in allusion to the same theological polemic of Qur'an 9:30 found in al-Khudri's narration of the hadith of theophany that Ibn 'Arabi notes how "words of disbelief" (*kalimāt kufr*) return and afflict the people who uttered them on the Day of Resurrection. Here, he asserts that "such is the case with the disbelief (*al-kufr*) and blasphemy (*al-sabb*) spoken by the Jews and Christians with respect to God."[89] Elsewhere in *The Meccan Openings*, Ibn 'Arabi similarly refers to the Jews and Christians as perpetrators of disbelief (*kufr*), since they "particularized" a universal relationship with God specifically to themselves:

> All disbelief occurs only by the particularization (*takhṣīṣ*) of (a universal) relationship (to God) like the Jews and the Christians said about themselves over others from the people of religions and sects (*al-milal wa al-niḥal*): "*We are the sons of God and His beloved ones*" [Qur'an 5:18]. So, after they affiliated (themselves) with Him in this (particularized) way, they generalized this relationship (as absolute), even though that—in reality—was mistaken. Thus, God said to them: "*Why then does He punish you for your sins? On the contrary, you are only human beings from among those whom He created*" [Qur'an 5:18]. God, the most high, says the relationship is one, so why particularize yourselves in it over others?[90]

The Qur'anic verse that Ibn 'Arabi invokes in this passage is indeed preceded by another verse that specifically calls the deification of Jesus disbelief (*kufr*): "*Those who say that God is the Messiah, son of Mary have disbelieved*" (Qur'an 5:17). In *The Ring Stones of Wisdom*, Ibn 'Arabi directly refers to this particular verse within his well-known disavowal of the Christian doctrine of incarnation (*ḥulūl*). Here, Ibn 'Arabi observes that the fact that Jesus gave life to the dead

> has led some of them to assert the doctrine of incarnation (*bi al-ḥulūl*) and that he is God. For that, they are associated with disbelief (*al-kufr*), which is concealment (*al-sitr*), because they conceal God who (in reality) gives life to the dead in the human form of Jesus. And the Most High said: "*Those who say that God is the Messiah, son of Mary have disbelieved*" [Qur'an 5:17].[91]

Despite the fact that Ibn 'Arabi's position around the Christian doctrine of the Trinity appears to be more ambivalent,[92] the presence of such polemical religious discourse within Ibn 'Arabi's writings—as well as in the subsequent commentary tradition of his school—has led Tim Winter to assert that "the idea that Ibn 'Arabī's school commended a religious pluralism of a kind acceptable in late modern Europe seems to ignore both the nature of religion in the medieval world and the specific teachings of the Shaykh himself."[93]

Approaching The Interpreter of Desires *from the Muhammadan Station*

Given Ibn 'Arabi's broad Euro-American reception as a proto-religious pluralist—along with a general neglect of his theological polemics against Judaism and Christianity—it is not surprising that the celebrated verses of *The Interpreter of Desires* and their interreligious references have been repeatedly read as "a call for universality," as Sells himself contends in his 1984 analysis mentioned above.[94] Perhaps one of the best current examples of this interpretive legacy is the work of the prolific Perennialist scholar Reza Shah-Kazemi,[95] who often refers to Ibn 'Arabi's lines in defense of a universalist reading of Ibn 'Arabi and Islam.[96] In *Paths to Transcendence: According to Shankara, Ibn Arabi, and Meister Eckhart*, for example, Shah-Kazemi quotes the celebrated verses and then comments:

> In the lines above, *the religions are . . . seen as so many forms of the supra-formal*, whose essential nature is infinite Beatitude; thus, the knowledge that only the Essence is absolutely Real *is accompanied by the contemplative appreciation of all sacred forms as aspects or modes of this Essence.*[97]

Not only are all religions one but also, according to Shah-Kazemi's reading of Ibn 'Arabi, they are "so many forms of the supra-formal"—that is, *so many forms of God* as "the Essence." Like Izutsu above, here Shah-Kazemi interprets Ibn 'Arabi as equating the divine itself with all of the world's historical "religions."

Shah-Kazemi goes on to infer that these lines articulate the "witnessing of the Divine in the diverse forms of religion."[98] In his more recent work, *The Spirit of Tolerance in Islam*, Shah-Kazemi notes that in his celebrated verses Ibn 'Arabi "is simply transcribing, in poetic and mystical mode, the essential message of the Qur'ān as regards the religious Other."[99] In connection with this message, Shah-Kazemi then mentions verse 3:84, which I translate as follows:

> *Say: we have faith in God and what has been sent down upon us, and in what was sent down upon Abraham, Ishmael, Isaac, Jacob, and the tribes (of Israel), and in what was given to Moses, Jesus, and the prophets from their Lord; we do not distinguish between any of them, and to Him we are of those who submit* (muslimūn).

Shah-Kazemi goes on to note how Ibn 'Arabi describes Qur'an 3:84 in *The Meccan Openings* as "the key to all knowledge" and as "the culminating point in his spiritual ascent."[100]

Shah-Kazemi is certainly correct in noting that in *The Meccan Openings* Ibn 'Arabi claims that he received verse 3:84 as the culmination point in his spiritual journey. In one of his two ascension narratives contained in this massive work, Ibn 'Arabi engages this verse at the point when he claims to have attained the Muhammadan Station. After spiritually recapitulating Muhammad's famous "nocturnal voyage" (*isrā'*) and heavenly ascension (*mi'rāj*) through the seven heavens, Ibn 'Arabi arrives at "*the lote tree of the furthest boundary*" (*sidrat al-muntahā*) (Qur'an 53:14), where the Qur'an asserts that Muhammad himself attained to the presence of God.

It is at this point in Ibn 'Arabi's own ascension narrative that he boldly claims God "sent down" (*anzala*) upon him, in revelatory fashion, verse 3:84, which as translated above proposes a correspondence between "*what has been sent down upon us*" and the revelation sent to the biblical patriarchs and prophets along with an assertion that "*we do not distinguish between any of them.*" After thus receiving Qur'an 3:84, Ibn 'Arabi immediately asserts:

> So in this verse, He gave me all of the verses and brought the affair home to me, and He made this verse the key to all knowledge for me.[101]

In *Paths to Transcendence*, Shah-Kazemi thus claims that Ibn 'Arabi's reception of verse 3:84 implies "the assimilation of the principle of the universality of revealed religion."[102] Indeed, Shah-Kazemi further asserts that in receiving verse 3:84 as "the key to all knowledge," Ibn 'Arabi "understood that there is *no distinction between the prophets at the highest level of religion*, and also *that the respective revelations vouchsafed them are consequently all to be accepted as valid*."[103] This is a critical assertion, not only because much of Shah-Kazemi's argument for Ibn 'Arabi's universalism rests upon it, but also—and more important—because the claim that Ibn 'Arabi accepted the validity of all revealed religions forms the basis of the Perennialist argument itself. Yet, rather ironically, it is what Ibn 'Arabi continues to say in this particular ascension narrative that shows how his own so-called universal vision is entirely different from, *and ultimately opposed to*, such common universalist claims.

After declaring that he has received Qur'an 3:84 as "the key to all knowledge," Ibn 'Arabi announces:

> Thus, I knew that *I am the sum total* of those who were mentioned to me (*majmūʿ man dhukira lī*). By this, the good news came to me that I (had now attained) the Muhammadan Station (*muḥammadī al-maqām*)[104]—that is, I am of those who inherit the comprehensiveness of Muhammad (*jamʿīat muḥammad*), may God bless him and grant him peace. Indeed, he was the final messenger to be sent revelation. God gave him the comprehensive words (*jawāmiʿ al-kalim*) and favored him in six things that no other messenger of any other community was favored.[105] His messengership is universal because of the universality (*ʿumūm*) of the facets of these six. So, no matter which direction you proceed from, you will only find the Light of Muhammad (*nūr muḥammad*) bestowed generously upon you. None acquires except from it, and no divine messenger has conveyed except by way of it.[106]

Like much of *The Meccan Openings*, Ibn 'Arabi here writes in what Norman O. Brown has called "the apocalyptic style"—that is, "*totum simul*, simultaneous totality; the whole in every part."[107] Thus, from the allusions in this small passage where Ibn 'Arabi announces his attainment of the Muhammadan Station—which I will refer to from here on as his "attainment passage"—we can distill many of the most important anthropological and cosmological assertions that inform Ibn 'Arabi's position regarding the religious Other. Indeed, as Shah-Kazemi rightly intuits, Ibn 'Arabi's attainment passage also provides the metaphysical basis needed to understand Ibn 'Arabi's celebrated verses in *The Interpreter of Desires*.

Yet, by unpacking its main ideas, it quickly becomes apparent that Shah-Kazemi's attempt to interpret the attainment passage as a type of inclusive religious universalism reveals more about his own Schuonian preunderstanding than it does about Ibn 'Arabi's position itself.

The Theme of "Comprehensiveness" within Ibn 'Arabi's Logos Orientation

In opposition to Shah-Kazemi's assertion that Ibn 'Arabi understood Qur'an 3:84 as implying that "there is no distinction between the prophets at the highest level of religion," in the attainment passage of *The Meccan Openings* quoted above, Ibn 'Arabi boldly announces that he himself is "*the sum total* of those who were mentioned to me" (*majmūʿ man dhukira lī*). Here, it is important to appreciate the difference between Ibn 'Arabi's distinctionless totalization of the prophets mentioned in 3:84 and Shah-Kazemi's assertion that Ibn 'Arabi is "consequently" validating each revelation separately. It is very clear through Ibn 'Arabi's use of the Arabic relative pronoun *man* ("those who") that when he claims to be "*the sum total*," he is speaking about the biblical patriarchs and prophets specifically mentioned in Qur'an 3:84 rather than their attendant revelations. Instead of asserting any kind of interreligious validity, Ibn 'Arabi here clearly describes a rather forceful *vision of subsumption*. Indeed, the subsumption of all previous prophets (and their attendant knowledge) in Muhammad is a common, yet less discussed, theme within Ibn 'Arabi's discourse. In the attainment passage, Ibn 'Arabi refers to this central idea as "the comprehensiveness of Muhammad" (*jamʿīat muḥammad*).

A corollary assertion that goes hand in hand with the idea of Muhammad's "comprehensiveness" is Ibn 'Arabi's oft-repeated reminder that the Prophet claimed to have been given "the comprehensive words" (*jawāmiʿ al-kalim*), which he also includes in the attainment passage quoted earlier. This attribution, like much of the extra-Qur'anic material that informs Ibn 'Arabi's metaphysics, comes directly from the canonical hadith. The phrase *jawāmiʿ al-kalim* is found in several hadith narrated by Abu Hurayra, such as the one in *Ṣaḥīḥ Muslim* that Ibn 'Arabi directly refers to in the attainment passage. In this hadith, Muhammad claims that God "favored him in six things that no other messenger of any other community was favored."[108] The normative understanding of Muhammad's "comprehensive words" is based on an internal definition found within a similar hadith, which asserts that God combined for the Prophet "in one saying (*al-amr*) or two the many sayings (*al-umūr al-kathīra*) that were written in the books that came before him."[109] Yet, in Ibn 'Arabi's larger metaphysical anthropology and cosmology, the idea of "the comprehensive words" takes on a much more cosmic meaning. In *The Meccan Openings*, Ibn ʿArabi explains that in this phrase,

> "words" is the plural of "word," and the words of God are not exhausted (*kalimāt allāh lā tanfad*),[110] so Muhammad was given knowledge of that which does not end. Thus, he had comprehensive knowledge of the realities of the known (*ḥaqāʾiq al-maʿlūmāt*), which is a divine attribute belonging only to God. . . . So, he is the tongue of the Real, His hearing, and His sight, and this is the highest of divine ranks.[111]

Thus, for Ibn ʿArabi, "the comprehensive words" signify the comprehensive knowledge of the Prophet Muhammad as the human embodiment of the "Muhammadan Reality" (*ḥaqīqa muḥammadiyya*)—what Ibn ʿArabi refers to in the attainment passage as the "Light of Muhammad" (*nūr muḥammad*).[112]

This idea plays a central role in *The Ring Stones of Wisdom*, where early on Ibn ʿArabi explains how the spiritual "reality" of Muhammad—that is, the *ḥaqīqa muḥammadiyya*—serves as the abiding source of knowledge for all the prophets:

> Every single prophet from Adam to the Final Prophet takes only from the niche of the Seal of the Prophets (*khātam al-nabiyyīn*), even though his physical existence comes last—indeed, by his own reality he is (abidingly) existent—as his words relate: "I was a prophet when Adam was between water and clay."[113]

Each of the twenty-seven chapters of *The Ring Stones of Wisdom* is named according to a specific divine "wisdom" (*ḥikma*) that is related to a "word" (*kalima*), or attribute, of God manifested by a particular prophet who is in turn a manifestation of the Muhammadan Reality. Indeed, in *The Meccan Openings*, Ibn ʿArabi asserts (via the same non-canonical hadith quoted in the passage above) that Muhammad had attained to his station "when Adam was between water and clay,"[114] and so when God taught Adam all of the divine names (as described in verse 2:31 of the Qur'an), "Muhammad *already* had knowledge of the comprehensive words—and all of the names (of God) are from the words."[115] Thus, as the Qur'anically enunciated "Seal of the Prophets,"[116] Muhammad is for Ibn ʿArabi the locus of manifestation for all divine names, thereby forming the archetype of the "Perfect Human Being" (*al-insān al-kāmil*) whose physical manifestation is cosmographically situated as the spiritual "pole" (*quṭb*) of the universe.[117]

Indeed, the cosmogonic role of the Muhammadan Reality as analogous to the Hellenic concept of the "Word" or *Logos* was systematically treated in Affifi's aforementioned *Mystical Philosophy of Muḥyid Dīn-ibnul ʿArabī*, where he christens Ibn 'Arabi's metaphysics "the first Muslim Logos-doctrine."[118] The Muhammadan Reality is here understood as the generative and rational principle of the universe and is, according to Affifi, theoretically distinguishable from the historical Prophet.[119] Yet, such differentiations are not always so clear-cut within Ibn 'Arabi's discourse itself. For example, in *The Meccan Openings,* Ibn 'Arabi cosmically links the historical figure of Muhammad with the divine nature of the Qur'an itself by enunciating three specific points: (1) the hadith report of the Prophet's wife 'A'isha that claims Muhammad "was the character of the Qur'an" (*kāna khuluquhu al-qur'ān*),[120] (2) the Qur'anic verses that call both the character of the Prophet and the Qur'an "tremendous" (*'aẓīm*),[121] and (3) the theological tenet (most notably among the Ḥanbalīs) that the Qur'an, as the speech or "Word of God" (*kalām allāh*), is one of God's attributes.[122] After listing these three components, Ibn 'Arabi boldly exclaims: "It is as though the Qur'an assumed the bodily form called Muhammad."[123] Even further blurring the boundaries between the Qur'an as an attribute of God and the person of Muhammad, Ibn 'Arabi concludes: "The Qur'an is the Word of God and it is His attribute. Thus, Muhammad in his totality was an attribute of the Real (*al-ḥaqq*), Most High, so '*whoever obeys the Messenger has obeyed God*' [Qur'an 4:80]."[124]

It is precisely such indeterminacy between the divine and its *logos*-oriented Muhammadan "reflection" that forms the fulcrum around which the metaphysical ideas of "comprehensive" perfection and the "Perfect Human Being" pivot in Ibn 'Arabi's discourse. In *Sufi Aesthetics*, Cyrus Ali Zargar shows how Ibn 'Arabi's professed "religion of love" (*dīn al-ḥubb*) mentioned in the last line of the celebrated verses closely parallels the Persian "School of Passionate Love" (*madhhab-i 'ishq*), which emphasizes the contemplation of God through the famous practice of "witness play" (*shāhid bāzī*)—that is, the "witnessing" (*shuhūd*) of the human form.[125] As Zargar notes, according to Ibn 'Arabi, "the greatest witnessing of existence is that which is most comprehensive."[126] In Ibn 'Arabi's discussion on Adam in *The Ring Stones of Wisdom*, he establishes that the human being is superior to all created things in comprehensiveness and thus "serves as the supreme mirror in which God witnesses himself."[127] Thus, as the perfect locus of the divine names and most complete reflection of God, Muhammad is, for Ibn 'Arabi, *the most comprehensive* of all human beings.[128]

Reinterpreting The Interpreter

As I discussed at the start of this chapter, a substantial part of Ibn 'Arabi's modern aura of "enlightened" universalism has much to do with how his small collection of amorous poems, *The Interpreter of Desires*, has been interpreted by contemporary Western scholars. Written in the erotic style of the Arabic love lyric (*nasīb*) in honor of Niẓām—apparently, a beautiful and learned daughter of a scholar Ibn 'Arabi befriended in Mecca—it is not surprising that such amorous poetry coming from a supposedly pious mystic raised eyebrows. In response, Ibn 'Arabi wrote a highly metaphysical commentary, *The Treasury of Lovers: A Commentary on the Interpreter of Desires* (*Dhakhā'ir al-a'lāq: sharḥ tarjumān al-ashwāq*), to reveal its hidden mystical allusions and thus preserve his honor as a Sufi.[129]

While Nicholson's 1911 translation includes glosses of *The Treasury of Lovers*, he proclaims that Ibn 'Arabi's commentary, while sincere, took "refuge in far-fetched verbal analogies" that ultimately descended "from the sublime to the ridiculous." According to Nicholson, this was due in part to Ibn 'Arabi's "entering into trivial details," which Nicholson added was characteristic of Arabs who were "apt to exaggerate details at the expense of the whole."[130] Following this rather typical Orientalist racialism, Nicholson lets his readers know that he has only translated "the interesting and important passages" from the commentary.[131] Thus, in his recent article "The Religion of Love Revisited," Chittick re-examines *The Treasury of Lovers* in greater detail to rectify general misunderstandings regarding the celebrated verses and Ibn 'Arabi's famous profession to "follow the religion of Love."[132] As such, Chittick concludes that

> [Ibn 'Arabi's] Religion of Love is not quite what most people imagine it to be. It certainly implies openness to the beauty of God's creation along with love and compassion for all of God's creatures, but more than anything else it is a program of action, *that of putting the Sunna into practice* on the two basic levels discussed in classical Sufism, the Shariʿa and the Tariqa, with the aim of reaching the Haqiqa, which is the Divine Reality Itself.[133]

From the level of so-called authentic Sufi *praxis*, Chittick's description is most likely an accurate articulation of how Ibn 'Arabi would describe "the religion of Love." In the remainder of this chapter, I also revisit *The Treasury of Lovers* to shine light on Ibn 'Arabi's celebrated verses. Yet, here I am concerned to throw into relief *a different level* of enunciation at work in the celebrated verses that has to do with their discursive production of power and how that particular configuration, or "politics," is often discarded as *unessential*. Rather than *merely* "a program of action . . . putting the Sunna into practice," as Chittick asserts, in what follows I argue that these verses simultaneously involve a much more radical *discourse of subsumption*. That is, situated within a *logos*-oriented language-game, Ibn 'Arabi's celebrated verses pay tribute to the creative power of Muhammad and the ontological triumph of his reality.

While I will return to Ibn ʿArabi's famous line professing a heart that "*has become capable of every form*" momentarily, here I begin with Ibn ʿArabi's commentary on what is frequently taken to be "religious" imagery in the lines that follow (as translated by Nicholson): "a convent for Christian monks, / And a temple for idols and the pilgrim's Kaʿba and the / Tables of the Tora and the book of the Koran." Thus, in *The Treasury of Lovers*, Ibn ʿArabi explains that he used the symbol of a "convent for Christian monks" because the heart is like a convent where monks worship. Similarly, he says that he employed "a temple for idols" to represent "the realities (*al-ḥaqāʾiq*) sought by humanity, who exist internally, and through whom God is worshiped."[134] As is the case throughout *The Interpreter*, Ibn ʿArabi here makes use of the poetic topos of "infidelity," known in the Persian poetic tradition as "*kufriyyāt.*" In this trope that is traceable back to the Arabic discourse of Manṣūr al-Hallāj (d. 922), the poet praises non-Islamic traditions such as Christianity or Zoroastrianism or, more radically, exalts "heresy and unbelief (*kufr*)" and "the idolatrous temple-tavern."[135] However, when Ibn ʿArabi states that idol worship represents the seeking of "realities," which in his terminology represent the specific qualities of the divine names,[136] the Andalusian Sufi's famous idea of "the god created in the beliefs" is uniquely invoked.[137] Here, as perfectly reflected in Ibn ʿArabi's oft-used example of the "hadith of theophany" discussed above, the devout only recognize a god that is created solely within their own particular mental projections or beliefs. Indeed, referring to this hadith, Ibn ʿArabi explicitly states in *The Meccan Openings* that people "only worship what they believe (*iʿtaqadū*) pertaining to the Truth (*al-ḥaqq*), worshiping merely a creation (*makhlūq*)." "And so," according to Ibn ʿArabi, "there is none but the worshiper of idols (*fa-mā thamma illā ʿābid wuthun*)."[138] As Chittick notes:

> Ibn al-ʿArabī frequently calls the idols inside everyone's heart "the gods of belief." . . . In a certain respect, it is the god of my belief that keeps me in my own station, for it is my understanding of this god that has tied my heart in a knot. *Progress on the path to God demands negating the gods of all beliefs* while recognizing their limited utility.[139]

Thus, from the internal idols of the heart, Ibn ʿArabi goes on in *The Treasury of Lovers* to comment that "the Kaʿba" represents the heart encircled by "celestial spirits" (*al-arwāḥ al-ʿulwiyya*) and is thereby given the capacity for angelic insight, while "the Tora" represents a heart inscribed with the Hebraic sciences of Moses.[140] Yet, it is Ibn ʿArabi's elucidation of "the book of the Koran" that is the most metaphysically revealing, and, not insignificantly, one of the most inadequately treated in Nicholson's gloss of *The Treasury of Lovers*, which follows: "'The book of the Koran,' because his heart has received an inheritance of the perfect Muhammadan knowledge."[141] Yet, Ibn ʿArabi's original exegesis is more detailed. Referring to himself in the third person, Ibn ʿArabi states:

> Since his heart inherited the perfected Muhammadan knowledges (*al-maʿārif al-muḥammadiyya al-kamāliyya*), he made them into a book, and he established them within the station of the Qur'an because Muhammad attained the station of "I was given the comprehensive words" (*ūtītu jawāmiʿ al-kalim*[142]).[143]

Here, Ibn ʿArabi appears to allude to the same realization enunciated in his attainment passage from *The Meccan Openings* quoted above where he realizes the Muhammadan Station and thus inherits "the comprehensiveness of Muhammad" *because* the Prophet had been given "the comprehensive words." As I also note above, in *The Meccan Openings* Ibn ʿArabi additionally links the historical figure of Muhammad with the divine nature of the Qur'an, going as far as to state: "The Qur'an is the Word of God and it is His attribute. Thus, Muhammad in his totality was an attribute of the Real (*al-ḥaqq*), Most High." In light of these claims, Ibn ʿArabi's assertion in *The Treasury of Lovers* regarding his heart's inheritance of "the perfected Muhammadan knowledges" as established "within the station of the Qur'an" becomes especially significant. Not only does the "station of the Qur'an" come last in the list of interreligious references, but also it reflects the "perfected" nature of "the comprehensiveness of Muhammad." Indeed, as is additionally evinced in the attainment passage of *The Meccan Openings*, Ibn ʿArabi's reference to "the station of the Qur'an" in terms of the comprehensive nature of Muhammad refers to his realization that he was "*the sum total*" of the biblical patriarchs and prophets specifically mentioned in verse 3:84 of the Qur'an, which as he claims was "the key to all knowledge."

Returning once more to Ibn ʿArabi's commentary in *The Treasury of Lovers*, after noting that "I follow the religion of Love" refers to the Qur'anic verse "*Say: If you love God, follow me, then God will love you*" (3:31)—a verse that has been traditionally interpreted as depicting an instance where Muhammad invited a group of either idolaters, Jews, or Christians to Islam[144]—Ibn ʿArabi states:

> For this reason, he has called it "the religion of love" (*al-dīn ḥubb*) and professed it. For he meets the burdens of his beloved with acceptance, contentment, and love—hardship and discomfort having been removed from them in every way. Thus, he said "whatever way [Love's camels] take," that is, whatever path they follow—whether agreeable or not—we are

> content with all of them. And his saying "that is my religion (*dīnī*) and my faith (*īmānī*)" means that there is no religion (*dīn*) higher for one who is indebted to Him through Him and who is transcendently commanded by Him than a religion founded upon love and longing.[145]

Here, Ibn ʿArabi situates the religion of love in a fairly normative way according to the general ethos of classical Sufism and its emphasis on longing for God as the Beloved—a Beloved for whom he is willing to endure every hardship. Yet, it is the next set of lines—again severely neglected by Nicholson—that return to the above notion of the station of the Qur'an and the motif of "the comprehensiveness of Muhammad":

> And this is a special prerogative for the Muhammadans (*al-muḥammadiyyīn*)—for indeed Muhammad, may God bless him and grant him peace, is alone from among all of the prophets in the station of perfect love (*maqām al-maḥabba bi kamālihā*). He is chosen (*ṣafī*), a confidant (*najī*), and a friend (*khalīl*), as well as all of the other meanings (*maʿānī*) of the stations of the prophets; yet, he is beyond them all. Indeed, God took him as a darling (*ḥabīb*), that is, (both) lover (*muḥibb*) and beloved (*maḥbūb*), and his heirs are on his way.[146]

Here, it is first necessary to note Ibn ʿArabi's mention of "the Muhammadans" (*al-muḥammadiyyīn*), which as Sells points out was mistranslated by Nicholson as merely "Moslems."[147] Indeed, Chittick comments that in Ibn ʿArabi's vocabulary,

> the Muhammadans are the perfect human beings par excellence, those who stand in the highest station of spiritual perfection, a station that was achieved only by the Prophet and a few of his great followers. He commonly says that the Muhammadans stood in "the station of no station" (*maqām lā maqām*), meaning that they achieved union with God, thus transcending all the stations on the path, all the individual perfections that human beings can realize. Their station embraces every possible human perfection, that is, every possible manifestation of divine perfection. *Since the Muhammadans have gone beyond all stations and internalized all the perfections designated by the stations, they cannot be limited to one station or another.*[148]

Although Ibn ʿArabi does not make specific mention of it in his commentary, Chittick is no doubt correct in relating Ibn ʿArabi's notion of "the station of no station" (*maqām lā maqām*) to his assertion, as quoted above, in *The*

Treasury of Lovers that "the religion of love" is "a special prerogative for the Muhammadans," since as Chittick has thoroughly shown elsewhere, the station of the Muhammadan was specified by Ibn ʿArabi in *The Meccan Openings* as "the station of no station."[149] Sells too makes this connection in his 1984 article where he asserts that the term "Muhammadians" for Ibn ʿArabi "does not refer to Muslims but rather to those who have achieved *the station of no station and who refuse to bind themselves to any one prophetic wisdom*."[150] Yet, Sells's statement here appears to imply that in such a "station of no station," Muhammadans "refuse" to be associated with "any one prophetic wisdom," or religious dispensation, *whatsoever*, thus seemingly including Islam. Indeed, Sells furthers this implication by immediately adding that "Schimmel, who relies on Nicholson in her interpretation, has mistakenly identified the 'religion' referred to in the verses with Islam when, in fact, as is made clear throughout Ibn ʿArabī's writings, *very few Muslims are Muhammadians*."[151] Yet, in the passage from *The Treasury of Lovers* quoted directly above, Ibn ʿArabi specifically expounds on the *particular excellence* of the Prophet himself, who has achieved a unique perfection out of all the prophets in "the station of perfect love" as one who is "chosen (*ṣafī*), confidant (*najī*), and a friend (*khalīl*), as well as all of the other meanings of the stations of the prophets." These three qualities refer to the traditional attributes used in association with Adam, Moses, and Abraham, respectively.[152] As such, Ibn ʿArabi's mention of these attributes in *The Treasury of Lovers* qualifies the so-called station of Muhammad's "perfect love" as embodying the entirety of divine realities contained within all of the preceding prophets—what Ibn ʿArabi here refers to as the "*meanings* (*maʿānī*) of the stations of the prophets."[153] Thus, rather than a station that "*refuse[s] to bind . . . to any one prophetic wisdom*," as Sells suggests, in this passage "the station of perfect love" *subsumes* all prophetic wisdom in the name of Muhammad himself.

In such terms, the last line in the same passage from *The Treasury of Lovers*, "and his heirs are on his way," is especially significant since it parallels statements about a Muhammadan inheritance made in Ibn ʿArabi's commentary above on "the book of the Koran" and in the attainment passage of *The Meccan Openings*—that is, Ibn ʿArabi's assertion that "his heart inherited the perfected Muhammadan knowledges" and that he "was among the heirs of the comprehensiveness of Muhammad," respectively. In all such references, Ibn ʿArabi asserts that the special station of the Muhammadan saint inherits the *logos*-oriented perfection of the Prophet. Just as Ibn ʿArabi acknowledges the Qur'anic enunciation of this perfection of Muhammad as the "Seal of the Prophets," he famously situates himself as the "Seal of the Saints" (*khātam al-awliyāʾ*)—that is, the supreme "spiritual" manifestation of the Muhammadan Reality as the highest Muhammadan saint.[154] Thus, directly after the aforementioned passage quoted from *The Ring*

Stones of Wisdom that identifies Muhammad as "the niche" from which all the prophets derive their knowledge, Ibn 'Arabi states that the Seal of the Saints was likewise "a saint while Adam was between water and clay."[155] As such, Ibn 'Arabi notes that the Seal of the Saints "takes from the Origin and is the witness (*al-mushāhid*) of all degrees (of reality)."[156] It is precisely from this sense of witnessing all of the divine self-manifestations and thus containing *in toto* all the "meanings" of the *Logos*—that is, the "comprehensive words" of Muhammad as a manifestation of "the Word of God"—that Ibn 'Arabi's celebrated verses of *The Interpreter* should be understood.[157] Indeed, as Chittick notes in relation to the station of no station, the Muhammadan "passes from station to station, never losing a positive attribute after having gained it. One by one, in perfect harmony, *he assumes the traits of the divine names*. Having reached the highest station, *he owns all stations*."[158] Chittick thus concludes: "The Muhammadan friend of God inherits his knowledge, stations, and states *directly from the Prophet Muḥammad*."[159] Thus, if we are to read Sells's assertion generously—that Muhammadan saints "*refuse to bind themselves to any one prophetic wisdom*"—then we must simultaneously add the critical proviso: *except* for the prophetic wisdom of Muhammad, which in Ibn 'Arabi's language-game is none other than the revelation of Islam qua the ultimate dispensation of the primordial "religion (*milla*) of Abraham."[160]

In light of this, we can now return to the enigmatic phrase that opens the celebrated verses: "*My heart has become capable of every form*." Ibn 'Arabi begins his commentary on this line in *The Treasury of Lovers* by relating how the Arabic word for heart, *qalb*, is called such "because of its constant transformation (*taqallub*)." Here, both terms "heart" and "constant transformation" are derived from the same root *q-l-b*, which means to "alter," "invert," "turn," "move," and so forth. Ibn 'Arabi then explains:

> This is so, since the heart diversifies (*yatanawwuʿ*) according to the diverse inrushes (*tanawwuʿ wāridāt*) upon it. Its diverse inrushes correspond to the diversity of its states (*aḥwāl*), and the diversity of its states are through the diversity of divine self-manifestations (*al-tajalliyāt al-ilāhiyya*) in accord with its secret (*sirr*).[161]

Given that *The Treasury of Lovers* was written apologetically for a reader already familiar with Ibn 'Arabi's metaphysical grammar, his normally dense prose is here even more so. Indeed, much of what Ibn 'Arabi concisely glosses in his commentary is expanded at length in later writings.[162]

For example, in *The Meccan Openings*, Ibn 'Arabi explains this same phenomenon in a slightly different way through one of his other favorite metaphors—how nondelimited, and thus transparent, substances like water or polished glass take on the color of delimited things, as symbolized by either their colored vessels or contents, respectively. Here, Ibn ʿArabi deploys the latter example and begins by using the same root *q-l-b* to express the constant transformation (*taqallub*) of the heart:

> The heart constantly transforms (*yataqallabu*) from state to state, as God, who is the Beloved (*maḥbūb*), is "*every day upon some affair*" [Qur'an 55:29]. So the lover (*muḥibb*) is diversified in the object of his love in accordance with the diversity of the Beloved in His acts, just as the polished and transparent glass cup is diversified according to the diversity of the liquid in it. So, the color of the lover is the color of his Beloved.[163]

At the end of Ibn ʿArabi's commentary on the line "*My heart has become capable of every form*," he notes that the diversification of the states of the heart "is referred to by the revealed tradition (*al-sharʿ*) as transmutation (*al-taḥawwul*) and continual change (*al-tabaddul*) in the forms."[164] This is a direct reference to al-Khudri's narration of the hadith of theophany found in *Ṣaḥīḥ Muslim*, which I discussed above, where God appears to his believing Muslim servants.[165]

Elsewhere, in the chapter on the "heart wisdom" (*hikma qalbiyya*) of the prophet Shuʿayb in *The Ring Stones of Wisdom*, Ibn ʿArabi elaborates on the diversity of forms in the heart. He does this through the discourse on belief by noting (as partially quoted earlier) that when "God lifts the veil from between Himself and His servant, the servant sees Him in the form of his belief. So, *He is the same as his belief*."[166] Ibn ʿArabi's bold assertion here—that is, that God is the same as the servant's "belief"—clearly does not mean that God in His absolute essence is the same as such beliefs, but only that such beliefs bind, or "knot," the reality of the believer to particular "forms." Thus, Ibn ʿArabi concludes:

> Neither the heart nor the eye witnesses anything of the Real (*al-ḥaqq*) except the form of its own belief. Thus, the Real is contained within the form of the belief that the heart encompasses. It is this that manifests to (the heart) so that it is known by (the heart). So, the eye sees only the believed Real (*al-ḥaqq al-ʿitiqādī*)—and the diversity of beliefs is no secret.[167]

From Ibn ʿArabi's variegated, yet interrelated, descriptions of "the heart," it is clear that when *The Interpreter of Desires* mentions the "forms" that the poet's heart is capable of, it is talking about the phenomena of a heart in its various states, which are interconnected with how God manifests to the heart through belief. Yet, it is here where it is easy to make Ibn ʿArabi speak for a plurality of religions, rather than simply of beliefs, or similarly, to assume that the latter necessarily entails the former. Indeed, Ibn 'Arabi follows the aforementioned passage in *The Ring Stones of Wisdom* by stating:

> So, whoever limits Him, denies Him in other than what he limits Him, but affirms Him in his limitation of Him when He manifests Himself (*tajallā*). Yet, the one who releases Him from limitation will never deny Him, and thus affirms Him in every form He Himself transmutes (*yataḥawwalu*) into. As such, He grants him from Himself the form of His self-manifestation (*tajallī*) over and over, since the forms of self-manifestation are infinite.[168]

Elsewhere in *The Ring Stones of Wisdom*, Ibn 'Arabi states that "there are only beliefs and all are correct (*muṣīb*)," and similarly, if a person truly "understood al-Junayd when he said 'the color of water is the color of its vessel,' then he would grant every believer their belief and perceive God in every form and every belief."[169] As such, Ibn 'Arabi famously warns:

> Beware of delimiting yourself by a specific *belief* (*ʿaqd*) and disbelieving all else, for much good will pass you by—in fact, the knowledge of the affair itself will pass you by. So, be in yourself the primordial matter of all forms of *beliefs* (*muʿtaqadāt*) since God, the Most High, is too wide and great to be restricted by one *belief* (*ʿaqd*) over another.[170]

From just these examples it becomes apparent how easily such statements can be read within a Perennialist interpretive lens of religious universalism, easily sliding from the idea of "belief" to that of "religion." Indeed, as was quoted at the start of this chapter, Nicholson also translated the passage above in his preface of *The Interpreter of Desires* under the subheading "*Religion*," thereby directly correlating belief and religion in Ibn 'Arabi's thought. Along the same lines, but a bit more conspicuously, this passage was translated by Izutsu, who rendered derivations of *ʿ-q-d* as "religion" rather than "belief"—again smuggling in the modern idea that religion is defined as *a system of beliefs* or, in Izutsu's words, a "system of dogmas."[171] Thus, Izutsu renders this same passage from *The Ring Stones*:

> Beware of being bound up by a particular *religion* [*ʿaqd*] and rejecting all others as unbelief! If you do that, you will fail to obtain a great benefit. Nay, you will fail to obtain the true knowledge of the reality. Try to make yourself a (kind of) Prime Matter for all forms of *religious belief* [*muʿtaqadāt*]. God is wider and greater than to be confined to one particular *religion* [*ʿaqd*] to the exclusion of others.[172]

Here, Izutsu's translation of the term *ʿaqd* as "religion" is *severely misleading*, since, as previously mentioned, the Arabic meaning is geared toward the notion of restricting, or "knotting," God in some kind of conceptual form, or "belief," and not the modern Protestant notion of religion itself as "a system" or set of beliefs. The theomonistic prohibition of not limiting God to a particular conceptual form is *very different* than the contemporary universalist prohibition of not limiting salvation to a particular religious form. Conflating these two prohibitions is to conflate the attributes of God and the various religious dispensations, which is to deify every religion as a manifestation of God—a conception that forms a basic axiom within Schuonian Perennialism. As Seyyed Hossein Nasr notes in summation of Schuon's thought: "Each religion comes from the Absolute and possesses an archetype which determines its earthly reality."[173]

In *Paths to Transcendence*, Shah-Kazemi quotes Izutsu's above passage verbatim.[174] Yet, in an older article published two years prior, Shah-Kazemi notes the problematic nature of Izutsu's word choice of "religion" in this very same passage and instead replaces it with the word "creed."[175] Nonetheless, Shah-Kazemi here asserts that Izutsu's translation "adequately conveys the clear intention behind this warning to believers not to restrict God to the form of their own belief," and thus

> for Ibn Arabi, *there is but one religion, which comprises diverse modes of revelation and different rulings*, according to the requirements of different human collectivities addressed by the one and only Divinity.[176]

Here, Shah-Kazemi repeats a foundational claim of Schuon, namely, that "what determines the difference among forms of Truth is the difference among human receptacles,"[177] and again asserts that not only did Ibn ʿArabi hold to the notion of a *religio perennis*—an "eternal Religion," in the words of Izutsu—but also that this religion is found concurrently within every historical religion. Thus, like Izutsu, Shah-Kazemi conflates Ibn ʿArabi's theomonism, which recognizes that all beings ultimately worship one God, with the much different assertion that all historical religions share an underlying essence.

An Ontology of God or "Religion"?

In light of the analysis above, we can see how when Ibn ʿArabi claims his heart "capable of every form," instead of asserting that he is capable of every "religion," or *religious form*, as is often claimed, he is asserting that as the Seal of the Saints he is like Muhammad in his perfected comprehensive capacity to ontologically witness all of the names, meanings, and forms that make up the "form" (*ṣūra*) of the divine itself.[178] While Corbin rightfully observes that this is "the religion of the gnostic . . . whose *heart* has rendered itself capable of receiving all theophanies because it has penetrated their *meaning*," he nevertheless anachronistically projects a contemporary conception of universalism conflating belief with religion onto Ibn 'Arabi where "the 'Form of God' is for him no longer the form of this or that faith exclusive of all others, but his own eternal Form."[179] Corbin tellingly calls this transition "the passage from *the dogmatic religion* of the 'God created in the faiths' to the religion of the gnostic."[180] Although appreciative of Corbin's genius, Schimmel was more critical, observing that Ibn 'Arabi's claim to a "heart capable of every form" was the "highest self-praise" and an "acknowledgement of an illumination that is far beyond the 'illumination of the names.'"[181]

Whether exclusive self-praise or something more in keeping with the decorous sensibilities of classical Sufism, like self-annihilation before the face of God, what is clear is that Ibn 'Arabi's claim is certainly lofty. In such exalted (and no doubt *exalting*) terms, he often refers to the hadith: "God created Adam upon His own form (*ṣūra*)."[182] After invoking this hadith in his later treatise *Revelations in Mosul* (*al-Tanazzulāt al-mawṣiliyya*[183]), Ibn 'Arabi enunciates lines very similar to his celebrated verses of *The Interpreter of Desires*. In a chapter regarding the obligation of ritual purification for prayer, and the use of water for it, he states:

God created (*faṭara*) my form (*ṣūratī*) upon his,
 so I am every form.
God entrusted His two affairs within me until
 I became a wall (*sura*) differentiating His two foundations:[184]
In my outward (*ẓāhirī*) there is distress and punishment
 Yet, in my inward (*bāṭinī*) is veiled mercy (*raḥma mastūra*).
I encompass His Torah and His Gospels
 His Qur'an and His Psalms.[185]

Like Ibn 'Arabi's claim in *The Interpreter of Desires* that his "heart has become capable of every form," here too he is all forms. Yet in the verses from *Revelations in Mosul*, Ibn 'Arabi makes an internal distinction between the "two foundations" of reality—God's Outward (*ẓāhir*) and Inward (*bāṭin*). In the Outward there is the reality of punishment and torment, but in the Inward there is the promise of mercy. Here, Ibn 'Arabi articulates the profound, cosmic dualism of the monotheistic traditions, radically internalizing the wisdom of God's revelations *in toto*: "*I encompass His Torah and His Gospels His Qur'an and His Psalms.*"

Ibn ʿArabi thus continues in this passage from *Revelations in Mosul* to further his theomonistic identification with the divine by stating: "I am everything with Him!"[186] Indeed, he goes even further: "When I claim that I am a lord (*rabb*), God lets down (*asdala*) his veils (*sutūrahu*) over my face!"[187] But then, he immediately adds:

> Yet, His law (*sharʿuhu*) comes and addresses my very essence (*dhātī*),
> Oh heedless one, you have been ignorant of His commands!
> God has made obligatory grace and punishment,
> according to the manifest claims upon humanity.[188]

It is such dialectical tension between outward and inward, sobriety and ecstasy, and transcendence and immanence that indelibly marks Ibn ʿArabi's theomonistic language-game. Yet, Ibn ʿArabi is no al-Hallaj, who ultimately was unable to reconcile between the theophanic self-identification of lordship and the outward sharia. As Carl Ernst notes, "Hallajian infidelity" was marked by the insistence on the "full application of legal discrimination on the social level; anyone who follows the path taken by Hallaj must himself be prepared to accept the legal consequences."[189] Thus, Hallaj's "self-blame and desire for martyrdom" was the result of an apparent incongruence between ultimate reality (*ḥaqīqa*) and the sharia.[190] In the aforementioned section from *Revelations in Mosul*, however, Ibn ʿArabi seeks to balance the "infidelity" of *ḥaqīqa* alongside the law within a dyadic tension.[191] Yet even more boldly, Ibn ʿArabi claims that for attained mystics like himself, there is *in reality* no such tension; that is, such theophanic self-witnessing is completely within the bounds of the law. He states:

> If someone like me says "I am a lord,"
> Oh my friend—is that a major sin (*kabīra*)?
> No, it is my right, for He and I are one!
> I did not even commit a minor sin (*ṣaghīra*).
> How can I commit a minor or major sin,
> when I am holy (*al-quds*) and possessor of exaltation (*al-ʿalā*) and sovereignty (*al-sarīr*)?[192]

Indeed, Ibn ʿArabi succinctly articulates this idea in the same passage in *The Ring Stones of Wisdom* cited earlier where he compares himself as the Seal of the Saints to Muhammad as the Seal of the Prophets. Here, Ibn ʿArabi notes that his "inherited" perfection of the Seal of the Saints as the "Saint-Heir" (*al-walī al-wārith*)—a statement that echoes Ibn ʿArabi's previously quoted claim as heir to the Muhammadan Station in *The Interpreter of Desires*—is only one of the perfections of Muhammad, who is "Saint-Messenger-Prophet" (*al-walī al-rasūl al-nabī*).[193] As exemplified in his own ecstatic utterance in *Revelations in Mosul* above, and his subsequent qualification, the outward importance of the law—and as we shall see in chapters 2 and 3 *its attendant absolutism*—is for Ibn 'Arabi an integral part of his hierarchical metaphysics and religious cosmography. It is thus evident that Ibn 'Arabi's celebrated claim of having a heart "capable of every form" who follows the "religion of love" is in fact a claim to inherit the unique *comprehensive perfection* of the Prophet Muhammad as God's singular beloved. Rather than articulating prophetic equivalence or the universal transcendence of outward religious form, such perfection is a subsumption of all revealed knowledge and thus a forceful assertion of the spiritual sovereignty of Muhammad from both socio-historical and metaphysical perspectives.

Conclusion: The Interpreter of Desires *or the Desires of the Interpreter?*

The modern image of mysticism as the universal "core" of all religions that transcends the worldly politics of religious rivalry is nowhere more apparent than in universalist and Perennialist interpretations of Ibn 'Arabi's celebrated verses, which are hardly ever treated as an enunciation of power (along with knowledge). Directly imbricated with this hermeneutical commonplace is Ibn 'Arabi's discourse on belief—a foundational idea present throughout his writing, claiming an individual's heart as the locus of the Real via "the form of his belief."

As I have shown, Ibn 'Arabi's heart "capable of every form" is a heart capable of every divine truth *because* it directly inherits the comprehensiveness and subsumptive power of the Prophet Muhammad. Yet, this discourse is commonly taken to be a call for religious universalism where "every form" of belief is understood as every "religious form"—often additionally conflating the form of God with that of religion itself. When Ibn 'Arabi states that if a person truly "understood al-Junayd when he said 'the color of water is the color of its vessel,' then he would grant every believer their belief and perceive God in every form and every belief,"[194] he is often read as promoting a universalist outlook that accepts all religions as valid paths to God. In this chapter, I have argued that such an understanding is based in part on anachronistic readings that substitute the idea of "belief" with that of "religion." Yet what remains unacknowledged in such readings is that Ibn 'Arabi wrote these passages from the point of view of an enlightened witness to God's oneness, articulated not to celebrate the religions of Others, but to enunciate God's absolute sovereignty. In other words, such readings conflate Ibn 'Arabi's theomonistic idea of "God" as the *only* worshiped with "religion" as having something to do with the process of worshiping that *only* one. This conflation has led to the "strong misreading" (in the Bloomian sense)[195] that Ibn ʿArabi is claiming not only the unity of God but also the unity of all religions.

When Ibn ʿArabi discourses on "the divinity of beliefs," he is therefore not theorizing about the transcendent unity of religions as is commonly supposed, but rather about the human projection of ideational images upon the transcendent. Since human beings are created in the "image" or *form* of God, such projections do in fact reflect particular attributes of God, and as such are "true." Thus, the Andalusian Sufi makes his famous claim (as quoted above): "There are only beliefs and all are correct." Yet, Ibn ʿArabi held that individual beliefs as distinct images or forms can never be wholly "True"—that is, they can never contain the totality of God. For him, the only individual locus "capable" of such a feat is the cosmic Muhammadan heart that subsumes all meanings, forms, and beliefs within its *logos*-centered comprehensiveness. As Ibn ʿArabi notes in *The Meccan Openings*, only one with "perfect composition" (*al-kāmal al-mizāj*) encompasses all beliefs.[196] Such encompassment, however, is not simply a privatized mystical notion in Ibn ʿArabi's discourse, but plays out within a particular political cosmography in his own situated regime of power and knowledge production.[197] It is toward this politico-metaphysical discourse that our camels now must turn.

2

Return of the Solar King

Political mysticism . . . is exposed to the danger of losing its spell or becoming quite meaningless when taken out of its native surroundings, its time and its space.

ERNST H. KANTOROWICZ, *The King's Two Bodies.*[1]

IN A FAMOUS letter written in the year 1212 to the Seljuk sultan of Anatolia, ʿIzz al-Dīn Kaykāʾus I (r. 1211–20),[2] Ibn ʿArabi advised the newly enthroned king not to allow the Christians under his protection more socio-religious freedom than legally mandated by the sharia for the "Protected People" (*ahl al-dhimma*).[3] At the start of the letter, the Andalusian Sufi urges the king to "take care lest some day I find you among the most debased of Muslim leaders—those whose actions '*led them astray in the life of this world while they considered what they were doing to be good*' [Qur'an 18:104]."[4] Ibn ʿArabi sternly rebukes Kaykaʾus for persisting in violating divine prohibitions (*ḥudūd*) and further warns him not to mistake God's "respite" (*imhāl*) for "inattention" (*ihmāl*), for at death regret will be of no avail.[5] Ibn ʿArabi then turns to the abject state of the sultan's kingdom:

> The calamity that Islam and Muslims are undergoing in your realm—and few address it—is the raising of Church bells, the display of disbelief (*kufr*), the proclamation of associationism (*shirk*), and the elimination of the stipulations (*al-shurūṭ*) that were imposed by the Prince of Believers, ʿUmar ibn al-Khaṭṭāb, may God be pleased with him, upon the Protected People.[6]

Not only does the Andalusian Sufi here suggest that Christians living within Kaykaʾus's domain are disbelievers who profess the most heinous form of infidelity according to Islamic tradition (and indeed according to Ibn ʿArabi himself[7])—that is, associating partners with God or *shirk*—but he also goes on to detail a long litany of discriminating provisions that the sultan should enforce. Ibn ʿArabi here repeats a version of what is variously referred to as "the Pact of ʿUmar" (*ʿahd ʿumar* or *ʿaqd ʿumar*) or "the Stipulations of ʿUmar" (*shurūṭ ʿumar* or *al-shurūṭ al-'umariyya*)—a document of debated authenticity, which in exchange for the protection and partial socio-religious freedom of the Protected People demands that they submit to an extensive list of restrictions designed to show their subordinate status within Muslim society.[8] Thus, Ibn 'Arabi includes such proscriptions as "the prohibition of establishing in the city or the surrounding area a church, convent, cell, or hermitage for monks," as well as the prohibitions of imitating Muslim dress, using Muslim names, riding on saddles, taking up arms, displaying crosses, and performing loud liturgical recitations in the presence of Muslims.[9] Additionally, this list reiterates Ibn 'Arabi's initial concern regarding *shirk*, stating plainly that the Protected People "should not manifest associationism,"[10] again implying that they are—or at the very least have the potential to be—polytheistic in their doctrine or worship.[11] To add insult to injury, Ibn 'Arabi even rehearses the pact's stipulations of identification, or "distinguishing marks" (*ghiyār*), for non-Muslims: "they must trim their forelocks, keep their manner of dress the same wherever they are, and fasten girdles (*zanānīr*) around their waists."[12] By way of conclusion, Ibn 'Arabi repeats the dire warning that "if any thing from among what has been thus stipulated is violated, then there is no protection for them and it is permitted for the Muslims to deal with them as people of rebellion and sedition."[13] Finally, Ibn 'Arabi authoritatively seals the pact in his letter to Kayka'us with a disputed hadith on the proscription of church building and repair: "In Islam, there is no building of churches and no repairing what has fallen into ruin from them."[14]

Although this missive is included in Ibn 'Arabi's magnum opus, *The Meccan Openings* (*al-Futūḥāt al-makkiyya*), most scholars who defend his universalism as religiously inclusive ignore it altogether or dismiss it as a political concession. Often, this letter is explained away by the insistence that such religiously exclusive statements are somehow separate from Ibn 'Arabi's "authentic" mysticism. For example, in R. W. J. Austin's introduction to the now-classic translation of Ibn 'Arabi's *Fuṣūṣ al-ḥikam, The Bezels of Wisdom*, he notes that Ibn 'Arabi's reply to Kayka'us "is very revealing of the *nonmystical* side of his character, since he advised Kay Kaus to impose on them the full rigor of Islamic Law."[15] Similarly, Ibn 'Arabi's preeminent Western biographer, Claude Addas, notes that "even though he did recognize the validity of all creeds, and *a fortiori* of all monotheistic traditions, Ibn 'Arabi was nevertheless perennially aware, in those dark days, of the fact that Christianity was becoming a threat to Islam on all fronts."[16]

Even William Chittick—one of the foremost Western experts on Ibn 'Arabi and noted for depicting him "as a mainstream Sunni thinker" and thus emphasizing his "respect for the revealed Law"[17]—downplays the significance of such polemical discourse (although without ever acknowledging it directly).[18] In his oft-quoted 1994 work *Imaginal Worlds: Ibn al-ʿArabī and the Problem of Religious Diversity*, Chittick thus states:

> One would expect to find among the Sufis a clear exposition of the universality of revealed truth without the reservations expressed by most other Muslims. *But the Sufis had to take into account the beliefs of their contemporaries.* Even Ibn al-ʿArabī, who was not afraid to attack the limitations of the juridical and theological mentalities, often defends a literal reading of the Koranic criticisms of the People of the Book, *without suggesting that by "Christians" or "Jews" the Koran means anyone other than the contemporary practitioners* of those religions.[19]

According to Chittick here, Ibn ʿArabi's criticism of "the People of the Book" (*ahl al-kitāb*)—the Qur'anic term used to designate (at the very least) Jews and Christians—is at once cautiously conservative and decidedly situational: what qualms the Qur'an might have had against the People of the Book should be understood as part of its particular socio-historical context, and therefore Ibn ʿArabi did not view such criticism as relevant in other times and places.[20] As I will discuss at length below, Chittick thus emphatically claims that Ibn ʿArabi rejects the classical Islamic juridical position of abrogation (*naskh*), which asserts that Islam superseded all previous revelation. Rather, according to Chittick, Ibn ʿArabi recognizes the simultaneous and contemporaneous validity of all revealed religions.[21]

Besides the varying degrees of disavowal by Western scholars that authoritarian and exclusionary positions actually hold a place in Ibn ʿArabi's metaphysics in any meaningful way, his correspondence with the Anatolian sultan has also engendered strong condemnation, albeit more rarely in contemporary Euro-American contexts. For example, the Spanish Roman Catholic priest and Islamicist Miguel Asín Palacios (d. 1944) referred to Ibn ʿArabi's letter to Kayka'us as exuding "political hatred for the Christians."[22] Commenting more recently on the same issue, the Protestant minister and scholar of religion Carl-A. Keller asserts: "It is the tragedy of [Ibn ʿArabi's] faithfulness toward Islam that he was unable to work out different practical consequences of his spiritual insight."[23] Similarly, the Islamicist Giuseppe Scattolin, who is also a Roman Catholic priest and Comboni missionary, observes that it is precisely such types of stipulations as "the Pact of ʿUmar"—that is, those that enforce the sharia over non-Muslims—that are fundamental to Islamist discourse today. As such, Scattolin calls Ibn ʿArabi's Sufism "a type of 'simplified and reductive' mysticism, based as it is on a 'simplified and reductive' vision of other religions."[24] Although coming from the opposite side of the hermeneutical spectrum from those who offer apologies for Ibn ʿArabi, such critical readings (all notably from Christian scholars who are also ordained clergy) at bottom carry similar presuppositions of what a "true" religious mystic should be, namely, a universalist who celebrates the religious beliefs of the religious Other while avoiding the entanglement of "this-worldly" politics and interreligious polemics.

Yet, rather than a political comedown from a sublime spirituality, in this chapter I argue that Ibn 'Arabi's normative treatment of the Protected People in his letter to Kayka'us forms part of a wider metaphysics—that is, his ontological and epistemological understanding of reality—which is *itself* inherently political and has at its cosmological center the solar image of the Prophet Muhammad as cosmic king around whom the entire universe turns and whose station triumphs over, *and ultimately subsumes*, all previous religions and their laws. Here, I am not simply arguing that Ibn 'Arabi's mode of Sufism was "politically relevant,"[25] which it no doubt was, but rather that his so-called universalism is *entirely* dependent upon a specific political cosmography without which it ceases to be coherent.

In what follows, I primarily explore sections of Ibn 'Arabi's multivolume work *The Meccan Openings* that reflect his positions on abrogation and Islamic supersessionism and reveal an underlying exclusivism often overlooked in contemporary universalist treatments of Ibn 'Arabi's metaphysics. Indeed, in many such discussions, his positions are instead touted as a means of overcoming the exclusivist implications of traditional absolutism.[26] One of the problems that has faced a deeper critical reception of Ibn 'Arabi in the West is that his sprawling opus has not yet been fully translated into a European language.[27] Ibn 'Arabi's revised handwritten manuscript of *The Meccan Openings* totaled 560 chapters within thirty-seven volumes, and while he claimed the final order to be inspired, "it was also," as Michel Chodkiewicz trenchantly notes, "an intangible order."[28] Indeed, in some ways, reading *The Meccan Openings* is not dissimilar to reading the Qur'an: subjects are not treated in linear fashion, and conceptual keys for particular ideas and themes are scattered like pearls throughout its oceanic expanse. Thus, what Ibn 'Arabi might have to say about a particular topic in one chapter of *The Meccan Openings* may only be the tip of the iceberg, thus requiring further exploration within its voluminous depths.

Ibn 'Arabi, Marshall Hodgson, and the Western Idea of Mysticism

Before more closely examining the details of Ibn 'Arabi's ideas on abrogation and Islamic supersessionism, I think it will be helpful to first look at how the acclaimed scholar of Islam Marshall Hodgson (d. 1968) understood him within the larger category of Islamic mysticism. Although always useful, Hodgson is particularly helpful here because his work has served as the gold standard of post-Orientalist scholarship in Islamic studies for the latter half of the twentieth century.[29] Indeed, Hodgson has been called "a true visionary" in his anticipation of issues and concerns "a generation before the rest of the academic world."[30] In his now-classic multivolume work on Islamic history, *The Venture of Islam*, Hodgson consciously resists what he calls "the usual Westernistic image of world history" by offering a nonessentialist reading of Islamic history as indispensable, and thus refusing to submit to a Eurocentric clash of civilizations theory long before anyone had thought to name it as such.[31]

Hodgson aimed to bring to light the "ingrained misperceptions" that he believed aided in distorting the Islamic studies of his day, and he was hugely successful in doing so.[32] Yet, there were still places where his own held presuppositions were arguably distorting. One such area was his idea of Sufism and its relationship to Ibn 'Arabi.[33] While Hodgson did bring to the fore the importance of the sharia in Ibn 'Arabi's discourse,[34] which was in itself ahead of its time, he nevertheless had a particular depoliticized, universalist, and transhistorical preunderstanding of religious experience that he considered to be authentically "mystical"—a preunderstanding that seems to have colored his idea of Sufism in general.[35]

In *The Venture of Islam*, Hodgson identifies "two main types of piety within Islam": kerygmatic and mystical.[36] While Hodgson's notion of kerygmatic (i.e., "proclamatory" from the Greek *kerygma*, "proclamation") is at times ambiguous, he appears to mean by it a mode of traditional Muslim piety oriented around historical and social concerns that sought to proclaim the divine fulfillment of prophetic history along "with its positive moral commitments."[37] This orientation was enunciated in terms of "moral exclusivity" through allegiance to what was understood to be the only true community of authentic revelation:

> Only in that community was there truth and validity; but whoever shared in its allegiance was by that fact not only socially but cosmically on a plane above those who refused allegiance, on a plane where the only true difference among the faithful was in degree of piety. The Muslims felt themselves the defenders of the faith of Abraham in the midst of re-paganized dhimmî communities.[38]

Within such a so-called kerygmatic orientation, the exalted status of the biblical prophets (including Jesus as one of them) was necessarily recognized. Yet, according to Hodgson:

> in practice, pious Muslims could not acknowledge that the traditions derived from the moments of revelation granted to those other prophets

> had more than a limited legal validity as compared with the tradition arising from the revelation to Muḥammad. The others were all quite hopelessly corrupted. . . . The messengership of former prophets was but a pale corollary of Muḥammad's.[39]

Clearly, Hodgson felt that the exclusivism of this type of dogmatic subjectivity was spiritually shallow. As an alternative path, he described "a more individualistic piety" concerned "with more personal problems, which a pious man met when he tried to deepen and purify his inward worship."[40] Thus, according to Hodgson, such piety "became frankly mystical."[41] Hodgson further categorized this mystical metamorphosis as being "inspired, above all, by subjective inward awarenesses emerging as the selfhood matured, [while] *the historical, the political role* of the Muslim Ummah came to play a minimal role in it."[42] After thus semantically linking the terms "historical" and "political," Hodgson concludes by asserting that "this less historically-oriented Muslim movement was called *Ṣûfism*."[43] Even though Hodgson categorically distinguishes between the kerygmatic (as politico-historical) and the mystical (as internal), he also admits their historical linkage. Such linkage is best exemplified by Ibn ʿArabi's influential predecessor Abū Ḥāmid al-Ghazālī (d. 1111), who, according to Hodgson, assigned to Sufis "a function in validating a kerygmatic, historical vision as well as a *more properly inward* mystical role."[44]

Nevertheless, Hodgson held Ibn ʿArabi's hermeneutical approach to be distinctly nonkerygmatic and geared toward the "mystical relationship of the soul to the divine, and particularly with the relationships implied in the term 'love' " without undue concern for either history or politics.[45] According to Hodgson, this unconcern was symptomatic of a type of "philosophically inclined" mysticism that favored " 'unitive' formations" exemplified by Ibn ʿArabi and his Persian predecessor Shahābuddīn Yaḥyā Suhrawardī (d. 1191). "In contrast even to Ghazâlî," Hodgson avers, "neither was historically minded. . . . [T]heir universe was essentially timeless, as was their religion. For them, the great, concrete Muslim state had disappeared from philosophy as effectively as from the political map."[46]

As progressive as Marshall Hodgson's treatment of Islam was, and still is, his definition of "mysticism" and "mystical" as essentially nonkerygmatic and referring "in the first instance, to inward personal experience"[47] reveals a particular set of Euro-American presuppositions regarding what counts as "authentic" religiosity. While the association between religious subjectivity and "the interior life" has been a part of the Western conception of piety since Augustine, it has become increasingly central to the modern European understanding of "spirituality."[48] Not only was the Protestant Reformation responsible for emphasizing the individual relationship with God over that of the collective, but also, as William

Cavanaugh notes, the very distinction between religion and politics was itself instigated in the sixteenth and seventeenth centuries by the transference of power from the church to the new sovereign state. The so-called wars of religion were thus "fought by state-building elites for the purpose of consolidating their power over the church and other rivals."[49] While the church was deeply involved in such violence, the birth of the modern state was the real catalyst for these upheavals rather than religious fanaticism.[50]

Nevertheless, the assertion that the European wars of religion are evidence that public religiosity and its attendant absolutism causes violence has been, in Cavanaugh's words, a "creation myth for modernity"—a myth not only used as justification for Western secularism, but one also "inextricably bound up with the legitimation of the state and its use of violence."[51] In the face of the myth of religious violence, the Enlightenment impetus to relegate religion to a mode of private belief secluded from the socio-political realm was sanctioned as critical for Western progress. Thus, the modern turn toward the subject along with the increasing privatization of religion produced a particular, *and enduring*, conception of mysticism as an internal refuge from the political, transcendently dissociated from metanarratives of particularism and cosmologies of power.

Indeed, one of Hodgson's most illustrious colleagues was the influential historian of religion and Islamic studies scholar Wilfred Cantwell Smith, who was a Professor of Comparative Religion at Harvard University and served as the head of the world-renowned Harvard Center for the Study of Religion. As an ordained minister, former missionary, and graduate of Princeton University, Smith was emblematic of religious studies during Hodgson's scholarly generation.[52] Although every scholar working in the field today remains indebted to his seminal insights, Smith's notions regarding what constituted authentic spirituality can almost serve as a template for our inherited Western presuppositions regarding mysticism as "authentic" religion. These ideas are perhaps nowhere more concisely articulated with respect to Sufism than in a small passage from Smith's seminal 1957 work *Islam in Modern History*. Here, Smith states:

> Sufism differs from the classical Sunni *Weltanschauung* radically; and not least in its attitude to history, the temporal mundane. It stresses the individual rather than society, the eternal rather than the historical, God's love rather than His power, and the state of man's heart rather than behavior. It is more concerned that one's soul be pure than one's actions be correct. Some Sufis thought the Law unimportant. Most regarded it as a private discipline guiding the person towards transcendent fulfillment, and paid little heed to its function in ordering society, in marshaling history into a prescribed pattern.[53]

Ibn ʿArabi and the Political Moment of Exclusion

More recently, Omid Safi has forcefully challenged received traditions of Sufism as read through the specular reflection of the Western lens—a lens that consistently privileges Protestant categories of the "quest for a personal experience of God" over larger social, political, and institutional frameworks of power.[54] In contradistinction to such privatized constructions of religion, Safi argues that in medieval Persia, Sufis

> were intimately involved in the task of using their sanctity to rearrange, improve, challenge, and remain responsible for the affairs of the visible universe. Their social interactions far from nullify their credentials as "mystics" but in fact reinforce their status as holders of both *wilāya* (power and authority) and *walāya* (intimacy with God).[55]

Safi thus warns that "if our understanding of mysticism is based on a private experience of the Divine held in isolation from a social life, then we are bound to misconstrue the social significance of premodern Muslim mystics."[56]

Although Ibn ʿArabi both attempted and claimed to have effectively wielded political power,[57] my argument in this chapter is not about Ibn ʿArabi's political influence per se. Rather, I wish to show how his metaphysics cannot be decoupled from the broader socio-political concerns of his medieval context, as is often claimed. The distinction of the former from the latter depends on how we understand the idea of the political. For example, Addas claims that "generally speaking, in the corpus of Ibn ʿArabī's works we never find him adopting a political position."[58] Here, Addas specifically refers to Ibn ʿArabi's general silence regarding the political wrangling among contemporaneous ruling elites, such as the announcement that Jerusalem had been surrendered in 1229 to the Christians by the Ayyūbid sultan of Egypt al-Kāmil (d. 1238), or the betrayal of the Ayyūbid sultan of Damascus al-Nāṣir Dāwūd (d. 1258) by his uncle al-Ashraf (d. 1237). "The fact that in his writings he chose not to discuss these circumstantial issues," Addas asserts, "was simply because they held no place in the message God had instructed him to transmit to future generations."[59] Although Addas admits that Ibn ʿArabi does sometimes comment on the so-called political, such as his aforementioned missive to the sultan of Anatolia Kaykaʾus, she nevertheless argues that Ibn ʿArabi's discourse conveys a universal metaphysics, both transcultural and transhistorical, thus decoupled from the political issues of his day.

Yet, to define "the political" as merely having to do with the affairs of statecraft and governance, as Addas seemingly does, neglects a deeper politics that runs through Ibn ʿArabi's metaphysics that is directly linked to the particular socio-political context of his metaphysical milieu. In acknowledging this broader sense, the political theorist Chantal Mouffe asserts that

> the political cannot be restricted to a certain type of institution, or envisaged as constituting a specific sphere or level of society. It must be conceived as a dimension that is inherent to every human society and that determines our very ontological condition.[60]

As such, Mouffe understands the political as metaphysical. In other words, for Mouffe, the political is ontologically part of *the relational nature* of social identity in "*that the condition of existence of every identity is the affirmation of a difference*."[61] Mouffe's forceful insight of "difference" as the defining characteristic of social identity—and thus "the political"—is based on a reformulation of Carl Schmitt's infamous delineation of the political as the agonistic dialectic between friend and foe. As Mouffe contends, "By drawing our attention to the centrality of the friend/enemy relation in politics, Schmitt makes us aware of the dimension of the political that is linked to the existence of an element of hostility among human beings."[62]

Mouffe's relational conception of the political, however, importantly differs from Schmitt in its recognition of social identity as simply constituted by the "difference" posed by a relational "other" rather than the Schmittian necessity of war's "possibility" for the distinction between friend and enemy, and hence the existence of the political itself.[63] As Hugh Nicholson notes, according to Mouffe's relational conception of social identity,

> all forms of collective identity are constituted by difference; a group's sense of identity is constituted by the other against which it defines itself. Social identity therefore has an "us" versus "them" structure; it presupposes, in other words, *a political moment of exclusion*.[64]

It is precisely this political moment of exclusion that plays a critical role in Ibn 'Arabi's metaphysics and is nowhere more apparent than in his understanding of the doctrine of abrogation (*naskh*).

Ibn 'Arabi and the Aporia of Abrogation

In more specialized discussions, Ibn 'Arabi's position on abrogation has been repeatedly used to argue for his supposed inclusive religious universalism in opposition to normative Islamic discourses of exclusive supersessionism. As Reza Shah-Kazemi asserts: "We can . . . turn to Ibn Arabi for a useful Sufi means of overcoming one of the obstacles to wholesome dialogue between Muslims and members of other faiths: *the traditional legal notion of the abrogation of other religions by Islam*."[65] Part of the assumed foundation of what Shah-Kazemi rightly calls "the traditional legal notion" of abrogation, and its political corollaries, was an absolutist conception of the Islamic dispensation as superseding all previous religious laws. While the category of abrogation commonly denotes an *intra*-textual supersession of certain canonical textual prescriptions or prohibitions by other such texts within the Islamic discursive tradition itself, its usage here denotes an interscriptural process where the laws of an entire religious dispensation supersede and cancel a previous one. Just as medieval Christians understood Christianity as superseding Judaism, medieval Muslim scholars understood Islam as superseding the dispensations of the People of the Book. As John Burton notes, "To Muslim scholars, the abrogation of Judaism and Christianity by Islam was obvious."[66] Indeed, this supersessionist position was characteristic of Ibn 'Arabi's entire intellectual milieu.

Not only did Ghazali unquestionably believe that the Islamic abrogation of previous dispensations was a manifestation of the divine will,[67] but also even the irenic Muḥammad ibn ʿAbd al-Karīm al-Shahrastānī (d. 1153), who has been described as an early proponent of "an ecumenical Muslim worldview,"[68] staunchly held to the doctrine of abrogation. At the end of his theological treatise *The Furthest Limits in the Knowledge of Theology* (*Nihāyat al-aqdām fī ʿilm al-kalām*), Shahrastani's description of the progressive abrogation of each revealed religion until the advent of Muhammad is a classic example of such discourse and worth quoting here. After conducting a lengthy rebuttal against the Jewish claim that it is impossible for God to change His mind and abrogate the Jewish dispensation after He had given the Jews the Torah,[69] Shahrastani concludes:

> Each revealed law is abrogative (*nāsikha*) and clothes itself in another form until it ends at the perfection of all of the revealed laws, and they are all sealed by the Seal of the Prophets. There is nothing after the perfection and rectitude (*al-istiqāma*) except for the Hereafter (*al-maʿād*) and the Resurrection (*al-qiyāma*): "My advent and the hour is as (close) as these two (fingers)."[70] So, the creation is completed there and the command is completed here. Just as the creation is sealed by the perfection of the state of the sperm as a complete human being, so too is the revealed law (*al-sharīʿa*) sealed by the perfection of the state of the first revealed law (*al-sharʿ al-awwal*) as a completely perfect religion (*dīn tāmm kāmil*): "*Today I have perfected your religion for you, completed My favor upon you, and sanctioned for you Islam as a religion*" [Qur'an 5:3]. We

> are contented with God as a lord, with Islam as a religion (*dīn*), with Muhammad the chosen one (*al-muṣṭafā*), may God bless him and grant him peace, as a prophet, with the Qur'an as a book, with the Kaʿba as a qiblah, and with the believers as our brothers.[71]

Similarly, one of Ibn 'Arabi's most important Andalusian predecessors,[72] Ibn Barrajān (d. 1141), who was also from Seville, was "a firm believer in the dogma of 'supersessionism' whereby Islam supersedes or abrogates Christianity, just as the latter is understood to have superseded Judaism."[73] "Salvation in the afterlife" for Ibn Barrajan was thus "only possible within the framework of the Qurʾānic message brought by Muḥammad. *All other religions are devoid of salvific efficacy*."[74]

Because of Ibn 'Arabi's repeated emphasis on the Qur'anic notion that Muslims are to believe that all pre-Islamic revelations are sent as true divine messages from one God, it is often assumed that Ibn 'Arabi believes all revelations to be contemporaneously "valid" and thus *not superseded* by Islam. Since Ibn 'Arabi mentions Jews and Christians by name so infrequently, one can argue (as Chittick is quoted arguing at the start of this chapter[75]) that Ibn 'Arabi only refers to them in terms of the historical context of the Qur'anic revelation. Such Qur'anic criticism, so the argument reasonably goes, was never meant to be more than the censure of specific groups during the lifetime of Muhammad, since other Jews and Christians are indeed praised within the Qur'an.[76] Thus, in *Imaginal Worlds*, Chittick rightly notes that "the Koran declares that the essential message of every prophet is the same, while the details of each message is unique."[77] It is from this assertion, however, that Chittick makes a rather large interpretative leap, concluding: "*Hence the universality of religious truth is an article of Islamic faith*."[78] As might be imagined, such an absolute and ambiguously rendered statement of Islamic universalism would present a particular challenge for premodern, normative Islamic theology, and Chittick immediately qualifies his statement by adding: "It is true that many Muslims believe that the universality of guidance pertains only to pre-Koranic times, but others disagree."[79]

Although Chittick does not state which Qur'anic verses he is referring to here, Qur'an 3:84—which as mentioned in chapter 1 was (re)revealed to Ibn 'Arabi himself when he attained to the Muhammadan Station at the end of his spiritual ascension—is exemplary.[80] As we recall, this verse exhorts Muhammad and those who follow him to assert faith in God and the Qur'an, while simultaneously asserting faith "*in what was sent down upon Abraham, Ishmael, Isaac, Jacob, and the tribes (of Israel), and in what was given to Moses, Jesus, and the prophets from their Lord.*" Qur'an 3:84 thus categorically proclaims: "*we do not distinguish between any of them.*"

According to Chittick, Ibn ʿArabi "*frequently affirms the validity of religions other than Islam*, and in so doing he is *simply stating the clear Koranic position*."[81] Indeed, this interpretation of Ibn ʿArabi's understanding of the religious Other is characteristic of the type of Perennialist universalism that I wish to trouble here. As one of the foremost Western experts on Ibn ʿArabi, Chittick's meticulous and erudite translations have become the standard source for the majority of academic and popular references to him in English. As such, Chittick's assertions as to the universal, nonpolitical nature of Ibn ʿArabi's metaphysics have been particularly influential.

While chapter 3 will specifically interrogate such universalist ideas of religious "validity," in what follows I demonstrate how Ibn ʿArabi's so-called affirmation of religions other than Islam is fully in alignment with the classical discourse of Islamic supersessionism and not necessarily as inclusively "universal" as has been imagined. The following example from *The Meccan Openings* is a good illustration of Chittick's preceding assertion. Here, Ibn ʿArabi states:

> As for a revealed law (*sharʿ*) previous to us, it is not required of us to follow it except for what our law has confirmed from it, even though it is a true revelation for those to whom it was addressed. We do not say that it is false (*bāṭil*); rather, we believe in God, and his messenger and what was revealed to him and that which was revealed before him from the Book and the law.[82]

Here, of course, Ibn ʿArabi does recognize the "truth" of former revelations, as does the Qur'an,[83] yet it is a category mistake to interpret such recognition as the belief that all religions are contemporaneously valid along with Islam. This, however, is the argument that Chittick repeatedly makes.

In his 1992 book *Faith and Practice of Islam: Three Thirteenth Century Sufi Texts*, Chittick translates and comments on "three Persian texts written from a Sufi perspective" by a contemporaneous, or nearly so, follower of Ibn ʿArabi's metaphysics—either his stepson and preeminent disciple Ṣadr al-Dīn Qūnawī (d. 1274)[84] or, more likely according to Chittick, the similarly named Naṣīr al-Dīn Qūnawī. Regardless, these texts, as Chittick states, "are perhaps the earliest examples" of the school of Ibn ʿArabi.[85] The following passage appears in the first treatise, *The Rising Places of Faith (Maṭāliʿ-i īmān)*:

> As for the people of the creeds, they follow the prophets step by step. They acknowledge the Ocean of the Unseen through the Shariahs of the messengers, hobbling their rational faculties with the cord of commands and prohibitions. *And now of those Shariahs, only the authority of our own*

> *Prophet's Shariah—which has abrogated the other Shariahs—remains on the face of the earth.*[86]

In this passage, Qunawi first acknowledges that true believers ("the people of the creeds") accept the validity of previously revealed, prophetic laws ("Shariahs"). This statement thus echoes many verses of the Qur'an,[87] as well as the quoted passage of Ibn 'Arabi above: "we believe in God, and his messenger and what was revealed to him and that which was revealed before him from the Book and the law." Yet, Qunawi then immediately asserts that those very same revealed laws that he acknowledges in the preceding sentence have been abrogated *in their entirety* by the sacred law of Muhammad. Qunawi thus concludes with the absolutist and exclusory assertion that the revealed law of Islam is *the only one* that remains valid in the entire world.

In his commentary on this passage, however, Chittick seeks to mitigate Qunawi's absolutism, asserting that "although the Kalām authorities tend in the direction of exclusivism, many Sufis stress universality."[88] Even though in the introduction, as I noted above, Chittick claims that the text in question is perhaps the earliest example of Ibn 'Arabi's school, he nevertheless appears to assert here that on the issue of abrogation, Qunawi is closer to the exoteric theologians than he is with the "universal" discourse of Ibn 'Arabi. Chittick thus argues:

> Ibn al-'Arabī reminds his readers that Muslims are required to have faith in the "messengers and the scriptures"—that is, all the messengers and scriptures from Adam down to Muhammad. Muhammad, as he has told us in a sound hadith, was sent with "the all-comprehensive words," so his religion includes within itself the fundamental teachings of all religions. *This all-inclusiveness of Islam proves that other religions have not been abrogated. If they were, how could they be part of Islam?*[89]

As a proof text in support of his assertion that, for Ibn 'Arabi, "other religions have not been abrogated," Chittick translates the following passage from chapter 339 of *The Meccan Openings* (*Futūḥāt* III, 153):

> All the revealed religions [*sharā'i'*] are lights. Among these religions, the revealed religion of Muhammad is like the light of the sun among the lights of the stars. When the sun appears, the lights of the stars are hidden, and their lights are included in the light of the sun. Their being hidden is like the abrogation of the other revealed religions that takes place through Muhammad's revealed religion. Nevertheless, they do in fact exist, just as the existence of the light of the stars is actualized. This explains why we

> have been required in our all-inclusive religion to have faith in the truth of all messengers and all the revealed religions. They are not rendered null [*bāṭil*] by abrogation—that is the opinion of the ignorant.[90]

It is clear that Chittick puts a lot of stock in this single extract, since it has been published verbatim in at least two other places besides *Faith and Practice of Islam*.[91] Most notably, Chittick employs the exact passage and translation in his aforementioned book *Imaginal Worlds*, published two years after *Faith and Practice of Islam*, as support for another version of the same argument: although Ibn 'Arabi—like the Qur'an—sometimes takes the People of the Book to task for specific misinterpretations or distortions, "*he does not draw the conclusion that many Muslims have drawn*—that the coming of Islam abrogated (*naskh*) previous revealed religions."[92] Glossing his own translation, Chittick instead claims that for Ibn 'Arabi, "Islam is like the sun and other religions like the stars. Just as the stars remain when the sun rises, *so also the other religions remain valid when Islam appears*."[93]

The idea that Ibn 'Arabi rejected the normative Islamic supersessionism of his day—*a doctrine that* (as Chittick himself admits) *was even held by the earliest members of his own school*—and embraced all religions as valid has therefore become a prominent fixture in more recent universalist treatments of his thought. Since 9/11, there has been an increasing spate of publications *directly quoting* Chittick's above translation from chapter 339 used as a proof text to support this contention.[94] Yet, if read closely, the passage itself appears to contain an aporia. While first affirming that the idea of "abrogation" is real—"Their being hidden *is like the abrogation of the other revealed religions that takes place through Muhammad's revealed religion*"—the passage goes on to claim that such abrogation does not actually cancel the laws of the previous religions: "They are not rendered null [*bāṭil*] by abrogation."

Yet, Chittick's assertions in *Faith and Practice of Islam* and *Imaginal Worlds* (i.e., for Ibn 'Arabi "*other religions have not been abrogated*" and that Ibn 'Arabi "*does not draw the conclusion that many Muslims have drawn—that the coming of Islam abrogated* [naskh] *previous revealed religions*," respectively) proclaim a definitive resolution without ever addressing the original contradiction in the first place. Yet, these assertions do not amount to an argument; they are merely instances of special pleading that do nothing to help us understand why Ibn 'Arabi appears to contradict himself. Indeed, there seems to be more to this story than can be gleaned from this passage alone.

In 1996, Nuh Keller also had this sense. A popular American expatriate Sufi shaykh and translator known for his public defense of Ibn 'Arabi's "orthodoxy,"[95] Keller took Chittick to task for leaving out of the aforementioned abrogation passage from chapter 339 of *The Meccan Openings* a crucial remaining section—a section that when read in tandem with Chittick's above translation seems to imply a very different meaning. Keller's translation of Ibn 'Arabi's subsequent text, which begins a few lines before Chittick's translation ends, reads as follows:

> This is why we are required by our universal law to believe in all prophetic messengers (*rusul*) and to believe that all their laws are truth, and did not turn into falsehood by being abrogated: that is the imagination of the ignorant. So all paths return to look to the Prophet's path (Allah bless him and give him peace): if the prophetic messengers had been alive in his time, they would have followed him just as their religious laws have followed his law. For he was given Comprehensiveness of Word (*Jawami' al-Kalim*), and given [the Qur'anic verse] "Allah shall give you an invincible victory" (Qur'an 48:3), "the invincible" [*al-'aziz*, also meaning rare, dear, precious, unattainable] being he who is sought but cannot be reached. When the prophetic messengers sought to reach him, he proved impossible for them to attain to—because of his [being favored above them by] being sent to the entire world (*bi'thatihi al 'amma*), and Allah giving him Comprehensiveness of Word (*Jawami' al-Kalim*), and the supreme rank of possessing the Praiseworthy Station (*al-Maqam al-Mahmud*) in the next world, and Allah having made his Nation (*umma*) "the best Nation ever brought forth for people" (Qur'an 3:110). The Nation of every messenger is commensurate with the station of their prophet, so realize this.[96]

Indeed, this immediately following section that Chittick saw fit to leave out reiterates the comprehensive nature of Muhammad's prophethood, as discussed in chapter 1, and its incorporation of all prophetic paths and realities—as Chittick himself alludes to in his commentary in *Faith and Practice of Islam* noted above. Thus, the one line that most plainly controverts Chittick's repeated argument is Ibn 'Arabi's assertion that "all paths return to look to the Prophet's path. . . . *[I]f the prophetic messengers had been alive in his time, they would have followed him just as their religious laws have followed his law*." Clearly, this is a contradiction since Chittick argues that Ibn 'Arabi's universalism is transhistorical—that is, "*the other religions remain valid*"—whereas the section that Keller translates (and Chittick neglects) implies that Muhammad's law has indeed superseded what came before it.

Yet, even with the additional translation that Keller brings to our attention, the aporia remains. If Ibn 'Arabi's position is indeed a recapitulation of the classical Islamic juridical position of abrogation of all previously revealed religions and their laws (as evinced by Keller's translated passage asserting that the previous prophets would have followed Muhammad "just as their religious laws have followed his law"), then why does Ibn ʿArabi state in the first part of the passage (as Keller *himself* translates): "we are required by our universal law to believe in all prophetic messengers (*rusul*) and *to believe that all their laws are truth, and did not turn into falsehood by being abrogated*"? Indeed, if their laws *are* "truth" and have not been turned "into falsehood," would not Chittick's universalist argument that they remain valid as contemporaneous religions be reasonable? The answer *must* be yes. So how then is such an aporia to be reconciled?

The Political Cosmology of Abrogation in The Meccan Openings

The way through the apparent paradox of abrogation in Ibn ʿArabi's discourse is found in an extended discussion in chapter 12 of *The Meccan Openings*, which Ibn ʿArabi entitles:

> On Knowledge of the Rotation of the Celestial Sphere (*dawrat falak*) of our Master Muhammad, blessings and peace be upon him, which is the Rotation of Dominion (*dawrat al-siyāda*)—Time has Returned (*istadāra*) to its Original Condition on the Day God, Most High, Created It.[97]

The last part of this seemingly enigmatic title is taken directly from a hadith where the Prophet is reported by his companion Abū Bakra to have said during the so-called Farewell Pilgrimage (*ḥajj al-wadāʿ*): "time has returned (*istadāra*) to its original condition on the day God created the heavens and earth."[98] In the hadith, Muhammad announces the prohibition of intercalation (*al-nasīʾ*)—that is, the pre-Islamic practice in which the sacred months were postponed or transposed for material or political advantage, thus making the exact month ambiguous.[99] Muhammad's Farewell Pilgrimage thus rectified the month of Dhū al-Ḥijja, subsequently restoring the calendar to primordial time.

Taking the notion of Muhammad's rectification of primordial time in the aforementioned hadith to its cosmic extreme, in chapter 12 Ibn ʿArabi constructs an elaborate cosmology based on the figure of Muhammad in politico-metaphysical terms. Here, Ibn ʿArabi situates the spiritual reality of the Prophet as the cosmic axis around which the seven heavens rotate through cyclical time and according to their correlated commands, thus expounding verse 41:12 of the Qur'an, which states: "*And God completed seven heavens in two days and revealed in each heaven their command.*"

Throughout chapter 12, Ibn ʿArabi emphasizes Muhammad's primordial kingship as the cosmogonic source of all previous prophetic knowledge and law up until his own physical manifestation as the final prophet. Muhammad is thus described at the very beginning of the chapter as "king (*malik*) and master (*sayyid*) while Adam was still between water and clay."[100] Thus, at the end of the prologue of chapter 12, Ibn ʿArabi summarizes the cosmic and supersessionary significance of Muhammad, his revelation, and his community (*umma*):

> There is no celestial sphere more vast than that of Muhammad, blessings and peace be upon him, because he has been given all-comprehensiveness (*al-iḥāṭa*), which is only given to one from God's community specified by Him through the decree of supersession (*al-tabaʿiyya*). So we [as Muslims], in turn, have been given all-comprehensiveness over the remaining communities, and that is why we "*bear witness for humanity*" [Qur'an 2:143]. Thus at the time of the ascendant star of his birth, God gave Muhammad revelation commanded from the heavens that He did not give to anyone else.[101]

Yet, it is in the ensuing treatment of the fourth heaven—the cosmological location of the Sun—where Ibn ʿArabi reveals the core of his thought regarding the relationship between the dispensation of Islam and all other religions. In clear opposition to Chittick's assertion above that Ibn ʿArabi denied the abrogation (*naskh*) of other faiths by Islam, thus claiming their enduring validity, Ibn ʿArabi emphatically states that it is from the fourth heaven that God commands Muhammad's law to abrogate and supersede all previous religions. Ibn ʿArabi here states:

> And from the commanded revelation in the fourth heaven (*al-samāʾ al-rābiʿa*) is the abrogation (*naskh*) of all of the (previously) revealed laws (*jamīʿ al-sharāʾiʿ*) by Muhammad's revealed law (*sharīʿa*) and the triumph (*ẓuhūr*)[102] of his religion (*dīn*) over all of the religions (*adyān*) of the messengers who preceded him and each revealed book.[103]

Indeed, this is the only section in *The Meccan Openings* that Ibn ʿArabi uses the term "religion" (*dīn*) in the plural (*adyān*),[104] and it is telling that he does so to express the superiority of Muhammad's revealed law over all other religions. He continues:

> The only ruling (*ḥukm*) of God that remains from the religion (*dīn*) of the (previous) religions (*adyān*) is what Muhammad has firmly determined for it by his confirmation (*taqrīr*);[105] so, it is (now) of Muhammad's law

> and his universal messengership (*ʿumūm risāla*). If there remains a ruling other than this, then it is not from the ruling of God except for among the People of the Indemnity Tax (*ahl al-jizya*) in particular.[106] However, as we said, it is not (in reality) a ruling of God, because He named it "invalid" (*bāṭil*).[107]

Here, it is necessary to pause and note that Ibn ʿArabi himself appears to contradict the earlier quoted passage on abrogation from chapter 339 of *The Meccan Openings* (translated by both Chittick and Keller) where Ibn ʿArabi asserts that it is only the opinion of "the ignorant" that the religions prior to Islam are "invalid" (*bāṭil*). While the meaning of this apparent contradiction will be made clear below, for now I want to focus on what proves to be the critical element of this passage, namely, Ibn ʿArabi's mention of "the People of the Indemnity Tax"—that is, the People of the Book—as somehow encompassing an "exception" to the legal classification of "invalidity" assigned to previous religious laws after the coming of Islam. Thus, directly after Ibn ʿArabi states that in fact God has named any remaining ruling "invalid," he asserts:

> So, the (previous ruling) is *against* the one who has followed it, not *for* him (*fa huwa ʿalā man ittabaʿahu lā lahu*).[108] This is what I mean by the triumph of Muhammad's religion (*dīn*) over all of the religions (*adyān*), like al-Nābigha[109] in his panegyric said:
>
> Do you not see that God has given you such a superior rank (*sura*),
> that you see every king below you groveling (*yatadhabdhab*)?
> For you are a sun, and the kings stars;
> when the sun rises, there is no longer a single star apparent.[110]
>
> This is the rank of Muhammad, may God bless him and grant him peace, and the rank of the revealed law that he brought among the prophets and their revealed laws, God's peace be upon all of them.
>
> Indeed, the light of the stars is subsumed (*indaraja*) within the light of the sun. So, the day is ours, but the People of the Book only have the night, that is, if "*they offer the indemnity tax* (jizya) *willingly, in a state of humiliation*" [Qur'an 9:29].[111]

In light of the text above from chapter 12 of *The Meccan Openings*, Chittick's use of a single passage from chapter 339 of the same multivolume work (i.e., *Futūḥāt* III, 153) in *Faith and Practice of Islam* and *Imaginal Worlds* as a proof text for

Ibn 'Arabi's position on abrogation emerges as critically incomplete and thus forcefully misleading. Here, it becomes clear that the sun and stars metaphor mentioned in chapter 339 is only an allusion to the poem by al-Nābigha al-Dhubyānī (one of the six famous pre-Islamic Arabic poets) directly referenced in chapter 12. This "ur-passage" thus clarifies Ibn 'Arabi's doctrine of abrogation, which here asserts that all religious dispensations have been rendered "invalid" from on high—that is, from the fourth heaven—by the manifestation of Muhammad's revelation. Indeed, as noted earlier, Ghazali also held that the abrogation of the previous religions by Muhammad's revelation was an expression of the divine will.[112]

Yet, for Ibn 'Arabi, things are not so simple. He *also* asserts in the ur-passage from chapter 12 that the legal classification of "protection" (*dhimma*)—as made operative through the payment of the indemnity tax (*jizya*) and its attendant humiliation and subjugation—allows for the continuation of Jewish and Christian law, albeit in an impeded fashion. Thus, in the passage that Chittick translates from chapter 339, Ibn 'Arabi can emphatically state that the revealed religions—here, Judaism and Christianity—"are not rendered null [*bāṭil*] by abrogation." Yet, the question remains just what kind of validity do such religions really have, if they can, according to Ibn 'Arabi, only function as subsumed—that is, subjugated—within the sun of Muhammad's dispensation? Indeed, as Ibn 'Arabi asserts, "the day is ours, but the People of the Book only have the night." Moreover, the allotment of even only "night" is, as Ibn 'Arabi makes clear by quoting the final words of Qur'an 9:29, one that is *only made viable* through the humiliation of the indemnity tax:

> *Fight from among those who were given the Book—those who do not believe in God or in the last day, do not hold to be prohibited what God and His Messenger have declared to be so, and do not follow the religion of truth—until they offer the indemnity tax willingly, in a state of humiliation* (ṣāghirūn).

Ibn 'Arabi's reference to this Qur'anic call for the subjugation of the People of the Book by force of arms—in combination with his initial exaltation of "the triumph" of Muhammad's religion and al-Nabigha's verse extolling the triumphant king over his groveling vanquished—renders contemporary constructions of Ibn 'Arabi as a "universalist," such as Chittick's, deeply problematic.

Rather than simply an anomaly in Ibn 'Arabi's discourse, the idea that the People of the Book are allowed as "the protected people" (*ahl al-dhimma*) to continue to follow their laws *because* of their willing subjugation, and thus subsumption, within the Muhammadan sharia emerges as a coherent element within Ibn 'Arabi's metaphysical discourse. This particular idea—what I refer to as the "qualified subjugation" of the People of the Book—is mentioned in several places in *The Meccan Openings.* In one particularly telling passage, Ibn 'Arabi discusses the case of miraculously long-lived saints who were regents (*awṣiyāʾ* / s. *waṣī*) of past prophets but were still alive during the advent of Muhammad and received his revealed knowledge through the enigmatic figure of "Khiḍr, the companion of Moses."[113] As such, Ibn 'Arabi relays the story of Ibn Barthamlā, who reportedly testified to the prophecy of Muhammad in front of an envoy of the caliph 'Umar, even though he was a saintly regent of Jesus. Referring to Ibn Barthamla as a "monk," Ibn 'Arabi thus states:

> Do you think that monk remained on the rulings of the Christians? No, by God, the sacred law (*sharīʿa*) of Muhammad, may God bless him and grant him peace, is abrogative (*nāsikha*)! For he states, may God bless him and grant him peace, "If Moses were alive it would be impossible for him not to follow me."[114] And similarly, when Jesus descends he will only lead us from us, that is, by our way (*sunna*) and he will only judge us by our law (*sharīʿa*).[115]

Yet, Ibn 'Arabi goes on to qualify this statement:

> This monk was of the Christ-like saints (*ʿīsawiyyīn*) who inherit from Jesus, upon him be peace, until the time of Muhammad's mission. So when Muhammad, may God bless him and grant him peace, was sent, this monk worshiped God by Muhammad's law (*sharīʿa*). God taught him knowledge from His presence (*ladunhu*) by the mercy He gave to Muhammad. Thus, he inherits the Christ-like condition also through Muhammad and remains a Christ-like saint (*ʿīsawī*) on two sacred laws (*al-sharīʿatayn*). Do you not see that this monk had given an account of Jesus's descent, may God bless him, and when he will kill the pig and break the cross?[116] Do you think that he continues (on the opinion) that the meat of the pig is permissible? So this monk remains Christ-like on two laws, and he has a double reward—a reward for following his prophet and a reward for following Muhammad, may God bless him and grant him peace; he is waiting for Jesus to descend.[117]

In these passages, Ibn 'Arabi discusses a special situation of a saint who originally was Christian but because of the appearance of Muhammad was obliged to adopt his law. Thus, in the previous passage, Ibn 'Arabi relates a hadith of the Prophet that appears multiple times throughout *The Meccan Openings*: "If Moses were alive it would be impossible for him not to follow me."[118] In the same vein, Ibn

'Arabi here references another hadith he is fond of repeating, asserting that when Jesus descends he will judge by the sharia of Muhammad.[119] Yet, although Ibn Barthamla becomes a Muslim as it were—even, according to Ibn 'Arabi, following Qur'anic dietary prohibitions—he remains a Christian but renews his status as an "heir" (*wārith*) of Jesus through the intermediary of Muhammad.[120]

Ibn 'Arabi goes on to note that during the time when Ibn Barthamla was seen by the Companions of Muhammad,

> they did not ask him about his state in Islam and faith, nor did they ask from which of the sacred laws does he worship, because the Prophet, may God bless him and grant him peace, did not command them to ask such questions. We know for certain that the Prophet, may God bless him and grant him peace, did not confirm anyone in their associationism (*shirk*) and that he knew that God—out of His mercy and grace—took responsibility to teach (some) servants from His presence (*ladunhu*) knowledge that He revealed upon the Prophet, may God bless and grant him peace.[121]

Here we can sense Ibn 'Arabi's apprehension regarding an imagined interlocutor questioning the theology of such a monk—was he guilty of associating partners with God? Ibn 'Arabi's attention to this concern shows that he took this question seriously. Indeed, in Ibn 'Arabi's day not only were Christians commonly accused of such a grave offence,[122] but it is also the case, as quoted in the introduction to this chapter, that Ibn 'Arabi himself condemned the Christians living within the realm of Kayka'us for "the proclamation of associationism (*shirk*)." Yet, here Ibn 'Arabi assures his readers that this could not have been the case for Ibn Barthamla, since this particular monk was a spiritual heir of Muhammad, which would not have been possible had he been guilty of associationism. Moreover, God would not teach such a person directly from His presence.[123]

At this juncture in the passage, Ibn 'Arabi begins to broaden the discussion to the People of the Book in general:

> If he is one who pays the indemnity tax (*al-jizya*), we would say that the Muhammadan law (*al-sharʿ al-muḥammadī*) has confirmed his religion for him as long as he gives the indemnity tax—this is a specific matter of Muhammad's universal messengership (*ʿumūm risāla*). Indeed, with Muhammad's appearance the only law that remained was his law, which confirms the People of the Book's law as long as they give the indemnity tax.[124]

Here, when the discussion finally settles down to a more general conversation about the People of the Book, we find a succinct confirmation of Ibn 'Arabi's doctrine of qualified subjugation found within the Nabigha passage above—that is, by obeying the Qur'anic command of humiliation through paying the indemnity tax, the People of the Book are subsumed into the Muhammadan dispensation and allowed to remain upon their law.[125]

Elsewhere in a section from chapter 10 of *The Meccan Openings*, Ibn ʿArabi elucidates how all of "the prophets in the world were Muhammad's deputies (*nuwwāb*) from Adam to the last of the messengers, peace be upon them."[126] Once again, Ibn ʿArabi makes recourse to the doctrine of qualified subjugation as part of his metaphysical cosmography of supersessionism. Here, Ibn ʿArabi concisely recapitulates his entire metaphysical cosmology of Muhammad beginning with "his rank as a spirit (*rūḥ*) before God's engendering human bodies" as he was "a prophet when Adam was between water and clay."[127] Thus, according to Ibn ʿArabi, the "spiritual presence (*rūḥāniyya*)" of Muhammad "was with every prophet and messenger" during their prophetic career, and "he brought them assistance through his pure spirit, which manifested within their revealed laws (*al-sharāʾiʿ*) and branches of knowledge (*al-ʿulūm*) during the time of their existence as messengers."[128] Ibn ʿArabi explains that because Muhammad "did not exist in the sensory world in the beginning, each law is associated with whom it was sent. Yet in reality, each is the revealed law of Muhammad (*sharʿ muḥammad*)."[129] Thus, Ibn ʿArabi clarifies that even though Muhammad's spiritual presence—that is, the Muhammadan Reality (*ḥaqīqa muḥammadiyya*)—was in effect the source of these laws, they were still abrogated by the coming of Muhammad's sharia when he physically manifested:

> As for God (having) abrogated (*nasakha*) all of the laws by Muhammad's law, this abrogation (*al-naskh*) does not disregard (the fact that) the previous revealed laws (*sharāʾiʿ*) were from his revealed law (*sharʿ*). For indeed, God has made us witness to his outward law as revealed to him, God bless him and grant him peace, in the Qur'an and the Sunna that abrogation (*al-naskh*) is with our (community's) consensus (*ijmāʿ*), and we are in agreement (with this) provided it is understood that the previous abrogated law was Muhammad's law sent by him to us (through previous prophets). So that which comes later abrogated that which came before. Thus, this abrogation, as found in the Qur'an and the Sunna, alerts us to the fact that all of the previous revealed laws (*sharāʾiʿ*) that have been abrogated were not separate from Muhammad's law.[130]

In this passage, Ibn ʿArabi's conception of Muhammadan supersessionism—which, it should be noted, is very similar to Shahrastani's passage on abrogation quoted earlier—emerges *as a metaphysical tautology*: while all prophetic laws are in essence Muhammad's law, they are nevertheless in the end abrogated by Muhammad's final dispensation. That is, of course, except for the laws of the People of the Book, which Ibn 'Arabi again mentions here. Thus, Ibn 'Arabi clarifies that "when Jesus, peace be upon him, will descend at the end of time, *he will rule by other than his own law*, or rather, *with a portion of what he ruled with in the time of his own message*."[131] As such, Ibn 'Arabi asserts that Jesus's "rule will be by the Muhammadan Law (*al-sharʿ al-muḥammadī*) as established today," but "the protected people (*ahl al-dhimma*) from the People of the Book" will follow their own law as long as they "*give the indemnity tax willingly, in a state of humiliation*" [Qur'an 9:29].[132]

The Muhammadan Return as Solar King

Throughout his overlapping discussions of abrogation, supersession of previous revelations, and the doctrine of qualified subjugation, Ibn 'Arabi consistently uses metaphors of divine governance in relation to Muhammad and his legal dispensation. For example, in the same section from chapter 10 covered in the preceding discussion, Ibn 'Arabi asserts that "if Muhammad, God bless him and grant him peace, had been sent during the time of Adam, then the prophets and all of humanity would be physically under the ruling (*ḥukm*) of his revealed law (*sharīʿa*) until the Day of Resurrection."[133]

According to Ibn 'Arabi, all of the prophets were sent to specific communities and none were sent universally (*ʿāmma*) except for Muhammad. This is so, Ibn 'Arabi reasserts, because "he is the king (*al-malik*) and the master (*al-sayyid*) . . . and his dominion (*mulk*) spans from the time of Adam to the time when he was sent, may God bless him and grant him peace, until the Day of Resurrection." "What emerges from all of this," Ibn 'Arabi concludes, "is that Muhammad is king (*malik*) and master (*sayyid*) of all the children of Adam, and that all of those who preceded him were under his dominion (*mulk*) and his followers (*tabaʿ*), and those who ruled previously were his deputies (*nuwwāb*)."[134]

Indeed, the idea of Muhammad as "king and master" is a recurrent theme in *The Meccan Openings*—one that, as I noted above, initiates chapter 12, wherein the cosmology of abrogation is detailed. Indeed, it is again in chapter 12 that Ibn 'Arabi quotes Nabigha's poetic solar metaphor of a triumphant monarch over lesser, groveling kings: "For you are a sun, and the kings stars." As we have seen, it is this very same solar metaphor that Ibn 'Arabi directly refers to elsewhere in *The Meccan Openings*, including Chittick's oft-quoted translation from chapter 339, which he uses as a proof text for the clearly misleading assertion that Ibn 'Arabi rejects Islamic supersessionism and the doctrine of abrogation. As such, Ibn 'Arabi's cosmological symbolism of the Prophet Muhammad's kingship and rule, and its attendant abrogation and subsumption of all previous prophetic revelations and laws, is certainly amplified, if not perhaps inspired, by Nabigha's solar metaphor itself. Yet, the politico-religious trope of solar kingship is ancient and persistently present throughout the literature of Near Eastern civilizations. Out of all the celestial bodies, in the preclassical era it was the sun that served as a consistent model for kingship.[135] Indeed, in his definitive study on classical astrology and religion, Franz Cumont recounts that according to the ancient Semitic Chaldean system,

> the Sun moves in the midst of the heavenly spheres. It occupies the central position among the seven circles of the universe. The other planets appeared to revolve round it, or rather to escort it, and astrologers delighted to point to the Royal Sun advancing in the midst of his satellites, as earthly princes, whose tutelar star he is, march encircled by their guards.[136]

It is therefore no accident that Ibn ʿArabi locates the celestial home of the sun, "the fourth heaven" (*al-samāʾ al-rābiʿa*), as the "heart of the world and heart of the heavens."[137] In the chapter on Idrīs (often identified with the Biblical prophet Enoch) in *The Ring Stones of Wisdom*, Ibn ʿArabi states: "The highest of places is the place around which the millstone (*raḥā*) of the world of the spheres rotates, and it is the Sphere of the Sun (*falak al-shams*)."[138] As the cosmic hub around which the entire firmament turns, Ibn ʿArabi thus claims that the Sphere of the Sun is "the pole (*quṭb*) of the spheres," which holds "an elevated place" (*rafiʿ al-makān*).[139]

While Ibn ʿArabi states that the "spiritual station of Idrīs" (*maqām rūḥāniyyat idrīs*) is connected to the "exaltedness of the place" (*ʿulū al-makān*) of the Sphere of the Sun, he asserts further (in parallel language): "as for exaltedness of the rank (*ʿulū al-makāna*), it belongs to us—that is, the Muhammadans."[140] As Chodkiewicz observes, "the model par excellence of [the] Muḥammadan . . . is Ibn ʿArabī himself."[141] Thus, in this passage, Ibn ʿArabi makes a subtle allusion to his own rank as the highest Muhammadan saint,[142] *and thus his own station*—that is, the Muhammadan Station—within the Sphere of the Sun itself.[143]

Yet because, as I noted above, Ibn ʿArabi cosmologically positions the Sphere of the Sun as the cosmic "millstone" and "pole," it is clear that his claim for the "exaltedness of the rank" of both himself and "the Muhammadans" is more broadly linked to Muhammad himself, whom Ibn ʿArabi describes in *The Meccan Openings* as the ultimate spiritual axis or pole: "As for the one (true) pole (*al-quṭb al-wāḥid*), he is the spirit of Muhammad (*rūḥ Muḥammad*), blessings and peace be upon him, who is the spiritual support (*al-mumidd*) for all of the prophets and messengers, peace upon them all."[144] It is in this sense that Ibn 'Arabi aligns the Sphere of the Sun as the cosmic pole around which the whole universe turns with Muhammad himself as its anthropomorphous fulcrum upon which the entire spiritual hierarchy of creation pivots. Indeed, it is precisely the merging of Muhammad with the cosmic pole that Ibn 'Arabi's previously noted title for chapter 12 of *The Meccan Openings* refers: "On Knowledge of the Rotation of the Celestial Sphere of our Master Muhammad, blessings and peace be upon him, which is the Rotation of Dominion. . . ."

Let us recall that it is in chapter 12 where Ibn 'Arabi relates it is from within the fourth heaven—the Sphere of the Sun—that the divine command issues for the Islamic abrogation of all other previously revealed religions. Indeed, chapter 12 is also where Ibn 'Arabi quotes Nabigha's solar metaphor of a triumphant monarch. In a synoptic passage found elsewhere within *The Meccan Openings*, Ibn 'Arabi summarizes the spiritual supremacy of the Prophet Muhammad in terms of Nabigha's metaphor of a solar king. Here, Ibn 'Arabi states:

> Know that since God made the waystation (*manzil*) of Muhammad—blessings and peace be upon him—that of lordship (*siyāda*), he is master (*sayyid*). He who is other than him is of (his) subjects. We have thus understood that he is matchless, for indeed subjects cannot compare to their kings—they have a particular waystation as subjects do theirs.[145]

Ibn 'Arabi goes on to relate the now-familiar assertion that Muhammad has held his sovereign station before the creation of Adam. He thus claims that through his unique "station of the comprehensive words" (*maqām jawāmiʿ al-kalim*), Muhammad has been the source of "spiritual support (*al-mumidd*) for every Perfect Human Being (*insān kāmil*)," beginning with Adam through "a continuous succession of vicegerents" until Muhammad's physical birth "in order for the ruling property of his rank to manifest through the confluence of his two configurations (*nash'atayn*)."[146] By "confluence of his two configurations," Ibn 'Arabi here means the meeting of Muhammad's spiritual "reality" (i.e., the *ḥaqīqa muḥammadiyya*) and his physical form. As such, Ibn 'Arabi asserts, "*When he appeared, it was like the sun subsumed in its light all light*."[147] He thus concludes:

> So he confirmed from his revealed laws (*sharāʾiʿ*)—that is, laws that he directed his (prior) deputies (to reveal)—what he confirmed and he abrogated from them what he abrogated. Thus, his care for his community (*umma*) appeared through his presence and manifestation—although the entire human and fiery (*al-nārī*)[148] world is his community. Yet, Muhammad's (particular dispensational) community is attributed

> with special characteristics. God made them "*the best community ever to be brought forth for humanity*" [Qur'an 3:110]. This grace was bestowed through the manifestation of Muhammad's two configurations (simultaneously). So, one of the graces given to this community over the other communities is that God bestowed upon this community the rank of Muhammad's vicegerents before his (physical) manifestation.[149]

In this important passage, Ibn 'Arabi consolidates his argument regarding the subsumptive nature of Muhammad by historicizing his spiritual aspect within the abrogative power of his revealed law. His conclusion that the Muslim religious dispensational community is superior to all others is not merely grounded in his reference to Qur'an 3:110, but is here tied to the subsumptive nature of the primordial Muhammadan *Logos* made flesh, *as it were*, through its physical manifestation as a law-giving Prophet. Muhammad's ultimate appearance in the world—returning cosmic time to its primordial position, and thus ushering in the triumph of Islam—brings to the fore Ibn 'Arabi's notion of history as grounded simultaneously in political difference and ontological wholeness.

Conclusion

Chittick's repeated deployment of a small passage from chapter 339 of *The Meccan Openings* (i.e., *Futūḥāt* III, 153)—and its attendant solar metaphor—as a proof text for Ibn 'Arabi's rejection of abrogation has formed the basis for an entire post-9/11 interpretive field on Ibn 'Arabi and the religious Other. Through the various publications that have reproduced verbatim Chittick's translation, as well as repeating his universalist reading of Ibn 'Arabi,[150] the idea that the Andalusian Sufi rejected the classical doctrine of Islamic abrogative supersessionism has received wide popular and scholarly acceptance. For example, in a 2016 conference held at George Washington University, Chittick's exact translation of the abrogation passage from chapter 339 (as quoted earlier) was read verbatim in a talk entitled "The Quran and the Perennial Philosophy" by the Ibn 'Arabi scholar Caner Dagli (along with a few additional lines from the succeeding passage). Dagli goes on to quote Shah-Kazemi's interpretation of Ibn 'Arabi's position regarding Islamic supersession and abrogation as follows (Shah-Kazemi also quotes Chittick's translation from chapter 339 before this passage):

> For Ibn ʿArabī, the fact that one's own religious Law sustains the traveller upon the path does not signify that other Laws are intrinsically incapable of sustaining other communities in their spiritual journey—even if all

> other religions are deemed to be eminently comprised within Islam, seen as the final, all-comprehensive way.[151]

Dagli continues to quote another article by Shah-Kazemi (which again cites Chittick's translation of the abrogation passage from chapter 339):

> To believe that pre-Qur'anic religions lose their efficacy is thus to render meaningless the avowed function of Islam to be a "confirmation" and "protection" in relation to those religions: if the religions are inefficacious as vehicles of salvation, there is no point in confirming and protecting them. They should simply be cast into the dustbin of religious history along with other degenerate religious traditions, according to the logic of those who believe that "abrogation" equals "nullification"—the "ignorant," as Ibn ʿArabī calls them.[152]

Dagli concludes by arguing that one cannot simply selectively pick quotes from Ibn 'Arabi to prove his absolutism. To drive his point home, Dagli invokes the work of Frithjof Schuon and the example of his many criticisms against Christian doctrines (such as the Trinity, the papacy, the mother of God formulation, and the *Filioque*) and notes that if these criticisms were quoted in isolation

> to someone who was unfamiliar with his body of work, . . . they might conclude that Schuon was an exclusivist, but thinkers must be judged in accordance with their general metaphysics and everything relevant that they've written or said on a particular subject. *What I mean is it's very difficult to turn Ibn 'Arabi into a strict abrogationist and exclusivist if we take his entire body of work into view*.[153]

Indeed, Dagli's final assertion here—that it is "very difficult to turn Ibn 'Arabi into a strict abrogationist and exclusivist *if we take his entire body of work into view*"—points precisely to the main thrust of my argument in this chapter and indeed this entire study: that is, to read Ibn 'Arabi as adhering (anachronistically) to a Perennialist view of inclusive universalism is to strongly misread "*his entire body of work*."[154] As I have argued in chapter 1, Ibn 'Arabi's idea of "religion" has very little to do with "belief" (as religion is generally understood in the West today) and much more to do with law. And as I have shown throughout this chapter, as well as in chapter 1, the religious Other for Ibn 'Arabi is totally subsumed within the legal authority of both the Qur'an and the Prophet Muhammad. Indeed, this is fully borne out by Ibn 'Arabi's repeated reference (including in Chittick's proof text from chapter 339) to the solar metaphor found directly within Nabigha's panegyric verses quoted in chapter 12 of *The Meccan Openings* in straightforward support of abrogation and the *logos*-oriented subsumption of all previously revealed laws within Muhammad's law. Indeed, according to Ibn 'Arabi, such forceful—and *cosmic*—subsumption is an *essential* aspect of Muhammad's solar nature as the all-comprehensive manifestation of God's light.

As Ibn 'Arabi repeatedly asserts, the religions of the Protected People are indeed abrogated by the appearance of Muhammad's sharia, and their laws are thus technically invalidated. And yet, these same laws are in fact permitted to remain operative, but *only if* the People of the Book pay the *jizya*, or indemnity tax, commanded by the contentious words of verse 9:29 of the Qur'an (directly quoted by Ibn 'Arabi in chapter 12), which order Muhammad to fight the Jews and Christians until they submit to his law and consent to pay the *jizya* "*in a state of humiliation.*" As I will discuss in more detail in the following chapter, elsewhere in *The Meccan Openings* Ibn 'Arabi specifically mentions that "the Followers of the Books who pay the indemnity tax" (*aṣḥāb al-kutub bi al-jizya*) have the possibility of attaining eternal happiness. Yet, such salvific efficacy granted by Ibn 'Arabi appears to be solely determined by *obedience* to the revelation of Muhammad and *not* due to any particular soteriological power of Judaism, or Christianity, or their respective scriptures.[155] Thus, rather than an ecumenical offering, Ibn 'Arabi's repeated emphasis of the indemnity tax and its relation to the liminal validity of the People of the Book forms the discursive basis for a "grammar of universal monarchy," the key component of which is "the celebration of mastery over a multiplicity of lesser lords and subject populations and *their need to pay homage and tribute to the supreme ruler*."[156] Indeed, it is this selfsame triumphant grammar that Ibn 'Arabi employs with the inclusion of the Pact of 'Umar in his letter to the Seljuk sultan Kayka'us, with which this chapter began. As Mark Cohen observes, medieval Muslims "explained the stipulations of the Pact of 'Umar as an elaboration of the commandment in Sūra 9:29 to 'humble' (*ṣaghār*) the People of the Book."[157]

Rather than being an anomalous political concession, Ibn 'Arabi's concern to repeatedly articulate the subsumption of the People of the Book in the radiant face of the Muhammadan *logos* throws into relief a political cosmology that informs his entire metaphysics. And it is precisely this cosmology that should give us pause when we attempt to engage Ibn 'Arabi's ideas on the religious Other. "Political mysticism," as Ernst Kantorowicz observes in the epigraph that heads this chapter, is easily misread "when taken out of its native surroundings, *its time and its space*." Indeed, when Ibn 'Arabi's metaphysical thought is dissociated from its socio-historical context, it is often anachronistically misconstrued (or conveniently appropriated) as a premodern version of inclusive religious universalism. Yet, reading Ibn 'Arabi's metaphysics as transhistorical *because* transcendent—as if independent from its own complex political time and place—paradoxically produces interpretations that have wide-ranging political implications.[158] In the next chapter, I begin to address how particular Western mapping strategies of transcendence have formed such interpretations (in comparison with Ibn 'Arabi's own metaphysical cartography) in order to more critically examine what kinds of cosmographic maps they, *in turn*, have the potential to authorize.

3

Competing Fields of Universal Validity

Is there not in all religions more or less of
the true nature of religion . . .?

FRIEDRICH SCHLEIERMACHER,
On Religion: Speeches to Its Cultured Despisers.[1]

It has become impossible to provide an effective defense
for a single religion against all the others . . . ; to
persist in doing so . . . is a little like wishing to maintain the
Ptolemaic system against the evidence of verified and
verifiable astronomical data.

FRITHJOF SCHUON, *Logic and Transcendence.*[2]

One is not born traditional; one chooses to become
traditional by constant innovation.

BRUNO LATOUR, *We Have Never Been Modern.*[3]

WRITING IN 1909 under the pseudonym Palingénius at the start of a career as one of the most influential twentieth-century European esotericists,[4] René Guénon (d. 1951) disparaged the popular spiritualism of his day, the "so-called doctrines" of which "are only materialism transposed onto another plane" and thus "always lead to absurd consequences."[5] In its stead, Guénon proposed an esoteric quest for "gnosis," which he claimed to be beyond the purview of any type of systematization: "Gnosis, in its broadest and highest sense, is knowledge; true gnosticism cannot be a particular school or system, but must above all be the search for the integral Truth."[6] According to Guénon, the only reliable guide for the attainment of gnosis was "the orthodox Tradition contained in the sacred books of all peoples."[7] Such "orthodox Tradition" was "the same everywhere, despite the various forms it takes to adapt to every race and era."[8] Throughout the next decade, Guénon increasingly dissociated himself from the occult movement of *fin-de-siècle* France by further developing his concept of "orthodox Tradition,"[9] which he came to call the "Primordial Tradition" (*la Tradition primordial*). The Primordial Tradition would eventually become synonymous with such terms as *philosophia perennis, sophia perennis,* and *religio perennis* that marked the contemporary esoteric movement of Perennialism developed by the Swiss-German metaphysician Frithjof Schuon (d. 1998).[10]

Indeed, Guénon and Schuon are commonly viewed as the "dual originators and expositors"[11] of what is variously referred to as Traditionalism or Perennialism.[12] It has even been asserted, in evangelical-like fashion, that "Guénon was the pioneer, and Schuon the fulfillment."[13] No doubt, Perennialism developed from an intellectual movement into a full-fledged "initiatic tradition" when Schuon took on the mantle of spiritual guide, or *shaykh*, for the ʿAlāwiyya Sufi order at the end of 1936,[14] which became the ʿAlāwiyya Maryamiyya in the mid-1960s due to his special devotion to the Virgin Mary.[15] After Guénon's death in 1951, "Schuon gradually assumed the role of the premier expositor of the *philosophia perennis*."[16]

Yet, Schuon critically distinguished his version of Perennialism from Guénonian Traditionalism. Unlike the strict French Catholic childhood of his predecessor, Schuon was brought up in the Lutheran Church in Basel, Switzerland, until he converted to Catholicism at the age of fourteen at the request of his dying father. His early interest in Orientalism was complemented by a wide reading in German romanticism from his father's library.[17] Schuon's ecumenical upbringing in tandem with his interest in German romanticism no doubt influenced his evolution from the more insular ethos of Guénon's metaphysics and its rejection of the "anti-traditional" West. Schuon's most significant difference with Guénon revolved around the validity of Christian initiation. He strongly disagreed with Guénon's contention that the church had lost its early connection to esotericism.[18] Indeed, Schuon's redemption of Euro-American forms of spirituality within the Traditionalist framework included "orthodox" Protestantism, by which Schuon meant Lutheranism and that according to him, "incontestably manifests a Christian possibility—a limited one, no doubt, and excessive through certain of its features, but not intrinsically illegitimate and therefore representative of certain theological, moral, and even mystical values."[19] In a 1982 letter, Schuon wrote regarding Lutheranism: "It cannot be pure heresy. . . . Its priorities are simplicity, inwardness and trust in God; nothing else touched me in my early childhood."[20]

Indeed, Schuon's ecumenism came to uniquely define his approach, which, as Paul Sérant notes, "above all intends to show the profound agreement between Eastern and Western traditions."[21] Nevertheless, the importance of "the Guénonian message" as a precursor to Schuon's lifework and self-image is without question and was contextualized by Schuon himself in spiritual terms.[22] Thus, as John Herlihy observes, Guénon's emphasis on the Primordial Tradition as the source of the "world religions"

> prepared the way for an understanding of what Frithjof Schuon described as "the transcendent unity" of the world's religious traditions, wherein

> each religion casts the same universal truth within the mold of an individual form that suits a particular mentality and a given era.[23]

Here, Herlihy makes direct reference to Schuon's 1948 publication *The Transcendent Unity of Religions* (*De l'Unité transcendante des Religions*), the title of which as mentioned in the introduction to this book has become emblematic of Schuon's lifework and is often associated with the teachings of Ibn 'Arabi. For example, in his 2010 monograph on Sufism, the French Perennialist Éric Geoffroy claims that *The Transcendent Unity of Religions* is in reality an "allusive" presentation of Ibn 'Arabi's ideas.[24] Similarly, Seyyed Hossein Nasr, who is openly an initiate of Schuon's ʿAlāwiyya,[25] uses Ibn 'Arabi's celebrated verses from *The Interpreter of Desires* (*Tarjumān al-ashwāq*) to describe Sufism as the Islamic vehicle for attaining the Schuonian ideal of transcendent religious unity:

> The Sufi is one who seeks to transcend the world of forms, to journey from multiplicity to Unity, from the particular to the Universal. He leaves the many for the One and through this very process is granted the vision of the One in the many. For him all forms become transparent, including religious forms, thus revealing to him their unique origin. *Sufism or Islamic gnosis is the most universal affirmation of that perennial wisdom which stands at the heart of Islam and in fact of all religion as such.* It is this supreme doctrine of Unity—which is itself unique (*al-tawḥîd wâḥid*)—*that the Sufis call the "religion of love" and to which Ibn 'Arabî refers in his well-known verses in the Tarjumân al-ashwâq*. This love is not merely sentiment or emotions, it is the realized aspect of gnosis. *It is a transcendent knowledge that reveals the inner unity of religions.*[26]

Schuon himself likewise referenced Ibn 'Arabi's famous lines in his best-known monograph on Islam, *Understanding Islam*,[27] as a proof text for the universal validity of religions. Noting that each religion speaks an "exclusive language" because the differences among religions correspond to the differences among groups of people, Schuon claims that "if the religions are true it is because each time it is God who has spoken, and if they are different, it is because God has spoken in different 'languages' in conformity with the diversity of the receptacles."[28] Thus anticipating the demurral of the "orthodox," Schuon invokes the metaphysical authority of Ibn 'Arabi and his celebrated verses as "Islamic" evidence for the Guénonian-inspired notion of "universal orthodoxy":

> We know all too well, and it is moreover in the natural order of things, that *this thesis is not acceptable on the level of exoteric orthodoxies, but is so*

> *on the level of universal orthodoxy*, that to which Muhyiddin Ibn 'Arabi, the great enunciator of gnosis in Islam, bore witness in these terms: "My heart is open to every form: it is a pasture for gazelles, and a cloister for Christian monks, a temple for idols, the Kaaba of the pilgrim, the tables of the Torah, and the book of the Quran. I practice the religion of Love; in whatsoever direction His caravans advance, the religion of Love shall be my religion and my faith."[29]

Given such associations of the Schuonian "transcendent unity of religions" with Ibn 'Arabi's discourse, it is perhaps not surprising that both Guénon and Schuon—as the "dual expositors" of Perennialism—have been compared to the Andalusian Sufi himself.[30] Furthermore, such associations go some way in explaining why post-9/11 the conceptual legacy of Schuonian Perennialism has been so intertwined with the thought of Ibn 'Arabi, interfaith dialogue, and pluralistic approaches to the Qur'an.[31] Yet, the academic use of Schuonian Perennialism to present Ibn 'Arabi's ideas has not simply been a post-9/11 phenomenon.

As William Chittick recently pointed out, Nasr's "strong endorsement of the writings of Schuon" in three books published in the mid-1960s by Harvard University Press proved "instrumental in bringing the traditionalist school to the notice of official academia."[32] In *Three Muslim Sages*, the first of Nasr's Harvard publications, he spends an entire chapter focusing on Ibn 'Arabi, where he forcefully asserts that "all attempts at a profound rapprochement with the other religions made by Muslims today can and *should be based* on the rich foundations prepared by Ibn 'Arabī and Rūmī."[33] Yet, as late as 1986 in the first installment of a widely respected three-part scholarly article on Ibn 'Arabi, James Morris lamented that there was still no adequate introductory study of the "essential 'rhetorical' aspect of Ibn ʿArabī's writings," which "unites many methods, styles, and traditional subjects in view of certain recurrent spiritual intentions."[34] Morris, however, immediately qualified this assertion, claiming that

> the best illustration of the needed sensitivity to that crucial dimension of Ibn ʿArabī's writing, usually phrased in terms of comments on "Sufism" in general, *is to be found in the various collections of essays by F. Schuon on Islamic subjects*. . . . However, *those reflections generally presuppose a great familiarity with both the writings of Ibn ʿArabī* and the broader Sufi traditions of which they are a part.[35]

More recently, Morris notes "the profound effect of the abundant writings of F. Schuon in applying the central ideas of Ibn 'Arabī to *articulating* (but in the long run also deeply shaping) an understanding of the spiritual dimensions of religious life."[36] Morris further claims that Schuon's particular application of Ibn 'Arabi's ideas has profoundly appealed

> to several generations of philosophers and theologians seeking to develop a comprehensive, non-reductive "philosophy of religions" enabling mutual understanding and active co-operation between the followers of different religious traditions and the increasing number of citizens who do not consciously identify exclusively with any particular historical tradition.[37]

And yet, Morris concludes, "Because of the peculiar vagaries of academic opinion and respectability, this wide-ranging influence is rarely mentioned publicly . . ., *but is to be found virtually everywhere*."[38]

Indeed, in an article on Ibn 'Arabi's "approach to religious diversity" published in a collection of essays for Frithjof Schuon's eightieth birthday, Chittick himself notes that "anyone familiar with the *philosophia perennis* will certainly recognize a number of its basic teachings" within Ibn 'Arabi's "traditional metaphysics."[39] While Chittick has denied being a "traditionalist" or "a member of any school of thought," he does admit to having "learned a great deal from authors who are commonly called 'traditionalist,' such as Frithjof Schuon."[40] In an online interview originally published in Swedish, Chittick discussed Schuon's aforementioned notion of "the transcendent unity of religions." According to Chittick, "the Koran among all the world's scriptures has by far the clearest expression of the transcendent unity of religions."[41] Chittick goes on to discuss the issue of abrogation (*naskh*) and takes the same position for a general interpretation of the Qur'an as he does in *Faith and Practice of Islam* and *Imaginal Worlds* regarding his interpretation of Ibn 'Arabi's position dealt with in chapter 2:

> Most modern-day Muslims find it difficult to accept this unity because preachers have told them that Islam "abrogated" the previous religions, and most classical theologians took that position. But the Koran certainly does not say that it abrogated them. This is a theological opinion, by no means accepted by all Muslim scholars over history. . . . [W]hen the Koran says that it has come to "confirm" the previous messages, it means that it is confirming their truth *and their continuing efficacy and legitimacy*.[42]

It is precisely the idea of a continued "efficacy and legitimacy" for "the previous religions" that demarcates the universalist claims of Traditionalism and Schuonian Perennialism. Indeed, in his 2007 anthology of essays, *Science of the Cosmos, Science of the Soul*, Chittick himself identifies the position of "universal validity" with Nasr and Schuonian Perennialism:

> Nasr, of course, does not write only about Islam, but also about other religions as well. Like Schuon and Coomaraswamy, he claims *universal validity* for a point of view that he and they usually call "traditional" and that observers have often called "traditionalist" or "perennialist."[43]

In his article "Is there a Perennial Philosophy?," the renowned scholar of religion Huston Smith, who was also an open exponent of Schuonian Perennialism, explains this idea of universal validity by noting that "the differences in revelations 'flesh out' God's nature by seeing it from different angles. They supplement our view without compromising the fact that each angle is, in its own right, adequate, containing (in traditional locution) '*truth sufficient unto salvation*.'"[44] As I brought to light in chapter 1, such an idea of universal validity forms an essential component of the Perennialist interpretation of Ibn 'Arabi's celebrated verses contained within *The Interpreter of Desires*. And as I further brought forth in chapter 2—and will flesh out in what follows—such recourse to the concept of validity often forms a subtext for Chittick's approach to Ibn 'Arabi and thus marks his interpretation as particularly Perennialist. Indeed, it is worth noting that in an article arguing for Schuon's Islamic credentials, Nasr himself includes Chittick in a list of ten well-known American and European scholars of Islam, "all of whom," according to Nasr, "were deeply influenced by Schuon's works."[45]

Scholars who unapologetically situate themselves within the worldview of Schuonian Perennialism, such as Reza Shah-Kazemi,[46] can thus effectively use Chittick's translations to present a specific Perennialist image of Ibn 'Arabi that conveniently leaves out a particular mode of polemical discourse found within his writings—a discourse that is too important to disregard, especially for any discursive analysis that attempts to historicize Ibn 'Arabi's ideas. Those committed to the Perennialist framework, however, will no doubt respond that the Andalusian Sufi's metaphysics transcends history and thus rises above the more *mundanely secular* issues of politics, authority, and religious polemics. I maintain, however, that while Ibn 'Arabi's view of the religious Other may trouble our modern sensibilities, such a transhistorical approach essentializes and depoliticizes his complex metaphysical ideas—ideas that are fully inscribed by the discursive locality of their historical origins.

The Transcendent Religious A Priori: A Perennialist Imperative

In his 1972 essay "Islam and the Encounter of Religions," mentioned in the introduction of this book, Seyyed Hossein Nasr laid out what he felt was at stake in the contemporary study of religion. The "essential problem" with such a field of study, according to Nasr, "is how to preserve religious truth, traditional orthodoxy, the dogmatic theological structures of one's own religion *and yet gain knowledge of other traditions and accept them as spiritually valid ways and roads to God.*"[47] Given Nasr's intellectual and spiritual standing in the Perennialist movement as, in the words of Chittick, "the foremost living member of the traditionalist school,"[48] such a *prescriptive challenge* for the study of religion should not be taken as empty rhetoric likely to go unheeded by those who follow his lead. In fact, the Perennialist scholar Shah-Kazemi has dubbed Nasr's 1972 essay as "one of the most important contemporary expressions . . . of the principle of the 'transcendent unity of religions' from the point of view of the Islamic tradition as a whole."[49] Indeed, it was in this same essay, as quoted earlier, that Nasr compared Ibn 'Arabi's "religion of love" with Schuon's emblematic theme of "transcendent unity."

The doctrine of the transcendent unity of religions has been used by Perennialists to argue that within the Qur'an and the esoteric writings of the Sufis, there is an acknowledgment of a deeper religious unity marking all revealed traditions as equally valid. This is so, the standard Perennialist argument goes, in spite of (or perhaps, more realistically, without fully appreciating) the triumphant assertion of abrogative supersessionism that was held by most scholars of the medieval Islamic tradition, which, as was shown in chapter 2, included Ibn 'Arabi. Thus, Nasr, in the passage quoted earlier from his 1972 essay, asserts that "Sufism or Islamic gnosis is the most universal affirmation of that perennial wisdom which stands at the heart of Islam and in fact *of all religion as such.*" He then, as we recall, invokes Ibn 'Arabi's "religion of love" as most representative of this perennial wisdom—that is, as the true religion within all outward religious forms. Yet in order to universally validate "all religion as such," Nasr following Schuon must transcend historical religious difference by arguing for a transcendent a priori as "true religion," which in this case is represented by "perennial wisdom" (i.e., *sophia perennis*) and Ibn 'Arabi's quintessential "religion of love."

Nasr's Perennialist recourse to a transcendent religious a priori is indeed a prominent feature of universalist religious discourse. Yet, while Nasr's Perennialist position has been compared to other essentialist modes of religious pluralism, particularly the pluralist thought of John Hick, the discursive analytical value of such comparisons has been limited because of their tendency to devolve into theological debate. Part of the issue here is that the Perennialist recourse to "tradition" and its insistence on the divinity of all religions as upholding "the irreducible character—the divinely willed uniqueness—of each of the revealed religions" creates an aura of authenticity against the comparatively "modern" pluralism of Hick, which, according to Shah-Kazemi, "seeks to eliminate these differences for the sake of a unity."[50] Such an ostensible divide between the "traditional" and the "modern" leads Adnan Aslan in his comparative analysis of Nasr and Hick to note:

> It is certainly a problematical task to compare Hick, whose philosophy of religion bears the stamp of the idealism of Kant and the empiricism of Hume, *with Nasr, whom it is hard to situate within any mainstream philosophical orientation of the West, with the possible exception of Neoplatonism*. The two thinkers differ entirely in their conceptions of knowledge: Hick's concept is basically constituted from elements of post-Enlightenment philosophy, while Nasr's is constituted by the principles of Islamic faith and the perennial philosophy.[51]

While Aslan tries to further nuance his discussion on Nasr by noting that Perennialism "is a modern discourse, to a certain extent an ideological attempt to discover the significance of traditions," he goes on to state that for Perennialists, "Ibn 'Arabi and [Meister] Eckhart are the main expositors of the *sophia perennis*."[52] While "they are traditional" because "they presented their traditions from the mystical perspective of which they were a part," they are not, according to Aslan, Perennialists because "they did not write about their religions in order to convince modern people."[53] Aslan thus concludes that "the traditional point of view is not traditional in the sense that traditional people understood it."[54] Thus, in the end Aslan's analysis falls flat because it is circular. Although he is correct to note that Perennialism is a modern discourse, the idea that premodern people did not write for modern people is both a truism and tautological. More important, it does not help us to understand the discursive structures that make Perennialism particularly modern.

Indeed, Schuonian Perennialism shares with Hickian pluralism a particular modern conception of religions that can be likened, as Hick himself does with his own theology, to a "Copernican revolution" that shifts the premodern, chauvinistic worldview of only one right religion to multiple religious worlds of equal validity.[55] Yet, while Hick's distinctive Kantian model posits a central, unknowable "Real," Schuon's universalism argues that the divine *makes itself known* through various religions and is thus knowable through a mode of experiential intellection, or "gnosis." Thus, in Hick's negative conception, the contrasting truth claims of each circling religious worldview are ultimately human cognitive creations and thus false in varying degrees.[56] Conversely, Schuon's positive perspective professes to acknowledge each conflicting religious claim as "providential" and variously (but not *absolutely*) true.

While the conclusion to this study endeavors to compare the discursive practices of Schuonian Perennialism with the religious reductionism of Kant in relation to their shared metaphysics of autonomy, here a comparison of Schuon with Friedrich Schleiermacher (d. 1834) is paramount in that it serves to first situate Schuonian Perennialism within its immediate discursive tradition of "anti-reductionist," or essentialist, religious universalism.[57] Admittedly, with the antipathy that both Guénon and Schuon held for liberal Protestantism, a comparison with Schleiermacher may seem strained.[58] Yet, at the level of discourse itself, such differences are surprisingly formal.[59] Indeed, Schuon's recognition of the transcendent unity and validity of distinctive and conflicting revealed religious traditions has perhaps its most coherent modern precursor in Schleiermacher.[60] Moreover, both positions concede that the conflicting practices, beliefs, and laws of religious traditions are simultaneously validated and transcended by an underlying religious "essence" that unites them.[61] Schuon has many names for this underlying essence, which he frequently calls the "perennial religion" (*religio perennis*)[62] or simply "religion as such."[63] Indeed, one Perennialist author goes so far as to claim that "Schuon writes with *sovereign authority* on the subject of *religion as such*."[64]

Yet, "the first book ever written *on religion as such*," according to Wilfred Cantwell Smith, was Schleiermacher's 1799 work *On Religion* (*Über die Religion*), whose subject matter was "not on a particular kind or instance and not incidentally, but explicitly on religion itself as a generic something."[65] Here, the idea of religion "constitutes a private, interiorized dimension of experience that, although manifested outwardly in varying forms, is shared across all religions regardless of their historical differences."[66] Yet, because Schleiermacher was keen to reject the Kantian reduction of religion to mere reason and morality, he was unwilling to disparage the various particular dispensational forms of religion throughout history and concede to the Enlightenment notion of a rational, "natural religion" the same for all people everywhere.[67] Thus, Schleiermacher posits that each religion was "one of the special forms which mankind, in some region of the earth and at some stage of development, has to accept."[68] As such, he asserts that

> *the positive religions are just the definite forms in which religion must exhibit itself*—a thing to which your so-called natural religions have no claim. They are only a vague, sorry, poor thought that corresponds to no reality, and you will find that *in the positive religions alone a true individual cultivation of the religious capacity is possible.*[69]

Thus, Nasr's above assertion that Ibn ʿArabi's "religion of love" is found at the heart of all religions tellingly echoes Schleiermacher's recourse here to a transcendent "religion" present within "the definite forms" of "the positive religions." As William Johnson notes, for Schleiermacher, "every particular, positive religion was ultimately founded upon *the Religion of the infinite*"—that is, "*the religious* a priori."[70]

In the following comparison between Schleiermacher and Schuon, I wish to look more closely at Schleiermacher's particular strategic use of a transcendent religious a priori to highlight a similar discursive strategy within Schuonian Perennialist discourse on religious validity. Establishing "true religion" as a transcendent a priori allowed Schleiermacher to circumvent the problem of religious difference and simultaneously argue for its necessity. Thus, for Schleiermacher, "religion could never be realized except in a concrete historical form. Historical Religions always possessed, therefore, the quality of imperfection."[71]

The discursive structure of the Schuonian Perennialist argument for orthodoxy as both divine *and* contradictory follows a similar logic, as Nasr notes:

> For Schuon orthodoxy is related at once to Truth and the formal homogeneity of a particular traditional universe. To speak of the Truth is also to speak of the possibility of error. To be orthodox is to be on the side of the Truth. But since the Truth has revealed itself not once and in only one formal language but many times in different "worlds" possessing their own formal homogeneity and language of discourse, the question of being on the side of the truth involves also the formal world in question. Schuon therefore defends Christianity as orthodox in itself while being heterodox from the point of view of Jewish orthodoxy and he explains why Buddhism is an orthodox religion, that is an embodiment of the Truth and means "provided" by that Truth to attain the Truth, while it is considered as heterodox from the perspective of Brahmanism.[72]

Here, Nasr openly engages an argument that forcefully counters what is commonly referred to as the Aristotelian law of noncontradiction, a logical principle that is the tacit assumption of normative theology. According to such basic logic, "the same thing cannot be both x and not-x at the same time and in the same way."[73] Yet, a theological or metaphysical perspective that claims to acknowledge all so-called orthodox truth claims as valid cannot operate from such a normative assumption. In addressing this conflict, Schuon argues:

> One could conceive, it is true, that *there might be only one Revelation* or Tradition for our human world and that diversity might be realized through other worlds, unknown to man or even unknowable by him; but this would imply a failure to understand that *what determines the difference among forms of Truth is the difference among human receptacles.* For thousands of years humanity has been divided into several fundamentally

> different branches constituting as many complete humanities, more or less closed in on themselves; *the existence of spiritual receptacles so different and so original demands a differentiated refraction of the one Truth*.[74]

In a similarly structured notion, Schleiermacher states:

> The whole of religion is nothing but the sum of all relations of man to God, *apprehended* in all the possible ways in which any man can be immediately conscious in his life. *In this sense there is but one religion*, for it would be but a poverty-stricken and halting life, if all these relations did not exist wherever religion ought to be. *Yet all men will not by any means apprehend them in the same way, but quite differently*. Now this difference alone is felt and alone can be exhibited while the reduction of all differences is only thought. You are wrong, therefore, with your universal religion that is natural to all, *for no one will have his own true and right religion, if it is the same for all*.[75]

In both of these arguments, Schuon and Schleiermacher respectively call upon a mode of discourse that seeks to transcend the principle of noncontradiction by arguing that for religion to be valid, different groups or individuals must experience religious truth differently. In Schuon, the differences among collective ontic capacities "*demand*" different refractions of one divine truth, while in Schleiermacher, one ontological truth is "*apprehended*" differently depending on the social context. While such subtle differences highlight the distinctive ontological assumptions of each author, the structure of the argument is identical.

In his study on postliberal theology, George Lindbeck has called this type of doctrinal model "experiential-expressivism." Following Bernard Lonergan, Lindbeck has identified several key aspects of such a model, all of which revolve around the notion that different religions are diverse objectifications or expressions of "a common core experience." Such a core experience is described by Lonergan as "'God's gift of love' or when fully present, as 'the dynamic state of being in love without restrictions' and 'without an object.'"[76]

Recalling again Nasr's 1972 essay and his passage on Islamic gnosis and Ibn ʿArabi quoted earlier, the connection of love with such a "common core experience" is implicit where "love" is claimed to be "the realized aspect of gnosis" qua "transcendent knowledge." Similarly, the Perennialist author Patrick Laude writes that Schuon's "perspective on Islam derived from gnosis, that is, a spiritual and supra-rational 'heart-knowledge' that finds its most direct expression in the primordial and universal wisdom referred to as *sophia perennis*."[77] Thus, the concept of "gnosis" as combining the experiential state of love with that of a "supra-rational" knowledge is a type of experiential intuition, or what Laude and Jean-Baptiste Aymard have elsewhere called "supraformal intuition."[78] In Schleiermacher's version of the experiential-expressivist model, he uses similar terms that express the common experience of religion; the closest one to the Perennialist "gnosis" is the Schleiermacherian "intuition" (*Anschauung*),[79] which, as John Oman in his preface to the original English translation of *On Religion* notes, is perhaps more exactly translated as "immediate knowledge."[80] While the first edition of *On Religion* emphasized intuition as central to the essence of religion, in later editions the notion of "feeling" (*Gefühl*) came to dominate Schleiermacher's categorization of religious essence.[81] Nevertheless, in the third and final edition, Schleiermacher speaks of "the unity of intuition and feeling"[82] and persists in categorizing intuition as embodying religion *as such*. For example, he states: "Intuition of the Universe . . . is the highest formula of religion, determining its nature and fixing its boundaries," and "to have religion is to have an intuition of the Universe."[83]

Thus, for both Schleiermacherian and Schuonian essentialist models of religion, the idea of religious experience qua intuitive knowledge is strategically deployed to transcend the differences of competing religious epistemologies and thus coherently posit an inclusive religious universalism. Yet, for such an experiential modality to satisfactorily engage with competing truth claims, a concomitant approach toward religious "symbols" must also be in place that authorizes such symbols to be both transcendently valid *and* transreligiously contradictory. Thus, Schleiermacher asserts that "thousands might be moved religiously in the same way, and yet each, led, not so much by disposition, as by external circumstances, might designate his feeling by different symbols."[84] Commenting further in a footnote, he states:

> Apart from the universal, divine connection of all things, we can say, for example, that if Christianity had had a great and preponderating Eastern extension, the Hellenic and Western being, on the contrary, kept back, without being essentially different, *it might have been contained in another type of doctrines*.[85]

Thus, for Schleiermacher, as Jacqueline Mariña observes:

> The purpose of doctrine is not to mirror the real but to give logical coherence to *a system of symbols*. If this is the case, *then it is possible that two differing religious systems of symbolic representation and the second order doctrines that systematize them can both be valid expressions of the experience* of ultimate mystery.[86]

Such symbolic relativity is also an inherent interpretive strategy of Schuonian Perennialism. As Schuon himself notes:

> If Revelations more or less exclude one another, this is so of necessity since God, when He speaks, expresses Himself in an absolute mode; but this absoluteness concerns the universal content rather than the form, to which it applies only in a relative and symbolical sense, *for the form is a symbol* of the content and so too of humanity as a whole, to which precisely this content is addressed. . . . Revelation speaks an absolute language because God is absolute, not because the form is absolute; in other words *the absoluteness of the Revelation is absolute in itself, but relative in its form*.[87]

By allowing absolute claims of revelation to be relativized through symbols, Schuon can thus assert that "with God, truth lies above all in the symbol's effective power of enlightenment and not in its literalness," and "the existence of dogmatic antinomies serves to show that for God truth is above all in *the efficacy of the symbol* and not in the 'bare fact.'"[88]

Yet, in terms of Ibn ʿArabi's discourse on religious authority, such claims of the symbolic as regnant over other discursive practices are difficult to sustain. Indeed, the notion that systems of symbols were the decisive factor that determined premodern religious dispositions and experience has been forcefully challenged by Talal Asad. In *Genealogies of Religion*, Asad argues that before the modern universalization of religion, "coercion was a condition for the realization of truth, and discipline essential to its maintenance."[89] Asad further notes that for the early Christian theologian and mystic Augustine of Hippo,

> it was not mere symbols that implant true Christian dispositions, but power—ranging all the way from laws (imperial and ecclesiastical) and other sanctions (hellfire, death, salvation, good repute, peace) to the disciplinary activities of social institutions (family, school, city, church) and of human bodies (fasting, prayer, obedience, penance). Augustine was quite clear that power, the effect of an entire network of motivated practices, assumes a religious form because of the end to which it is directed, for human events are the instruments of God. *It was not the mind that moved spontaneously to religious truth, but power that created the conditions for experiencing that truth*.[90]

Following Asad, in the remainder of this chapter, I interrogate the notion that for Ibn ʿArabi religious truth was arrived at through a gnostic response to a set of relative symbols devoid of absolute frameworks of power. This is not to deny the importance of transcendent experience in Ibn 'Arabi's thought, and Sufism more broadly.[91] Rather, I wish to cast into relief how Ibn 'Arabi's experience was fully integrated within his own historical and intellectual context. In other words, while Ibn 'Arabi's discourse is well known for its radical theomonism, as discussed in chapter 1, such theomonism was developed within the confluence of transmitted tradition and socio-political history. The claims that result from such a unitive worldview often appear to be at odds with the absolutism and practices of power present within Ibn 'Arabi's religio-political context. In Euro-American scholarship on Ibn 'Arabi, when such modalities of power are found embedded within his discourse, they are often explained away as accidental to his metaphysics. Yet, I argue here that for the economy of Ibn 'Arabi's ideas to remain solvent, both sides of this discursive coin must be tendered. As Asad trenchantly notes, a "consequence of assuming a symbolic system separate from practices is that *important distinctions are sometimes obscured, or even explicitly denied*."[92]

Revisiting Ibn 'Arabi's Idea of Abrogation Through the Lens of Schuonian Cosmology

At this juncture, let us briefly return to Chittick's *Imaginal Worlds: Ibn al-'Arabī and the Problem of Religious Diversity* and his commentary on the abrogation passage (i.e., *Futūḥāt* III, 153) from chapter 339 of *The Meccan Openings* (*al-Futūḥāt al-makkiyya*), which I discussed at length in chapter 2. Here, Chittick claims that Ibn 'Arabi "*does not draw the conclusion that many Muslims have drawn*—that the coming of Islam abrogated (*naskh*) previous revealed religions."[93] "Rather," Chittick asserts, for Ibn 'Arabi "Islam is like the sun and other religions like the stars. Just as the stars remain when the sun rises, *so also the other religions remain valid when Islam appears*."[94] It is directly after making this assertion, however, that Chittick importantly inserts the following coda not mentioned in chapter 2: "One can add a point that perhaps Ibn 'Arabī would also accept: *What appears as a sun from one point of view may be seen as a star from another point of view*."[95]

This seemingly inconsequential suggestion on second glance proposes something rather far-reaching: it suggests that Ibn 'Arabi would have agreed to a paradigm shift challenging *the entire basis* of his metaphysical cosmology. In other words, Chittick proposes that Ibn 'Arabi would accept a type of Copernican turn that completely inverts his hierarchical cosmology discussed in chapter 2.[96] Thus, Ibn 'Arabi's hierarchical planetary system is here decentered from its triumphant Muhammadan Sun—and its attendant supersession of Islam over all other religions—to a nonhierarchical and pluralist universe of multiple prophetic suns illuminating equally valid religious dispensations. Although the origins of such an idea are arguably ancient,[97] this particular mode of "cosmic pluralism" strikingly echoes the early modern universalist cosmology of the Italian Dominican friar Giordano Bruno (d. 1600).[98]

In his 1986 introduction to *The Essential Writings of Frithjof Schuon*, Seyyed Hossein Nasr stated something remarkably similar about Schuon's own work. Here, Nasr notes that Schuon "has written over and over again on . . . *how the sun of each religious cosmos is for that cosmos the sun while being a star in that spiritual firmament which symbolizes the Divine Infinity*."[99] An example of one such passage to which Nasr thus alludes was put forth in Schuon's fourth major work, *Gnosis: Divine Wisdom*.[100] Following an extended discussion of how revelations can exclude one another and still be simultaneously valid, Schuon encapsulates this "doctrine" within a solar metaphor of cosmic pluralism:

> This whole doctrine is clearly illustrated by the following example: *the sun is unique in our solar system, but it is not so in space; we can see other suns since they are located in space as is ours, but we do not see them as suns*. The unicity of our sun is belied by the multiplicity of the fixed stars *without thereby ceasing to be valid within the system that is ours under Providence*; hence the unicity is manifested in the part, not in the totality, which the part nonetheless represents for us; by the divine Will it "is" thus the totality, though only for us and only insofar as our mind, whose scope is likewise willed by God, does not go beyond forms; but even in this case the part "is" *totality as far as its spiritual efficacy is concerned*.[101]

The striking similarity between Schuon's above passage, Nasr's apparent gloss, and Chittick's additional commentary on Ibn 'Arabi's "proof text" on the validity of revealed religions should give us pause. Whether Chittick's statement that "*what appears as a sun from one point of view may be seen as a star from another point of view*" is a direct allusion to the similar assertions made by Schuon or Nasr, or merely an echo, is of little consequence; the symmetry between them and their distinctly modern commentary on an ancient metaphor clearly shows that Chittick is thinking about Ibn 'Arabi's passage on abrogation within the same Schuonian interpretive field that presupposes "the transcendent unity of religions" and its attendant notion of the "universal validity" of the *religio perennis* underlying all so-called orthodox religions.

Indeed, Chittick's previous commentary on the abrogation passage from chapter 339 of *The Meccan Openings* and its attendant assertion that Ibn 'Arabi held to a proto-Perennialist notion of universal validity has provided Shah-Kazemi with the authoritative basis necessary to further develop this rather technical argument into something of a bulwark for Perennialist and universalist interpretations of Ibn 'Arabi; as a result, this argument appears in the majority of his publications.[102] Directly relying on Chittick's translation of the abrogation passage from chapter 339 (and clearly his attendant assertion, quoted above, that Ibn 'Arabi "*does not draw the conclusion that many Muslims have drawn*—that the coming of Islam abrogated [*naskh*] previous revealed religions"), Shah-Kazemi states:

> In many places Ibn Arabi exalts the Quranic revelation above all others, but he does so in a nuanced manner, *making it clear that the historical appearance of Islam* (or: the final revelation of the one religion, "Islam," in the sense of universal submission) *did not nullify the efficacy of the earlier religions* (or: the earlier revelations of this one religion); *the commonly held view in Islamic exoterism, that Islam "abrogated"—in the sense of annulled or invalidated—all other religions is thus rejected*; for him, Islam's "abrogation" (*naskh*) of other religions means that Islam takes precedence over them, it "supersedes" them, in the literal sense of "sitting above" them.[103]

Here, Shah-Kazemi dissociates Ibn 'Arabi's notion of abrogation from "the commonly held view in Islamic exoterism," which invalidates "all other religions." Rather, according to Shah-Kazemi, Ibn 'Arabi's idea of abrogation simply means that "Islam" benevolently sits above them. In what can only be described as an ironic inversion, Shah-Kazemi immediately adds that Ibn 'Arabi therefore "*transforms the whole doctrine of abrogation from being a basis for the rejection of other religions into a decisive argument for the validity of the other religions.*"[104]

Thus, after quoting Chittick's translation of the abrogation passage from chapter 339, Shah-Kazemi draws the following conclusion:

> In other words, following the dictates of Islam and believing it to be the most complete religion can coexist with an awareness *that the other religions retain their enlightening function and their spiritual efficacy for their adherents*. The very real differences of conception, orientation, and ritual as exist between the religions are not ignored in this perspective; rather, one is urged to submit entirely to the form of one's own religion even *while recognizing its inevitable particularity and hence relativity*; thus *for Ibn Arabi there is no substantial contradiction between following the dictates of one's own "way"—in terms of which certain things may be forbidden—and accepting the intrinsic validity of another "way" which permits those same things.*[105]

Shah-Kazemi's summation here (variously repeated in the majority of his other works) is useful for its concise grafting of Schuon's above heliocentric model of the validity of all religions onto Ibn 'Arabi's doctrine of abrogation. Shah-Kazemi thus claims that Ibn 'Arabi subscribed to an essentialist discourse on religion that transcended the principle of noncontradiction by accepting the "intrinsic validity" of opposing religious rules and doctrines. Here, religious experience qua intuitive knowledge is implicit in Shah-Kazemi's assertion that "the other religions retain their *enlightening function* and their *spiritual efficacy* for their adherents." In the same way, Schuon's own cosmological model of multiply valid religious suns, as quoted earlier, links the different religious solar systems together by means of their "*spiritual efficacy*." As I also cite above, Schuon additionally links such "efficacy" with the enlightening power of religious symbolism as a *relative* modality of truth, thus making it open to contradiction while maintaining its validity: "the existence of dogmatic antinomies serves to show that for God truth is above all in the efficacy of the symbol." Elsewhere, Schuon makes a parallel cosmological argument:

> As every religion corresponds to a "divine subjectivity"—or "theophanic individuality"—it cannot be expected to be "objective" with regard to another religion, or at least not a priori or exoterically; for a religion as such—as a form precisely—*the elements of other religions are scarcely more than symbols or points of reference*, which can be used—most often in a pejorative or negative sense—within its own imagery and in keeping with its characteristic perspective. There are examples of this in ordinary experience: thus the appearance of things in space can give rise to an immutable symbolism even though the appearance may be different from another spatial point of view and may even reveal that the preceding appearance was an optical illusion. The earth seems flat, and the stars seem to revolve around it; the symbolism based upon appearances has nothing to fear, however, from their illusory character, which cannot invalidate it; the reality symbolized was before the symbol.
>
> No doubt God shows His solidarity with a form that has issued from His Word, but He could not be in solidarity with this form alone; what this means is that God always commits Himself to a given form sufficiently *but never exclusively*.[106]

Indeed, Shah-Kazemi similarly argues that Ibn 'Arabi enacted "the external prescriptions of the Law . . . *as symbols* relating to the principal realities they embody and intend."[107] Such a Schuonian proposition allows Shah-Kazemi to relativize Islamic legal prescriptions and decouple them with any notion of absolute truth. All legal prescriptions are therefore only symbols, or in Schuon's terms "points of reference," for an a priori set of "principal realities" (i.e., religious essences), which ultimately appear differently from different religious perspectives. By taking recourse to such symbolic relativity in relationship to religious law, Shah-Kazemi is thus able to circumvent the law of noncontradiction and "logically" argue that interreligious disparities among their legal rulings are merely accidental and ultimately inconsequential. Here, all religious laws—no matter how conflictive—are *spiritually efficacious* and thus *equally valid.*

Ibn ʿArabi and the Question of Pre-Qurʾanic Scriptural "Corruption" (*taḥrīf*)

Although Chittick's translation and commentary of the abrogation passage from chapter 339 of *The Meccan Openings* (*Futūḥāt* III, 153) has been used by Shah-Kazemi and others to variously argue for Ibn ʿArabi's *rejection* of the classical doctrine of Islamic supersessionism through abrogation (*naskh*),[108] additional textual evidence not presented by either Chittick or Shah-Kazemi shows this position to be clearly untenable. As I fully detail in chapter 2, Ibn ʿArabi holds that Jews and Christians are indeed able to observe their own religious laws on *the important condition* that they observe the Qurʾanic command of verse 9:29 and pay the indemnity tax (*jizya*), while enduring its proposed humiliation ("*until they offer the indemnity tax willingly, in a state of humiliation*") and subsequent subjugation. By doing so, according to Ibn ʿArabi, "the People of the Indemnity Tax" (*ahl al-jizya*) are subsumed within the Muhammadan sharia. As I quote Ibn ʿArabi in chapter 2:

> If he is one who pays the indemnity tax (*al-jizya*), we would say that the Muhammadan law (*al-sharʿ al-muḥammadī*) has confirmed his religion for him as long as he gives the indemnity tax—this is a specific matter of Muhammad's universal messengership (*ʿumūm risāla*). Indeed, with Muhammad's appearance the only law that remained was his law, which confirms the People of the Book's law as long as they give the indemnity tax.[109]

Yet, the qualified subjugation of the People of the Indemnity Tax along with their attendant backdoor entrance into the fold of Islam, albeit in an inferior "nocturnal" participation ("the day is ours, but the People of the Book only have the night, that is, if '*they offer the indemnity tax willingly, in a state of humiliation*'"[110]), presents a noteworthy variation on the theme of religious "validity." Here the external, or in Kantian terms, "heteronomous," imposition of Islamic law appears to counter the autonomy of gnosis as the validating factor within the universalist discourse of Schuonian Perennialism. Yet, before offering additional textual evidence and further analysis on this point, I think it would be helpful here to look at more basic Perennialist claims regarding Ibn 'Arabi's conception of the scriptural "validity" of pre-Qur'anic revelation as well as his neglected discourse on the subject.

According to Shah-Kazemi, "the knowledge *that all religions are united in their essence* was crystallized in Ibn Arabi's consciousness by one of the key Quranic verses proclaiming the message of all the prophets to be one and the same."[111] The verse referred to here is Qur'an 3:84, which I discussed in chapter 1.[112] As I detailed there, verse 3:84 is the very same verse that Ibn 'Arabi "received" when he attained to the Muhammadan Station at the end of his ascension recounted in *The Meccan Openings*. Shah-Kazemi thus asserts, as I also quote in chapter 1, that in receiving verse 3:84, Ibn 'Arabi "understood that there is no distinction between the prophets at the highest level of religion, and also *that the respective revelations vouchsafed them are consequently all to be accepted as valid*."[113] Shah-Kazemi similarly claims later in the same work that "*the universal validity of religion as such* was established for Ibn Arabi in his spiritual ascent."[114]

Yet, rather than interpreting this verse as a call for an inclusive religious universalism or the perennial validity of all "orthodox" religions, Ibn 'Arabi here clearly recounts what I describe in chapter 1 as a powerful *vision of subsumption*. Upon attaining the Muhammadan Station, Ibn 'Arabi claims that he at once knew that he was "*the sum total*" of the biblical patriarchs and prophets specifically mentioned in Qur'an 3:84, thus triumphantly indicating his Muhammadan comprehensiveness as the totality of all previous prophetic understanding.[115] Indeed, as I detailed in chapter 2, it is precisely this subsumptive quality of comprehensiveness that serves as the vehicle for the divinely mandated Muhammadan abrogation of all other preceding religious dispensations, since those previous dispensations are simply prior manifestations of the comprehensive Muhammadan Reality (*ḥaqīqa muḥammadiyya*), which are ultimately subsumed by the final advent of the Islamic dispensation through the historical prophecy of Muhammad.[116]

As such, Shah-Kazemi's interpretation of verses like Qur'an 3:84 as "*the universal validity of religion as such*" evinces an anachronistic preunderstanding based upon a contemporary, Western essentialist notion of religion that can be traced back to the Schleiermacherian model of experiential-expressivism discussed earlier. Yet, if we wish to better understand Ibn 'Arabi's engagement with texts such as Qur'an 3:84—and revelation more broadly—without the distortion of such a modern lens, it would seem imperative to take seriously his inherited hermeneutical *habitus*. Thus, from within the perspective of the wider interpretive field of Ibn 'Arabi's medieval context, the claim for the continuity of revelation and revealed law should only be understood as a manifestation of "perennial religion" in the most narrowly circumscribed terms—that is, a *continual process of prophetic renewal* of the only true, primordial "religion" (*al-dīn*).[117] As Norman O. Brown observes:

> Islam picks up and extends the notion, already present in Jewish (Ebionite) Christianity, of the unity of the prophetic spirit: *Christus aeternus, verus propheta ab initio mundi per saeculum currens*; the one true prophet, from age to age, from the beginning of the world; Adam, Noah, Abraham, Moses, Christ, Muhammad. The later prophet comes to reiterate the Eternal and Everlasting Gospel—the "seim anew," *Lex mosaica per Jesum prophetam reformata*, the mosaic law reformed by Jesus the prophet. The tradition gets de-formed and has to be re-formed. Thus "true Christianity" is identical with "true Judaism."[118]

Classical Muslim exegetes, as the Qur'anic scholar Jane McAuliffe clarifies, understood "true" Christianity as those pre-Islamic Christians who embraced "that vision of Christian scripture that sees in it a prefiguration of the final Prophet."[119]

Within this medieval prophetology of continuous renewal, the Qur'an was thus understood to be the final revelation of previously revealed books, all sent down from the same heavenly source—the "mother of the book" (*umm al-kitāb*).[120] However, according to the Qur'an, some of the Jews were guilty of scriptural *taḥrīf* (variously translated as "corruption," "alteration," or "distortion")[121] and *tabdīl* ("substitution," "replacement," or "change").[122] Yet, the exact meaning and ramifications of such assertions has been the subject of a long-standing debate among Muslim scholars.

In reference to Qur'anic passages in apparent support of the universal validity of other religions (e.g., Qur'an 3:84 discussed above), Shah-Kazemi himself notes, "many Muslims" assert "the unreliability of the 'sacred books' revealed before the Qur'ān . . . referred to as the doctrine of *taḥrīf* (alteration)."[123] As such, he argues that "while the Qur'an gives only a single actual instance of actual alteration (IV:46),"[124] it also unconditionally relates that in both Jewish and Christian scripture there is "*guidance and light*."[125] Shah-Kazemi goes on to make an argument for "*the continuing validity* of the revealed Scriptures of the People of the Book."[126] He states:

> While . . . the Qur'ān certainly castigates some of the People of the Book for some attitudes, this criticism does not extend to the sources of their tradition, sources which retain their value: otherwise the legal recognition and formal protection granted to them would be devoid of meaning, and their being referred to as "People of the Book" would be both inaccurate and illogical.[127]

Shah-Kazemi here takes a particular stand on a very old exegetical argument that dates back to the beginning of Muslim polemics against Jewish and Christian scripture regarding two distinct interpretations of what the Qur'anic accusation of *taḥrīf* implies. Although some polemicists argued that *taḥrīf* referred to the "corruption of the text" (*taḥrīf al-naṣṣ*) itself, others claimed that it referred only to a "corruption of the meaning" (*taḥrīf al-maʿānī*).[128]

In arguing that the sources of the People of the Book "retain their value," Shah-Kazemi not only directly supports a Schuonian framework for the universal validity of other religions but also endorses the exegetical conception that the Qur'an criticized the People of the Book for corrupting its texts only at the level of interpretation (i.e., *taḥrīf al-maʿānī*) and not for literally corrupting the text itself (i.e., *taḥrīf al-naṣṣ*).[129] While Shah-Kazemi's argument merely implies, but never claims, that Ibn 'Arabi took this particular view of *taḥrīf*, Chittick's treatment is at once more specific in such assertions and much less transparent about the exegetical debate it engages.

Even though Chittick never mentions the technical terminology involved in the debate, Shah-Kazemi's argument for *taḥrīf al-maʿānī* clearly echoes (in reverse order) the same assertions made by Chittick in *Imaginal Worlds* regarding Ibn 'Arabi and *taḥrīf*.[130] Here, in a section entitled "The Koranic View of Revelation" (which also contains Chittick's discussion of Ibn 'Arabi's view on abrogation discussed in chapter 2), Chittick states: "The Koran never criticizes the prophetic messages as such, but it often condemns misunderstandings or distortions by those who follow the prophets."[131] Chittick then acknowledges that Ibn 'Arabi confirms (in some sense) the Qur'anic assertion of scriptural "distortion" (i.e., *taḥrīf*): "The Shaykh sometimes criticizes specific distortions or misunderstandings in the Koranic vein."[132] At the end of this section, Chittick thus concludes:

> To maintain the particular excellence of the Koran and the superiority of Muhammad over all other prophets *is not to deny the universal validity of revelation* nor the necessity of revelation's appearing in particularized expressions. *Since all revealed religions are true in principle, the particular circumstances that lead one to suspect that they have been corrupted may change.*[133]

By claiming that Ibn 'Arabi's discourse confirms (by not denying) "the universal validity of revelation," Chittick, like Shah-Kazemi above, echoes the Schuonian notion of the continued "spiritual efficacy" of orthodox religions and "the transcendent unity of religions." In addition, Chittick's final statement refers again to *taḥrīf*, specifically arguing for the corruption of meaning (*taḥrīf al-maʿānī*): "Since all revealed religions are true in principle, the particular circumstances that lead one to suspect that they have been corrupted may change." Because the opposing idea of *taḥrīf al-naṣṣ* implies that the original text has been literally lost, Chittick's statement only makes sense in the context of a corruption of meaning since such meaning could arguably be recoverable in the right circumstances. In other words, because all the revelations as they exist in their contemporary forms are *essentially* true, they cannot be permanently corrupted, only misunderstood. Indeed, here Chittick's articulation of *taḥrīf al-maʿānī* echoes Perennialist discourse in important ways. For example, in his same article expositing the contours of Perennialism mentioned earlier, Huston Smith defines the nature of religious validity in similar terms by noting that "the great historical religions have survived for millennia, which is what we would expect if they are divinely powered."[134] According to this circular logic, the very continued existence of "the great historical religions" is itself sufficient proof of their universal validity.

Indeed, Ibn ʿArabi often makes assertions that could easily be read from within the Perennialist framework of the universal validity of religions. For example, in the first of two ascension narratives in *The Meccan Openings*, which offers an allegorical narration,[135] Ibn ʿArabi describes a symbolic vision at the foot of "*the lote tree of the furthest boundary*" (*sidrat al-muntahā*) (Qur'an 53:14) where three lesser rivers and their smaller tributaries emerge from a larger one. Here he relates that the larger river is the Qur'an, while the three emerging ones are the Torah, Psalms, and the Gospel, finally followed by the lesser revelations (*al-ṣuḥuf al-munzala*).[136] Ibn ʿArabi then makes a claim that at first glance appears to support a Schuonian model: he states that whoever has drunk from any of these rivers becomes an inheritor (*wārith*) of their respective prophets, for "all are true, since they are the words of God."[137] However, he further clarifies thus:

> "The ulama are the inheritors of the prophets" in what they have drunk from these rivers and tributaries. So commence (*ishraʿ*)[138] with the river of the Qur'an and you will triumph in each way of felicity (*saʿāda*), since it is the river of Muhammad, may God bless him and grant him peace, for whom prophethood was realized while Adam was between water and clay. And Muhammad was given the comprehensive words (*jawāmiʿ al-kalim*) and was sent to all people (*ʿāmma*). Thus, the branches of the rulings (*furūʿ al-aḥkām*) are abrogated (*naskh*) by him, but his ruling (*ḥukm*) is not abrogated by another.[139]

By following his assertion that whoever has drunk the scriptural rivers becomes an inheritor (*wārith*) of their respective prophets with the famous hadith "the ulama are the inheritors of the prophets,"[140] Ibn ʿArabi clarifies that he here is speaking about the religious "scholars" who have come *after* the advent of Muhammad (i.e., the Muslim ulama). Indeed, in *The Ring Stones of Wisdom* (*Fuṣūṣ al-ḥikam*), Ibn ʿArabi directly comments on this hadith, noting that even though the death of the Prophet put an end to law-giving prophethood (*nubūwat al-tashrīʿ*), God gave His servants the ability to continue, in a sense, such law-giving through legal reasoning (*al-ijtihād*). The "inheritance" to which this hadith refers, states Ibn ʿArabi, "is none other than the ulama's use of legal reasoning to arrive at rulings and thus legislate them."[141] Like Ibn ʿArabi's story of Ibn Barthamlā discussed in chapter 2, which claimed that after the advent of the Prophet Muhammad a saintly "heir" (*wārith*) of a prophet other than Muhammad will still *necessarily* follow the sharia of Muhammad since it abrogates previously revealed laws,[142] here Ibn ʿArabi instructs his readers to drink from the supreme river of the Qur'an, which he not only directly associates with Muhammad but also associates with the *abrogative power* of his sharia.

Thus, in his "visionary" passage above, Ibn ʿArabi's discourse appears to deploy a hadith in an "exoteric" fashion as part of the triumphal discourse of Muhammadan comprehensiveness discussed in chapter 2. As Morris importantly notes, a distinctive feature of Ibn ʿArabi's discourse is his "spiritual literalism," that is, Ibn ʿArabi's "constant insistence on the ultimate coincidence (not simply in outward formulation) between the precise, revealed literal formulations of the Koran and hadith and their essential spiritual truth and intentions as realized and verified by the saints."[143] Itzchak Weismann has similarly observed that a close examination of *The Meccan Openings* reveals that Ibn ʿArabi's "thought was basically a meticulous, though unbound by reason, *literal interpretation* of the scriptures."[144] It is thus my contention here, and throughout this book, that Ibn ʿArabi's "spiritual literalism" is nowhere more apparent than in his statements regarding *naskh* and *taḥrīf*—that is, the abrogative function of Muhammad's legal dispensation, as detailed in chapter 2, and the attendant idea that the pre-Qur'anic scriptures were distorted. In such discourse, Ibn ʿArabi appears to forcefully echo—albeit in a more "spiritualized" fashion—one of his most intellectually formidable religious heroes and fellow Andalusian, the famous Ẓāhirī scholar and polemicist Ibn Ḥazm (d. 1064).

After having a profound dream of Ibn Hazm in his early life in which he witnessed his Andalusian predecessor embracing the Prophet in a cloud of light,[145] Ibn ʿArabi assiduously studied and transcribed his works.[146] While the similarities between Ibn ʿArabi's approach to jurisprudence and the Ẓāhirī school of law have been the subject of much discussion, there are important differences between the two.[147] Where Ibn ʿArabi appears to have adopted (or likewise rejected) literalist Ẓāhirī methodology, he did so only in accordance with his primary goal of providing ease to Muslims by preserving as much of their freedom as possible within the limited confines of divine prescription.[148]

For Ibn Hazm, the "literal" (*ẓāhir*) meaning of the Qur'an must be adhered to unless a clear indication that another meaning was intended.[149] This literalist approach filled the silences in the text with God-given meaning and provided people not less, *but more* freedom of choice.[150] Indeed, it is this spirit of freedom in Ibn Hazm's approach that seems to have inspired Ibn 'Arabi.[151] And it is in this same spirit where we find a mystical echo of Ibn Hazm's approach to legal theory in Ibn 'Arabi's Qur'anic hermeneutics. As Adam Sabra observes, the Ẓāhirī scholar strove to obtain "the maximum utility from the fixed canon of sacred texts."[152] Thus, for Ibn Hazm, "when a word has more than one meaning, one must not restrict it to one meaning. *All possible meanings are valid*, provided they do not result in a logical absurdity."[153] Similarly, for Ibn 'Arabi, as Michel Chodkiewicz notes, "rigorous fidelity to the letter of Revelation does not exclude but, on the contrary, *it implies a multiplicity of interpretations*."[154] While it can be compellingly argued that Ibn 'Arabi's methodology often evinces more of a *promiscuity* than a "fidelity" to the Qur'anic Arabic he interprets,[155] it is nevertheless his discursive *claim* to fidelity within such a polysemic context that so closely resembles Ibn Hazm's method.

In light of this, it is not unreasonable to assume that some of Ibn 'Arabi's interpretive practices developed within the discursive aura of what Gerald Elmore refers to as the "avant-garde" movement of "Ḥazmism" in Seville, where Ẓāhirism "became the official law of the land" under the reform campaign of the Almohad caliph Abū Yūsuf Yaʿqūb al-Manṣūr (r. 1184–99) against the Mālikī school of jurisprudence.[156] As Camilla Adang notes, the tension between the Mālikīs and the Ẓāhirīs appears to have been formative for Ibn Hazm's own position regarding the abrogation (*naskh*) of Mosaic law by the sharia of Muhammad and the supremacy of Islam over Judaism:[157]

> Ibn Ḥazm's demonstration of the abrogation of the Mosaic law is not primarily meant to convince the Jews of the antiquated nature of their scripture, but seems above all aimed at reminding his fellow-Muslims that the only valid canonical law is the Islamic *sharīʿa* . . . and that it is therefore not permitted to follow the laws of Moses or any other prophet apart from Muhammad. This he deemed necessary, since he had noticed that a number of Muslims, or, to be more specific, Mālikīs, displayed tendencies which might be termed "Judaizing."[158]

In light of the historical tension between the Mālikīs and Ẓāhirīs in Ibn 'Arabi's native Seville and his deep affinity for Ibn Hazm's intellectual approach,[159] Ibn 'Arabi's aforementioned vision of a Qur'anic urtext at the foot of "*the lote tree of the furthest boundary*" takes on a particularly politico-metaphysical hue. Given the fact that the audience Ibn ʿArabi wrote for can be broadly defined as an intellectual Muslim elite "composed mainly of religious scholars,"[160] his more polemical statements regarding pre-Qurʾanic revelation do not appear to be made in dialogue with non-Muslims in an attempt to convert or debate them. Indeed, in a passage about the direct power of the Qurʾan for salvation and the limited utility of other sciences such as speculative theology (*kalām*) found in the introduction of *The Meccan Openings*, Ibn ʿArabi echoes Ibn Hazm and other formative Sufi theorists like Abū Ḥāmid al-Ghazālī (d. 1111):[161]

> The mighty Qurʾan is abundantly sufficient for the intelligent person, and for one who has a chronic disease it is a remedy and a healing. As God said: "*We reveal from within the Qurʾan that which is a healing and a mercy for the believers*" [Qurʾan 17:82]. It is a sufficient healing for one who has undertaken the way of salvation (*ṭarīq al-najāh*), has desired to ascend the ranks, and has left the sciences that produce perplexity and doubts, for they waste time and induce (God's) hatred.
>
> When that way is embraced, however, then such a person will seldom be safe from contentious wrangling or being preoccupied with his own (dialectical) rehearsal and refinement so that all of his free moments will be immersed in repelling imaginary opponents and refuting specious arguments that may or may not transpire.
>
> But if they do, then the sword of the sharia is the most repellent and cutting! "I have been commanded to fight people until they say 'there is no god but God' and until they believe in me and what I have brought." This is the Prophet's statement, may God bless him and grant him peace. He did not oblige us to argue with them when they are present; rather, (our recourse) is to struggle (*jihad*) and the sword if they resist what has been declared to them.[162]

While Ibn ʿArabi's language here straddles double registers of literalism and allegory, given the similar discursive bellicosity in his advice to Kaykāʾus, the Seljuk sultan of Anatolia, as discussed at the start of chapter 2, there is no reason to doubt his commitment to both. Yet, irrespective of how seriously his jihadist rhetoric was intended, his concern is clearly not to dialectically convince opponents who "resist." In light of such avowals, Ibn ʿArabi's emphatic claim in his ascension narrative, as quoted above, that by beginning "with the river of the Qurʾan," one "will triumph in each way of felicity" combined with his following statement that Muhammad's law abrogates but is not abrogated seems to be addressed primarily to his coreligionists who may have been tempted, like the Mālikīs according to

Ibn Hazm, to incorporate aspects of other religious practice or discourse into Islam—particularly that transmitted from the rabbinic tradition.[163]

Indeed, evidence for such a concern can be gleaned from a passage at the very end of chapter 257 in *The Meccan Openings*, where Ibn 'Arabi rails against the "Tales of the Prophets" (*qiṣaṣ al-anbiyāʾ*) or *Isrāʾīliyyāt* literature. As Gordon Newby notes, "the circulation of non-Islamic materials for use as the basis for Qur'ân commentary"—particularly that derived from rabbinic sources—"was present during Muḥammad's lifetime and saw a considerable increase in the two generations after his death."[164] This tradition was continued not only by early proto-Sufis such as al-Muḥāsibī (d. 857) who used such sources freely but also by later figures like Abū Nuʿaym al-Iṣfahānī (d. 1038) and Ghazali who also employed them.[165] While the embellishments of the storytellers (*quṣṣāṣ*) became a standard subject of scorn by the fourteenth century for scholars such as Ibn Kathīr (d. 1373),[166] many of the earliest critics of storytellers were Sufis like Abū Ṭālib al-Makkī (d. 996).[167]

In the following passage, Ibn 'Arabi, like his predecessor al-Makki, draws a line between the "assemblies of remembrance" (*majālis al-dhikr*),[168] which according to Prophetic tradition are visited by the angels, and the "lies" of the storytellers that result in angelic rejection. As such, Ibn 'Arabi urges the would-be "preacher" (*mudhakkir*)—literally, *the one who reminds, admonishes, or exhorts others*—"to avoid rubbish in his lesson," by which he means transmitting fabrications that the Jews allegedly made about their prophets commonly used in Qur'anic commentary (*tafsīr*):

> When the preacher (*al-mudhakkir*) knows that angels are attending his assembly, it is best for him to investigate the truth and not go into what the historians have narrated, on the authority of the Jews, about the (imagined) transgressions of those whom God praised and selected, and thus not take such narrations as commentary on the Book of God, saying, "the commentators have said...."
>
> It is not appropriate to present such rubbish as commentary on the Word of God like the tale of Joseph (*qiṣṣat yūsuf*) and David and those similar, peace be upon them, and Muhammad, may God bless him and grant him peace, by means of perverted interpretations and on the authority of people with baseless chains of transmission who said concerning God that which God has mentioned about them.[169] If the preacher relates the like of this in his assembly, the angels will abhor and eschew him, and God will abhor him as well. Sometimes a person is found whose religious practice inclines toward dispensations and who takes recourse to such

> things, saying: "If the prophets had fallen into situations like this, then who am I (not to do the same)?"
>
> By God, the prophets are far from what has been ascribed to them by the Jews, God curse them (*laʿanahum allāh*)! . . . So, the establishment of the sanctity of the prophets (*ḥurmat al-anbiyāʾ*), upon them be peace, and having shame (*al-ḥayāʾ*) before God is obligatory for the preacher who should not follow what the Jews have claimed to be the truth regarding the defects of the prophets, nor should he follow the fictions of the exegetes (who rely on such sources)—God forsake them (*khadhalahum allāh*)![170]

Although Ibn ʿArabi shows elsewhere that he is not adverse to polemical statements against the Jews and Christians, as I have already noted in the first half of this book,[171] here the topic of disrespect against the prophets seems to have raised Ibn ʿArabi's ire enough to warrant curses. And it is in these very curses, along with their apparent grounds, that we find a strong echo of the polemical style of Ibn Hazm, who often hurled similar imprecations.[172] Indeed, as Theodore Pulcini notes, "Perhaps the most impassioned charge Ibn Hazm brings against the Jewish scriptures is that they contradict the Islamic doctrine of *ʿiṣma*, i.e., they violate the principle that the prophets are immune from error and sin."[173] The following lines contained in Ibn Hazm's *Book of Appraisal on Religions, Heresies, and Sects* (*Kitāb al-fiṣal fī al-milal wa al-ahwāʾ wa al-niḥal*) similarly attack what he considered Jewish lies against the prophets in the Torah:

> Of David they say that he openly committed adultery with the virtuous wife of one of his soldiers. . . . Not to mention the lies they impute to Abraham, Isaac, Jacob and Joseph. . . . God's curse and His wrath be upon everyone who gives credence to any of these lies![174]

It was indeed Ibn Hazm's systematic polemical attack on Judaism and his specific allegations against the Jews that changed the way Muslim scholars approached the scriptures of the People of the Book. Not only was Mosaic law subject to abrogation (*naskh*) by the sharia of Muhammad, but also, according to Ibn Hazm, the text of the Torah itself had actually been irretrievably corrupted (i.e., *taḥrīf al-naṣṣ*).[175] Before Ibn Hazm, most scholars subscribed to the more moderate conception of scriptural corruption that held the meaning of the text to have been distorted (i.e., *taḥrīf al-maʿānī*), while the integrity of the text itself remained unchanged.[176] Indeed, Ibn ʿArabi's more immediate predecessor in Seville, Ibn Barrajān (d. 1141), subscribed variously to both positions.[177]

Thus, in contradistinction to Chittick's implied assertion in *Imaginal Worlds* that Ibn ʿArabi adhered to the more liberal view of *taḥrīf al-maʿānī*, as discussed earlier, the Andalusian Sufi appears to follow Ibn Hazm and the more extreme position of *taḥrīf al-naṣṣ*. While there are several statements in *The Meccan Openings* where Ibn ʿArabi emphatically asserts that the Qurʾan is protected from *taḥrīf* (and various analogous terms),[178] as opposed to "the other revealed books,"[179] perhaps his definitive ontological view is again found in chapter 12 just prior to a similar statement about abrogation (*naskh*) discussed in chapter 2. While the divine command for the abrogation of all other religious dispensations by that of Muhammad's emerges from the fourth heaven, its counterpart for the continued preservation from alteration (*taḥrīf*) of both the Qurʾan and Muhammad's sharia itself emerges from the first heaven:

> One of the specific commands of the first heaven is that no letter or word from the Qurʾan would be changed (*yabdul*). Thus, if Satan imposes a meaning upon its recitation that is not of it, whether by elimination or addition, then God will abrogate (*nasakha*) that—this is preservation (*ʿiṣma*) (from error).
>
> Also from the first heaven is the fixed state of permanence (*thabāt*): his sharia is not abrogated by another. Rather, it is definitively preserved and firmly established from every point of view, which is why every group affirms it.
>
> . . . Regarding another community of revelation, it has been said about them: "*They knowingly corrupted [the Word of God] after they understood it*" [Qurʾan 2:75]. So "God misguided them (*aḍallahum*) in full knowledge (of their true state)."[180] But for us, God took it (upon himself) to preserve His (Book of) Remembrance (*dhikrahu*). Thus, He said: "*We have sent down the Remembrance, and indeed We are its guardian*" [Qurʾan 15:9], because He is the hearing of the servant, his seeing, his mouthpiece, and his hand.[181] A community other than this one had been entrusted with guarding His Book, but they altered it (*ḥarrafūhu*).[182]

In addition to Ibn ʿArabi's assertion regarding the overall preserved status of both the Qurʾan and its revealed law, following Qurʾan 2:75, he declares that a previous religious community was guilty of alteration. Yet, he does not specify which type of alteration—*taḥrīf al-maʿānī* or *taḥrīf al-naṣṣ*—was committed. There is, however, another passage in *The Meccan Openings* that unequivocally reveals that Ibn ʿArabi again follows Ibn Hazm in this regard, believing it to have been the latter—that the text of the Torah itself was purposefully and irretrievably altered.

This particular passage appears in the second ascension narrative in *The Meccan Openings* (i.e., chapter 367)[183] and comes in the final section where Ibn 'Arabi describes his visionary experience after he attained to the "Muhammadan Station" (*muḥammadī al-maqām*), as mentioned in chapter 1.[184] It is in this section that he narrates a long list of visions of particular types of knowledge—each beginning with "And I saw . . . " (*wa ra'aitu*). As Morris notes, this list differs from similar listings in the other chapters contained in the section of "spiritual abodes" (*faṣl al-manāzil*) of *The Meccan Openings*[185] (in which chapter 367 is included) in that "it contains a number of Ibn 'Arabî's most fundamental metaphysical theses."[186]

Yet, no mention of the following passage is made by Morris, or any other universalist scholar of Ibn 'Arabi that I am aware, since its synthesis of the highest mode of visionary experience with a clear disavowal of the authenticity of the Torah is a circle rather difficult to square for those who wish to imagine Ibn 'Arabi universally accepting the validity of the religions of his day. Here, Ibn 'Arabi states:

> And I saw (*wa ra'aitu*) the Torah and the specific knowledge that God wrote in it by His own hand. But I was astonished at how, even though He wrote it by His own (single) hand, God did not protect it from substitution (*al-tabdīl*) and corruption (*al-taḥrīf*) by the Jews, the companions of Moses, who changed (*ḥarrafa*) it. Just as I was so astonished, I was spoken to secretly; I heard the address, but what is more, I saw the very speaker, and I witnessed him in an expansive mercy in which I stood and which surrounded me. He said to me: "More astonishing than that, is that He created Adam by his two hands and He did not protect him from disobedience and forgetfulness—where is the rank of one hand compared to that of two?" How astonishing indeed! The two hands were turned only towards his clay and his nature. And because Satan whispered to him, the whispering came only to him from the direction of his nature. And Satan is created from part of what Adam was created from.[187] It was only by his own nature that Adam forgot and yielded to the whispering, and it was upon his nature that the two hands were turned. For that reason, He did not protect Adam from the disobedience of his own offspring, which he carried within his own clay.
>
> So, do not be astonished by the Jews changing the Torah, since the Torah was not changed in its pure form, but rather change has befallen it by their writing it and their verbalizing it. This was referred to by the Word of God when He said: "*They knowingly corrupted it after they understood it*" [Qur'an 2:75]. The Jews knew that the Word of God was understood

> (by many) among them, yet what they disclosed in their transcription (of the Torah) contradicted what was in their hearts and what was in their revealed book (*muṣḥafihim al-munzal*). They only changed it when they copied it from the original, while knowledge of the original remained for those scribes and their scholars.
>
> Thus, even though Adam was with the two hands (of God), he disobeyed by himself—he was not protected like the Word of God, which is even more astonishing. Rather, the Word of God was preserved (*ʿuṣima*) because it is a (divine) ruling (*ḥukm*). And the ruling is inviolable (*maʿṣūm*), but its abode is with the scholars. So what was with the scholars was changed, which they did for their followers. And Adam is not a ruling of God, so it is not imperative for him to be preserved in himself, but preservation (*al-ʿiṣma*) is imperative in what is conveyed from his Lord with respect to the ruling when he was a messenger, and so it is for all of the messengers. This is noble knowledge (*ʿilm sharīf*).[188]

In this passage, remarkable for its amalgamation of visionary experience and polemical theology, Ibn ʿArabi explains the metaphysical reasons behind the apparently astonishing fact that the Torah could have been physically changed even though, as "the Word of God," it must be inviolable (*maʿṣūm*). Yet more amazing, according to Ibn ʿArabi, is how Adam disobeyed God, even though he was made with both of God's hands. Thus, in a notably sober mood, Ibn ʿArabi sets forth an argument distinguishing God's transcendent perfection in opposition to the nature of His creation, no matter how enlightened.

Al-Ṭabarī (d. 923) was perhaps the first to argue that in addition to a genuine Torah, which was burned, lost, and then miraculously restored by Ezra,[189] there was a second text written by a group of rabbis and mistakenly taken as the original by the Jews of al-Tabari's day.[190] Ibn Hazm similarly held that the Torah was destroyed and rewritten by Ezra. Instead of a miraculous restoration, however, Ezra radically changed the Torah into an invalid forgery.[191] Against this extreme assertion of *taḥrīf*, Ibn Hazm anticipated objections that would argue, as Shah-Kazemi does above, that the Qur'an itself claims that the Torah contains "*guidance and light*" (Qur'an 5:44). While such a divine Torah exists, according to Ibn Hazm, it is not the one possessed by the Jews. Rather, the true Torah along with the Gospel was taken up by Jesus when he ascended to heaven.[192] Although Ibn ʿArabi does not rehearse this particular narrative in the passage above, he clearly holds the same idea—that is, while the Torah remains intact "in its pure form," the written (and subsequently verbalized) form was changed. The metaphorical paradox, of course, is that Adam, as both a messenger and a human being, is the channel of a protected divine message and the simultaneous cause of its corruption.

Moreover, there is an unspoken subtext on the superiority of Muhammad here, whose own revelation (as discussed above) is the only one granted preservation in both the heavenly and earthly realms. Indeed, it is to this special nature of the Muhammadan dispensation and its apparent ability to remain preserved—but also to redeem prior dispensations—that we now turn.

The Efficacy of Subjugation: A Heteronomous Model

We have now come full circle to the question of Ibn 'Arabi's position on the "validity" of religions other than Islam and the problem presented by "the People of the Indemnity Tax" in chapter 2. Having decidedly established Ibn 'Arabi's discursive position regarding scriptural corruption (*taḥrīf*)—in addition to abrogation (*naskh*)—it is now possible to more fully situate the limited validity Ibn 'Arabi gives to the People of the Indemnity Tax and conclusively determine if such validity has *any* correspondence to the universalism of Schuonian Perennialism and its claim that all orthodox religions contain "truth sufficient unto salvation," to use Huston Smith's descriptive locution quoted earlier.

In another passage from *The Meccan Openings*, which I briefly mention at the close of chapter 2, Ibn 'Arabi qualifies the relationship of the People of the Book to Islam through their payment of the indemnity tax (*jizya*). Here, not only does Ibn 'Arabi again sanction what I dubbed in chapter 2 as their "qualified subjugation," but he also relates that through such subjugation the People of the Book are granted salvific "felicity" (*sa'āda*). In the following passage, Ibn 'Arabi specifically discusses "the Followers of the Books who pay the indemnity tax" (*aṣḥāb al-kutub bi al-jizya*) and states:

> Their remaining upon their religion (*dīn*) was prescribed (*shrara'*) by God for them on the tongue of Muhammad, may God bless him and grant him peace. So their giving the indemnity tax (*al-jizya*) benefits them if it is taken under the threat of force and as a humiliation for them, since (under such conditions) they have fulfilled their obligation.[193] This, then, is their portion from the revealed law (*al-sharī'a*) (of Muhammad), and they are allowed to remain upon their divine law (*shar'*), which is, as such, Muhammadan law (*shar' muḥammadī*). So they attain to a state of felicity (*yas'adūn*) by that, but those who exceed the proper bounds will be punished from the law that they are upon.[194]

Thus, despite his various admonishments of the People of the Book for their unbelief (*kufr*) and associationism (*shirk*),[195] here Ibn 'Arabi asserts that through the fulfillment of the Qur'anic command of humiliation, Jews and Christians can presumably be spared the torments of Hell.[196]

While this passage succinctly confirms the argument proffered in chapter 2—that according to Ibn 'Arabi, Judaism and Christianity can only be considered "valid" religions if their adherents follow Qur'an 9:29 and "*offer the indemnity tax willingly, in a state of humiliation*"—it additionally throws into relief how Ibn 'Arabi understands such validity. In sharp contrast to the Schuonian notion of the "spiritual efficacy" of all "orthodox" religions via transcendent gnosis of their various symbolic truths, the spiritual efficacy of Judaism and Christianity is for Ibn 'Arabi here shown to be solely determined by *obedience* to the revelation of Muhammad rather than any particular "truth sufficient unto salvation" that Ibn 'Arabi grants to the Torah or Gospel. Thus, the payment of the indemnity tax by the People of the Book "under the threat of force and as a humiliation" fulfills *their particular* Qur'anic scriptural "obligation," and they are thus coercively subsumed within the cosmographical sovereignty of Muhammad.

Conclusion: An Interpretive Field Revealed

In this chapter, I have sought to identify some key components of the Schuonian Perennialist strategy of universal religious validity. As we have seen, this strategy seeks to transcend the Aristotelian law of noncontradiction through recourse to two particular ideas: (1) a purported modality of religious experience that goes beyond rational thought through what can be called intuitive knowledge or "gnosis," and (2) a worldview that holds religious symbols critical to all religious forms as both true and nonabsolute—that is, symbolically relative.

I have also shown how the Schuonian Perennialist reading of Ibn 'Arabi adheres to this strategy of validity by imagining that his approach to other religions confirms the Perennialist idea of universal validity and transcendent unity. Yet, to do this, such a reading must invert Ibn 'Arabi's hierarchical Muhammadan cosmology into a model of cosmic pluralism that is at once symbolically relative and applicable to all contemporaneous, "orthodox" religious cosmologies. Finally, I posed the question of whether the validity that Ibn 'Arabi gives to the People of the Indemnity Tax confirms the Perennialist conception of religious validity. By looking at Ibn 'Arabi's notion of scriptural "corruption" (*taḥrīf*), in addition to revisiting his idea of abrogation (*naskh*) already established in chapter 2, I demonstrated that he understood previous scriptures to have been *textually* corrupted (*taḥrīf al-naṣṣ*) and unrepresentative of their original purity, since God had not protected them via the heavenly sphere of the first heaven as was the case with the Qur'an. Thus, rather than supporting the efficacy of Judaism and Christianity in terms of scriptural truth or experiential "gnosis," the spiritual efficacy that Ibn ʿArabi granted the People of the Book was predicated purely on their ability to obey the Qur'an and thus enter through the back door, so to speak, of the Muhammadan sharia. For Ibn ʿArabi, these contemporaneous religious traditions achieve prophetic validity only by a fully heteronomous process of forceful obedience to the Islamic sharia. Thus, in alignment with Asad's observations about premodern Christianity, religious truth for Ibn ʿArabi is expressed through "practical rules attached to specific processes of power and knowledge."[197] Indeed, as I mentioned in chapter 1, Ibn ʿArabi defined "religion" (*dīn*) as "obedience" (*inqiyād*)[198]—a definition that replicates a theological principle at work within early Islamic technical terminology.[199]

Although Ibn ʿArabi did not focus on interreligious polemics like his intellectual predecessor Ibn Hazm, the evidence that I have presented in this chapter shows that his metaphysical ideas were forged within a *habitus* of religious rivalry and constituted through frameworks of absolutism. As Jacques Waardenburg observes:

> Just as the Qurʾān had been declared to be the uncreated and infallible Word of God, in the second half of the ninth century C.E., so Muhammad's status as the infallible seal of the prophets proclaiming definite truth was fixed. The three issues of *naskh*, *tahrīf*, and *prophethood* . . . formed the basis for the *mutakallimūn*'s polemics against Christianity, as they did for their polemics against Judaism.[200]

As I have shown, Ibn ʿArabi's conceptualization of his contemporaneous religious Others is grounded precisely within a metaphysical cosmology heavily constituted by these three main polemical issues—that is, *naskh, taḥrīf,* and *prophethood.*[201]

In spite of repeated Perennialist claims that Ibn ʿArabi upheld the continued validity of all religions after the advent of Islam (and by doing so transcended the Aristotelian law of noncontradiction), the evidence that I have offered in this chapter provides much support for a reassessment of his supposed religious "universalism." Yet, scholars working within the interpretive field of Perennialism have sustained Ibn ʿArabi's discursive image as an inclusive universalist in the face of long-observed discrepancies between his ideas and the Schuonian conceptual claim for the transcendent validity of all religions.

Indeed, in all of his works that interpret Ibn ʿArabi through a Perennialist framework, Shah-Kazemi, like Chittick himself, never broaches the subject of Ibn ʿArabi's well-known letter to the Seljuk sultan of Anatolia. Yet, as mentioned at the beginning of chapter 2, Ibn ʿArabi's hostility to the Christians displayed in the missive was noted early on and with not a little pique by the Catholic scholar Miguel Asín Palacios in his 1931 work on Ibn ʿArabi, *El Islam cristianizado*.[202] Moreover, Reynold Nicholson's study of ʿAbd al-Karīm al-Jīlī (d. after 1408) and his work *al-Insān al-kāmil* first published in 1921 has long been regarded as an important early contribution to Western scholarship on Ibn ʿArabi and his school.[203] As one of Ibn ʿArabi's most important interpreters, Jili articulated much of the same discourse. While Nicholson admits that Jili criticizes Christianity, albeit "mildly and apologetically," he notes that Ibn ʿArabi "*is more critical and orthodox* than Jílí."[204] Still, according to Nicholson, Jili not only recognizes Islam as "the crown of religions"[205] but also accepts (precisely like Ibn Hazm and Ibn ʿArabi) the idea of *taḥrīf* in its more extreme form—that is, the actual corruption of the text (*taḥrīf al-naṣṣ*). Thus, Nicholson glosses Jili: "*It is true that the Jews and Christians suffer misery, but why is this? Because they have altered God's Word and substituted something of their own*."[206]

Yet, even more germane to the legacy of Perennialism is the absolutist interpretation of Ibn ʿArabi by Ivan Aguéli (d. 1917), the Swedish painter, anarchist, esotericist, and Sufi extraordinaire who introduced Guénon and Schuon to Ibn ʿArabi's metaphysics. While studying at the famous al-Azhar university in Cairo, Aguéli was initiated into a branch of the Shādhiliyya Sufi order by ʿAbd al-Raḥmān ʿIllaysh (d. 1921),[207] who was for a time an associate of Amir ʿAbd al-Qādir al-Jazāʾirī (d. 1883) in Damascus. Famous as the leader of the resistance against the French occupation of Algeria, ʿAbd al-Qadir "proved to be the most influential interpreter of Ibn ʿArabī in his time."[208] Thus, as Mark Sedgwick notes, the "Traditionalist emphasis on Ibn al-Arabi, then, derives ultimately from the Amir Abd al-Qadir."[209] After surveying Aguéli's Arabic letters, the Swedish Islamicist H. S. Nyberg (the first Western scholar to publish a critical edition of several important treatises by Ibn ʿArabi[210]) asserted that Aguéli was an "expert on Muḥyi ʾd-Dīn ibn al-ʿArabī."[211] Not only did Aguéli have a direct influence on Guénon as his initiator into ʿIllaysh's Sufi order, but also Aguéli's views on Ibn ʿArabi and Sufism were put forth in a series of articles published in Guénon's journal *La Gnose* under Aguéli's Muslim name ʿAbdul-Hādī.[212]

Due to his long-term interest in theosophy and his engagement with Guénon's French occultist milieu, much of what would come to be standard Schuonian Perennialist doctrine can be found in Aguéli's writing, such as the division between esoteric and exoteric and the importance of initiation. Indeed, even the notion of the "Marian Initiation" (*l'initiation marienne*), where the adept, like the Qur'anic Virgin Mary, experiences direct initiation, can be found first in Aguéli.[213] Yet in spite of such esoteric leanings, as Meir Hatina notes, Aguéli imbued "Sufism with an orthodox hue," which "also encompassed Ibn ʿArabi himself."[214] Thus, Aguéli would call Ibn ʿArabi "the most Muslim of all Muslims"[215] and depict him as "the purest of ʿulamaʾ in adherence to the unity of Allah and the path of His Prophet."[216] Although Aguéli expounded on the similarities between Islam and Taoism, he viewed Islam as superior. Even though they were both "primordial" religions, Taoism was, according to Aguéli, purely esoteric, while Islam was "esotero-exoteric" and therefore complete.[217] Other religions, however, such as Christianity and Buddhism, were qualitatively inferior since they rejected "collective reality"—social justice being imperative for Aguéli—while "Brahmanism" was also inferior because it "is only local, at least in practical terms, while Islam is universal."[218] Indeed, Aguéli time and again praises Islam as the most integral and universal religion known to human history. Moreover, in accordance with Ibn ʿArabi's own cosmology, as I have shown here and in the previous chapters, Aguéli's discourse is constituted by a hierarchical prophetology of Muhammad. For example, Aguéli states:

> we consider the prophetic chain to be completed, *sealed*, with Muḥammad, the Prophet of Arabs and non-Arabs, because he is its culmination. The prophetic spirit is the doctrine of the "Supreme Identity," the All-One in metaphysics, the Universal Man in psychology, and the Integral Humanity in social organization. It began with Adam and was completed by Muḥammad.[219]

Yet, as I have argued earlier, it is clear that Schuon made a Copernican turn toward a cosmic pluralism away from such a totalizing cosmology centered around the Prophet. While Guénon may have begun such a modification with his idea of a Primordial Tradition dissociated from any particular religious form, Schuon's conception of "the transcendent unity of religions" marked a decisive paradigm shift that opposed Aguéli's absolutist reading of Ibn ʿArabi.[220]

Indeed, Schuon would later call such exclusive absolutism "dogmatism," which, although a natural manifestation of "divine subjectivity," is "limitative" and not "pure truth."[221] As such, for Schuon the traditional Islamic locution that "the Prophet is 'the best of men' or 'of creation'" amounts to a "dogmatic assertion, which is self-evident in Islam."[222] Thus, "the role of esoterism," according to Schuon elsewhere, "is to surmount dogmatist disequilibriums and not prolong or refine them."[223] Indeed, this was Ibn ʿArabi's error precisely, which caused his thought to be, according to Schuon, "discontinuous, isolating, and over-accentuating"; while Ibn ʿArabi's so-called esotericism was often sublime, his exotericism was just as often tied to "ordinary theology"—that is, Semitic heteronomy and its attendant fideistic literalism.[224]

Schuon's Copernican turn thus appears to have been more a move away from normative Sufism as a whole, and not Ibn ʿArabi's thought in particular. As Schuon notes:

> Our starting point is *Advaita Vedânta*, and not a voluntarist, individualist, and moralist anthropology, with which ordinary Sufism is unquestionably identified; and this is true whether or not it is to the liking of those who wish our "orthodoxy" to consist in feigning an Arabo-Semitic mentality, or falling in love with it.[225]

Schuon's obvious disdain for an "Arabo-Semitic" heteronomy has been smuggled back into contemporary Perennialist readings of Ibn 'Arabi, yet only as dissociated from Ibn 'Arabi's discourse itself. Such readings repeatedly disavow Ibn 'Arabi's connection to more heteronomous and "normative" theological principles that were typical of his juridico-religious milieu.

Thus, in a rather ironic turn, contemporary Perennialist discourse has seemingly decoupled itself from Schuon's own ambivalence about Ibn 'Arabi and taken on a life of its own as an interpretive field. Indeed, the assertions of the Perennialist authors surveyed throughout this chapter evince adherence to specific discursive rules laid out in Schuon's Copernican turn, marked by a move from a hierarchical religio-centrism to a multireligious model united by the transcendent religious a priori of the "perennial religion" (*religio perennis*)—that is, "religion as such." This assimilation of Ibn 'Arabi's discourse into Schuonian universalism seems to have been fueled, at least in part, by the ideological mission of Nasr, as quoted earlier, "to preserve religious truth, traditional orthodoxy, the dogmatic theological structures of one's own religion and . . . gain knowledge of other traditions *and accept them as spiritually valid ways and roads to God*." From the vantage point intimated by such a universalist directive, which ultimately takes its lead from Schuon himself, the cosmic pluralism of Schuonian Perennialism seems worlds away from the cosmological absolutism of Ibn 'Arabi. Yet, when we dig more deeply into Schuon's own discursive treatment of Ibn 'Arabi, we paradoxically find a buried order of exclusivist absolutism—an absolutism not so different from that openly professed by the Andalusian Sufi, but one additionally burdened by the discursive practices of nineteenth-century Aryanism and racialism more broadly. We turn now to chart the contours of this little-explored region of the Schuonian interpretive field.

4

Ibn 'Arabi and the Metaphysics of Race

The notions that we so willingly see as transcendental, aprioristic, or original are almost always those that are most deeply buried in our own cultural memory.

DANIEL DUBUISSON, *The Western Construction of Religion: Myths, Knowledge, and Ideology.*[1]

And when, in play, he stole their veils,
He wished to see himself in Truth's naked ray.

FRITHJOF SCHUON, *Songs without Names.*[2]

AS I DISCUSSED IN the previous chapter, the elaboration of the Perennial Philosophy (*philosophia perennis*)[3] in the second half of the twentieth century by Frithjof Schuon remains one of the most dominant discursive fields in the contemporary Western reception of Ibn 'Arabi. While they were centuries and cultures apart, it is not surprising that Schuon is often compared to Ibn 'Arabi.[4] Not only did Schuon seemingly share a religious and mystical vocation with the Andalusian Sufi,[5] but also, like Ibn 'Arabi, Schuon's extensive oeuvre is held by many experts as one of the most profound metaphysical legacies of his age.[6] The title of Schuon's first major metaphysical treatise, *The Transcendent Unity of Religions*, has become emblematic of Schuon's entire philosophy enunciating the existence of a timeless truth unifying and validating all so-called orthodox religious forms beyond the limits of exoteric exclusivity. Not only is *The Transcendent Unity of Religions* Schuon's most iconic work, but also, as I mentioned in the introduction to this book, it is often taken to be based on the doctrine of "the Unity of Being" (*waḥdat al-wujūd*) traditionally associated with Ibn 'Arabi.[7] Indeed, as discussed in chapter 3, the entire intellectual foundation of Schuon's metaphysics is commonly claimed to be based on Ibn 'Arabi's ideas.[8]

As both a prolific author and the spiritual leader, or shaykh, of the first organized "traditional" European Sufi order (*ṭarīqa*),[9] Schuon spent more than sixty years expositing his particular brand of universalism, while discreetly guiding several communities in Europe and America, thus earning him a small but committed following. In 1991, however, the American Schuonian community in Bloomington, Indiana, came under strain when "allegation[s] of 'thought control' and 'sexual rites'" were leveled against Schuon by a disgruntled disciple, eventually leading to an indictment.[10] Although the charges were dropped because of insufficient evidence, negative publicity of the episode compromised Schuon's reputation.[11]

Since Schuon's death in 1998, however, his thought has undergone something of a renaissance, aided by a steady stream of new translations of his works issued by the Perennialist publishing house World Wisdom in Bloomington. Moreover, in the wake of 9/11, Perennialist thinkers have sought to bring to a larger audience what they view as the contemporary relevance of Schuon's so-called transcendent universalism—often in connection with the thought of Ibn 'Arabi—for spreading religious tolerance and engaging in interfaith dialogue. The work of the Perennialist scholar Reza Shah-Kazemi, as already introduced and discussed in the previous chapters of this book, is suffused with such ideas. Indeed, Shah-Kazemi regularly uses the thought of Ibn 'Arabi, and those in his school, as an example of the transhistorical truth of Schuonian Perennialism, which he holds to be "the most eloquent and compelling contemporary expression" of universalism.[12]

Yet, such easy linkage between Schuon and Ibn 'Arabi in the name of "the oneness of religions . . . on the transcendent plane"[13] belies a much more complex and fraught discursive relationship. While it is true that Schuon's esoteric erudition obliged him to acknowledge Ibn 'Arabi's metaphysical genius, Schuon's universalist avowal of "the relativity of forms" as "the transcendent" truth also impelled him to censure the Andalusian Sufi's Islamic absolutism. As I noted in the conclusion to chapter 3, in a 1989 letter Schuon identifies his own esoteric perspective through the nondual framework of "*Advaita Vedânta*" over and above "ordinary Sufism," which he decries as "a voluntarist, individualist, and moralist anthropology" associated with "an Arabo-Semitic mentality."[14] Although James Cutsinger, the foremost academic expert on Schuon, has defended such statements as simply emphasizing the fact that Schuon's "message refuses to be domesticated in the interest of any sectarian aim and cannot be limited by any formal enclosure,"[15] a close reading of Schuon's corpus shows otherwise.

Indeed, careful attention to the discursive practices and strategies contained within Schuon's writings reveals that his message arrived *already* domesticated in a sectarianism particular to the formal enclosure of his own Eurocentrism—an enclosure that has been conveniently ignored or metaphysically justified by his apologetic interpreters. As such, in this chapter I argue that underlying Schuon's so-called universalism is a hegemonic discourse of religious authenticity founded within nineteenth-century Aryanism and its attendant understanding of race as reflective of both physiological *and* spiritual difference. Thus, for Schuon, Ibn

'Arabi, like many Muslim mystics, succumbed to a "Semitic" propensity for a subjectivism that lacked the enlightened objectivity necessary to consistently discern the transcendent formlessness of essential truth from religious particularism. Yet, such enlightened objectivity is, according to Schuon, inherent in the so-called Aryan metaphysics of Vedanta and Platonism. In fact, Schuon's discourse regularly presents as self-evident the metaphysical superiority of a direct and active Aryan "intellection" over that of a so-called passive Semitic "inspirationism." Yet, rather than a transcendent and symbolic nomenclature innocent of its discursive history of racism—as Schuon's loyal devotees often claim[16]—in what follows I throw into relief how Schuonian universalism harbors a buried order of politics ironically constituted by and through long-held European discursive strategies of racial exclusion. Such strategies are not simply empty linguistic survivals, but instead substantively inform the core of Schuon's metaphysics, providing the impetus to denude Ibn 'Arabi of his own Islamic exclusivism and distill from him a Vedantic essence—that is, a pure esotericism capable of transcending the so-called Semitic veils of exoteric religious form. As such, Schuon effectively de-Semitizes Ibn 'Arabi to legitimize his own Aryan ideal of authentic religion, *the religio perennis*.

Interrupting Hagiographic Authority: Approaching a Discursive Analysis of Schuon

As part of the aforementioned posthumous Schuonian renaissance, there has been a burgeoning hagiographic literature on Schuon,[17] who in this discursive arena is often declared—as the renowned scholar of religion Huston Smith put it—"the spiritual prophet of our time par excellence."[18] As Cutsinger observes in the introduction to his 2013 anthology of Schuon's writings, *Splendor of the True: A Frithjof Schuon Reader,* those who continue to praise Schuon "in the grandest terms . . . represent the considered judgment of several of the academy's most prestigious and influential names."[19] Here, Cutsinger himself comes out, as it were, as a committed Schuonian and relates that his apologetic goal in compiling his anthology is to present some of

> the evidence that has led Schuon's defenders to draw what must otherwise seem excessively flattering conclusions concerning his stature and significance, *while challenging his critics—and the religious studies community as a whole—to give his work a much fuller and more sustained examination than it has so far received.*[20]

Indeed, as I initially highlighted in the prologue of this book, Cutsinger argues that to give Schuon's work the "sustained examination" it deserves,

> we must entertain the possibility . . . that Schuon was someone who actually knew what he was talking about, someone who had apprehended the Truth—with that capital "T" . . . *in a way that cannot be accounted for in terms of sheerly natural causes or purely human phenomena.*[21]

Here, Cutsinger rather evangelically rehearses a commonplace claim among faithful Schuonians—that Schuon did not understand his material from a "natural" or "human" perspective, but instead directly "apprehended the Truth." Cutsinger goes on to explain that true spiritual knowledge, or "gnosis," involves a total identification with divine "Truth" through "a faculty that Schuon calls the Intellect."[22] Indeed, Seyyed Hossein Nasr, who is himself arguably one of the twentieth century's most prominent religious thinkers,[23] had years earlier similarly claimed that "Schuon seems like the cosmic intellect itself impregnated by the energy of divine grace."[24] Cutsinger crucially defines Schuon's conception of the "Intellect" as the "power of immediate or intuitive discernment . . . *unaffected by the limitations of historical circumstance.*"[25] Thus, according to Cutsinger, to read Schuon "*as if* his insights were tied to certain formulations of language . . . is to misinterpret the *evident authority* of his work."[26]

Cutsinger's proclamation of Schuon's "evident authority" in tandem with his claim that Schuon's divinely inspired power of Intellect was "unaffected by the limitations of historical circumstance" and freed from the "formulations of language" should give us serious pause. Besides the obvious challenges to Schuon's ethical authority as a spiritual leader posed as a result of the anecdotal evidence brought forth in connection with the 1991 scandal mentioned earlier,[27] there are other questions of discursive authority that underscore what is at stake in my present argument. If we concede, along with Nasr, that Schuon's discourse itself reveals a "timeless message,"[28] then we must also grant it *transcendent authority*.

In the following chapter I take up a sustained and careful critique of Schuonian Perennialism in its relation to Schuon's elucidation of Ibn 'Arabi. In so doing, I also offer a response to Cutsinger, who has "kindly invited [his colleagues] to bring their preferred methodology to the table and to be as critical as they wish."[29] Rather than criticizing Schuon's socio-religious subjectivity in ethico-political terms,[30] here my "preferred methodology" aims to remain at the level of discourse by analyzing practices that create political subjectivities. In other words, I focus on how Aryanist discursive practices found within Schuon's writings *function* as strategies for authorizing authentic religious subjects—and thereby excluding Others. While such strategies are, in the words of Russell McCutcheon, "properly termed political" because they project how "human beings ought to interact with one another in a certain manner from within certain social arrangements,"[31] it does not necessarily follow that all such strategies are indications of what

McCutcheon has identified in the works of Mircea Eliade as a "*totalized* political program" and "a potent and explicit political manifesto."[32] Yet, the danger inherent within arguments for a transhistorical authenticity based on Aryan racio-spiritual typologies should be obvious—especially within a discourse that claims for itself divine authority.[33] Thus, while I leave others to speculate on Schuon's political alliances,[34] in this chapter I follow McCutcheon's more broad objective of understanding how scholarly works "can be informed by a particular political and social context and can carry with them sociopolitical implications."[35]

The Primacy of Metaphysics: Transcendent Universalism or *Situated Exclusivism?*

With the publication of *The Transcendent Unity of Religions* (*De l'Unité transcendante des Religions*) in 1948 and the death of his "Traditionalist" predecessor René Guénon in 1951,[36] Schuon promptly became "the great expositor of esoterism and the *sophia perennis* of his day."[37] As its title suggests, Schuon's iconic treatise claims that all religious forms are unified in their transcendent, essential nature—the *religio perennis*. This is so, according to Schuon, because "it is metaphysically impossible" that any given religious form "should possess a unique value to the exclusion of other forms; *for a form, by definition, cannot be unique and exclusive*."[38] Schuon explains his logic further:

> The exoteric claim to the exclusive possession of the truth comes up against the axiomatic objection that there is no such thing in existence as a unique fact, for the simple reason that it is strictly impossible that such a fact should exist, *unicity alone being unique and no fact being unicity*; it is this that is ignored by the ideology of the "believers," which is fundamentally nothing but *an intentional and interested confusion between the formal and the universal*.[39]

Setting aside the apparent logical fallacy of this argument,[40] what Schuon here asserts is that because the unitive reality of the divine is *alone* unique, there can thus be no other unique "facts" in creation. Therefore, normative religious creeds—that is, "the ideology of the 'believers'"—and their exclusive truth claims are necessarily partial, since the only true singularity is the ultimate truth of "unicity." Schuon thus concludes: "pure and absolute Truth can only be found beyond all its possible expressions."[41] Yet for Schuon, the truth of "unicity" can, *in fact*, be fully expressed. Accordingly, it is only through "a doctrine *that is metaphysical* in the most precise meaning of the word"—that is, as proceeding "*exclusively from the Intellect*"—that the "intentional and interested confusion" of normative religion is transcended and ultimate truth realized.[42] Thus, Schuon importantly asserts that "*intellectual intuition is a direct and active participation in divine Knowledge* and not an indirect and passive participation, as is faith."[43] As Cutsinger suggests above, "the Intellect"—and its attendant mode of "intellectual intuition"—emerges for Schuon as the key to "divine Knowledge," which is thus analogous to his "metaphysics" of transcendent unity. Indeed, as Schuon would later note, "our position is well known: it is fundamentally that of *metaphysics*, and this science is by definition *universalist*."[44]

Schuon's early valorization of metaphysics as encapsulating his universalist "science" of divine Knowledge would take on added significance in a work published nearly ten years after *The Transcendent Unity of Religions*. In this 1957 monograph tellingly entitled *Castes and Races* (*Castes et Races*), Schuon asserts that "if *the white race can claim a sort of pre-eminence*, it can do so only through the Hindu group which in a way *perpetuates the primordial state of the Indo-Europeans* and, in a wider sense, that of *white men as a whole*."[45] Schuon further notes that such a "primordial state" of the white man is preserved by the Hindus because they "surpass every other human group by their contemplativity and *the metaphysical genius* resulting from this."[46]

While the assertion of such Hindu-Indo-European-white metaphysical supremacy seems paradoxical enough given Schuon's claims in *The Transcendent Unity of Religions* for the impossibility of exclusive form, it appears all the more so given the fact that when *Castes and Races* was published, more than twenty years had passed since Schuon, under the Muslim name ʿĪsa Nūr al-Dīn Aḥmad al-Shādhilī al-ʿAlawī, had taken on the spiritual leadership of the European branch of the ʿAlāwiyya Sufi *ṭarīqa*, as initially noted.[47] Yet, the preeminence that Schuon affords the "metaphysical genius" of "the Hindu group" in terms of "the primordial state of the Indo-Europeans" in *Castes and Races* is also, although ironically, reflected in his racialized deprecation of Sufism. In his only work specifically dedicated to the subject, *Sufism: Veil and Quintessence* (*Le Soufisme: voile et quintessence*, 1980), Schuon faults "Sufi metaphysics" for being linked to the "*anti-metaphysical* and moralizing creationism of the monotheistic theologies," which ultimately keep it from admitting "*the principle of relativity*," that is, the transcendent unity of religions.[48] "The innermost motive of Muslim mysticism" is thus, according to Schuon, "*fundamentally more moral than intellectual* . . . in the sense that *Arab* or *Muslim*, or *Semitic, sensibility* always remains more or less volitive, hence *subjectivist*."[49] Indeed, in the same passage Schuon asserts: "We do not believe we are overstylizing things in taking the view that *the Aryan tends to be a philosopher whereas the Semite is above all a moralist*."[50] As evidence of such an assertion, Schuon thus claims that one need only "compare the *Upanishads*, the *Yoga-Vasishtha*, and the *Bhagavad Gītā* with the Bible, or Hindu doctrines with Talmudic speculations."[51]

As the few examples above evince, Schuon's original universalist epistemology—as discursively represented through the terminology of "metaphysics," "the Intellect," "intellectual intuition," and "contemplativity"—was early on directly imbricated with a so-called Aryan spiritual typology, including "the Hindu group," "the Indo-Europeans," and "white men as a whole." Moreover, such typology is posited as superior to an "*Arab* or *Muslim*, or *Semitic, sensibility*" notable for its "anti-metaphysical" characteristics such as moralism, volition, and subjectivism. Although Schuon's esoteric basis in Hinduism, and more specifically the Vedanta, has a specific resonance with that of his Traditionalist forerunner Guénon, it is clear that such Aryan spiritual typology is the result of a broader array of discursive influences.[52] The same holds true for the *fin-de-siècle* French occultism from which modern Perennialism sprang, such as the esotericism of the Theosophical Society.[53] Indeed, in this chapter I bring to light how Schuon's Aryanist discourse is founded upon the discursive practices evinced in what Léon Poliakov dubbed the nineteenth-century "Aryan myth"[54] as infamously elaborated by Ernest Renan (d. 1892) and his well-known contemporaries such as Christian Lassen (d. 1876), Arthur de Gobineau (d. 1882), and Houston Stewart Chamberlain (d. 1927). The discursive genealogy of this particular racialist knowledge regime can be traced to the nascent nationalism of German Romanticism and Friedrich Schlegel's (d. 1829) ethnocentric identification with ancient India.[55] Although it is clear that German Romantic literature, and Orientalism more broadly, had an enduring impact on Schuon's intellectual identity, it is not my intention to claim the direct influence of any one author or text on his thought.[56] Rather, in what follows I throw into relief how Schuon uses *a particular set* of discursive practices developed within nineteenth-century Aryanism, which ideologically frames his construction of "pure" esotericism and thus Ibn ʿArabi's delimited place within it.

Schuonian Discursivity and the Nineteenth-Century Aryan Myth

Although the term "Aryan"—from the Sanskrit *ārya*, meaning "noble"—was originally self-referentially employed by ancient Sanskrit and Persian speakers, at the start of the nineteenth century European philologists began to use the term to refer to the Indo-European language group. By the middle of the century, "Aryan" had come to signify a particular race in opposition to its "Semitic" Other.[57] This process of semantic transmogrification was greatly aided by the Romantic philology of Schlegel, who in an 1808 treatise on India hypothesized (erroneously) that "Greek and Latin, as well as the Persian and German languages" originated from

Sanskrit.[58] Moreover, Schlegel asserted that cultural history was best perceived through a "metaphysical interpretation" of the grammatical structure of language itself, claiming Sanskrit to be "*almost entirely a philosophical or rather a religious language* and perhaps none, not even excepting the Greek, *is so philosophically clear and sharply defined*."[59] Rather predictably, Schlegel adds: "We find nothing in Arabic, or Hebrew, agreeing with the Indian grammar."[60] Thus, as George Mosse trenchantly notes, Schlegel "set down the maxims of an Aryan superiority exemplified by linguistic roots."[61]

At midcentury, Schlegel's incipient Aryanism would emerge fully formed in Arthur de Gobineau's *Essay on the Inequality of the Human Races* (*Essai sur l'inégalité des races humaines*, 1853–55). Here, Gobineau states:

> The *superabundance of philosophical and ethnological terms* in Sanscrit corresponds to the genius of those who spoke it as well as its richness and rhythmic beauty. *The same is the case with Greek while the lack of precision in the Semitic tongues is exactly paralleled by the character of the Semitic peoples.*[62]

Renan would further theorize the relationship between language and race by asserting the existence of "linguistic races"[63] and argue that in the later development of humanity "*language took almost entirely the place of race in the division of humanity into groups*; or, to put it in another way, the word 'race' assumed a different meaning. *Language, religion, laws, and customs, came to constitute the race far more than blood.*"[64] Indeed, it was through such claims of an inherent linkage between language, race, and religion that Renan could famously reassert the superiority of the Aryan intellect, which "differed essentially" from the Semitic and thus "*contained in the germ all the metaphysics* which were afterwards to be developed through the Hindoo genius, the Greek genius, the German genius."[65] For Renan the particular "genius" of the Aryan spirit is its metaphysical "search for the truth," while the inadequacy of the "Semitic spirit" is precisely its incapacity for metaphysics, which manifests in a "fearful shallowness" that closes the Semitic mind "to all subtle ideas."[66]

In his aforementioned work *Castes and Races*, Schuon affirms the category of "race" as infused with higher spiritual significance beyond physiology:

> *It is not possible . . . to hold that race is something devoid of meaning apart from physical characteristics*, for, if it be true that formal constraints have nothing absolute about them, forms must none the less have their own sufficient reason; *if races are not castes, they must all the same correspond to*

> *human differences of another order, rather as differences of style may express equivalence in the spiritual order whilst also marking divergencies of mode.*[67]

Moreover, Schuon recapitulates the Renanian notion of "linguistic races," stating that the Semites and Aryans constitute not only a "linguistic group" but also "a psychological group and *even a racial group*."[68] Schuon also echoes Renan's contentions of a superior Aryan spirit in the quest for "truth" in opposition to the Semitic spirit that veils it. "It is perhaps not too hazardous to say," Schuon ventures, "that *the Aryan spirit . . . tends a priori to unveil the truth* whereas *the Semitic spirit*, whose realism *is more moral than intellectual, tends toward the veiling of the divine Majesty*."[69]

The idea of the metaphysical superiority of the so-called Aryan spirit in relation to Hinduism—or more esoterically conceived as "the Vedanta"[70]—formed a large part of the Romantic fascination with India. A key German influence for Renan and his contemporaries in this respect was the work of Schlegel's successor, the Indologist Christian Lassen, whose conception of Aryan philosophical supremacy over that of the Semite linked the highest mode of Aryanism with the *whitest* castes of India.[71] Houston Stewart Chamberlain, the notorious "seer of the Third Reich,"[72] would note that Lassen "proves in detail his view that the Indo-European race is 'more highly and more fully gifted,' that in it alone there is 'perfect symmetry of all mental powers.'"[73] Thus, Chamberlain asserts that "the Aryan Indian . . . *unquestionably possesses the greatest talent for metaphysics* of any people that ever lived" and that the thought of "the Hindoo" is "*metaphysically the deepest in the world*."[74] Chamberlain further claims: "The most perfect expression of absolutely mystical religion is found among the Aryan Indians."[75]

In a strikingly similar avowal, Schuon states: "The most direct doctrinal expression of the *sophia perennis* is undoubtedly *Advaita Vedānta*."[76] Indeed, the Indian "*Veda*" is for Schuon a superior scriptural form that "does not give orders to the intelligence," like the "*enslaving*" revelation of the Semites, "but awakens it and reminds it of what it is."[77] Thus, for the Aryan, according to Schuon, "intellectual certainty has priority here *over a submissive faith*."[78] Yet more important, the Aryan "tendency to intellection" is not simply determined externally by the epistemological nature of the Vedic scriptural tradition, since in Schuon's understanding "what determines the difference among forms of Truth *is the difference among human receptacles*."[79] While I will return to this important aspect of Schuon's esoteric cosmology below, here it is sufficient to note that, according to Schuon, the different "mental conditions" of each racial "group" self-determine the "refraction" of Truth of their particular revelation.[80] Indeed, in *Castes and Races*, Schuon directly states: "*A revelation always conforms to a racial genius*."[81] Elsewhere, Schuon claims that "diverse Revelations do not really contradict one another since they do not apply to the same receptacle . . .; *a contradiction can arise only between things situated on the same level*."[82] For Schuon, then, the superior quality of Aryan intellection is not simply *a result* of its distinctive revelation, that is, the "Veda," but the mark of a particular racio-spiritual disposition that is in itself *the cause* of its own revelation and thus ontologically superior. Thus, while both Aryan "intellectionism" and Semitic "inspirationism" are according to Schuon "sacred," Semitic inspirationism is "derived from a particular grace *and not, like intellection, from a permanent and 'naturally supernatural' capacity*."[83]

Such an Aryan " 'naturally supernatural' capacity" is further elaborated in Schuon's appropriation of the Hindu term "avatar." Like Renan, Schuon repeatedly uses the idea of avatar as a synonym for prophet.[84] While Renan suggests subtle distinctions between avatar and prophet, noting that while the avatar is a divine incarnation, the prophet is a chosen instrument of revelation,[85] Schuon categorizes such difference as "major and minor *Avatāras*, complete and partial incarnations," respectively.[86] Schuon goes on to importantly clarify the difference between the two through a comparison between Jesus and Muhammad: "Christ, who *identifies the divine Message with himself*, belongs to the first of these two categories whereas the Prophet, who *passively receives* the Message that God 'causes to descend,' belongs to the second."[87] In other words, Aryan "intellection" as a " 'naturally supernatural' capacity" is in accordance with Schuon's category of "major" Avatara, whom Christ embodies as a divine manifestation, whereas Semitic inspirationism as a *passive influx* of grace accords with his notion of "minor" Avatara and the Arab Prophet. Such distinctions revolve around the crucial idea that the "genius" of the Semitic race is dissociated from the "Semitic spirit" itself. As Maurice Olender notes in the context of Renanian discourse: "Although the Hebrew did indeed recognize that God is one, that truth descended upon him: he had no responsibility in the matter. *His monotheism was in no sense a product of his mind*."[88]

Elsewhere, Schuon further elucidates the distinction between Muhammad and Christ in Aryanist terms:

> Since it was not necessary for Muhammad to present himself—any more than Abraham and Moses—as the Manifestation of the Absolute, he could, like them, remain *wholly Semitic in style*, a style which attaches itself meticulously to human things, not scanting even the smallest; *whereas in Christ*—paradoxically and providentially—*there is an element that brings him closer to the Aryan world*, that is, *a tendency in his nature toward the idealistic simplification of earthly contingencies*.[89]

Here, Schuon's classification of Muhammad's "Semitic" style posits a mentality that is attached "meticulously to human things" in opposition to Christ's "Aryan" tendency toward a Platonic "idealism"—that is, a metaphysical realm that transcends the human world of material reality.[90] Such a comparison between the Semitic "worldly" Muhammad and the Aryan "formless" Christ is once more a forceful reiteration of an Aryanist conceit, here deprecating a Semitic "materialism" notable for its voluntarism, ritualism, and lack of metaphysics. As Chamberlain succinctly states: "Pure materialism is the religious doctrine of the Arab Mohammed."[91] Indeed, after apologizing for what may strike the reader as "ill-sounding," Schuon clarifies in a footnote that "we shall say that Christ, who was destined to be an '*Aryan god*', has himself, by way of anticipation, *a certain Aryan quality,* which shows itself *in his independence—seemingly 'Greek' or 'Hindu'—toward forms.*"[92] Schuon elsewhere maintains that the language of Christianity is "*on the whole more 'Aryan' than that of Moslem piety, hence more direct and more open.*"[93]

Schuon's perception of Christianity as more or less "Aryan" is—like much of his comparative religionist discourse—yet another iteration of a nineteenth-century Aryanist commonplace. The idea that Jesus was an Aryan and not a Jew became popular around the turn of the twentieth century and was ultimately adopted in Germany by National Socialists who wished to appear congruent with Christianity.[94] Renan's ideas proved once again to be formative in this arena with his controversial work *The Life of Jesus* (*Vie de Jésus*, 1863), which in the words of Olender "saved Jesus from Judaism."[95] Indeed, Renan situated Jesus's true home in Galilee, whose "free life" was "like perfume from another world."[96] Conversely, Jerusalem as representative of Judea was a city of "littleness of mind" and "*contributed in no respect to refine the intellect.*" "It was," according to Renan, "something analogous to *the barren doctrine of the Mussulman fakir.*"[97]

Following Renan, Chamberlain's section "Christ not a Jew" in his infamous anti-Semitic work *Foundations of the Nineteenth Century*[98] begins with the claim that Jesus's "advent is not the perfecting of the Jewish religion but its negation."[99] Chamberlain thus asserts that the "formalism" of the Jews "choked" the "genuine religion" that Jesus opened up.[100] Thus, Chamberlain inquires "where is the people, which, awakened by Christ to life, has gained for itself the precious right of calling Christ its own? *Certainly not in Judea!*"[101] Unsurprisingly, Chamberlain transposes the lineage of Jesus's religion from Semitic Judea to Aryan India and the Vedanta.[102] In this too, he follows Renan's lead, who saw in Christ's predecessor, John the Baptist, the "life of a Yogi of India," which was "so opposed to the spirit of the ancient Jewish people" that it more resembled the "*gourous* of Brahminism."[103] For his part, Schuon precisely recapitulates the sentiments above, situating Jesus's proper spiritual place in India rather than Judea, noting that

> Jesus has the function of a regenerator: he is the great prophet of inwardness, and as such he should have been accepted by Israel as Isaiah was;

however, *this acceptance presupposed a spiritual suppleness more fitting of India than Judea.*[104]

Ibn 'Arabi and the Schuonian Imperative of Esoteric "Objectivity"

Regardless of their personal attachment to Jesus, it is clear that Renan's and Chamberlain's Aryan appropriation of him was necessary for their message to be accepted within their respective Christian milieus. Likewise, Schuon could not afford to ignore Ibn 'Arabi's importance within Guénonian Traditionalism. While Guénon identified the "primordial tradition" directly with Vedanta,[105] which Schuon enthusiastically commended him for,[106] he *also* acknowledged that Ibn 'Arabi expressed such truth "in almost identical terms," but in a way consonant with "Judaism [as] . . . nothing but a particular way of expressing the idea of universal manifestation and its relation with the Principle."[107] Indeed, Guénon's first encounter with Islam was through the metaphysical hermeneutics of Ibn 'Arabi's thought via the interpretation of Ivan Aguéli (d. 1917)—the well-known Swedish painter, anarchist, and esotericist. Aguéli was initiated as "ʿAbdul-Hādī" into a branch of the Shādhiliyya Sufi order by ʿAbd al-Raḥmān 'Illaysh (d. 1921). As I noted in my brief discussion on Aguéli at the conclusion of chapter 3, 'Illaysh had been an associate of the famous nineteenth-century Sufi Amir ʿAbd al-Qādir al-Jazāʾirī (d. 1883), who led the resistance against the French occupation of Algeria.[108] Not only did Aguéli have a direct influence on Guénon as his initiator into 'Illaysh's Sufi order,[109] but also, as Mark Sedgwick notes, "the real significance of this encounter was *the transfer into Traditionalism of the central position taken by Ibn al-Arabi* in Damascus."[110]

Thus, in the Traditionalist milieu, Ibn 'Arabi's thought is commonly taken to be, as noted by the distinguished Arabist and Perennialist Martin Lings (d. 2005), "basically identical with the Sufi perspective in general."[111] In the light of such renown, Schuon seemingly had little choice but to acknowledge Ibn 'Arabi's metaphysics in the highest terms, identifying him as "the great enunciator of gnosis in Islam"[112] and even as a direct expression of none other than the *religio perennis* itself.[113] Yet, Schuon also takes Ibn 'Arabi to task for "divergent interpretations—one esoteric and the other exoteric"[114] and elsewhere disparages the "unevenness and contradictions" in his thought "owing above all to his at least partial solidarity with ordinary theology."[115]

Thus, when discussing Ibn 'Arabi's elevation of Muhammad's rank over that of Joseph in *The Ring Stones of Wisdom* (*Fuṣūṣ al-ḥikam*),[116] Schuon asserts: "one has a right to expect a more nuanced and *objective perspective* in an esoteric context."[117] Similarly, Ibn 'Arabi's auto-exegetical statement that his "religion of love is the prerogative of Muslims; for the station of the most perfect love has been imparted exclusively to the Prophet Muhammad and not the other Prophets"[118] is derided by Schuon as an "*abrupt and unintelligible denominationalism.*"[119] Schuon thus protests that "one might expect an esoterist not to enclose himself in this concept-symbol but, since he has opted for the essence, *to take into account the relativity of forms* . . . and to *do so in an objective and concrete*, and not merely metaphorical, manner—or else remain silent, for pity's sake."[120]

Such corrective reprimands evince not only an exasperation with Ibn 'Arabi's recourse to Islamic normativity but also, and more important, a perceived infringement of a supposed esoteric axiom—that is, the "objective" truth of "the relativity of forms." To explain such a shocking transgression by a metaphysician who should know better, Schuon further asserts that "one is obliged, however, to take note of the *de facto* existence of two esoterisms, one partially formalistic and the other perfectly consistent, all the more so as facts cannot be at the level of principles."[121] Schuon elucidates this idea elsewhere in an essay appropriately entitled "Two Esoterisms."[122] In explicating its first sense, Schuon employs esotericism in opposition to its binary "exotericism." Here, esoteric truth is a "*non-formal and metaphysical*" mode of "*intellection*" that originates from the very "*nature of things*" and is opposed to the "formal and theological truth" of "Revelation," which is by implication "legalistic or obligatory truth."[123]

Schuon's second definition of esotericism further reifies the concept, giving it a unique autonomy decoupled from any relationship to its exoteric Other. Here, esotericism "is not, in its intrinsic reality, *a complement* or a half."[124] Rather, for Schuon, "*esoterism as such is metaphysics*"; indeed, it is "*the total truth as such*."[125] As "the total truth," this pure form of esotericism is inherently different than an "esoterism of a particular religion," since such an esotericism "tends to adapt itself to this religion and thereby enter into theological, psychological and legalistic meanders foreign to its nature."[126]

While Vedanta is for Schuon "an intrinsic esoterism,"[127] Sufism falls into the category he referred to as "an esoterism-complement, that is, an esoterism found alongside a religious system of a sentimental character," which he relates to "the Semitic spiritualities in their general manifestation."[128] Thus, in *Sufism*, Schuon declares: "From the doctrinal point of view Sufis seek—whether consciously or not—to combine two tendencies, Platonism and Asharism."[129] Here, Platonism, like Vedanta, is an example of "true metaphysics" where "the true, the beautiful, and the good are such because they manifest qualities proper to the Principle, or to the Essence."[130] Yet in the path of Sufism, Platonism is combined with the "ordinary" theological tradition of Ashʿarism, which according to Schuon is not only voluntaristic but also "viscerally moralistic and therefore individualistic."[131]

Thus, Schuon asserts that "Sufism obviously approaches pure *gnosis* to the extent it is Platonic . . . and it departs from it to the extent it capitulates to Asharism."[132] Schuon concludes this discussion by pointing out how the doctrine of *waḥdat al-wujūd* ("the Unity of Being"), which as I noted earlier is traditionally associated with Ibn 'Arabi, is tainted with an Ashʿarī voluntarism since in it "everything that exists is 'good' because it is 'willed by God.'" Schuon thus asserts, "Here the most vertiginous metaphysics is combined with the most summary Asharism."[133] Elsewhere, Schuon directly equates Ibn 'Arabi's related occasionalism to "the Hanbalite and Asharite negation of secondary causes and natural laws."[134] Here, Schuon reproaches Ibn 'Arabi for a hermeneutical approach to the Qur'an that is "*independent of every question of dialectic*," thus resulting in opposing esoteric and exoteric interpretations that "give the impression of being confused."[135] According to Schuon, such apparent confusion reveals a weakness in Ibn 'Arabi's metaphysical argumentation, which Schuon ascribes to Ibn 'Arabi's particular brand of Islamic fideism that colors his monistic absorption and hinders a clearer discernment worthy of his "metaphysical intention."[136]

Indeed, Schuon's reductive portrayal of Ashʿarī voluntarism and occasionalism serves throughout his work as a symbol of a wider typology where "the negation of secondary causes and natural laws that is characteristic of Asharism" is a trait common to "*all Semitic theologians.*"[137] As such, it should come as no surprise that for Schuon the reason Platonism is contrary to Ashʿarism is because Plato "*belonged intellectually to the Aryan world*, and his doctrine *is like a distant modality of Brahmanism*."[138] According to Schuon, this Aryan-Vedantist typology facilitated in Plato "the actualization of pure intellection" as opposed to the fideism of al-Ashʿarī.[139] Indeed, elsewhere Schuon clarifies that this difference is due to an *inherent* Aryan capacity for "dialectic" and thus "objectivity":

> Greeks and especially Hindus have *long possessed the instrument of dialectic*, for it corresponds to *their sense of objectivity*, whereas *it was missing among the early Semites, as well as for nascent Islam*.[140]

In another work Schuon similarly notes that "the reasoning of Semites" is based merely on a "dogmatic" certitude and a wish to "communicate and reinforce what is evident," thus opposing "Greeks and Hindus" whose mode of reasoning is "*a dialectic* that is concerned with *doing justice to the nature of things*."[141] Here, Schuon invokes an intellectualist discourse similar to the Stoic philosophy of "natural law" as marked by the notion that the intrinsic rationality of the universe—that is, "the nature of things"—is a reflection of divine reason, or *logos*, and accessible to humans through their higher intellect.[142] Schuon thus concludes that "the weakness of certain arguments of Sufis themselves" is explained by the

Semitic lack of objectivity—that is, Semitic voluntarism—because Semitic logic "is not impartial and has ceased to be anything more than *an extrinsic factor*."[143]

Unsurprisingly, Schuon's opposition to Semitic voluntarism through an intellectualist appeal to "natural law" aligned with Hindu and Greek thought is similarly found in Chamberlain, who asserts that "while the Indian taught the negation of will, . . . *religion is for the Semite the idolization of his will*."[144] In another passage, Chamberlain opposes both Islamic and Jewish voluntarism by identifying the "Indo-European" with the law of "nature":

> *The abnormally developed will of the Semites* can lead to two extremes: either to rigidity, as *in the case of Mohammed*, where the idea of the unlimited divine caprice is predominant; or, *as is the case with the Jews*, to the phenomenal elasticity, which is produced by the conception of their own human arbitrariness. *To the Indo-European both paths are closed. In nature he observes everywhere the rule of law.*[145]

Indeed, the oft-repeated dichotomy in Schuon's writings between a purported Aryan philosophical "objectivity" and a moralistic, "subjective" Semitic Other vividly echoes the discourse of Lassen, Renan, and Chamberlain where the supposed "subjective" sentimentality of the Semitic mentality does not have the necessary self-distance to experience higher forms of poetic and philosophical thought.[146] Thus, according to Chamberlain, "religion" for the Aryan has nothing to do with "morals"; rather, "*he is thinker and poet*."[147] In *Castes and Races*, Schuon echoes Chamberlain precisely, stating that "*the white man is essentially a poet*."[148] Following Gobineau's tripartite racial typology,[149] Schuon continues: "As for the black man, he is neither a cerebral type nor a visualizer but vital, and so a born dancer; he is profoundly vital as the yellow man is delicately visual, *both races being existential rather than mental as compared to the white race*."[150]

Schuon elsewhere claims that while "Platonists and Vedantists" are concerned with "a metaphysical description of the Real," the "Semites, on the other hand, *stress a subjective way of attaining what is*; the Real is enclosed in a dogma."[151] Similarly, in *Sufism*, Schuon states that "*Aryans are objectivists* . . . while *Semites are subjectivists*. . . . It is the difference between intellectualism and voluntarism."[152] In such terms, Schuon makes the following ontological claim: "The *prerogative of the human state is objectivity*," and that "*objectivity is a kind of death of the subject* in the face of the reality of the object."[153] Thus, according to Schuon, "*Objectivity is none other than the truth*, in which the subject and the object coincide, and in which *the essential takes precedence over the accidental*."[154] It is therefore unmistakable that "objectivity" for Schuon is analogous to his above notion of "esoterism" as "*the total truth as such*"; both concepts accordingly fall within the special province of the Aryan, who not only possesses a unique " 'naturally supernatural' capacity" for "intellection" but also—by way of an inherent "objectivity"—analogically represents the most complete expression of "the human state."

De-Semitizing Ibn 'Arabi: Finding Vedanta through the Naked Virgin

As I have shown, for Schuon the primary problem with so-called Semitic subjectivism is its inability to distinguish the underlying formlessness of the Real from the contingent dogmas presented by the various religions. Like his Aryanist predecessors, Schuon linked this Semitic "confusion" with the inherent nature of monotheistic "inspirationism," which was incapable of the higher-order, metaphysical insight necessary for objective knowledge. Indeed, as I noted at the start, this was precisely Schuon's critique of Sufism, which he claimed is linked to the "*anti-metaphysical and moralizing creationism* of the monotheistic theologies," thus keeping it from sufficiently acknowledging "*the principle of relativity*."[155]

Although Schuon repeatedly asserted the importance of maintaining "traditional" religious form, it seems that he did so only as a formal means to acknowledge its ultimate *relativity* and thus legitimize its transcendence. As Schuon states in a 1983 letter:

> A condition of the legitimacy of a spiritual school or community is the presence of the traditional form; in our case, Islam. Nevertheless, the more conscious one is of the supra formal nature of spiritual Truth and Reality, the more conscious one must be also of the *relativity of the traditional form*; and according to the spatial or temporal circumstances, *one must in one fashion or another manifest this consciousness*.[156]

In an earlier letter, Schuon appears to have theorized his above call to "manifest" the "consciousness" of the relativity of formal religion as "a moving away from the *Religio formalis* by virtue of a moving towards the *Religio perennis*."[157] Here, Schuon importantly explains that the "*Religio perennis* is the body," while "the *Religio formalis* is the garment."[158] Thus, while Schuon admits that Islam forms "the providential ground" for his so-called *ṭarīqa* (literally "way" in Arabic and, as noted above, traditionally used to denote a Sufi order), he specifies that "the goal" of "the work" is "not the Islamic form as such, but precisely esoterism, and from this it follows that our *Tarīqah* as [a] vehicle of esoterism could not simply be absorbed in the Islamic form."[159]

In the same letter, Schuon relates that the "Holy Virgin in a new form, corresponding directly to esoterism" came to him as part of an answer to his early search for "how esoterism as such could manifest and assert itself anew."[160] Indeed, Schuon changed the name of his *ṭarīqa* to the ʿAlāwiyya Maryamiyya in the mid-1960s in response to repeated experiences and visions of the Virgin Mary, which marked a transition to the mature stage of Schuon's esoteric theory and the exposition of the *religio perennis*.[161] Schuon understood "the domain of Mary, the Virgin Mother" to be on a level where separate religious "*systems as such lose much of their importance* and where by way of compensation *the essential elements they have in common are affirmed, elements which, whether one likes it or not, give the systems all their value*."[162] This "new form" of the Virgin is, according to Schuon, "a form that in a certain way *includes India in it* and at the same time belongs to the proto-Semitic world; *which thus rises above all theological and liturgical particularization*."[163] Thus, Schuon often equates the Virgin with the "incarnation of divine Femininity"[164] and its Hindu manifestation, the "Supreme *Shakti*,"[165] which precedes all forms and "overflows upon them all, embraces them all, and reintegrates them all."[166]

In extending the metaphysical association of the "new form" of the Virgin to include India and Hinduism, Schuon brings Mary into discursive alignment with his own self-identification as "the messenger" of a new esoteric *ṭarīqa*. In a letter written in 1980, Schuon speaks of himself in the third person and claims that he is "the human instrument for the manifestation of the *Religio perennis* at the end of time," further noting that "the messenger who brought the *Tarīqah* to Europe . . . is more a proto-Aryan than a European."[167] Indeed, Schuon goes on to reiterate, and specifically emphasize, that he is "above all a proto-Aryan and through this deeply rooted in the Hindu spirit, since indeed it has in a certain way kept alive the proto-Aryan spirit."[168] In another letter written the following year, Schuon further explains the characteristics of his "Aryanism":

> In my letter . . . *I mentioned my Aryanism*; this becomes clearer when one considers that it is *the following characteristics which make up Aryanism*: a sense for the plurality of the Divine Hypostases and for their relative autonomy; a sense for the holiness or for the divinity, so to speak, of Nature, hence the reverencing of Nature, be it the veneration of forests, mountains or streams, or the worship of the sun; then a sense for the divinity of the whole universe, and consequently "pantheism" so-called or "immanentism"—not in the modern philosophical

> sense, of course—and with it, all-embracing esoterism and the mystery cults; then too—and this properly belongs under the heading of "polytheism"—the cult of Divine Femininity; and lastly the fine arts, namely the representation of living creatures and consequently the worship of images. *All this has been preserved in the highest degree in the Hindu civilization.*[169]

Tellingly, Schuon's list of Aryan "characteristics" in this passage draws upon explicit nineteenth-century Aryanist conceits regarding what "proto-Aryans" were thought to have believed.[170] Moreover, the direct link made by Schuon here between "the cult of Divine Femininity," "the fine arts," "the worship of images," and "Hindu civilization" is not fortuitous.

Indeed, as part of Schuon's new spiritual relationship with the Virgin Mary, he began to paint her partially or totally naked.[171] Schuon related these images of the Virgin to Hinduism: "In my paintings of the Virgin a tendency towards Hinduism, towards Shaktism if you will, manifests itself."[172] Moreover, Schuon theorized this distinctive genre as "sacred nudity," which he equated with "a return to the essence" as he states in an interview: "It is said, in India, that nudity favors the irradiation of spiritual influences. . . . In an altogether general way, nudity expresses—and virtually actualizes—a return to the essence, the origin, the archetype, thus to the celestial state."[173] Thus, returning to the aforementioned letter in which Schuon notes that the new esoteric form of the Holy Virgin "*includes India*," he similarly comments:

> And here we touch once again upon *the mystery of sacred nudity*; *for dress is form, or particularity*, at least in the respect considered here. If the protecting mantle is an essential component of the Holy Virgin, then this holds true for her long, down-streaming hair as well, for this is her natural mantle.[174]

It is thus through the metaphysics of "sacred nudity" and the above conceptions of the Virgin as "corresponding directly to esoterism" and "above all theological and liturgical particularization" that Schuon's distinction between the *religio perennis* as "the body" and the *religio formalis* as "the garment" is made explicitly clear. Schuon's conceit of "sacred nudity" thus nostalgically seeks a return to what he elsewhere refers to as "the Golden Age" before "the Semitic religions" found it "necessary *to clothe* [the truth] in an argument *efficacious for certain mentalities*."[175]

Indeed, in another 1981 letter, Schuon expounds on the reasons for the unique nature of his *ṭarīqa* as not only because of "our purely esoteric perspective" but also "the fact of the contents of our consciousness, given us by our Western origin; and then the Vedanta as a metaphysical foundation."[176] Schuon continues to assert that "our point of departure is the quest after esoterism and not after a particular religion; after the pure and total Truth, not after a sentimental mythology."[177] In seemingly direct relation to this statement, Schuon further on asserts that while the nondual Vedantic philosophy of "Shankara is altogether clear and unambiguous; Ibn 'Arabī, on the contrary, is uneven, tortuous, obscure and ambiguous, despite all his merits. *Quite generally we recognize in Hinduism the great resonance of the primordial religion.*"[178] Schuon thus asserts: "we take our stand on Shankarāchārya, not on an Ibn 'Arabī; *the latter we accept only insofar as we find in him something of the Vedānta.*"[179]

As early as 1975, in *Form and Substance in the Religions* (*Forme et substance dans les religions*), Schuon had indeed "found" in Ibn 'Arabi "something of the Vedānta" through recourse to the Virgin Mary. Here, Schuon notes:

> Muhyiddin Ibn Arabi, after declaring that his heart "has opened itself to all forms," and that it is "a cloister for monks, a temple of idols, the Kaaba," adds: "I practice the religion of Love"; now *it is over this formless religion that, Semitically speaking, Sayyidatna Maryam presides, thus identifying herself with the Supreme Shakti.*[180]

In a footnote, Schuon qualifies this statement by noting that while Ibn 'Arabi specifies that the "religion of Love" is "Islam," he was "doubtless obliged to do so in order to avoid a charge of heresy, and he could do so in good conscience by understanding the term *islâm* in its direct and universal meaning."[181]

In light of this, Schuon's reference in the same work to "the 'Marian' or 'shaktic' *aspect* in the path of Ibn Arabi"[182] emerges as a discursive strategy that subtly decouples Ibn 'Arabi from his *Other*, Semitic "aspect." This decoupling is facilitated not only by the establishment of a metaphysical link between Ibn 'Arabi and an Aryanized Mary but also through Schuon's categorization above of Ibn 'Arabi's "religion" as "formless," as well as his designation of Ibn 'Arabi's religious identification with Islam as merely opportunistic. As "the universal *Shakti*," Mary "personifies" for Schuon "the *Sophia Perennis*"[183] and "the feminine aspect of the *Logos*."[184] Thus, it is not insignificant that Schuon should choose to associate Ibn 'Arabi with Mary qua *Logos*, even though Ibn 'Arabi famously identified himself as "the Seal of Muhammadan Sainthood" (*khātam al-walāya al-muḥammadiyya*) and thus the principal manifestation of the Muhammadan *Logos* on Earth—that is, the Muhammadan Reality (*ḥaqīqa muḥammadiyya*)[185]—the esoteric nature of which Schuon himself had written in detail.[186]

The Underlying Racialism of the Underlying Religion

Sedgwick has argued that Schuon's universalism, although present at the start of his career, developed over time out of a more or less "orthodox" Islamic perspective—a "deviation" marked by an increasingly forceful critique of Islam and turn toward a universal esotericism with features of a "new religious movement."[187] More recently, however, Renaud Fabbri apologetically contends that because of Schuon's "function" as "the paracletic spokesman of the *sophia perennis*," his universalist position has necessarily been consistent from the beginning, thus marking the "underlying continuity in his personality."[188] In a letter written in 1981, Schuon would seem to confirm, at least in part, Sedgwick's position. Here he divides the history of "the *Tarīqah*" into three phases; the first lasting until 1942 was characterized by "the spell of Guénon and also *the psychic atmosphere of exoteric Islam*."[189] Although Sedgwick dates Schuon's self-estrangement from Islam as late as 1978,[190] it is significant that Schuon's major discursive production did not begin until the start of his self-identified "second phase" after 1942 in which he notes that the "spell" of exoteric Islam "was broken."[191] While this phase was marked by the "descent of the Themes"[192] and "a certain *barakah* stemming from Hinduism and the American Indians," it was also, according to Schuon, a liberation from an

> increasingly unbearable prejudice that would see in me nothing more than the tool of Guénon and the commentator of Ibn ʿArabī; that would even make of me a champion of the Islamic faith and pseudo-esoteric Mahdism. Whereas we had been seeking esoterism![193]

The third phase began, according to Schuon, in 1965 with "the coming of the Holy Virgin" and "the fact that, proceeding from an inner vision, I painted the Virgin and wrote Arabic poems, or rather prayers, to her."[194]

Nevertheless, instances in Schuon's early writing appear to lend credence to Fabbri's apologetic assertion above regarding an "underlying continuity in his personality." For example, in a 1932 letter, just prior to his conversion (and thus before the three aforementioned phases of his *ṭarīqa*), Schuon confessed his hesitations about Islam to a friend in language strikingly similar to his later work:

> How could you think that I would wish to come to God "through Mecca," *and thereby betray Christ and the Vedanta?* . . . Do I have to explain to you once again *that either we are esoterists and metaphysicians who transcend*

> *forms*—just as Christ walked over the waters—and who make no distinction between Allah and Brahma, *or else we are exoterists, "theologians"—or at best mystics—who consequently live in forms like fish in water*, and who make a distinction between Mecca and Benares?[195]

Indeed, Schuon's first published article was written soon after in Mostaganem, Algeria, during his one-time visit with Shaykh Al-ʿAlawī in 1933. Entitled "The Ternary Aspect of the Monotheistic Tradition" (L'aspect ternaire de la tradition monothéiste) and published in *Le voile d'Isis*, it "evoked, for the first time, the notion of the 'essential and transcendent unity' of the three monotheistic religions."[196] This article would eventually become the sixth chapter in *The Transcendent Unity of Religions*, which has been called "his first major doctrinal book."[197]

It is thus in Schuon's most iconic work that he first laid out what he understood to be the proper objective perspective through which Ibn ʿArabi should be received. Here, Schuon discusses "the universality of religion," which, he notes,

> is clouded over by all sorts of historical and geographical contingencies, so much so that certain people freely doubt its existence; for instance, we have heard it disputed somewhere that Sufism admits this idea, and it has been argued that Muḥyi 'd-Din ibn ʿArabī denied it when he wrote that Islam was the pivot of the other religions.[198]

"The truth is, however," Schuon continues, "that every religious form *is superior to the others in a particular respect*, and it is this characteristic that in fact indicates the sufficient reason for the existence of the form."[199] Schuon goes on to claim that "this point of view finds its prototype in the Koran itself; in one place the Koran says that all the Prophets are equal, while elsewhere it declares that some are superior to others."[200] Schuon then notes that this latter Qur'anic declaration (i.e., 2:253, 17:55) is interpreted by Ibn ʿArabi to mean "*that each Prophet is superior to the others* by reason of a particularity that is peculiar to him."[201] While it is not entirely clear what specific text (if any) Schuon based this innovative interpretation on,[202] such a Bloomian "strong misreading"[203] of Ibn ʿArabi is an early example of Schuon's "principle of relativity" noted earlier and his "Copernican turn" as discussed in chapter 3. Here, Schuon's ostensibly nonhierarchical prophetology, which treats each prophetic tradition as an independent solar system, replaces Ibn ʿArabi's hierarchical cosmology where all of the prophets orbit around Muhammad as the universal ruler.

Yet, in contradistinction to Schuon's claim of prophetic relativity, Ibn ʿArabi offers a much more hierarchical interpretation of Qur'an 2:253 and 17:55 within the chapter on Ezra in *The Ring Stones of Wisdom*. Here, he notes that each prophetic community is ranked in degree according to their own excellence, while each prophet is ranked with his particular community, thus forming a necessary link between the particular knowledge of a prophet and the needs of his respective community.[204] In his outstanding translation, Caner Dagli (whose recent defense of a Perennialist interpretation of Ibn 'Arabi I discussed in chapter 2)[205] renders this section as follows:

> Know that the Messengers, may they receive God's blessings—with respect to their being Messengers, not with respect to their being saints and knowers—occupy a hierarchy as occupied by their communities. The knowledge with which they were sent was possessed by them only in the measure of what that messenger's community needed, nothing more or less. The communities are ranked in excellence, some excelling others. In terms of the knowledge proper to messengerhood, the messengers are ranked in excellence in accordance with the rank of their communities. This is spoken of in His Words, transcendent is He, *Some of those messengers We have favored above others* [Qur'an 2:253]. Similarly, they also are ranked in excellence—as regards the knowledge and determinations that stem from their essences—in accordance with their preparedness, spoken of in His Words, *We have favored some of the prophets above others* [Qur'an 17:55].[206]

In a footnote specifically addressing Ibn 'Arabi's quotation in this passage of Qur'an 2:253 (i.e., *Some of those messengers We have favored above others*), Dagli states that every messenger "must be given knowledge that will be adequate to the community to which he is sent. *Since the communities themselves occupy a hierarchy* and have differing needs, the knowledge given to the messenger *qua* messenger will vary as well."[207] Yet, in a subsequent footnote after Ibn 'Arabi's quotation of Qur'an 17:55 (i.e., *We have favored some of the prophets above others*), Dagli contradicts both his previous comment and his own translation by echoing Schuon's assertion of prophetic relativity, thus noting: "Ibn al-'Arabī is saying that as individuals the prophets also are different from one another, *each possessing certain strengths in relation to the other prophets*."[208] There is no indication in the text, however, that Ibn 'Arabi makes any attempt to relativize prophetic strengths; rather, Ibn 'Arabi's interpretation of Qur'an 2:253 and 17:55 is in this particular instance literal and unequivocally hierarchical.[209] Dagli continues by claiming that the fact that Ibn 'Arabi discerns "a different wisdom in each of the prophets" in *The Ring Stones* indicates that he "sees something special in each of them."[210] While one could hardly argue with this truism, it neglects to underscore (in the same relativizing manner as Schuon does earlier) the entire *raison d'être* of *The Ring Stones* itself, which as mentioned in chapter 1 is to situate each individual prophet as a "word" (*kalima*) of God within "the comprehensive words" (*jawāmiʿ al-kalim*) of Muhammad, both spiritually and physically—that is, as the *logos*-orientated reflection of the Muhammadan Reality (*ḥaqīqa muḥammadiyya*) and as "the Seal of the Prophets."[211] This sentiment is repeated several times by Ibn ʿArabi in *The Ring Stones*,[212] but perhaps most fittingly summarized in the first section from the chapter on Muhammad:

> His wisdom is that of singularity because he is the most complete creation of the human species (*al-nawʿ al-insānī*). Thus, this affair begins and is sealed by him—for he was a prophet when Adam was between water and clay, and then by his elemental configuration (*nashʾa*) he became the Seal of the Prophets. . . . He was, peace be upon him, the greatest proof of his Lord, for he was given the comprehensive words, which were the appellations named by Adam.[213]

While throughout this book I have provided numerous instances where Ibn ʿArabi articulates such a prophetic hierarchy in relationship to the unique universality and subsequent superiority of Muhammad, here I offer one final example. In the following passage from *The Meccan Openings*, not only does Ibn ʿArabi once again enunciate this prophetic hierarchy, and Muhammad's superior position within it, but he additionally expresses *in no uncertain terms* its logical consequence necessitating obedience to the Prophet:

> Each prophet was only sent specifically to a designated people because each one has a precisely suited composition (*mizāj*) (for a particular group). However, Muhammad, blessings and peace be upon him, was only sent by God with a universal message to all of humanity in its entirety. He only received the like of this message because he has a universal composition that encompasses the composition of every prophet and messenger. Indeed, he has the most balanced and perfect of compositions and the most upright configurations (*nashʾāt*). . . . You know the degree of your low standing compared to the composition of Muhammad, blessings and peace be upon him, in knowledge of his Lord. So, adhere to faith, follow him, and make him your leader![214]

In addition to Schuon's admonishment of Ibn ʿArabi's declaration of Muhammad's superiority over other prophets and exclusive claim to the religion of love, noted earlier, Schuon elsewhere spurns similar arguments regarding the superiority of

Muhammad and the universality (and thus supersession) of his religion over all others. While "self-evident in Islam," according to Schuon, such a "dogmatic assertion" that Muhammad is " 'the best' . . . can be said of every other Messenger within the framework of his own Message" and thus "every integral religion necessarily possesses such an incomparable quality, for *otherwise it would not exist*."[215] Thus, Schuon assures us that if Ibn 'Arabi did make statements apparently holding to the exclusivity of Islam, this is simply because he was obliged to do so since he "belonged to the Islamic civilization and owed his spiritual realization to the Islamic *barakah* and the Masters of Sufism, in a word, to the Islamic form of religion."[216]

While Schuon's ostensibly "generous" reading of Ibn 'Arabi appears to be infinitely more inclusive than the Andalusian Sufi's own arguments for the superiority of the Muhammadan *Logos* and Islam, a closer and contextualized analysis of Schuon's position proves otherwise. Schuon rejects Ibn 'Arabi's Islamic conception of one universal religion with Muhammad at its center, not only on metaphysical grounds, but also—and perhaps more fundamentally—on ethno-racial ones. In *Gnosis: Divine Wisdom*, while Schuon concedes that it is possible to conceive "that there might be only one Revelation or Tradition for our human world," he argues, as I quoted in part earlier, that such an assertion is in actuality "a failure to understand that what determines the difference among forms of Truth is the difference among human receptacles."[217] Although this conception of diversity looks very similar to Ibn 'Arabi's assertion in *The Ring Stones* that prophetic knowledge is based on the needs of the particular community each prophet is sent to, Schuon adds a racio-spiritual component:

> For thousands of years humanity has been divided into several fundamentally different branches constituting as many complete humanities, more or less closed in on themselves; the existence of spiritual receptacles so different and so original demands a differentiated refraction of the one Truth. Let us note that this *is not always a question of race, but more often of human groups*, very diverse perhaps, but nonetheless *subject to mental conditions* which, taken as a whole, *make of them sufficiently homogeneous spiritual recipients*.[218]

Importantly, Schuon understood differences among "human groups" *not solely* in the context of race, but more completely in a context of "natural castes."[219] As he states above, each "human group" has a particular "*mental condition*" that makes them "sufficiently homogeneous." Indeed, Schuon directly asserts in *Castes and Races*, as partially quoted earlier, that "*a revelation always conforms to a racial genius*, though this by no means signifies that it is restricted to the specific limits of the race in question."[220] Thus, Schuon forcefully echoes the discourse of his nineteenth-century predecessors on race. Indeed, in *Castes and Races*, Schuon precisely recapitulates such racial stereotypes in relation to imagined metaphysical qualities. For example, Schuon states:

> The black race bears in itself the substance of an "existential wisdom"; it asks for few symbols; it needs only a homogeneous system: God, prayer, *sacrifice and dancing*. Fundamentally the black man has a *"non-mental" mentality*, whence the "mental" importance for him of what is *corporeal, his physical sureness and his sense of rhythm*. . . . [The black man's] eyes are slightly prominent and heavy, warm and moist; their look reflects the beauty of the tropics and combines *sensuality—and sometimes ferocity—with innocence*.[221]

Schuon goes on to state: "However paradoxical it may seem, *it is the intelligence rather than the body of the negro which is in need of rhythms and dances*, and that precisely because his spirit has a plastic or existential and not an abstract way of approach."[222] In spite of self-assurances regarding his racial objectivity,[223] Schuon here spiritualizes—and thus *re-essentializes*—hackneyed racialist notions equating blackness with irrationality, physicality, sensuality, rhythmicity, violence, and "native primitivism."[224] Indeed, as Colin Kidd has observed, "Just as racialists ascribed distinctive intellectual qualities (or failings) to particular races, so they also associated particular racial groups with certain spiritual characteristics."[225] In such nineteenth-century treatments, "race was not simply a matter of external physical differences but of deep psychic differences, *which manifested themselves in the varieties of religion found throughout the world*."[226] Thus, in the same passage from *Gnosis* quoted above, where Schuon asserts that the difference "of spiritual receptacles . . . *is not always a question of race, but more often of human groups . . . subject to mental conditions*," he goes on to state:

> This being so, we can say that *the diverse Revelations do not really contradict one another since they do not apply to the same receptacle* and since God never addresses the same message to two or more receptacles having a divergent character, that is, corresponding analogically to dimensions that are formally incompatible; *a contradiction can arise only between things situated on the same level*. The apparent antinomies between Traditions are like differences of language or symbol; *contradictions are an aspect of the human receptacles, not of God*; diversity in the world *is a result of its remoteness from the divine Principle*.[227]

Through what appears to be recourse to racialist premises, Schuon here once again contravenes the Aristotelian law of noncontradiction—a fundamental strategy of the Perennialist discourse of transcendent unity discussed in chapter 3.[228] If it is indeed true, as Schuon claims here, that "*a contradiction can arise only between things situated on the same level*" and that "the diverse Revelations *do not really contradict one another*," then it stands to reason that for Schuon each "group" of so-called "human receptacles" is situated on a different spiritual "level." If we further concede to Schuon that "*diversity* in the world *is a result of its remoteness from the divine Principle*," then by necessity some so-called groups are closer to God than *Others*.

Let us here recall, as I quote earlier, that according to Schuon, after "the Golden Age," the Semitic religions were forced "to clothe [the truth] *in an argument efficacious for certain mentalities*." Notwithstanding his proclamations against Gobineau and Chamberlain, who held that German blood was bound by a racial soul,[229] Schuon notes that there is "a fundamental tendency in the Gospel that responds with particular force to *the needs of the Germanic soul: namely, a tendency toward simplicity and inwardness, hence away from theological and liturgical complication, [and] formalism*."[230] In a related vein, Schuon argues in *Gnosis* that the idea of a single universal religion (as Ibn 'Arabi claims for Islam) is in fact "*contrary to the nature of things*."[231] This is so, he contends, because

> *the ethnic diversity of humanity* and the geographical extent of the earth suffice to render highly unlikely the axiom of one unique religion for all and on the contrary highly likely—to say the least—*the need for a plurality of religions*; in other words *the idea of a single religion does not escape contradiction if one takes account of its claims to absoluteness and universality*, on the one hand, and *the psychological and physical impossibility of their realization*, on the other, not to mention the antinomy between such claims and the necessarily relative character of all religious mythology; *only pure metaphysics and pure prayer are absolute and therefore universal.* As for "mythology,"[232] it is indispensable—apart from its intrinsic content of truth and efficacy—for enabling metaphysical and essential truth to "gain a footing" in a given human collectivity.[233]

In light of the above, it would seem that Schuon's conception of the "transcendent unity of religions" is ironically based on a much more *existential* foundation—that is, "*the ethnic diversity of humanity*." According to Schuon, such diversity makes religious pluralism necessary, *not* because of an inherent good of plurality in itself, but because human racio-spiritual difference makes the functionality of a single exoteric religion an impossibility. In other words, certain racio-spiritual dispositions, such as "the German soul," are in need of more esoterically oriented religions, like Christianity. Yet here we encounter a second irony: while Schuon claims in the previous passage that "*the idea of a single religion does not escape contradiction if one takes account of its claims to absoluteness and universality*," he also asserts that "*only pure metaphysics and pure prayer are absolute and therefore universal*."

Even though Schuon claimed, as I noted earlier, that Islam formed "the providential ground" for his manifestation of "*the supra formal nature of spiritual Truth*," he nevertheless rejects Ibn 'Arabi's recourse to Muhammad as a universal prophet. As Schuon importantly notes in *Logic and Transcendence*, "according to Islam," Muhammad is the "synthesis" of all of the prophets "since he is thus the first in his celestial reality he is the last in time, according to the principle of inverse reflection."[234] Although Muhammad's synthesis is, according to Schuon, taken as a "unique and supereminent quality" by Muslims, it is in reality "*quite contingent*" and "entirely in line with henotheist logic, for it is in just the same way—because of a given quality shared with the Absolute—that Vishnu, Shiva, or other divinities become alternatively or separately the supreme God."[235] Citing Max Müller's employment of the term "henotheism" as "a cult involving several divinities, each of whom is looked upon as the supreme God while it is worshiped,"[236] Schuon thus argues that Muhammad's supremacy is relative to his specific sphere of *logos*-centered influence, or what Schuon here calls Muhammad's "cosmic sector." Understood through such a strategy of relativity, Schuon is thus able to reorder the cosmic hierarchy of *logoi*. He thus states:

> Just as the chronological posteriority of the Arab Prophet may—or must—be interpreted in the cosmic sector of Islam as marking the principial anteriority of the Muhammadan *Logos*, so the human femininity of the Blessed Virgin, hence her subordination, can indicate a real *celestial superiority* in a particular connection: given *the spiritual and cosmic supereminence* of the personage, femininity appears in this case as the inverted reflection of pure essentiality, which amounts to saying that in her "transcendent body" (*dharmakāya*) *the Virgin is the virginal Mother of all the Prophets*; she is thus identified with divine Femininity or the Wisdom that was "in the beginning."[237]

As I discussed earlier, Schuon's discourse is notable for denuding the Virgin Mary of her Semitic clothing and reimagining her within an Aryanist language-game as "the universal *Shakti*" and the personification of "the *Sophia Perennis*." In the passage above, Schuon similarly announces the "*celestial superiority*" of the Virgin Mary as higher and even more anterior than Muhammad (whom he importantly refers to as "the *Arab* Prophet"), since she is the "virginal Mother of all the Prophets." If we recall Schuon's previous argument in *Gnosis* regarding the "need for a plurality of religions" *because* of "the ethnic diversity of humanity," then his replacement of "the Arab Prophet" with "the virginal Mother of all the Prophets" emerges as a cosmological map deeply inscribed by a particular ethnoracial hierarchy. Following such logic, if there are multiple religions because of the ethnic diversity of humanity, then having an Arab prophet personified as the *Logos* would signify not only the superiority of the Islamic "religious mythology" but also that of the Semitic Arabs. Yet, Schuon notes in the passage quoted from *Gnosis* earlier that all "claims to absoluteness and universality" from such religious mythologies are relative, while "only *pure metaphysics and pure prayer are absolute and therefore universal*." Thus, Schuon's assignment of the Virgin to the supreme cosmic position qua mother of the prophets in tandem with his self-identification with Aryan metaphysical "purity" in essence makes her the mother of all of humanity and all races, thus positioning her—and thereby Schuon—as *prior to* and *thus above* the limiting factors of race, authorizing him to take up the self-determined position of "the human instrument for the manifestation of the *Religio perennis* at the end of time"—that is, the ultimate arbiter and interpreter of religious "Truth" ("with that capital 'T'" as Cutsinger himself asserts at the start of this chapter).

In a related cosmological mapping strategy in *Sufism*, Schuon refers to an iconic passage in *The Ring Stones of Wisdom* dealing with Ibn 'Arabi's famous concept of "the divinity of beliefs" discussed at length in chapter 1.[238] Regarding this particular passage, Schuon asserts that "among the statements made by Ibn Arabi," it is "*the one most directly in conformity with the esoteric perspective*."[239] Although Schuon quotes a longer section from the final chapter on Muhammad in *The Ring Stones*, the thrust of his commentary revolves around the following passage of Ibn 'Arabi (here rendered by Schuon):

> The believer . . . praises only the Divinity contained within his belief. . . . The Divinity in whom one believes is (so to speak) fashioned by him who conceives (*nādhir*), and it is therefore (in this respect) his work; the praise addressed to what he believes is praise addressed (indirectly and with regard to conceptualization) to himself.[240]

Schuon thus notes that "it is important to understand here that the image of the 'believer who praises himself' *must be applied above all, according to the logic of things,* to a given religious point of view and therefore *to a given collectivity*."[241] Yet, rather than following "the logic of *things*," Schuon's apparent slippage from particular mental projections concerning God to religious collectivities once again echoes the logic of post-Enlightenment modernity, which (as I argued in chapter 1) tends to construe each particular religion as "a set of beliefs to be confessed."[242] In other words, Schuon here simply perpetuates the post-Enlightenment commonplace that reduces religion *to* belief. Moreover, as we recall, instead of understanding all religions as "true" in an absolute sense, Schuon understands them as only *relatively* true—that is, as *mythologies* designed "for enabling metaphysical and essential truth." Indeed, Schuon's deployment of Ibn 'Arabi's discourse on belief here *relativizes* all religions except for that of so-called esotericism.

As such, in concluding his discussion of Ibn 'Arabi's discourse on belief, which as noted above Schuon claimed as "*directly in conformity with the esoteric perspective*," he states:

> It follows from these considerations that God is the same for all the religions only in the divine "stratosphere," not in the human "atmosphere"; in this "atmosphere" each religion has its own God for all practical purposes, *and there are as many Gods as there are religions*. In this sense it could be said *that esoterism alone is absolutely monotheistic*, it alone recognizing only one religion under diverse forms.[243]

Schuon thus appropriates Ibn 'Arabi's discourse on belief in the service of what he described in *Logic and Transcendence* earlier as a "henotheistic logic"—a representative "Hindu" doctrine of many gods that relativizes all notions of divine supereminence within a wider esoteric cosmology of competing "cosmic sectors." In such a henotheistic cosmology, Ibn 'Arabi's identification with the Qur'anic dispensation and the Muhammadan *Logos* as the universal prophetic "synthesis"[244] is transmogrified once again into an identification with "esoterism alone" as the *only* "absolutely monotheistic" path since "it alone recognize[s] only one religion under diverse forms." Thus, recalling Schuon's previously quoted assertion that "diversity in the world *is a result of its remoteness from the divine Principle*," here Schuon effectively classifies the *religio perennis* (i.e., the "esoteric" or *transcendent* unity of all religions as personified by the Virgin Mary) as *the only* mode of consciousness that fully encompasses ultimate truth, subsuming and superseding all other religions.

Finally, it must be noted that Schuon's closing statement above is remarkable not only for its unabashed absolutism ("esoterism alone is *absolutely monotheistic*"), but also for its explicit deification of "religion" as implied by the adjective "monotheistic" ("it alone recognizing *only one religion* under diverse forms"). Here, the normative idea of monotheism as *belief in one God* is categorically replaced with the idea of *belief in one religion*. Indeed, as I noted in chapter 1, there is a tendency within the interpretive field of Schuonian Perennialism to conflate God and the modern concept of "religion" itself—a tendency that appears to be a result of the essentialism inherent in the very notion of a *religio perennis*.[245] The intellectual history of such conflation was first traced by Wilfred Cantwell Smith in his classic 1962 work *The Meaning and End of Religion*, in which he showed how the abstract idea of religion has been constructed and increasingly reified in Western modernity.[246] Commenting on Smith's seminal insights regarding the "almost idolatrous" nature of such modern "reification," Carl Ernst more recently observes how this phenomenon "has given rise to a subtle but momentous shift of perspective in which people speak of believing in Christianity or in Islam, as opposed to believing in God."[247]

Conclusion

As the Seal of Muhammadan Sainthood and the principal manifestation of the Muhammadan Reality on Earth, Ibn 'Arabi took the cosmological *and* historical superiority of the Prophet as seriously as he took the purity of his own Arab pedigree; indeed, his spiritual "vocation" depended on them both.[248] While Schuon clearly understood such ultimate prophetic and cosmic authority Ibn 'Arabi conferred upon Muhammad, he chose to openly reject this prophetology in the way he cosmologically mapped the Andalusian Sufi. In enunciating "the 'Marian' or 'shaktic' aspect in the path of Ibn Arabi," Schuon imagined another cosmic figure to associate Ibn 'Arabi with—one more aligned with the so-called formlessness of Aryan metaphysics. In literally painting this "shaktic" image of Mary as naked, Schuon denudes her of her Semitic clothing, for, as he notes, "*dress is form.*" Thus, by asserting that Ibn 'Arabi's "religion of love" is presided over by the "Supreme *Shakti*," Schuon endeavors to remove the Semitic "style" of Muhammad—the *religio formalis*—from Ibn 'Arabi while simultaneously seeking to "find in him something of the Vedānta"—that is, the pure Aryan metaphysics of the *religio perennis*.

Under Schuon's interpretive gaze, Ibn 'Arabi is thus effectively appropriated as the Seal of Marian Sainthood—a saint who is imagined to transcend the particularities of religious form, thus encompassing the Schuonian ideal of objectivity. Echoing the discursive practices of nineteenth-century Aryanism, Schuon situates such objectivity as the preeminent quality of pure esotericism, which he consistently juxtaposes to Semitic "subjectivism"—an orientation marked by its particularity and inability to differentiate the underlying truth of all religions from their contingent forms. Schuon held such subjectivist "confusion" to be imbricated with the "theological, psychological, and legalistic" elements of religion and thus incapable of the esoteric acknowledgment of "*the principle of relativity*," that is, "the transcendent unity of religions."

Hugh Nicholson has observed that all inclusive universalist schemes are inevitably ideological in their attempt to mask their own particularism. Such discourse "declares a radical break with religious exclusivism, but does so only through an act of exclusion that it fails to acknowledge."[249] While Schuon's elucidation of Ibn 'Arabi has been widely interpreted by *both* supporters and detractors as a discourse that seeks to unify *or* homogenize religious diversity within a purported underlying religious essence, Schuon's own discursive practices evince a much more complicated and ironic appropriation marked by a universalization of nineteenth-century racialist categories as signifiers of Semitic difference in opposition to a single Aryan truth. Schuon's racialist understanding of revelation—where "*revelation always conforms to a racial genius*"—posits religious form itself as burdened with the limitations and particularisms of racial Others. Indeed, for Schuon, Muhammad qua "the Arab Prophet" is hampered by a Semitic mentality attached "meticulously to human things" in opposition to Christ, whose divinity displays an "Aryan quality" marked by an "*independence*—seemingly 'Greek' or 'Hindu'—*toward forms*." Thus, Schuon replaces Muhammad as "the Arab" *Logos* with the "*celestial superiority*" of Mary qua "*the virginal Mother of all the Prophets*" who is "identified with . . . the Wisdom that was 'in the beginning.'" Here, the Aryan image of Mary is made transcendently *prior* to religion and, as such, to race. In Schuon's discourse, Aryan superiority is thus translated as metaphysically linked to the underlying essence of all (*Other*) religions and thus all (*Other*) races. By thus *transcending* religion and race—as situated above them—Schuon holds his own superior Aryan intellection as ultimately wielding the "permanent and 'naturally supernatural' capacity" to *interpret* (and thus *reign over*) them as "the human instrument for the manifestation of the *Religio perennis* at the end of time." Indeed, it is ultimately through Ibn 'Arabi's discourse on belief that Schuon ironically reifies (and subsequently *deifies*) his own system of belief—that is, the *religio perennis*—as the *only* religious path that "*is absolutely monotheistic*, it alone recognizing *only one religion* under diverse forms."[250]

Rather than an inclusive universalism that accepts all religions as valid, Schuonian Perennialism emerges as hegemonically supersessionist, subtly authorizing its own perfection, while classifying the religions of Others as *necessarily* incomplete. As such, Schuon's radically selective reading of Ibn 'Arabi's discourse, and subsequent Aryanist construction of his "Marian" image, is a lucid example of what McCutcheon has called the "cosmogonic" activity of the "'art' of hermeneutics," where a "very particular present" is universalized through ideological appeals to "mythic time."[251] Thus, Schuon's self-identification with Aryanism and its superior *because primordial* objectivity naturalizes historically situated *and racially inflected* presuppositions within an exclusivist universalism that in the end fails to go beyond the religious particularism it claims to transcend.

Conclusion

MAPPING IBN ʿARABI AT ZERO DEGREES

The mark of the true church is its universality.
IMMANUEL KANT, *Religion within the Bounds of Bare Reason.*[1]

Profane thought is always the portrait of an individual even when it is mingled with some glimmerings of knowledge, as must always be the case since reason is not a closed vessel.
FRITHJOF SCHUON, *Logic and Transcendence.*[2]

Metaphysics—the white mythology which reassembles and reflects the culture of the West: the white man takes his own mythology, Indo-European mythology, his own *logos*, that is, the *mythos* of his idiom, for the universal form of that he must still wish to call Reason.
JACQUES DERRIDA, *Margins of Philosophy.*[3]

IN THE PRECEDING pages I have discussed critical ways that scholars working from within (as well as on the margins of) the interpretive field of Schuonian Perennialism have mapped out Ibn ʿArabi's universalism in contradistinction to the Andalusian Sufi's own cosmological mapping of the religious Other. In tandem with textual comparisons between Ibn ʿArabi and those of his Perennialist interpreters, I have endeavored to identify and trace the formative contours of Schuon's own universalist cartography. In chapter 3, I compared Schuonian discourse to the nonreductive, religious universalism of Schleiermacher to contextualize the Perennialist reception of Ibn ʿArabi within the modern tradition of religious essentialism—that is, the concept of a universal religious essence underlying all historical religions. In chapter 4, I demonstrated how Schuon's conflicted reception of Ibn ʿArabi strikingly echoes racialist discursive practices of nineteenth-century Aryanism—a conceptual lineage that held its own notion of what counts for the universal and, more important, *who is most capable* of discerning it. In the conclusion that follows, I revisit the broader concerns alluded to in the introduction of this study regarding the nature of universalism itself and how the conceptual lineage of its modern Euro-American formation bears upon contemporary reading practices of Ibn 'Arabi and "religion" more broadly. As such, I discursively situate key elements of the Schuonian language-game within a deeper genealogy of German idealism to show foundational resonances with a Kantian metaphysics of autonomy and its attendant universalism.

As I noted in chapter 3, Schleiermacher is famous for developing the first systematic treatment of religion as an essence unique to itself. Yet, Schleiermacher's romantic reliance on intuition and feeling to describe the essence of religion was directly related to a larger Kantian tradition. Simply put, Kant famously argued that certain knowledge of the "noumenal" realm (i.e., the divine "*as such*") was impossible through conceptual experience even though *the practical idea* of God was ethically necessary. Thus, as Grace Jantzen notes, "Schleiermacher, and the religious Romantics who followed him, sought to escape the Kantian strictures by affirming that while God could not be discovered in thought, it is possible to experience God in pure preconceptual consciousness."[4] Nevertheless, it is clear that Kant *also* believed there is an essence of "religion"—only he situated it within moral reason as opposed to Schleiermacher's romantic notion of intuition and feeling. Thus, as Jantzen notes, "what was up for debate in Schleiermacher's thinking was not whether such an essence *could be* postulated but *rather in what it could be said to consist*."[5]

Although the metaphysical perspectives of Kantianism and Schuonian Perennialism are situated at *polar ends* of a rather vast continuum regarding the human potential for knowledge of the divine, in what follows I set aside these differences and focus instead on their shared intellectual genealogy of religious universalism.[6] As such, I trace how their discursive practices are imbricated within a particular grammar of what George Lakoff and Mark Johnson have called "metaphorical thought."[7] Building off of the Copernican metaphor I developed in chapter 3 in relation to how Schuonian universalism decenters Ibn 'Arabi's hierarchical cosmology, the ensuing analysis is framed against the metaphorical backdrop of the Copernican age and its imperial cartographic perspective. While I adumbrate this backdrop in broad strokes, the heart of my analysis centers on a comparison of Schuonian and Kantian language-games. Here, I not only argue that Schuon shares with Kant the philosophical and religious metaphorics of Platonic idealism situated within a common Euro-Christian tradition, but that Schuon's exposition on the *religio perennis* also *functionally* echoes Kant's creation of a "universal" religion defined through the primacy of internal autonomy over its Kantian opposite of "heteronomy"—that is, *externally received* religious form devoid of true morality and systematically symbolized in Kant's late writings by Judaism *itself*. Reading Schuon alongside of Kant in this way thus suggests how deeply the Kantian conceptual grammar of universalism—including its attendant Othering of Judaism qua "the heteronomous"—is embedded within Perennialist interpretive approaches to religious universalism and the metaphysics of Ibn 'Arabi. Indeed, the force of this inherited conceptual lineage proves even more remarkable given the fact that Schuon roundly disavowed Kant's philosophy in shrill terms.[8] In the end, I show how the discursive formations of Schuonian universalism paradoxically harbor absolutist modalities of supersessionism that are similar to those openly posited by Ibn 'Arabi. The exclusivism inherent within such discourse brings into view the historically constituted and situated nature of all claims to inclusive or "transcendent" universalism and the localized forms of religious subjectivity they authorize.

Copernican Cartography and the Hubris of Zero Degrees

The idea that there exists a "universal beyond time and space" has been a seminal conceit in European imperialism since the end of the fifteenth century.[9] The modern European attempt to find an objective, "universal" perspective "independent of its ethnic and cultural center of observation" has been dubbed by Santiago Castro-Gómez "*the hubris of zero degrees*."[10] Here, Castro-Gómez alludes to the agenda announced at the start of the 1884 International Meridian Conference in Washington, DC, "to create," according to the conference chair, Rear Adm. C. R. P. Rogers, "a new accord among the nations by agreeing upon a meridian proper to be employed *as a common zero* of longitude and standard of time throughout the world."[11] The meridian thus agreed upon was at the Royal Observatory, Greenwich, England.[12]

Building on the work of Enrique Dussel and Walter Mignolo, Castro-Gómez observes that such a European positionality of "zero degrees" emerged as the result of the Spanish conquest of America and the imperial need for cartographic precision. Like the astronomical revolution of Copernicus, which transcended the confines of geocentric cosmology, European cartographers of the sixteenth century transcended the cartographic depiction of an ethnocentric world contained within a circular boundary. As Castro-Gómez notes, such a shift in perspective

> completely revolutionizes the scientific practice of cartography. In making the point of observation invisible, *the geometric center no longer coincides with the ethnic center*. Instead, cartographers and European navigators who now possess precise instruments of measurement, begin to believe

> that a representation made from the ethnic center is prescientific, since it is related to a specific cultural particularity.[13]

It was from this new notion of perspective, dissociated from an "ethnic center," that the Western conceit of "truly scientific and 'objective' representation" emerged as the "universal point of view"—"a sovereign gaze external to the representation."[14] Indeed, Slavoj Žižek has called such positionality "the privileged *empty point of universality*" through which the acknowledgment of "the Other's specificity is the very form of asserting one's own superiority."[15] Such universality assumes a clear view of "absolute knowledge," which, as Mignolo posits, amounts to "knowledge that hides its own geopolitical grounding."[16]

As a seminal, and self-described, inheritor of this Copernican innovation of cartographic perspective, Kant's radical form of "transcendental"[17] idealism definitively broke from the premodern metaphysical conception of innate ideas as transcendent a priori, while it nevertheless retained the metaphysical possibility of a necessary and universal a priori knowledge solely through autonomous reason (i.e., through conceptual categories) and its cognition *of* external objects (as opposed to the *heteronomous effect* of objects on the self). This is what David Pacini has called the "Kantian 'critical standpoint,' " which replaces the traditional "idea that the world constitutes me with the idea that I constitute the world."[18] Kant thus charted a new course between classical metaphysics and empirical science, comparing his own innovation to that of Copernicus.[19]

Schuon's universalism is likewise inscribed by what I described in chapter 3 as a self-conscious Copernican turn away from a premodern hierarchical religio-centrism to a heliocentric model of religious unity made possible through recourse to what could be thought of as a similar "transcendental" religious a priori, mediating between classical metaphysics and modern religious pluralism.[20] As Schuon himself asserts:

> It has become impossible to provide an effective defense for a single religion against all the others by declaring the rest anathema without exception; to persist in doing so—unless one is living in a society that is still medieval, in which case the question does not arise—is a little like wishing to maintain the Ptolemaic system against the evidence of verified and verifiable astronomical data.[21]

Rather than the premodern, confessional understanding of heteronomous religious form as absolute for the religious subject, here the a priori category of the essence of religion *as such*—that is, the *religio perennis*—is absolute, by which all external religious forms are constituted as so many manifestations of the divine.

While both Kantian and Schuonian universalist cosmologies thus appear to reflect a similar Copernican turn where notions of an autonomous, a priori universal perspective form the bases of two (albeit very different) religious epistemologies, following the insight of Castro-Gómez I argue that these respective discourses *also* metaphysically reflect the *imperial cartography* formed within the Copernican age itself and the hegemonic universalism it produced. In such Copernican or imperial mapmaking, the cartographer is transposed from an ethnic location to a universal Archimedean metaposition. From this ethnically decentered position, the imperial cartographer is removed from the realm of the Other. Thus, while claiming scientific "objectivity," imperial mapmakers of the Copernican age pictorially and discursively colonized geo-political space through naturalizing hierarchies of civilizational and religious difference in Euro- and Christocentric terms.[22] As Mignolo notes, this cartographic "colonization of space (of language, of memory)" formed "a larger frame of mind in which the regional could be universalized and taken as a yardstick to evaluate the degree of development of the rest of the human race."[23] Like the Žižekian notion of the "empty point of universality," such a *hubris of zero degrees* concealed its own situated position of enunciation and exported local European history as universal truth. Thus universalized, such world-ordering "would become the epistemological base that gave rise to the anthropological, social, and evolutionist theories of the Enlightenment."[24]

Although sixteenth-century European imperialism was therefore important in the Western conceptualization and production of the Other,[25] it was the paradigm shift of Cartesian mind–body dualism in the seventeenth century that philosophically informed a discursive reduction of social subjectivities "to physical dimensions and correlates."[26] Indeed, as James Byrne points out:

> The major effect of mind-body dualism was a privileging of the rational, intellectual and abstract over the physical, sensuous and practical. This in turn reinforced the trend in Western thought—*a trend which had roots in a particular Christian anthropology*—to view the body as the locus of error, weakness and sin.[27]

Indeed, Cartesian mind–body dualism and its attendant primacy of reason "*over the physical, sensuous and practical*" was indeed a major problem for Kant and his contemporaries.[28] By way of a solution, Kant sought a dual freedom: an a priori rational autonomy that justified not only a "freedom from metaphysical illusion"[29] but also a freedom from all empirical and subjective sources of reality. The Kantian transcendental ideal of autonomy thus contends that there is a universal modality of reason that remains independent of and unconstituted by the external world, yet constitutive of it.[30] Indeed, the universal power that Kant sought to harness through his idea of "the *autonomy* of pure reason"[31] framed not only his mature philosophy but also his later conception of "pure" moral religious subjectivity—a subjectivity he fully fleshed out in his tellingly entitled work *Religion within the Bounds of Bare Reason* (*Die Religion innerhalb der Grenzen der blossen Vernunft*), published in 1793. Yet, to appreciate Kant's particular religious language-game articulated here (and its attendant *prelapsarian* metaphorics), it is necessary to read it, *as it was intended*, not as *mere* philosophy (as somehow dissociated from religion), but as a work of "philosophical theology" in dialogical tension, *but not opposition*, to "biblical theology" as Kant himself clarifies.[32] As such, *Religion* must be read in light of its own politico-theological context, as well as its deep genealogy of "Christian anthropology" that Byrne importantly points to above.

Kant's Religion: Platonism, Christianity, and the Jewish Question

Kant's north-German Protestant university metaphysics, as Ian Hunter observes, was deeply infused with Christian Platonic anthropology.[33] Such an anthropology posited that while the human soul is created, it retains a trace of the divine image through its rationality and freedom. By freeing itself from "sensual slavery," the rational mind could attain to spiritual wisdom within the intelligible divine order through the indwelling Christ and divine law.[34] It was the divine order, and not the created world, that was understood to be the source of all knowledge. While Kant maintained this strict epistemological divide, he situated human reason, instead of a purported indwelling divinity, as pure rational being (*Vernunftwesen*) and therefore pure intelligence (*homo noumenon*).[35]

Thus, in *Religion*, Kant establishes human autonomous reason as self-regulating moral law—that is, "reason's inner voice of duty"[36]—in place of divine intelligence by invoking the Christian Platonic idea of the *Logos* as the divine archetype: "the idea of him emanates from God's essence; he is to that extent not a created thing but God's only begotten Son, 'the *word* (the *Let it be so!*) through which all other things are, and without which nothing exists that has been made.' "[37] As such, Kant claims that "to *elevate* ourselves to this ideal of moral perfection, i.e., to the archetype of the moral attitude in all its purity, is a universal human duty."[38] Indeed, the Kantian idea of the pure rational being, as Hunter notes, not only exists independently of space and time but also has a dual intellectual function: (1) to intelligize pure forms of experience and (2) to govern the will by thinking the form of its law.[39] It is through these intellectual processes that "Kant's *homo noumenon* or rational being is supposed to free himself from the 'sensuous inclinations' that otherwise tie the will of empirical man (*homo phenomenon*) to extrinsic ends or goods."[40]

Thus, in *Religion*, Kant theorizes this path to the autonomy of moral reason as the final phase of the development of religion in human history. Although presented as a philosophy of religion, *Religion* is equally a "history of reason" that prefigures Hegel's own dialectical teleology of history.[41] Kant therefore emplots a teleological historical narrative in *Religion* that culminates in the realization of autonomous reason. Beginning with a Hellenized Judaism, Kant's religion evolves into a Christianity whose progressively mature forms increasingly discard the restraints of external religious law and finally emerges as an autonomous form of "pure rational religion."[42] Kant's teleological, universalist approach to history can therefore be understood as an attempt to show a progressive development from *homo phenomenon* to *homo noumenon*, and his critique of religion theorizes this progression. Thus, in *Religion*, Kant states:

> It is . . . a necessary consequence of the physical and simultaneously of the moral predisposition in us—the latter being the foundation and simultaneously the interpreter of all religion—*for religion finally to be detached gradually from all empirical determining bases, from all statutes that rest on history* and that, by means of a church faith, unite human beings provisionally in order to further the good, and *thus for pure rational religion ultimately to rule over all*, "so that God may be all in all."[43]

Here, Kant posits a universal *religious essence* as a divinely given "moral predisposition" of the human being that has served as the foundation of all positive religions.[44] The purity and sole truth of this autonomous morality has facilitated the progressive detachment of the positive religions from their historical accretions—that is, their scriptural laws. This emancipatory metanarrative finds its telos in the salvific emergence of a "*universal rational religion* and thus . . . a (divine) ethical state on earth."[45]

Kant goes on to clarify that because we cannot know God in and of God's self, we can only approach God through our own moral sensibilities: "This idea of a moral ruler of the world is a task for our practical reason. We are concerned to know not so much what God is in himself (what his nature is) as what he is for us as moral beings."[46] Such a statement perfectly exemplifies Kant's "Copernican" stance toward religion—a stance where, as Stephen Palmquist explains, "instead of viewing historical faith as the core and moral action as the secondary element, Kant views the latter as the core and locates the former on the periphery."[47]

It is from this moral theological perspective that Kant therefore asserts that "the universal true religious faith" is *triune*: it has faith in a God that is a "*holy* legislator," "*benign* governor," and "*just* judge."[48] What is important here is that Kant subsequently notes that this *universal true faith* "offers itself on its own to *any human reason* and is, therefore, *found in the religion of most civilized peoples.*"[49] According to Kant, this is the reason most so-called civilized religious traditions have a conception of a triune God. Indeed, in a footnote, Kant offers "the religion of *Zoroaster*," "the *Hindu* religion," "the *Egyptian* religion," and "the *Gothic* religion" as direct examples. More important, however, Kant states that "even the *Jews* seem to have pursued these ideas in the last time periods of their hierarchical constitution."[50] This is so, Kant argues, because they accepted the title of "son of God," but only differed from Christians in their rejection of Jesus as a truthful claimant.[51]

Yet it is not Kant's provocative, if simply ignorant, assertion regarding Jewish theology that concerns me here, but his more discrete proposition that the Jews could be counted as a "civilized" people *only* "in the *last time periods* of their hierarchical constitution," when they supposedly took up the idea of a triune godhead. This is to say—in accordance with Kant's prior declaration—that they were originally uncivilized *because* they lacked such triune theology and were thus *necessarily* without "any human reason." While Kant, *in the end*, agrees that "Christianity arose from Judaism," he does so only within the context of the later history of Judaism when "*this otherwise ignorant people* had already been reached by much foreign (Greek) wisdom."[52] Indeed, "the Greek philosophers' moral doctrines of freedom," Kant contends, "*shocked the slavish mind*" of the Jew.[53] Kant thus notes that such Greek teachings enlightened Judaism and provided it with the morality and autonomous reason necessary to facilitate the coming of Jesus.[54] Indeed, perhaps Kant's most infamous (if not *his most disregarded*)[55] assertion in *Religion* is his categorical assertion that "*Judaism is properly not a religion at all.*"[56] Because the Hebrew Bible supposedly contains no conception of a "future life,"[57] Kant's rather puritan textual reductionism led him to assume Judaism was not ethically but *only* politically situated and thus "*a sum of merely statutory laws*, on which a state constitution was based."[58] Indeed, even the invocation of "the name of God" in the Jewish tradition, according to Kant, does not make Judaism a religion, since in this theocratic context God is "venerated merely as a secular regent who makes no claim at all concerning and upon conscience."[59] Kant thus describes Judaism as "*an irksome* but dominant church faith *devoid of moral aim* (a faith whose *slavish service* can serve as example of any other on the whole *merely statutory faith*, the like of which was universal at that time)."[60]

In the second division of *Religion*, entitled "Historical Presentation of the Gradual Founding of the Dominion of the Good Principle on Earth,"[61] Kant maps out "not only a succession in time, but equally *the ascent of the rational principle toward full self-consciousness*."[62] In this teleological metanarrative, where Christianity ultimately becomes the "*true universal church*,"[63] Kant refuses to admit Judaism *any* historical role in the emergence of such universal religion. Indeed, according to Kant, "the *Jewish* faith stands in no essential connection whatsoever, i.e., in no unity according to concepts, with this . . . history we want to examine."[64]

Given Kant's open opposition to any religious tradition of "statutory faith" as emblematically epitomized in Judaism, it should come as no surprise that Jesus serves in Kant's historical teleology of reason as the founder of "the first true church."[65] According to Kant, Jesus brought only "*pure teachings of reason*."[66] Rather than demanding "the observance of external civic or statutory church duties," like Judaism, Jesus taught that "only the pure moral attitude of the heart shall be able to make a human being pleasing to God."[67] Thus, Kant asserts that Christianity arose as "*a pure moral religion* in place of an ancient cult."[68] Since Christianity was bound "*to no statutes at all*," it contained "*a religion valid for the world*, not for one single people."[69] Thus, in the final section of *Religion* entitled "On the Pseudoservice of God in a Statutory Religion," Kant states:

> The true, sole religion contains nothing but laws, i.e., practical principles of whose unconditional necessity we can become conscious and which we, therefore, acknowledge as revealed through pure reason (not empirically).... Now, to regard this statutory faith (which is in any case restricted to one people and cannot contain the universal world religion) as essential to the service of God in general, and to make it the supreme condition of divine pleasure taken in human beings, is a *religious delusion* the pursuit of which is a *pseudoservice*, i.e., a supposed veneration of God whereby one acts directly contrary to the true service required by God himself.[70]

Indeed, in *Religion*, Kant seldom grows weary of describing Judaism as a "delusional" *because* "slavish" religion mindlessly observing revealed law and tradition in opposition to the pure revelation of reason. In fact, this dualism between statutory bondage and reasoned freedom informs the entire metaphorical language-game of *Religion within the Bounds of Bare Reason*—its framing metaphor equating the human moral predisposition with autonomous "bare rational faith."[71] For Kant, such religion "pure of all statutes, is inscribed in the heart of every human being."[72] By emplotting humanity's progressive liberation from scriptural bondage, Kant puts forth his own teleological salvation history of "bare reason." In perhaps the most iconic passage of *Religion*, Kant thus states:

> *The cloaks* under which *the embryo first formed* itself into the human being *must be cast off* if he is now to step into the light of day. The leading string of holy tradition, with its appendages—the statutes and observances—which in its time rendered good services, is little by little becoming dispensable, indeed in the end a fetter, *when he enters adolescence*. As long as he (the human genus) "was a child, he was astute as a child" *and knew how to combine with statutes—which had been imposed on him without his collaboration. . . . "But now that he becomes a man, he puts away what is childish."*[73]

Here, Kant sounds a clarion call for humanity to divest itself of its religious clothing or "cloaks"—that is, the restraints of traditional "statutes and observances." While such prescriptive veils were necessary in the beginning stages of human history, they must now in humanity's maturity be "cast off" in the naked light of truth.

Of course, commentators are quick to note that in the aforementioned passage Kant refers nearly verbatim to Paul's First Epistle to the Corinthians (13:11): "As long as he (the human genus) 'was a child, he was astute as a child. . . . But now that he becomes a man, he puts away what is childish.'"[74] Yet what has seemingly gone unnoticed is how this passage more broadly echoes chapter four of Paul's Epistle to the Galatians (1–11), which reads:

> My point is this: heirs, as long as they are minors, are no better than slaves, though they are the owners of all the property; but they remain under guardians and trustees until the date set by the father. So with us; *while we were minors, we were enslaved to the elemental spirits of the world. But when the fullness of time had come, God sent his Son, born of a woman, born under the law, in order to redeem those who were under the law*, so that we might receive adoption as children. And because you are children, God has sent the Spirit of his Son into our hearts, crying, "Abba! Father!" *So you are no longer a slave but a child*, and if a child then also an heir, through God.
>
> *Formerly, when you did not know God, you were enslaved to beings that by nature are not gods. Now, however, that you have come to know God*, or rather to be known by God, how can you turn back again to the weak and beggarly elemental spirits? How can you want to be enslaved to them

> again? *You are observing special days, and months, and seasons, and years.* I am afraid that my work for you may have been wasted.[75]

In terms of both tone and import, the beginning of chapter 4 of Galatians is much closer to Kant's passage above, whereas 1 Corinthians 13 addresses the importance of love. In this section of Galatians the problem Paul rails against is that his Christian followers have apparently been observing Jewish law, which he importantly equates with the subservience of *slavery*. Indeed, in Galatians 4:10 above, Paul complains that his followers are observing the Jewish calendar: "You are observing special days, and months, and seasons, and years."[76] As Ursula Goldenbaum notes, in Galatians:

> Paul is eager to draw a sharp line between Jews and Christians, and he does not shy away from abusing Jewish religion and law as incompatible with Christian faith. He calls the Jews "immature"—in obeying their law they were immature children and indistinguishable from servants; in contrast, Christians were led into freedom by Jesus Christ. The law is considered to have served as the "pedagogue," keeping us in line until the appearance of Jesus Christ, but no longer needed once the savior had come and set us free.[77]

In an insightful analysis, Goldenbaum traces how Kant's famous line and thesis "*Enlightenment is man's emergence from his self-incurred immaturity*"[78] that opens his 1784 essay "An Answer to the Question: 'What Is Enlightenment?'" draws upon German Lutheran readings of Galatians as part of a wider debate regarding Jewish emancipation. The policy of the Prussian state "towards Jews in the eighteenth century was characterized by attempts to keep the Jewish community small and their tribute payments high and to limit their economic activities to a few professions."[79] During Kant's day, Jewish disenfranchisement was made worse by Frederick the Great's 1750 *General-Privilegium*, which further limited the freedom of Jews in terms of property rights and trade.[80]

In 1782, only two years prior to Kant's famous essay on enlightenment, Joseph II of nearby Austria granted Jews unprecedented freedom in his Edict of Tolerance, which became the subject of heated debate in Prussia. A year later, Moses Mendelssohn, Kant's most famous Jewish interlocutor, published his treatise *Jerusalem*—a text that would prove seminal to the Jewish Enlightenment by presenting "the Jews as capable of morals, and thus ready to become citizens."[81] On the other side of the debate was the popular Enlightenment theologian Johann Salomo Semler. As Goldenbaum observes, Kant's discourse strikingly echoes that of Semler, who

> contrasted Christian religion, which he saw as universal and moral, with Jewish religion, seen *as particular and political with hardly any morals. Being bound by the Jewish statutory law, Jewish religion could not develop any further and thus remained essentially static*. . . . Christian religion had changed from its early beginning until the present time and it would further change in infinity, *becoming less and less dogmatic and more and more pure in terms of morals*.[82]

Indeed, for Semler, as with Kant, the infinite change that Christianity undergoes amounts to a teleological history where

> no particular Christian dogma could be taken as its essential religious truth. Its true and pure message lay rather hidden in all parts of its doctrine and emerged with increasing clarity throughout history. Only at the end of the world, pure morality would appear as its actual message. . . . *Because the historical process would lead to more and more morality, it would create finally one universal religion of humankind, making all human beings Christians*.[83]

As Goldenbaum notes, "the congruence" between Kant's ideas and those of Semler is "*almost literal*" and she therefore concludes that "there is sufficient evidence as well that Kant found his model for enlightenment in Semler's theology of history."[84] Moreover, Goldenbaum shows that Kant's notion of "immaturity" (*Unmündigkeit*) in his first line of "An Answer to the Question" is similarly derived from a common German Lutheran translation of the beginning of chapter 4 in Paul's Epistle to the Galatians, which I quote above. Thus, Kant's notion of enlightenment, which, according to Goldenbaum, "sees the development of pure morality as a progress within the history of Christianity, thus excluding Jews qua Jews from this process," is indebted to the enlightenment theological discourse of his day, which he first put forth in somewhat coded language in "An Answer to the Question" and then "explicitly states in his *Religion*" nine years later.[85]

While Kant does not use the word "immaturity" in *Religion* as he did in his essay on enlightenment, the notion of a progressive movement from immaturity to enlightened reason forms the millenarianist basis of the entire text. For my purposes here, this teleological evolution is best understood in Kantian terms as a historical progression from religious "heteronomy" to enlightened "autonomy." Although Kant does not use this binary pair in *Religion*, evidence for its logical extension is found in his *Critique of Practical Reason* by way of definition:

> The sensible nature of rational beings in general is their existence under empirically conditioned laws and is thus, for reason, *heteronomy*. The supersensible nature of the same beings, on the other hand, is their existence in accordance with laws that are independent of any empirical condition and thus belong to the *autonomy* of pure reason.[86]

Here, Kant defines "heteronomy" as human "existence under *empirically conditioned laws*"—that is, laws that are sensibly determined through external historical processes as opposed to those morally determined through internal reason. Similarly, in *Religion*, as I quote above, Kant asserts that as a consequence of the human "moral predisposition," religion will "*be detached gradually from all empirical determining bases, from all statutes that rest on history*." It is therefore quite clear that for Kant, positive religions—or what are sometimes referred to as "empirical religion[s]"[87]—are *empirically conditioned* by history and thus heteronomous. As such, Kant's definition of the binary pair autonomy/heteronomy can be directly mapped onto the narrative emplotted in *Religion*, where the heteronomously bound adherents of historical religions (symbolized first and foremost by Jews and Judaism) will naturally progress to enlightened autonomy by denuding their respective religions from "*all empirical determining bases*"—or in another translation, from "*all empirical grounds of determination*."[88] The *telos* of Kant's evolution of religious autonomy is thus attained, as Kant confirms in the same passage, when "the abasing distinction between *laypersons* and *clerics* ceases, and equality arises from true freedom" *because* "everyone obeys the (non-statutory) law that he prescribes to himself."[89] Indeed, this Kantian narrative on the teleological development of religious autonomy has helped to form how "enlightened" religious subjectivity is understood in the secular-liberal tradition. As Susan Meld Shell observes:

> Kantian autonomy ennobles liberal concepts of freedom and equality by grounding them in an objective moral principle—a principle that is deemed to be accessible to all ordinary human beings on the basis of reason alone and *that does not depend on a particular religious dispensation or the blind acceptance of authority*.[90]

The Metaphysics of Nudity in Kant and Schuon

As displayed most clearly in the titular framing metaphor of *Religion within the Bounds of Bare Reason*, as well as in Kant's iconic passage above beginning with

"*The cloaks* under which *the embryo first formed* itself into the human being *must be cast off* if he is now to step into the light of day," Kant employs what Mario Perniola has called a "metaphysics of nudity," which Perniola traces to Greek thought in contrast to a Hebrew "metaphysics of clothing."[91]

Although Perniola is quick to note that neither the Greek nor Hebrew tradition can be reduced to such rigid metaphysical categories, Perniola's insight regarding the Platonic tradition of metaphysical nudity is particularly helpful in my comparison of Kantian and Schuonian language-games, which as I noted above can both be understood as (radically) different interpretations of Platonic idealism situated within a common German Lutheran intellectual history.[92] Thus, as opposed to the symbolism of the ancient Near East, where nakedness was a mark of degradation and shame—and conversely, clothing symbolized divine splendor[93]—the Greek metaphysical perspective understood nudity as "clarity of vision."[94] This idea is fully formed in Plato's conception of truth, as Perniola notes:

> In the myth of the cave, the path that leads to truth moves progressively from a vision of shadows and specular images to the contemplation of ideas. The metaphor of the "*naked*" *truth* comes from a conflation of the concept of truth as visual precision and the idea that eternal forms are the ultimate objects of intellectual vision. From this foundation, the entire process of knowledge becomes an unveiling of the object, a laying it entirely bare and an illumination of all its parts.[95]

Yet, this Platonic metaphysical perspective of nudity takes as its ultimate object the soul and understands the body as an earthly obstacle. Thus, "only when the soul is naked—*psuchē gumnē tou sōmatos*, the soul stripped of the body (*Cratylus* 403b)—does it acquire complete freedom."[96] This idea is echoed in Paul's Epistle to the Colossians: "Put to death, therefore, *whatever in you is earthly* (3:5). . . . These are the ways you also once followed, when you were living that life. But now *you must get rid of all such things*. . . . Do not lie to one another, seeing that you have *stripped off* the old self with its practices (3:9)."[97]

Thus, in *Religion*, Kant echoes such a Christian Platonic metaphysics of nudity through the assertion, quoted above, that the human being's religious "appendages—the statutes and observances"—are "cloaks" of the material world that have been "*imposed on him without his collaboration*" and thus are "a fetter." Now that humanity has matured, such clothing "*must be cast off*"[98] so that the naked truth can be realized. Here, Kant's metaphorics also draw upon the anti-Jewish polemics of German Lutheran theology, thus making Judaism *the* "delusional" archetype of "pseudoservice" that serves no higher purpose than a heteronomous politics of coercion. As Kant writes in *Religion*, the subjects of the original "*Jewish* theocracy" were "attuned to no incentives other than the goods of this world," and thus "were capable of no other laws than partly such as imposed burdensome ceremonies and customs . . . in which an external coercion occurred and which were, therefore, only civil laws, the inside of the moral attitude not being considered at all."[99] Judaism is thus understood as *merely material*—having nothing to do with a pure and universal religion of reason. Thus, as part of Kant's "transcendentally" idealist language-game that sought to overcome epistemological dependence upon the material world through recourse to universal reason, the Jews became a metaphor for "the impurity of empirical reality, of 'matter.'"[100] As Michael Mack notes, it was precisely this Kantian discourse that essentialized "the Jewish as the 'heteronomous'" and thus set the stage for the nineteenth-century German stigmatization of Jews as *nonmodern* and thus politically corruptive.[101]

In his late 1798 work *The Conflict of the Faculties*, Kant once again makes recourse to a metaphysics of nudity in relation to Judaism, stating that although "dreaming of a conversion of all Jews (to Christianity in the sense of a *messianic* faith)"[102] is no longer sensible,[103] still

> we can consider it possible even in their case if, as is now happening, purified religious concepts awaken among them and *throw off the garb* of the ancient cult, which now serves no purpose and even suppresses any true religious attitude.[104]

After calling for Jews to thus *denude* themselves of the "garb" of their traditional observances, Kant goes on to explain that it is only their public acceptance of "the religion of *Jesus*" that would "call attention to them as an educated and civilized people who are ready for all the rights of citizenship and whose faith could also be sanctioned by the government."[105] Thus, Kant concludes:

> *The euthanasia of Judaism* is pure moral religion, *freed from all the ancient statutory teachings*, some of which were bound to be retained in Christianity (as a messianic faith). But this division of sects, too, must disappear in time, leading, at least in spirit, to what we call the conclusion of the great drama of religious change on earth (the restoration of all things), when there will be only one shepherd and one flock.[106]

As may be supposed from Kant's telling call for "the euthanasia of Judaism," it was indeed "partly on the basis of its own Kantian premises that German nationalism emerged as a specifically anti-Jewish movement."[107]

As I noted in my analysis of Schuon's Aryanist discursive practices in chapter 4, while Schuon understood clothing as *"form, or particularity,"*[108] he sacralized nudity as *"a return to the essence, the origin, the archetype, thus to the celestial state."*[109] Schuon's discourse thus strikingly echoes the above Kantian metaphorics and metaphysics of nudity as "pure" truth. Indeed, Schuon summed up his entire metaphysical approach through a metaphorized articulation of the binary between form and essence—that is, a movement away from "the *Religio formalis* [as] the garment" toward "the *Religio perennis* [as] the body."[110]

As I further show in chapter 4, Schuon's metaphorics of nudity, like that of Kant's, is *also* tied to a particular conceptualization of Semitic religious subjectivity. This perspective nostalgically longs for a return to the primordial truth of a "Golden Age" *before* its apparent veiling by Semitic subjectivity. As Schuon states:

> In the origin—in the "Golden Age"—*the truth pure and simple* was saving by itself, and this to a certain extent is the point of view of Platonism; later it was necessary to reveal the aspect most appropriate to its saving effect, and it was thus necessary *to clothe* it in an argument efficacious for certain mentalities, and *this is what the Semitic religions have done.*[111]

While Schuonian Perennialism is thus based on a discourse of decline from an ancient golden age and hope of a palingenetic return to an original state similar to "Platonism,"[112] the Kantian notion of "pure rational religion" is marked by a forward-looking, melioristic vision of history, which Kant himself likened to a "metamorphosis."[113] Yet these polar differences in metaphysical perspective notwithstanding, both Kant and Schuon evince a common metaphorical grammar in which Semitic religious subjectivity represents heteronomy, while a primary basis of "pure" autonomous or objective "truth" is located in "foreign (Greek) wisdom" for Kant and "Platonism" for Schuon.

Kantian Autonomy and the Schuonian Discourse of Relativity

For Kant, the difference between heteronomous and autonomous religion depends on the ability for any religion to be universalized. As Shell notes, for the Jews "to carry out ceremonial rites forever on the basis of an authority that cannot in principle be shared by man is to put heteronomy, as Kant conceives it, at the core of one's faith."[114] In *Religion,* because such heteronomous religion is based on the idea of a God who sends revelation and its attendant laws—and "acquaintance with these laws is possible not through our own bare reason but only through revelation . . . propagated among human beings through tradition or scripture"—then such religion is what Kant describes as merely "a *historical* faith" and "not *a pure rational faith*."[115] Thus, according to Kant, it is "the pure moral legislation" attained through "bare reason" that "is not only *the inescapable condition of all true religion as such, but it is also that which properly constitutes religion itself*, and for which statutory religion can contain only the means to its furtherance and expansion."[116] Historical faiths are therefore for Kant multiple and can have "*different and equally good forms*," while their "statutes, i.e., ordinances regarded as divine, . . . *are chosen and contingent*."[117] In other words, Kant sees outward religious form as relative and not essential. Thus, in his 1795 work *To Perpetual Peace*, Kant famously states:

> *Differences in religion*: an odd expression! Just as if one spoke of different *moralities*. No doubt there can be different kinds of historical *faiths*, though these do not pertain to religion, but only to the history of the means used to promote it, and these are the province of learned investigation; the same holds of different religious *books* (Zendavest, the Vedas, Koran, and so on). But there is only a single *religion*, valid for all men in all times. Those [faiths and books] can thus be nothing more than the accidental vehicles of religion and can only thereby be different in different times and places.[118]

Kant's assertion here, that historical faiths and their scriptures "*can thus be nothing more than the accidental vehicles of religion*," is representative of what Talal Asad has called "the missionary's standpoint."[119] As Asad explains:

> The missionary cannot reform people unless they are persuaded that *the formal ways they live their life are accidental to their being*, channels for which other channels can be substituted without loss. And thus from one religion to another, or from living religiously to living secularly.[120]

As I have alluded to in chapters 3 and 4, an essential component of Schuon's Perennialism is a discourse of "relativity," or what Schuon calls "the principle of relativity,"[121] which I discuss in chapter 3 as an integral ingredient for the coherency of Schuon's logical break with the Aristotelian law of noncontradiction through symbolism and in chapter 4 as another way of expressing Schuon's emblematic notion of "the transcendent unity of religions"—that is, the idea that the contradictory differences among external religious forms are ultimately nonessential to the underlying essence that unifies them.[122] As I noted in chapter 3, Schuon himself asserts that although "Revelations more or less *exclude* one another, this is so of necessity" because God "expresses Himself in an absolute mode" and such absoluteness "concerns the universal content rather than the form, to which it applies only *in a relative* and symbolical sense."[123] As such, Schuon states: "Revelation is absolute in itself, *but relative in its form*."[124]

Indeed, the similarities between Kant and Schuon regarding the so-called relativity of religious form are worth exploring in more detail here. In *Religion*, written two years prior to the aforementioned passage from *To Perpetual Peace*, Kant asserts the following:

> There is only *one* (true) *religion*; but there can be many kinds of *faith*.—One may say, further, that in the various churches, set apart from each other because of the difference in their kinds of faith, one and the same true religion may nonetheless be found.[125]

Here, like Schuon, Kant asserts that in essence, religion is absolute, but in form, it is varied. Thus, Kant goes on to state:

> It is therefore more fitting (as, indeed, it is actually more customary) to say, This human being is of this or that (Jewish, Mohammedan, Christian, Catholic, Lutheran) *faith*, than, He is of this or that religion. The latter expression should properly not be used even in addressing the general public (in catechisms and sermons); for, it is too scholarly and not understandable for them, as indeed the modern languages also do not supply for it any synonymous word. *The common man understands by it always his church faith, which strikes his senses, whereas religion is hidden inwardly and depends on moral attitudes.*[126]

Once again, Kant here makes the distinction between "faith," which he understands as *historically* occurring in various forms, and "religion"—that is, "*the true, sole religion*"—which he understands as "revealed through *pure reason* (not empirically)."[127]

And again, Schuon's language-game, although metaphysically distinct at the level of theory, is functionally identical. As I discussed in chapter 4, "*the ethnic diversity of humanity* and the geographical extent of the earth," according to Schuon, are the sources of "*the need for a plurality of religions*."[128] Schuon thus argues that the idea "of one unique religion for all . . . does not escape contradiction" since it posits an "absoluteness and universality," which opposes "the *necessarily relative character* of all religious mythology."[129] Like Kant's aristocratic "*true, sole religion*" that is only universally revealed through "*pure reason*" but not understood by the "common man," Schuon concludes that "only *pure metaphysics* and *pure prayer* are absolute and therefore *universal*."[130]

Thus, for both Kant and Schuon, the "pure" essence of religion—however individually perceived, either by reason or gnosis (respectively)—is marked by true autonomy, that is, a direct, internal realization of *naked truth* as opposed to an external, heteronomous revelation that is veiled by form. According to this Kantian and Schuonian perspective of autonomy, formal or historical religious traditions are received from outside of the self, and thus indirect and *nonessential.* In both Kant and Schuon, adherence to such heteronomous tradition is understood as ultimately "slavery" to an external form, while religious autonomy is the essence of freedom. Indeed, it is precisely Jewish adherence to heteronomous law and knowledge that, in the eyes of Kant (who as noted above echoes Paul [Galatians 4:1–11]), makes Judaism "that *slavish* faith (in days, confessions, and customs of the service of God)."[131]

In a striking echo of Kant's aforementioned assertions, Schuon similarly proclaims:

> For the Semite, everything begins with Revelation and therefore with faith and submission; man is a priori a believer and consequently a servant: intelligence itself takes on *the color of obedience*. For the Aryan by contrast . . . Revelation is not a commandment that seems to create intelligence ex nihilo while at the same time *enslaving it*, but appears instead as the objectification of the one Intellect, which is at once transcendent and immanent. Intellectual certainty has priority here *over a submissive faith*.[132]

While Semitic intelligence (no matter how divinely inspired) is, for Schuon, *enslaved* by external revelation, "Aryan thought" perceives the universal "nature of things" *itself*.[133] As I discussed in chapter 4, Schuon therefore categorizes Semitic intelligence as passively "subjective" and Aryan thought as naturally in tune with "objective" truth.[134] Here it is important to note that Schuon uses the idea of subjectivity in the common-sense notion of "being dominated by or absorbed in one's personal feelings, thoughts, concerns"[135] and is the antithesis of the Kantian notion of "transcendent subjectivity," which refers to an idealized "thinking subject" as the essential ground of cognition that constitutes objective reality through the universal validity of a priori reason.[136] As Jill Buroker importantly notes, such transcendental subjectivity "is not to be confused with the empirical subjectivity of contingent sensible qualities that vary from individual to individual."[137] Thus, in Kantian terms, Schuon's Semitic "subjectivity" should be understood as *merely* empirical subjectivity that predominantly relies upon *heteronomous* recourse to jurisprudence and ritual practice—what Schuon refers to in *Castes and Races* as a Semitic "*need for external activities.*"[138] In Schuon's deployment, Aryan objectivity "is none other than the truth,"[139] and Christ's "certain Aryan quality" is demonstrated "*in his independence—seemingly 'Greek' or 'Hindu'—toward forms*."[140] Like Kant's notion, quoted above, that Jews were "attuned to no incentives other than *the goods of this world*" and "*capable of no other laws than partly such as imposed burdensome ceremonies and customs*," Schuon claims that the Semitic "style" of Muhammad "*attaches itself meticulously to human things*"[141] and Semitic subjectivity is accidental and thus "*enclosed in a dogma*."[142]

Indeed, Houston Stewart Chamberlain (d. 1927), whose Aryanist discursive practices were compared to those of Schuon in chapter 4, was heavily influenced by Kantian idealist anthropology, going so far as to write an entire book on Kant that quotes from *Religion* as an anti-Semitic and pro-Aryan proof text.[143] In his earlier and more well-known work *Foundations of the Nineteenth Century* discussed in chapter 4, Chamberlain employs the Kantian "idealist" notion of pure religion against so-called Semitic religion:

> Wherever the Semitic spirit has breathed, *we shall meet with . . . materialism*. Elsewhere in the whole world religion is an idealistic impulse . . . but the imperious will [of the Semite] immediately lays hold of every symbol, every profound divination of reflective thought, *and transforms them into hard empirical facts*. And thus it is that with this view of religion *only practical ends are pursued, no ideal ones*.[144]

Here, Chamberlain follows the Kantian language-game of associating Judaism "as a group that has followed not the path of transcendental freedom but that of enslavement to the material world."[145]

Like Kant and Chamberlain, Schuon similarly associates materialism with the typology of the Semite as evinced not only in his aforementioned assertion regarding a Semitic "need for external activities," but also in his description of Muhammad's "Semitic" attachment "to human things" in contradistinction to Jesus's "Aryan" tendency "*toward the idealistic simplification of earthly contingencies*."[146] Thus, Schuon's notion of Aryan "*independence . . . toward forms*" is functionally analogous to Kant's "*autonomy* of pure reason" as separate from empirically conditioned sensibility.[147] Indeed, Schuon notes that the point is not to deny matter, "but *to remove oneself* from its seductive tyranny; *to distinguish in it the archetypal and pure from the accidental and impure*."[148]

Exclusive Inclusivity and the Accidental Nature of Relative Form

As I have shown, both Kant and Schuon display an analogous notion that commitment to an essentialist discourse of religious relativity is indicative of enlightened *autonomy*, while fidelity to a particular revelation and its law is *empirically* subjective and *heteronomous*—what Schuon in exasperation referred to in Ibn 'Arabi as "unintelligible denominationalism."[149] Indeed, even William Chittick himself is not opposed to employing the Schuonian discourse of "relativity" when necessary, such as when he states in his work on Ibn 'Arabi and religious diversity:

> The stress of a given religious community on a specific self-revelation of the Guide brings into existence its hard edges. God's guidance provides a (*relative*) divine justification for focusing on a single manifestation of the unqualified and nondelimited Real and ignoring others. But *to make absolute claims* for a revelation that by nature can only be one of many *brings about a certain imbalance and distortion* that modern-day observers quickly sense.[150]

Chittick's incongruous break with Perennialist antimodern "tradition" through deference here to the outside authority of "modern-day observers" against religious absolutism is telling and seems to be particularly constituted by a contemporary secular-liberal sensibility opposed to religious discourses of exclusivism. His clear Schuonian argument that there can only be "*relative*" and never "*absolute claims* for a revelation" rests on two premises: (1) there are "by nature" many (valid) religions, and (2) making such absolute claims "*brings about a certain imbalance and distortion*."

Since I have shown in detail in the first three chapters of this book that Ibn 'Arabi clearly *did make absolute claims* regarding the supersession of Islam and the Qur'anic abrogation of all previous revelations, I will not belabor these points again here. Rather, I wish to simply point out the unstable and situated logic of such a Schuonian argument for religious "relativity" at work in Chittick's above statement. Although such discourse is mobilized in the name of *inclusive* universalism and the "validity" of all religious laws, it nevertheless paradoxically ends up *excluding* those very same religious laws it ostensibly professes to include by denying the *absolute validity* of any given revelation. In other words, for a universalist insider, Chittick's argument may certainly seem valid, while for a committed (nonuniversalist) adherent of any particular revelation, this same argument would in many (*if not most*) cases be totally invalid. As Hugh Nicholson observes, "The effort to dissociate religion from exclusionary, 'us' versus 'them' relations ends up merely transposing the act of exclusion to a meta-level where the excluded 'other'—in the form of exclusivist theologies—is not immediately recognized."[151]

The work of the Perennialist scholar Reza Shah-Kazemi serves as an even more compelling example of the universalist paradox of *exclusive inclusivism* displayed by Chittick above. In *Paths to Transcendence: According to Shankara,*

Ibn Arabi, and Meister Eckhart, Shah-Kazemi legitimizes his well-rehearsed and oft-repeated Schuonian discourse of relativity—or "transcendence"—through recourse to the authority of both Ibn 'Arabi and Schuon:

> The forms of the traditions may be seen as so many paths leading to a transcendent essence, realized as one by the mystics only at the summit of spiritual realization; short of this summit *the differences between the traditions are to be seen as relative* but nonetheless real on their own level. The forms of the traditions, at one in respect of their single and transcendent essence, are expressions of this essence, and, for this very reason, should be taken seriously as paths leading back to the essence, rather than rejected on the basis of their unavoidable relativity in the face of the Absolute. *This conclusion is in accordance with the principles made explicit by Ibn Arabi . . . and also with the universalist perspective associated chiefly with the name of Frithjof Schuon.*[152]

In his universalist treatise on the Qur'an and interfaith dialogue, *The Other in the Light of the One*, Shah-Kazemi similarly grounds a discourse of relativity within the purview of Ibn 'Arabi and Schuon,[153] attempting to square the circle of what he himself refers to as "the paradoxical combination of particularism and universalism."[154]

In the introduction to *The Other in the Light of the One*, Shah-Kazemi confidently claims "the universalism expounded here upholds as irreducible the differences of outward religious forms, for these differences are seen as divinely sanctioned: they are diverse forms reflecting the principle of divine infinity, *not just accidental expressions of human diversity*."[155] Yet when he attempts to situate Ibn 'Arabi's thought from within such universalism, Shah-Kazemi qualifies his assertion thus:

> The oneness of the message . . . implies a diversity of formal expressions, these expressions not being reducible to each other on the formal plane, *even if they are considered, in their formal aspect, as "accidental" in relation to the "necessary" import of the supra-formal substance.*[156]

Here, Shah-Kazemi offers a typical Schuonian "esoteric" contradiction (conveniently resolved through the discourse of relativity) claiming that while the "formal expressions" of differing religions are indeed absolute and irreducible in relation to each other, *they are also* simultaneously reducible, and thus "accidental," in relation to their common "supra-formal substance"—a substance Shah-Kazemi goes on to identify as "religion as such" in contradistinction to "such and such a religion":

> While such and such a religion is distinct from all others, possessing its own particular rites, laws and spiritual "economy," *religion as such* can be discerned within it and within all religions; *religion as such being the exclusive property of none, as it constitutes the inner substance of all.*[157]

Echoing the selfsame Kantian essentialist discourse of religion as "pure reason" (quoted above)—that is, "There is only *one* (true) *religion*; but there can be many kinds of *faith*"—here Shah-Kazemi's "supra-formal substance" is none other than the unitive *essence* of religion itself (i.e., the *religio perennis*) that underlies all particular religious forms. Thus, in relation to his oft-repeated assertion regarding the simultaneous *absolute* and *accidental* nature of religious form, Shah-Kazemi is simply proposing a hierarchy of perspective, ultimately claiming that in the final comparison with the universal kernel of the *religio perennis*, the diverse particularities of competing religious forms are merely husks and thus *necessarily secondary*. As such, Shah-Kazemi ends up operationalizing Asad's aforementioned description of the "missionary's standpoint"—a standpoint where outward religious forms become "*channels for which other channels can be substituted without loss.*"

While I will return to the implications of Shah-Kazemi's ultimate missionary stance in a moment, it is essential to note that in *The Other in the Light of the One*, Shah-Kazemi continuously struggles with a Schuonian preunderstanding of Ibn 'Arabi's so-called universalism and the subsequent contradictions that follow. For example, immediately after his above assertion regarding the irreducibility of the diverse religions "on the formal plane" and their simultaneous reducibility in terms of a common "supra-formal substance," Shah-Kazemi attempts to conciliate such discursive dissonance by turning once again to the thought of Ibn 'Arabi in relation to the evidential authority of Islamic prophetology:

> One may assert, in accordance with Ibn ʿArabī's hermeneutical principles, that any attempt to abolish or ignore the formal differences between the revelations violates the divine intentionality; the diversity of revelations is divinely willed, and thus deploys rather than contradicts the unity of the message.
>
> The diversity of laws, paths, and rites, however, must not obscure the fact that the religion ordained through the last Prophet is nothing other than *the one religion that was ordained through all previous prophets.*[158]

Shah-Kazemi goes on to argue that for Ibn 'Arabi this "one religion" unites all religious dispensations within a single underlying "substance or principle."[159] Yet, as I have shown throughout this work, to associate such an inclusive and essentializing universalism with Ibn 'Arabi's hermeneutics is a "strong misreading"[160] of the Andalusian Sufi's prophetology and his attendant cosmography of religious difference. Rather than understanding this "one religion . . . ordained through all previous prophets" as a common esoteric core at the heart of all contemporaneous religious dispensations, Ibn 'Arabi clearly assents to the Islamic supersessionist view that Muhammad was *the ultimate* and *only universal* renewer of the primordial "religion of Abraham."[161] Although all previous messengers revealed afresh this primordial religion, for Ibn 'Arabi, it is fully preserved *solely* in the Qur'an, which is the only revelation to remain divinely protected from corruption. Indeed, as I demonstrated in chapters 2 and 3, Ibn 'Arabi adhered to the classical Islamic supersessionist doctrines of abrogation (*naskh*) and textual corruption (*taḥrīf al-naṣṣ*) of pre-Qur'anic revelations.

While Shah-Kazemi admits that for Ibn 'Arabi and other "normative" Sufis, "Islam in the particular sense would indeed be regarded as the most complete religion, *qua* religion, the final, comprehensive and universally binding revelation," he also asserts that these selfsame Sufis simultaneously affirm "the holiness, virtue and truth which are present in principle within other revealed traditions."[162] Yet, because of his reliance on Schuonian preunderstandings, as well as canonical misreadings within the interpretive field of Ibn 'Arabi, Shah-Kazemi's discourse gives way to slippage concerning how "religion" is defined between medieval and modern contexts. As I argued in chapter 1, Ibn 'Arabi defined religion primarily through the concept of obedience and *not* by the modern universalist notion of an underlying religious essence inhering in all revealed religions. Religion, *as such*, for Ibn 'Arabi, was marked by an external continuity of sacred prescriptions revealed by successive prophets beginning with Adam and ending with Muhammad. *As a matter of course*, Ibn 'Arabi affirmed the "holiness, virtue, and truth which are present *in principle* within other revealed traditions," but that says nothing about how he viewed the contemporary salvific efficacy of those traditions. Because all of the previous prophets were ultimately Muhammad's deputies (*nuwwāb*) as I discussed in chapter 2, Ibn 'Arabi certainly understood them to be perennially integral. Yet, *it does not follow*, as I have shown, that Ibn 'Arabi viewed the dispensations that such prophets revealed as similarly integral throughout the course of history. As I demonstrated in chapters 2 and 3, for Ibn 'Arabi, all dispensations other than that of Muhammad have been either entirely abrogated or rendered subject to the conditions of the indemnity tax (*jizya*) prescribed by verse 9:29 of the Qur'an. In either case, it is clear that Ibn 'Arabi understood the religious Other as totally subsumed within the purview of the Prophet

Muhammad and not religiously autonomous. In other words, Ibn ʿArabi's was a totalizing politico-metaphysical discourse, based around a perennial notion of the essence of Muhammad—that is, the "Muhammadan Reality" (*ḥaqīqa muḥammadiyya*)—and *not* a perennial religious essence. Although Shah-Kazemi, who here follows Chittick, importantly emphasizes Ibn ʿArabi's profoundly heteronomous recourse to Islamic law, Shah-Kazemi's and Chittick's attendant assertions that Ibn ʿArabi accepted all contemporaneous religious laws as equally valid *deny the very basis* of his (*universalizing*) Islamic universalism—that is, the absolute particularity of Ibn ʿArabi's heteronomy. That is to say, if each revealed legal tradition from every religion is equally absolute (as such Perennialist scholars claim), then the heteronomous formalities of each tradition are thereby *relativized* and rendered *nonessential.*

Indeed, in the same discussion of "religion as such" (i.e., "the one religion" or the *religio perennis*) referred to above, Shah-Kazemi once more attempts (and here "carefully") to circumvent critiques such as Asad's problematization of the missionary's standpoint—that is, the accusation that he is simply arguing for a notion of inclusive universalism where competing religious forms are *made* accidental and secondary to (ideological) conceptions of an essential unity:

> It must be carefully noted here that this view of a religious essence that at once transcends and abides within all religions *does not in the least imply a blurring of the boundaries between them on the plane of their formal diversity*. Rather, the conception of this "essential religion" presupposes formal religious diversity, regarding it not so much as a regrettable differentiation *but a divinely willed necessity*. . . . Each revealed religion is totally unique—totally "itself"—while *at the same time being an expression of a single, all-encompassing principle which integrates it within religion as such*. Each is thus different from all the others, in form, *and also identical to all the others in essence.*[163]

While the supposed harmony between particularism and unity among religious forms and essence is here (yet again) asserted, Shah-Kazemi's categorical slippage from *nonaccidental*—or "divinely willed necessity"—to "'*accidental*' in relation to the 'necessary' import of the supra-formal substance" exposes an underlying Schuonian discourse of religious authenticity. In his work *Echoes of Perennial Wisdom*, Schuon asserts that "*the essential takes precedence over the accidental*" and "*the Principle takes precedence over its manifestation*—either *by extinguishing it, or by reintegrating it*."[164] Thus, in the above passage, Shah-Kazemi directly echoes Schuon's privileging of religious essence—that is, "*a single, all-encompassing principle*," or the *religio perennis*—over all "accidental" religious forms.

Indeed, only several pages earlier Shah-Kazemi states with no apparent irony:

> *No one interpretation can therefore be put forward as right and true to the exclusion of all others.* One must repeat: to exclude the exclusivist reading is in turn to fall into a mode of exclusivism. Thus, a truly inclusivist metaphysical perspective must recognize the validity of the exclusivist, theological perspective, *even if it must also—on pain of disingenuousness—uphold as more compelling, more convincing, and even more "true," the universalist understanding of Islam.*[165]

Although Shah-Kazemi here begins by claiming the universal validity of all religious subjectivities, he then emphatically asserts that such a claim *must* include exclusivism—yet he does so only to immediately contradict himself in the very next sentence. While he thus claims that no particular interpretation can be said to be "*right and true to the exclusion of all others*," Shah-Kazemi is thereby compelled to admit that his universalist position is "*more compelling, more convincing, and even more 'true'*" than the exclusivist (and now *excluded*) Other. Thus, even Shah-Kazemi's careful attempt to embrace the exclusivist to avoid falling "into a mode of exclusivism" *fails*. Just as Kant's so-called universal religion of autonomous reason must reject heteronomous religious form as "accidental vehicles of religion," so too must Schuonian Perennialists exclusively reject similarly conceived *heteronomy* (i.e., exclusive attachment to particular religious dispensations) as ultimately less "true." As Kant's essentialist religion of "bare reason" (i.e., religion *as such*) ends up being a religion onto itself—that is "the true, *sole religion*"—so too does "*esoterism as such*," that is, the *religio perennis*, as "*the total truth*" for Schuonian Perennialists.[166] As Schuon himself states: "esoterism alone is absolutely monotheistic, it alone recognizing only one religion under diverse forms."[167]

As Wouter Hanegraaff observes, this type of a Perennialist position views exclusivist theologies as representing "'lower' levels in a hierarchy, or stages in a process of evolution towards genuine spiritual insight, which means that they are imperfect."[168] "It is difficult to see," Hanegraaff trenchantly adds, "how this should be distinguished from other forms of exclusivism or, in some cases, dogmatism."[169] Indeed, as Wendy Brown notes:

> The universal tolerates the particular in its particularity, in which the putative universal therefore always appears superior to that unassimilated particular—a superiority itself premised upon the nonreciprocity of tolerance (the particular does not tolerate the universal). It is the disappearance of power in the action of tolerance that convenes the hegemonic as the universal and the subordinate or minoritized as the particular.[170]

Shah-Kazemi's aforementioned special pleading—as *authorized by* a universalism ascribed to Ibn 'Arabi—attempts to argue that all revealed religions are contemporaneously united within one single religious essence, yet his allegiance to Schuonian Perennialism ultimately must disenfranchise nonuniversalist religious Others as less free, that is, (slavishly) attached to the *material* particularities of *relative form*. As Shah-Kazemi states elsewhere: "all 'religions' are true by virtue of the absoluteness of their content, *while each is relative due to the particular nature of its form*."[171] Put in Kantian terms, that which is absolute in all religions—that is, for Schuonians, the underlying transcendent essence of the *religio perennis*—is *pure truth*, yet the particular "statutes and observances" of each religion are secondary and therefore *less* true. Thus, for Schuonian Perennialists, those who heteronomously adhere to the laws of only one religion, while not recognizing the universal validity of the pure truth of other religions, are mired in the materiality of form and thus, *necessarily*, Other.

Conclusion

Throughout this book, I have shown how much of the Schuonian field of interpretation surrounding Ibn 'Arabi has attempted in varying degrees to separate his unitive mysticism from heteronomous modes of religious absolutism and its attendant political cosmography. Yet, rather than a manifestation of an ostensible "cosmic intellect"[172]—an intellect, as James Cutsinger suggests, that is "unaffected by the limitations of historical circumstance"[173]—Schuon's "universalist" cartography clearly bears the burden of his own socio-historical genealogy. This cartographic burden, as I have argued above, can be understood as a hermeneutics of religious autonomy, which finds its full form in the ideas of Kant as carefully systematized in his late work *Religion within the Bounds of Bare Reason*. Although such a hermeneutics has undergone meticulous and subtle refinement within the Schuonian field of interpretation—and especially regarding the thought of Ibn 'Arabi—it is not unique to Schuon or even to Perennialism, but is to be found at the very beginnings of Sufi studies in the West.

Indeed, the first European scholarly article solely dedicated to Sufism strikingly echoes a Kantian metaphysics and metaphorics of autonomy. In "A Treatise on Sufiism" (written in 1811 and published in 1819), Lt. James William Graham of the British East India Company relates that a Sufi may be "*a person of any religion or sect*."[174] Such a "mystery," according to Graham, lies in the fact of the Sufi's "total disengagement" from the sensory world, which entails "*an entire throwing off . . . of the practical mode of worship, ceremonies, &c. laid down in every religion*."[175] Yet, this process of "*throwing off* . . . the practical mode of worship"—what Graham also tellingly refers to as the "*pharisaical mode of worship*"[176]—only happens when the mind of the Sufi is "properly nurtured *and become[s] matured*" through "tuition and due reflection."[177] According to Graham, this marks the first stage of the Sufi path when the mind "*may throw off* those things which it was at first taught to revere, and enter into the view of a sublimer system."[178] It is from the view of this "sublimer system" that "*man arrives to a knowledge of his own nature*" and thus "*may himself then look upon those outward prescribed forms as nugatory*."[179]

Graham's interpretation of Sufism thus faithfully echoes the Kantian discourse of autonomy and its metaphorics of nudity and teleology of universal truth attained by gradually shedding the veils of religious form, which is inevitably associated with Semitic heteronomy—in Graham's words a "*pharisaical mode of worship*." As Carl Ernst has trenchantly noted, when British Orientalists "discovered" the "Sooffees" in the latter half of the eighteenth century in India, the term *Sufi-ism* was invented "as an appropriation of those portions of 'Oriental' culture that Europeans found attractive."[180] In terms of religion, perhaps the particular thing that eighteenth-century Europeans found *most* attractive was their own image. As Pacini observes, such thought marked a "shift from a conception of religion as conformity to the divine order of being to a conception of religion as conformity to the human ordering of ideas."[181] This "modern religion of conscience"—or "looking glass religion"—was based on the Kantian "view of the modern subject whose most enduring trait was its dissociation from the world around it, and what was more, its subsequent transformation of that world into an image of itself."[182]

Thus, in the Copernican cartographic revolution of such a Kantian looking-glass religion, the sanctified perspective of European subjectivity as an invisible "sovereign gaze"—or what Castro-Gómez also refers to as "the power of a *Deus absconditus*"—emerges as universalized truth.[183] Here, Kant's teleology of autonomous religiosity envisions "religion finally to be detached gradually from all empirical determining bases, *from all statutes that rest on history*."[184] In likewise fashion, the mapping strategy of Schuonian Perennialism—which claims an autonomous perspective based on "*the supra-formal substance*" within every religion—purports to transcend (and thereby *have power over*) the accidental, while those beholden to particular religious traditions are unwittingly controlled by such (*relative*) forms. Brown describes such strategic constructions as "*the autonomy of the subject from culture*—the idea that the subject is prior to culture and free to choose culture."[185] It is indeed the conceit of autonomy, and its attendant pretense to *culturelessness*, through which post-Kantian, Euro-American thought has removed itself from the map of history and universalized situated Western epistemology as truth *itself*. Such principles of autonomy continue to be employed in contemporary liberal discourse to legitimate the subordination of culture to the purported universal, while simultaneously perpetuating the claim that the political practice of universalization is not culturally imperialist since "as universals, these principles are capable of 'respecting' particular cultures," while "nonliberal orders themselves represent the crimes of particularism, fundamentalism, and intolerance, as well as the dangerousness of unindividuated humanity."[186]

Under the weight of practices that echo strategies of universalism found from Kant through nineteenth-century Aryanism—strategies that I have shown are embedded within Schuonian Perennialism—Ibn 'Arabi's recourse to revealed law is *tolerated* within Perennialist discourse *only* as long as he is anachronistically understood to "transcend" religious and political rivalry and thus pluralistically acknowledge the contradictory truth claims and practices of other traditions by situating them as *secondary* and *accidental*. This type of distinction between religion and politics is maintained, as Russell McCutcheon points out, by the presence of the "idealist dualism of essence/manifestation."[187] Thus, Kantian and Schuonian idealism both share discursive strategies that claim to pluralistically accept *the essential core* of every religion, but at the ultimate cost of religious and socio-historical *difference*. This approach universalizes an imagined, internal "esoteric" wisdom as primary, thereby dissociating "all connections and associations with larger issues of context, politics, and power."[188]

Denuded of all trace of historical particularity, autonomy thus becomes a modern marker of religious, ethnoracial, and civilizational superiority, while heteronomy represents those inferior Others still epistemologically encumbered by their own socio-historical garb. David Theo Goldberg has referred to such a metanarrative of Othering as "racial historicism," which "elevates Europeans and their (postcolonial) progeny over primitive or undeveloped Others as a victory of History, of historical progress, even as it leaves open the possibility of those racial Others to historical development."[189] Such racial historicism can be likened to what Ashwani Sharma has referred to as "whiteness as 'absent presence,'" which "seeks to stand for and be a measure of all humanity. *It operates as a universal point of identification that strives to structure all social identities.*"[190] Indeed, drawing on Emmanuel Levinas's philosophical defense of heteronomy and his notion of "ontological imperialism,"[191] Robert Young notes:

> In Western philosophy, when knowledge or theory comprehends the other, then the alterity of the latter vanishes as it becomes part of the same. . . . In all cases the other is neutralized as a means of encompassing it: ontology amounts to a philosophy of power, an egotism in which the relation with the other is accomplished through its assimilation into the self.[192]

Such a universalizing ontology of the self, as Gilles Deleuze and Félix Guattari note, can be understood as a mode of "European racism" that "never detects the particles of the other," but rather "propagates waves of sameness until those who resist identification have been wiped out (or those who only allow themselves to be identified at a given degree of divergence)."[193] Indeed, the debate about Jewish emancipation in nineteenth-century Germany discussed above was fueled by a project rooted within Kantian universalism and such an imposition of *sameness*. Because Jews were perceived as lacking the Kantian ideal of autonomous religious subjectivity, they were "excluded from an idealist body politic."[194] To become a member of the modern German state, Jews needed to "lose their otherness"[195]—that is, *to shed their clothes of historical difference*, in Kantian terms.

Thus, in both Kant and Schuon, calls to *cast off* religious form are tied to the assumed superiority of an imagined "white" European autonomous subjectivity—what Brown calls "the fiction of the autonomous individual"[196]—over and against a purported "slavish" heteronomy of Semitic religious subjectivity. Such clear discourse conflating autonomy with racial superiority is thus a stark and ironic indication that Kantian and Schuonian so-called modes of "pure" universalism and "objectivity" are in fact quite the opposite—that is, historically situated European presuppositions regarding what counts as authentically religious.

While Ibn 'Arabi enunciated a *universalizing* discourse of abrogation and the supersession of Islam over all other religions, both Schuon and Kant posited a universal religious essence or disposition accessible to all human consciousness and thus imagined their respective universalisms to be free of religious exclusivism and prejudice.[197] Yet, as I have shown in chapter 4, Schuon understood that his divinely inspired "message" of the *religio perennis* was out of all religions the only true "monotheistic" way of knowing God, rising above the confusion of belief and the passivity of faith."[198] As such, Schuon replaced the Muhammadan *Logos* with the Virgin Mary, who as the representative of the *religio perennis* holds "celestial supremacy" and "spiritual and cosmic supereminence."[199] Likewise, Kant understood his ostensibly Christian, universal religion of autonomous morality to be superior to all "historical" religions—thus claiming "*pure rational religion ultimately to rule over all*." Indeed, Kant's final call for the "euthanasia of Judaism" (as quoted above) through an inner conversion to "pure moral religion" was, according to Paul Rose, "in effect nothing more than a secularization of the old Christian idea that the Old Testament and the Jewish religion had been superseded by the New Testament and Christianity."[200]

Thus, in ironically similar ways to the absolute religious discourse of Ibn 'Arabi, Kant and Schuon offer their own versions of abrogative supersessionism. Yet unlike Ibn 'Arabi, their discourse is additionally racialist in particularly modern terms.[201] Where, as I have shown, Ibn 'Arabi is discursively open about his religious exclusivism, Kant and Schuon conceal theirs within so-called universal discourses that claim to holistically include all (*true*) religions by acknowledging their essential core. In the face of such schemas that obscure and thus naturalize their exclusivist presuppositions, Kantian and Schuonian universal assertions can only be construed as ideological.[202] The radical incongruity inherent within these discourses further calls into question the entire premise of religious universalism and the possibility of nonexclusivist religious identity. These paradoxical inconsistencies are indeed a confirmation (of the postmodern truism) that exclusivism is inherent within the construction of any claim to truth. Thus, in discussing such contradictions in other related examples of universalist theology, Nicholson observes that "the entirety of religious discourse and practice . . . *would appear to be implicated, either directly or indirectly, in relations of religious rivalry*."[203]

Just as Castro-Gómez argues that the universal taxonomical categories that emerged in the sixteenth century were the products of local European epistemology in the service of imperial designs, Kant's own discourse of universalism "pertains not," as Hunter puts it, "to universal truth, but to *a particular regional way* of acceding to truth as 'universal.' "[204] Such regional particularity is especially significant in the face of Kant's (and by extension Schuon's) embedded racism.[205] Thus, as Emmanuel Eze notes, the Kantian universal idea of pure human reason "colonizes humanity by grounding the particularity of the European self as center even as it denies the humanity of others."[206]

In the end, it would seem that both Kantian and Schuonian thought reflect the cartographic approach of early modern European imperialism and its attendant ideological conceit of a universal perspective that claims to transcend its own ethnocentric situatedness. It is precisely the discursive practices and grammar of this larger Eurohegemonic conceptual lineage of universalism—*along with its attendant religious, racial, and civilizational superiority*—that Schuonian Perennialism inherits and naturalizes within its interpretive field. While this study has shown that Ibn 'Arabi's mysticism was heteronomously constituted by his religious tradition and intellectual lineage, it has also shown that the modern Western conceit of "religion" as a universally transcendent essence cannot exist in vacuo. Although the long-standing European discursive tradition of autonomy claims a universal "empty" space, it would appear that not only nature but also the *nature of human discursivity* abhors such emptiness. "All knowledge," as Young warns, "may be variously contaminated, implicated in its very formal or 'objective' structures."[207] Indeed, as the history of European epistemology shows—and the Schuonian discourses on Ibn 'Arabi in the foregoing chapters corroborate—it is none other than the self-image of Western subjectivity that so often fills the void left by the transcendence it claims to have attained.[208]

Notes

PROLOGUE

1. Jorge Luis Borges, "On Exactitude in Science," in *Collected Fictions*, trans. Andrew Hurley (London: Penguin, 1999), 325.
2. A veritable cottage industry has arisen on this question, spearheaded by a debate that ran through most of the 1980s between Robert A. Segal and Donald Wiebe on one side and Daniel Pals on the other. This conversation thus served as the basis for the work of the theorist Russell T. McCutcheon, beginning with his *Manufacturing Religion: The Discourse on Sui Generis Religion and the Politics of Nostalgia* (New York: Oxford University Press, 1997). On the lengthy debate between Segal, Wiebe, and Pals see, for example, Robert Segal, "In Defense of Reductionism," *Journal of the American Academy of Religion* 51, no. 1 (1983): 97–124; Daniel Pals, "Is Religion a Sui Generis Phenomenon?," *Journal of the American Academy of Religion* 55, no. 2 (1987): 259–82; and Robert A. Segal and Donald Wiebe, "Axioms and Dogmas in the Study of Religion," *Journal of the American Academy of Religion* 57, no. 3 (1989): 591–605. See also Timothy Fitzgerald, *The Ideology of Religious Studies* (New York: Oxford University Press, 2000); and more recently William E. Arnal, Willi Braun, and Russell T. McCutcheon, eds., *Failure and Nerve in the Academic Study of Religion: Essays in Honor of Donald Wiebe* (Sheffield: Equinox Publishing, 2012).
3. Talal Asad, *Genealogies of Religion: Discipline and Reasons of Power in Christianity and Islam* (Baltimore: Johns Hopkins University Press, 1993), 29.
4. Norman Malcolm, *Wittgenstein: A Religious Point of View?*, ed. Peter Winch (Ithaca, NY: Cornell University Press, 1994), 82 (emphasis mine).
5. While the two terms are commonly used synonymously, Traditionalism is sometimes used to specifically designate the school of René Guénon, while Perennialism that of Frithjof Schuon. See Setareh Houman, *From the* Philosophia Perennis *to*

American Perennialism, trans. Edin Q. Lohja (Chicago: Kazi Publications, 2014), 8. The concept of a perennial philosophy (*philosophia perennis*) was first introduced by Agostino Steuco (d. 1548) in his work *De perenni philosophia* (1540). Although a Catholic bishop who served as the librarian at the Vatican Library, Steuco adhered to a type of "Platonic monism" and believed that true theology "is nothing other than the revealed truth which has been known to mankind from the earliest times." Charles B. Schmitt, "Perennial Philosophy: From Agostino Steuco to Leibniz," *Journal of the History of Ideas* 27, no. 4 (1966): 515, 518.

6. As Seyyed Hossein Nasr observes: "for Schuon religion is the principle [*sic*] reality of human existence not to be reduced to any other category although it is related to all other categories and domains of human thought and action." Seyyed Hossein Nasr, introduction to *The Essential Writings of Frithjof Schuon*, by Frithjof Schuon, ed. Seyyed Hossein Nasr (New York: Amity House, 1986), 4.
7. Jonathan Z. Smith, *Map Is Not Territory: Studies in the History of Religions* (Chicago: University of Chicago Press, 1993), 289–309.
8. Ibid., 309 (emphasis mine).
9. Wright's confessed "transgressive" reading of J. Z. Smith is that Smith's prominent criticism of Mircea Eliade should not be understood as "a wholesale rejection . . . of a Romantic approach to the academic study of religions," but rather an exchange of a different kind—that is, "Smith's Wordsworthian mode of epiphanic reflection for Eliade's late German Romantic mode of hierophanic or theophanic experience." Peter Matthews Wright, "After Smith: Romancing the Text When 'Maps Are All We Possess,'" *Religion and Literature* 42, no. 3 (2010): 95, 100.
10. Ibid., 108.
11. As Wright notes, "If there is a distinction to be made between scholar and adherent it is that the cartography of the scholar of religions after Smith represents an order of *mythography*: that is, a *critical* compilation of myths ('mythography')." Ibid., 108 (emphasis mine).
12. Mark Quentin Gardiner and Steven Engler demarcate three levels of mapping in religious studies: (1) the "zero-order" map of believers; (2) the "first-order" map, which "consists of what scholars say or write about the religions that they study"; and (3) the "second-order" map, which "consists of what scholars say or write about 'religion' in general, including their representations of the work of other scholars of religion." Mark Quentin Gardiner and Steven Engler, "Charting the Map Metaphor in Theories of Religion," *Religion* 40 (2010): 5–6.
13. As Eliade asserted, the authentic, scholarly hermeneutics of humanism "is more than instruction, it is also a spiritual technique susceptible of modifying the quality of existence itself. This is true above all for the historico-religious hermeneutics. A good history of religions book ought to produce in the reader an action of *awakening*." Mircea Eliade, *The Quest: History and Meaning in Religion* (Chicago: University Of Chicago Press, 1984), 62.

14. Steven M. Wasserstrom, *Religion after Religion: Gershom Scholem, Mircea Eliade, and Henry Corbin at Eranos* (Princeton, NJ: Princeton University Press, 1999), 97 (emphasis original). See also McCutcheon, *Manufacturing Religion*, 37–42, 70, passim.
15. Nasr, introduction to *The Essential Writings*, 16 (emphasis mine).
16. Alfred Korzybski, *Science and Sanity: An Introduction to Non-Aristotelian Systems and General Semantics* (New York: Institute of General Semantics, 1994), 58 (emphasis original).
17. William H. Starbuck, *The Production of Knowledge: The Challenges of Social Science Research* (Oxford: Oxford University Press, 2006), 13.
18. Milton C. Sernett, "Believers as Behavers: Religion and Group Identity," in *Introduction to the Study of Religion*, ed. T. William Hall (New York: Harper and Row, 1978), 220.
19. Ernesto Laclau, "Universalism, Particularism, and the Question of Identity," *October* 61 (1992): 87.
20. Ibid., 85.
21. James Cutsinger, introduction to *Frithjof Schuon, Splendor of the True: A Frithjof Schuon Reader*, ed. and trans. James S. Cutsinger (Albany: State University of New York Press, 2013), xxxii (emphasis mine).
22. Ibid., xxxv (emphasis mine).
23. I should note here that part of my aim in this book is to problematize such definitions of "gnosis"—a definition that seemingly echoes a post-Kantian obsession with autonomy, be it of Platonic intellect or Kantian reason. Rather than transcending heteronomy, I argue that such knowledge is always constituted *through* it.

INTRODUCTION

1. Naoki Sakai, "Modernity and Its Critique: The Problem of Universalism and Particularism," in *Postmodernism and Japan*, ed. Masao Miyoshi and H. D. Harootunian (Durham, NC: Duke University Press, 1989), 98.
2. Bulent Rauf quoted in Suha Taji-Farouki, *Beshara and Ibn 'Arabi: A Movement of Sufi Spirituality in the Modern World* (Oxford: Anqa Publishing, 2007), 98.
3. This problem has continued since the Orientalist creation of the term "Sufism" itself, where, as Carl Ernst recently notes, Sufis served as "something of a cipher, reflecting back the European concepts that early Orientalism could not avoid." Carl W. Ernst, "Early Orientalist Concepts of Sufism" (Paper given at the Dinshaw J. Irani Memorial Lectures, No. 2, K. R. Cama Oriental Institute, Mumbai, July 19, 2016), 25.
4. As Richard King observes, "Sustained scholarly conversation about 'religion' is itself what constitutes the field of the study of religion." Richard King, "The Copernican Turn in the Study of Religion," *Method and Theory in the Study of Religion* 25 (2013): 145.

5. Walter D. Mignolo, *The Darker Side of the Renaissance: Literacy, Territoriality, and Colonization* (Ann Arbor: University of Michigan Press, 1995), 237 (emphasis mine).
6. Alfred Korzybski, *Science and Sanity: An Introduction to Non-Aristotelian Systems and General Semantics* (New York: Institute of General Semantics, 1994), 58.
7. Mignolo, *The Darker Side*, 237.
8. Jean Baudrillard, *Simulacra and Simulation*, trans. Sheila Faria Glaser (Ann Arbor: University of Michigan Press, 1994), 1.
9. Léon Marillier, "The Primitive Objects of Worship," in *The International Monthly*, vol. 2 (Burlington, VT: Macmillan Company, 1900), 470. The "universalizing religions" are commonly identified as Buddhism, Christianity, and Islam; for example, see Milton C. Sernett, "Believers as Behavers: Religion and Group Identity," in *Introduction to the Study of Religion*, ed. T. William Hall (New York: Harper and Row, 1978), 218.
10. See C. T. Lewis and C. S. Short, "ūnĭversus," *A Latin Dictionary* (Oxford, 1958), 1933.
11. Marshall G. S. Hodgson, *The Venture of Islam: Conscience and History in a World Civilization*, vol. 1 (Chicago: University of Chicago Press, 1974), 125.
12. Frithjof Schuon, *Light on the Ancient Worlds* (Bloomington, IN: World Wisdom, 2006), 120.
13. Emmanuel Levinas, *Totality and Infinity: An Essay on Exteriority*, trans. Alphonso Lingis (The Hague: Martinus Nijhoff Publishers, 1979), 242.
14. Ibid.
15. As Robert Young puts it, "The other is neutralized as a means of encompassing it: ontology amounts to a philosophy of power, an egotism in which the relation with the other is accomplished through its assimilation into the self." Robert J. C. Young, *White Mythologies: Writing History and the West*, 2nd ed. (London: Routledge, 2004), 45.
16. Ulrich Beck, "The Truth of Others: A Cosmopolitan Approach," *Common Knowledge* 10, no. 3 (2004): 433.
17. David Martin, *Religion and Power: No Logos without Mythos* (Farnham: Ashgate Publishing, 2014), 178 (emphasis mine).
18. Mignolo, *The Darker Side*, 225.
19. For example, R. C. Zaehner, *Mysticism Sacred and Profane: An Inquiry into Some Varieties of Praeternatural Experience* (New York: Oxford University Press, 1961); Steven Katz, ed., *Mysticism and Philosophical Analysis* (New York: Oxford University Press, 1978); Wayne Proudfoot, *Religious Experience* (Berkeley: California University Press, 1985); Talal Asad, *Genealogies of Religion: Disciplines and Reasons of Power in Christianity and Islam* (Baltimore: Johns Hopkins University Press, 1993); McCutcheon, *Manufacturing Religion*; Timothy Fitzgerald, *The Ideology of Religious Studies* (New York: Oxford University

Press, 2000); Richard King, *Orientalism and Religion: Postcolonial Theory, India and 'The Mystic East'* (London: Routledge, 2002); and Daniel Dubuisson, *The Western Construction of Religion: Myths, Knowledge, and Ideology* (Baltimore: Johns Hopkins University Press, 2003).

20. Tomoko Masuzawa, *The Invention of World Religions: Or, How European Universalism Was Preserved in the Language of Pluralism* (Chicago: University of Chicago Press, 2005), 316n6.
21. Ibid., 316.
22. Wouter Hanegraaff calls this position the "religionist perspective," which he associates with Schuonian Perennialism and the "transcendent unity of religions." See Wouter J. Hanegraaff, *New Age Religion and Western Culture: Esotericism in the Mirror of Secular Thought* (Leiden: E. J. Brill, 1996), 5n17, 52n38. Regarding the presence of Traditionalist thought in current modalities of Islamic studies generally, see Carl W. Ernst, "Traditionalism, the Perennial Philosophy, and Islamic Studies," *Middle East Studies Association Bulletin* 28, no. 2 (1994): 176–81; and Setareh Houman, *From the* Philosophia Perennis *to American Perennialism*, trans. Edin Q. Lohja (Chicago: Kazi Publications, 2014), 377–83.
23. Nasr, introduction to *The Essential Writings*, 2 (emphasis mine).
24. Following Talal Asad and Walter Mignolo, I use the terms "Western" and "the West" throughout this study to signify a critical ideological construct of modernity. As Asad notes, even though the West is not a "verifiable" object or integrated totality, it remains a global signifier for "innumerable intentions, practices, and discourses" that relate to a unique historicity claiming to be "the universal civilization." More specifically, "the West," according to Mignolo, "refers to an economic and ideological configuration centered on capitalism, Christianity, and whiteness." Asad, *Genealogies of Religion*, 18–19; and Mignolo, *The Darker Side*, 435.
25. James Winston Morris, "Ibn 'Arabi in the 'Far West,'" *Journal of the Muhyiddin Ibn 'Arabi Society* 24 (2001): 106, 106n23.
26. See William Chittick, "Rūmī and *waḥdat al-wujūd*," in *Poetry and Mysticism in Islam: The Heritage of Rūmī*, ed. Amin Banani, Richard Hovannisian, and Georges Sabagh (New York: Cambridge University Press, 1994), 71, 75, 87, passim.
27. For example, see Éric Geoffroy, *Introduction to Sufism: The Inner Path of Islam* (Bloomington, IN: World Wisdom, 2010), 184, 187. See also Thierry Zarcone, "Rereadings and Transformations of Sufism in the West," *Diogenes* 47, no. 187 (1999): 116; and Houman, *From the* Philosophia Perennis, 215.
28. Under the Muslim name of ʿIsa Nūr ad-Dīn, Schuon headed a European branch of the Shādhiliyya-ʿAlāwiyya *ṭarīqa* founded by Ahmad al-ʿAlāwī in Mostaganem, Algeria, which he would later change to the ʿAlāwiyya Maryamiyya in the mid-1960s in response to his alleged visions of the Virgin Mary. See Mark J. Sedgwick, "The 'Traditionalist' Shâdhiliyya in the West: Guénonians and Schuonians," in *Une*

voie soufie dans le monde: la Shâdhiliyya, ed. Éric Geoffroy (Paris: Maisonneuve & Larose, 2005), 461–64.

29. Seyyed Hossein Nasr, "Frithjof Schuon and the Islamic Tradition," in *The Essential Sophia*, ed. Seyyed Hossein Nasr and Katherine O'Brien (Bloomington, IN: World Wisdom, 2006), 258.
30. William Stoddart, introduction to *The Timeless Relevance of Traditional Wisdom* by M. Ali Lakhani (Bloomington, IN: World Wisdom, 2010), xiv.
31. Schuon, *Light on the Ancient Worlds*, 120.
32. I define theomonism in chapter 1 as "the comprehension of the divine through the non-dual prism of a universal being that is self-manifesting within both creation and human consciousness." See p. 30 and chap. 1, n. 57.
33. Wouter J. Hanegraaff, "Tradition," *Dictionary of Gnosis and Western Esotericism*, ed. Wouter J. Hanegraaff (Leiden: Brill, 2006), 1133.
34. Ananda K. Coomaraswamy, "Eastern Wisdom and Western Knowledge," *Isis* 34, no. 4 (1943): 359.
35. Seyyed Hossein Nasr, *Sufi Essays* (Albany: State University of New York Press, 1991), 146 (emphasis mine).
36. Ibid., 146–47.
37. As Shah-Kazemi notes, his approach takes the Schuonian "principle of the 'transcendent unity of religions' . . . as one of its main points of departure." Reza Shah-Kazemi, *The Other in the Light of the One: The Universality of the Qur'ān and Interfaith Dialogue* (Cambridge: Islamic Texts Society, 2006), xvii–xviii, xvii n14.
38. Shah-Kazemi also asserts that his position can "be characterised as 'universalist': a position which shares with pluralism the basic premise that the major religious traditions are valid paths to salvation, but parts company with the pluralist in asserting that this salvific efficacy stems from the fact that these religions are divinely revealed, not humanly constructed." Shah-Kazemi, *The Other in the Light*, xxiv. See also Reza Shah-Kazemi, "The Metaphysics of Interfaith Dialogue: Sufi Perspectives on the Universality of the Quranic Message," in *Paths to the Heart: Sufism and the Christian East*, ed. James S. Cutsinger (Bloomington, IN: World Wisdom, 2002), 140–89.
39. Shah-Kazemi, *The Other in the Light*, 52, 140–209.
40. Mohammad Hassan Khalil, *Islam and the Fate of Others: The Salvation Question* (Oxford: Oxford University Press, 2012), 13, 20.
41. Ibid., 66.
42. Ibn al-ʿArabī, *Fuṣūṣ al-ḥikam*, ed. Abul Ela Affifi (Beirut: Dar al-Kitab al-ʿArabi, 1966), 94; see also Ibid., 169.
43. This threefold model is the usual typology used within studies on religious pluralism. Originally formulated by Alan Race, it was further developed by Gavin D'Costa. See Alan Race, *Christians and Religious Pluralism* (London: SCM Press, 1983); and Gavin D'Costa, *Theology and Religious Pluralism: The Challenge of Other Religions*

(Oxford: Blackwell, 1986). See also Marianne Moyaert, *Fragile Identities: Towards a Theology of Interreligious Hospitality* (Amsterdam: Rodopi, 2011), 14n3.

44. Khalil, *Islam*, 7, 11, 12.
45. According to Khalil, inclusivists "affirm that theirs is the path of Heaven but hold that sincere outsiders who could not have recognized it as such will be saved," while pluralists "assert that, regardless of the circumstances, there are several religious traditions or interpretations that are equally effective salvifically." In this schema inclusivists limit the ability of the religious Other to be saved more than pluralists do, since the latter categorically recognize other religions as equally salvific. Yet, according to Khalil, liberal inclusivists "assert that the category of sincere non-Muslims includes individuals who have been exposed to the message in its true form yet are in no way convinced. . . . For liberal inclusivists, if the message were never seen to be a possible source of divine guidance, it would make little sense to speak of a sincere response." See Khalil, *Islam*, 7, 11, 12, 55.
46. As Khalil states: "whereas various versions of this classification system concern truth claims, mine is strictly soteriological; whereas most define, for example, 'pluralists' as those who hold multiple religions to be equally salvific and equally true ontologically, I define 'pluralists' *simply as those who hold multiple religions to be equally salvific*." Khalil, *Islam*, 152n23 (emphasis mine).
47. Ibid., 55 (emphasis original).
48. See Ibn al-ʿArabī, *Fuṣūṣ al-ḥikam*, 178, 113.
49. For example, see Geoffroy, *Introduction to Sufism*, 184.
50. Muḥyī al-Dīn Ibn ʿArabī, *al-Futūḥāt al-makkiyya*, vol. 2 (Beirut: Dār Ṣādir, 2004), 36 (Fut. I, 405).
51. For example, see pp. 35–36, 55–56, and 109–113.
52. Khalil, *Islam*, 67.
53. William C. Chittick, *Imaginal Worlds: Ibn al-ʿArabī and the Problem of Religious Diversity* (Albany: State University of New York Press, 1994), 155 (emphasis mine).
54. Khalil, *Islam*, 67.
55. For a unique treatment that briefly discusses the potential soteriological implications of Ibn 'Arabi's accusations of Jews and Christians as "people of calumny, heresy, and misguidance" see Mahmoud al-Ghorab, "Muhyiddin Ibn al-ʿArabi amidst Religions (*adyân*) and Schools of Thought (*madhâhib*)," in *Muhyiddin Ibn 'Arabi: A Commemorative Volume*, ed. Stephen Hirtenstein and Michael Tiernan (Shaftesbury: Element, 1993), 222.
56. Ibn ʿArabī, *al-Futūḥāt*, vol. 1, 182 (Fut. I, 145).
57. Ibid. See pp. 73, 82, 101.
58. Sayafaatun Almirzanah, *When Mystic Masters Meet: Towards a New Matrix for Christian-Muslim Dialogue* (New York: Blue Dome, 2011), 213.
59. Hugh Nicholson, *Comparative Theology and the Problem of Religious Rivalry* (New York: Oxford University Press, 2011), 11 (emphasis mine).

60. See Jane Clark and Stephen Hirtenstein, "Establishing Ibn 'Arabī's Heritage First findings from the MIAS Archiving Project," *Journal of the Muhyiddin Ibn 'Arabi Society* 52 (2012): 1.
61. The fullest account of Ibn 'Arabi's biography is Claude Addas, *Quest for the Red Sulphur: The Life of Ibn 'Arabī*, trans. Peter Kingsley (Cambridge: Islamic Texts Society, 1993). Originally published as *Ibn 'Arabī ou La quête du Soufre Rouge* (Paris: Gallimard, 1989). However, Addas's following shorter work, *Ibn 'Arabi: The Voyage of No Return*, trans. David Streight (Cambridge: Islamic Texts Society, 2000) [Originally published as *Ibn Arabî et le voyage sans retour* (Paris: Seuil, 1996)], includes the previously unknown biographical account found in Ibn Shaʿār, *'Uqūd al-jumān* (15–16), which was first discussed by Gerald Elmore. See Gerald T. Elmore, "New Evidence," *Journal of the American Oriental Society* 117, no. 2 (1997): 347–49; and *Islamic Sainthood in the Fullness of Time: Ibn al-'Arabī's Book of the Fabulous Gryphon* (Leiden: Brill, 1999), 26–27.
62. Elmore, *Islamic Sainthood*, 20, 26.
63. That is, the Seal of Muhammadan Sainthood (*khātam al-walāya al-muḥammadiyya*) and the principle manifestation of the Muhammadan Reality (*ḥaqīqa muḥammadiyya*) on Earth. As Michel Chodkiewicz notes, Ibn 'Arabi understood his function as the Muhammadan Seal to be the historical manifestation of "the most inward and most fundamental aspect of the Muḥammadan Reality which is the source of all *walāya*." Michel Chodkiewicz, *Seal of the Saints: Prophethood and Sainthood in the Doctrine of Ibn 'Arabī*, trans. Liadain Sherrard (Cambridge: Islamic Texts Society, 1993), 125.
64. Addas, *Quest*, 44–45, 97–98.
65. Addas, *Ibn 'Arabi*, 17.
66. Ibid., 74–76.
67. Addas, *Quest*, 254–56.
68. In translating *Fuṣūṣ* as *Ring Stones*, I follow Caner Dagli, who points out that it is quite clear both in Ibn 'Arabi's usage and lexicographically that the Arabic term *faṣṣ* denotes the gem or signet that is placed within the bezel and not the bezel itself. See Caner K. Dagli, trans., *The Ringstones of Wisdom* (*Fuṣūṣ al-ḥikam*), by Ibn Al-ʿArabī (Chicago: Great Books of the Islamic World, 2004), 127n12. See also See Edward William Lane, *An Arabic-English Lexicon* (1877; reprint, New Delhi: J. Jetley, 1985), 2403.
69. Addas, *Ibn 'Arabi*, 117–18.
70. Hayden White, *Tropics of Discourse: Essays in Cultural Criticism* (Baltimore: Johns Hopkins University Press, 1978), 88 (emphasis original).
71. Seyyed Hossein Nasr, *An Introduction to Islamic Cosmological Doctrines: Conceptions of Nature and Methods Used for Its Study by the Ikhwān al-Ṣafā', Al-Bīrūnī, and Ibn Ṣīnā* (Bath: Thames and Hudson, 1978), 267.
72. Ibid.

73. Corbin believed the term "Arab" should be rejected entirely when referring to Ibn ʿArabi because of his spiritual connection with the Iranian wisdom of Suhrawardī and Shīʿism in opposition to "Averroism." As such, Corbin constructs his metanarrative of Ibn ʿArabi as "a living exemplification of Suhrawardī's 'Recital of Occidental Exile.'" According to Corbin, both Ibn ʿArabi and Rumi "are inspired by the same theophanic sentiment," and their spiritual lineages "converge toward the symbol of an identical archetype." Henry Corbin, *Alone with the Alone: Creative Imagination in the Sūfism of Ibn ʿArabī*, trans. Ralph Manheim (Princeton, NJ: Princeton University Press, 1998), 16–20, 67, 71, 110. Originally published as *L'Imagination créatrice dans le Soufisme d'Ibn ʿArabî* (Paris: Flammarion, 1958).
74. Corbin, *Alone with the Alone*, 67 (emphasis mine).
75. Within the Protestant and Enlightenment traditions, Judaism is often denigrated for its "legalism" *because* of its supposed (unreflective) focus on *works* of external obedience over an assumed superior mode of reasoned *faith*. "Lacking any immediate relationship with God, Jews and Judaism must compensate for this with the letter, mere form, body, outward religion and ceremonialism—all negative counterparts of the Enlightenment's ideal: spirit, inwardness, spontaneous ethics and private religion." Anders Gerdmar, *Roots of Theological Anti-Semitism: German Biblical Interpretation and the Jews, from Herder and Semler to Kittel and Bultmann* (Leiden: Brill, 2009), 579. As Hamid Algar trenchantly notes, "when reading the works of Corbin, one cannot fail to be reminded of the theories of bygone Orientalists such as Comte Arthur de Gobineau and Max Horten who attempted to analyze the intellectual history of Islam in terms of a putative clash between Aryan (=Iranian) and Semite (=Arab). Corbin transferred the dichotomy from the biological to the spiritual plane." Hamid Algar, "The Study of Islam: The Work of Henry Corbin," *Religious Studies Review* 6, no. 2 (1980): 89. In the conclusion to this book, I trace the larger context of such European biases through the Kantian categorization of heteronomy and his characterization of Judaism as its perfect symbol.
76. Stephen Schwartz, *The Other Islam: Sufism and the Road to Global Harmony* (New York: Doubleday, 2008), 63.
77. See Alexander Knysh, "Historiography of Sufi Studies in the West," in *A Companion to the History of the Middle East*, ed. Youssef M. Choueiri (Malden, MA: Blackwell Publishing, 2005), 108–18.
78. Schwartz, *The Other Islam*, 23.
79. Ibid., 111.
80. Addas, *Ibn ʿArabi*, 108 (emphasis mine).
81. Addas, *Quest*, 276–77.
82. Carl Schmitt, *The Concept of the Political*, trans. George Schwab (Chicago: Chicago University Press, 2007), 89.
83. Ibid., 90.
84. Grace M. Jantzen, *Power, Gender, and Christian Mysticism* (Cambridge: Cambridge University Press, 1995), 345 (emphasis mine).

85. Wilfred Cantwell Smith, *On Understanding Islam: Selected Studies* (The Hague: Mouton, 1981), 190.
86. Ibid. Elsewhere Smith notes: "The Ṣufī poet and mystic, on the one hand . . . has been sensitive to faith wherever it be found, and has given expression to his humane—and divine—vision . . . The systematizer, on the other hand, whether conceptually (*mutakallim*) or morally-legally (*faqīh*), has been largely exclusivist." Wilfred Cantwell Smith, *Faith and Belief: The Difference between Them* (Oxford: Oneworld Publications, 1998), 207n41.
87. Here, I follow William T. Cavanaugh and Peter Scott's definition of "political theology" as "the explicit attempt to relate discourse about God to the organization of bodies in space and time." See William T. Cavanaugh and Peter Scott, introduction to *The Blackwell Companion to Political Theology*, ed. Peter Scott and William T. Cavanaugh (Oxford: Blackwell Publishing, 2004), 2.
88. Mignolo, *The Darker Side*, 237.
89. Ibid.
90. See also Elka Weber, *Traveling through Text: Message and Method in Late Medieval Pilgrimage Accounts* (New York: Routledge, 2005), 11.
91. Amira Bennison, "Muslim Universalism and Western Globalization," in *Globalization in World History*, ed. A. G. Hopkins (New York: Norton, 2002), 75.
92. Peter Fibiger Bang with Dariusz Kołodziejczyk, "'Elephant of India': Universal Empire through Time and Across Cultures," in *Universal Empire: A Comparative Approach to Imperial Culture and Representation in Eurasian History*, ed. Peter Fibiger Bang and Dariusz Kołodziejczyk (Cambridge: Cambridge University Press, 2012), 16.
93. Ibid., 11.
94. Margaret Malamud, "Gender and Spiritual Self-Fashioning: The Master-Disciple Relationship in Classical Sufism," *Journal of the American Academy of Religion* 64, no. 1 (1996): 102.
95. Ibid., 90.
96. Ovamir Anjum, "Mystical Authority and Governmentality in Medieval Islam," in *Sufism and Society: Arrangements of the Mystical in the Muslim World, 1200–1800*, ed. John Curry and Erik Ohlander (New York: Routledge, 2011), 86.
97. Marshall G. S. Hodgson, *The Venture of Islam: Conscience and History in a World Civilization*, vol. 2 (Chicago: University of Chicago Press, 1974), 228. As Chodkiewicz notes, Ibn 'Arabi was not the first to think up the idea of a *quṭb* and his attendant spiritual hierarchy, but he was the first to organize such ideas within a coherent doctrine of sainthood (*walāya*). See Chodkiewicz, *Seal of the Saints*, 91–92.
98. Ibn ʿArabī, *al-Futūḥāt*, vol. 6, 65 (Fut. III, 350).

99. See Ibn ʿArabī, *al-Futūḥāt*, vol. 6, 243 (Fut. III, 514), and Ibn al-ʿArabī, *Fuṣūṣ al-ḥikam*, 64. See also Chodkiewicz, *Seal of the Saints*, 125; and Addas, *Quest*, 77–78, 200.
100. Ibn al-ʿArabī, *Fuṣūṣ al-ḥikam*, 64.
101. Ibn ʿArabī, *al-Futūḥāt*, vol. 5, 164 (Fut. III, 142). This statement originates from the non-canonical hadith: "I was a prophet when Adam was between water and clay (*kuntu nabī wa ādam bayna al-māʾ wa al-ṭīn*)." For a discussion of its authenticity and as "the main scriptural reference" for the concept of the Muhammadan Reality, see Chodkiewicz, *Seal of the Saints*, 60–69.
102. Ibn ʿArabī, *al-Futūḥāt*, vol. 5, 164 (Fut. III, 142).
103. See also Qur'an 16:123 (and similar 3:95 and 12:38).
104. "*law kāna mūsā ḥayy ma wasiʿahu illā an yatbaʿanī.*" A variation of this hadith can be found in the Musnad of Ibn Ḥanbal. See Aḥmad ibn Ḥanbal, *al-Musnad*, ed. Hamza A. al-Zayn vol. 11 (Cairo: Dār al-Ḥadīth, 1995), 500 (no. 14565). See also p. 74.
105. Ibn ʿArabī, *Al-Futūḥāt*, vol. 1, 170 (Fut. I, 135).
106. Qur'an 6:75–79. In verse 41:53, the Qur'an establishes contemplation of nature and the self as a means toward the confirmation that "*He is the Truth*" (*annahu al-ḥaqq*). Indeed, Ibn 'Arabi himself states that "at the time when we comprehend both of these matters together, only then will we realize God and it will become clear to us that *He is the Truth*." Ibn ʿArabī, *Al-Futūḥāt*, vol. 3, 347 (Fut. II, 298).
107. For example, Qur'an 2:135; 3:95; 6:161; 16:123.
108. Uri Rubin, "Ḥanīf," in *Encyclopedia of the Qur'ān*, vol. 2 (Leiden: Brill, 2002), 403.
109. Ibid.
110. Michel Chodkiewicz, "Toward Reading the *Futûhât Makkiyya*," in *The Meccan Revelations*, vol. 2, ed. Michel Chodkiewicz (New York: Pir Press, 2004), 32–33.
111. Ibid., 33 (emphasis mine).
112. Ibid.
113. Jacques Waardenburg, "The Medieval Period 650–1500," in *Muslim Perceptions of Other Religions: A Historical Survey*, ed. Jacques Waardenburg (New York: Oxford University Press, 1999), 22 (emphasis mine).
114. Ibid.
115. See Walter D. Mignolo, "Preface to the 2012 Edition," in *Local Histories/Global Designs Coloniality, Subaltern Knowledges, and Border Thinking* (Princeton, NJ: Princeton University Press, 2012), xv.
116. Sherman A. Jackson, "Islam(s) East and West: Pluralism between No-Frills and Designer Fundamentalism," in *September 11 in History: A Watershed Moment?*, ed. Mary L. Dudziak (Durham, NC: Duke University Press, 2003), 121.
117. Ibid., 123 (emphasis mine).
118. Richard H. Jones, *Mysticism and Morality: A New Look at Old Questions* (Lanham, MA: Lexington Books, 2004), 282, 358.

119. Jantzen, *Power, Gender, and Christian Mysticism*, 14.
120. It is important to note that when discussing such regimes of knowledge production—or in Foucauldian terms, "power/knowledge"—the notion of power "should not be understood as exclusively oppressive but as *productive*," since "power constitutes discourse, knowledge, bodies and subjectivities." Marianne Jørgensen and Louise J. Phillips, *Discourse Analysis as Theory and Method* (London: SAGE Publications, 2002), 13 (emphasis original).
121. Wendy Brown, *Regulating Aversion: Tolerance in the Age of Identity and Empire* (Princeton, NJ: Princeton University Press, 2006), 14.
122. Len Bowman expressed a similar concern regarding Perennialist readings of Catholic mysticism: "As a Catholic informed by medieval Franciscan mysticism, . . . I find many instances where perennialists misunderstand or do violence to my tradition by imposing elements of alien particular traditions as if they were universally normative." Len Bowman, "The Status of Conceptual Schemata: A Dilemma for Perennialists," *Aries* 11 (1990): 9–19. The attempt to regulate identity in this way, as Hugh Nicholson notes, is hegemonic in that it attempts to extend the influence of an idea of religion "beyond the circle of those whose basic outlook it expresses." Nicholson, *Comparative Theology*, 5.
123. The term "politics of nostalgia" was first coined by the historian Isaac Kramnick in his 1968 work *Bolingbroke and His Circle: The Politics of Nostalgia in the Age of Walpole* (Cambridge, MA: Harvard University Press, 1968). In the present context it was taken up in Armin W. Geertz and Jeppe Sinding Jensen, "Tradition and Renewal in the Histories of Religion: Some Observations and Reflections," in *Religion, Tradition, and Renewal*, ed. Armin W. Geertz and Jeppe Sinding Jensen (Aarhus: Aarhus University Press, 1991), 11–27; and more recently in McCutcheon, *Manufacturing Religion* (esp. 32–35).
124. Titus Burckhardt, *Introduction to Sufi Doctrine* (Bloomington, IN: World Wisdom, 2008), xiv (emphasis mine). First published as *Du soufisme: introduction au langage doctrinal du soufisme* (A. Bontemps, 1951).
125. Mignolo, *The Darker Side*, 18.
126. Burckhardt, *Introduction to Sufi Doctrine*, xv.
127. Frithjof Schuon, *Sufism: Veil and Quintessence: A New Translation with Selected Letters*, trans. Mark Perry, Jean-Pierre Lafouge, and James S. Cutsinger, ed. James S. Cutsinger (Bloomington, IN: World Wisdom, 2006), 41 (emphasis mine). See also discussion, pp. 148–49.
128. Patrick Laude, "Seyyed Hossein Nasr in the Context of the Perennialist School," in *Beacon of Knowledge: Essays in Honor of Seyyed Hossein Nasr*, ed. Mohammad Faghfoory (Louiseville: Fons Vitae, 2003), 250.
129. As Houman rather matter-of-factly observes without further comment in her extensive study on Perennialism: "Schuon . . . established the basis for a typology of the spiritual temperaments according to caste, that is, the degree of

contemplativity possessed by a human being, *and the particular qualities of his/her race, such as color*." Houman, *From the* Philosophia Perennis, 370 (emphasis mine).

130. Schuon, *Sufism*, 33.
131. Ibid., 28 (emphasis mine).
132. For example, see ibid., 27–28 (emphasis mine).
133. Olav Hammer, "Sufism for Westerners," in *Sufism in Europe and North America*, ed. David Westerlund (London: RoutledgeCurzon, 2004), 141.
134. Mark C. Taylor, introduction to *Critical Terms for Religious Studies*, ed. Mark C. Taylor (Chicago: University of Chicago Press), 15 (emphasis mine).
135. Etienne Balibar, *Masses, Classes, Ideas: Studies on Politics and Philosophy before and after Marx*, trans. James Swenson (New York: Routledge, 1994), 201 (emphasis mine).
136. Elizabeth A. Castelli, "Theologizing Human Rights: Christian Activism and the Limits of Religious Freedom," in *Nongovernmental Politics*, ed. Michel Feher, Gaelle Krikorian, and Yates McKee (New York: Zone Books, 2007), 685.
137. Here, I follow Brian Edwards's use of Harold Bloom's theory of influence through misreading. See Brian T. Edwards, *Morocco Bound: Disorienting America's Maghreb, from Casablanca to the Marrakech Express* (Durham, NC: Duke University Press, 2005), 92. Bloom himself first defined the concept of "strong misreading" as constitutive of "a theory of canonization" within poetry: "A strong poem, which alone can become canonical for more than a single generation, can be defined as a text that must engender strong misreadings, both as other poems and as literary criticism. Texts that have single, reductive, simplistic meanings are themselves already necessarily weak misreadings of anterior texts. When a strong misreading has demonstrated its fecundity by producing other strong misreadings across several generations, then we can and must accept its canonical status." Harold Bloom, *Agon: Towards a Theory of Revisionism* (New York: Oxford University Press, 1982), 285.
138. Muḥyi'ddīn Ibn Al-ʿArabī, *The Tarjumán al-Ashwáq: A Collection of Mystical Odes*, trans. and ed. Reynold A. Nicholson (1911; reprint, London: Royal Asiatic Society, 1978), 67.

CHAPTER 1

1. Donald S. Lopez Jr., "Belief," in *Critical Terms for Religious Studies*, ed. Mark C. Taylor (Chicago: University of Chicago Press, 1998), 34.
2. Abraham Joshua Heschel, *The Sabbath: Its Meaning for Modern Man* (Toronto: HarperCollins Canada, 1994), 5.
3. Muḥyi'ddīn Ibn Al-ʿArabī, *The Tarjumán al-Ashwáq: A Collection of Mystical Odes*, trans. and ed. Reynold A. Nicholson (1911; reprint, London: Royal Asiatic Society, 1978), 67.

4. Michael A. Sells, "Ibn ʿArabī's Garden among the Flames: A Reevaluation," *History of Religions* 23, no. 4 (1984): 287–88.
5. Nicholson, "Preface to the 1911 Edition," in *The Tarjumán al-Ashwáq: A Collection of Mystical Odes*, by Muḥyiʾddīn Ibn Al-ʿArabī, trans. and ed. Reynold A. Nicholson (1911; reprint, London: Royal Asiatic Society, 1978), vii.
6. Ignaz Goldziher, *Introduction to Islamic Theology and Law*, trans. Andras Hamori and Ruth Hamori (Princeton, NJ: Princeton University Press, 1981), 152. Originally published as *Vorlesungen über den Islam* (1910; reprint, Heidelberg: Carl Winter, 1925), 171.
7. Reynold A. Nicholson, *The Mystics of Islam* (Bloomington, IN: World Wisdom, 2002), 75 (emphasis mine).
8. Indeed, in his preface to the 1978 edition of *The Tarjumán al-Ashwáq*, the Perennialist scholar Martin Lings states that Ibn ʿArabi's thought is "basically identical with the Sufi perspective in general." Martin Lings, "Preface to the 1978 Edition," in *The Tarjumán al-Ashwáq: A Collection of Mystical Odes*, by Muḥyiʾddīn Ibn Al-ʿArabī, trans. and ed. Reynold A. Nicholson (1911; reprint, London: Royal Asiatic Society, 1978), xiii.
9. See Arthur J. Arberry, *An Introduction to the History of Ṣūfism: The Sir Abdullah Suhrawardy Lectures for 1942* (London: Longmans, Green and Co., 1943), 58.
10. Chris Lowney, *A Vanished World: Muslims, Christians, and Jews in Medieval Spain* (New York: Oxford University Press, 2006), 181, 265.
11. Annemarie Schimmel, *Mystical Dimensions of Islam* (Chapel Hill: University of North Carolina Press, 1975), 272.
12. Annemarie Schimmel, *As through a Veil: Mystical Poetry in Islam* (New York: Columbia University Press, 1982), 39.
13. Sells, "Ibn ʿArabī's Garden," 311n37 (emphasis mine).
14. Ibid. (emphasis mine).
15. See "belief," no. 4.a., *Oxford English Dictionary* (3rd Edition, September 2011) online version June 2017, accessed January 03, 2018, http://www.oed.com/view/Entry/17368.
16. Michael A. Sells, *Stations of Desire: Love Odes of Ibn ʿArabi and New Poems* (Jerusalem: Ibis Editions, 2008), 24 (emphasis mine).
17. "I profess the religion [*dīn*] of love. Wherever its caravan turns along the way, that is the belief [*dīn*], the faith I keep." Sells, *Stations of Desire*, 23, 73. Although he here uses a slightly different text from which Nicholson derived his classic translation, this is exactly how Sells renders these same two instances of *dīn* in his original article: "My religion [*dīn*] is love—wherever its camels turn / Love is my belief [*dīn*], my faith." Sells, "Ibn ʿArabī's Garden." 287. In *Mystical Languages of Unsaying*, Sells uses "creed" instead of "religion" and then "belief": "My creed [*dīn*] is love; / wherever its caravan turns along the way, / that is my belief [*dīn*], / my faith." Sells, *Mystical Languages of Unsaying* (Chicago: University of Chicago Press, 1994), 90.
18. As Richard Horsley observes, "because of the modern western reduction of religion to individual belief," the contemporary discipline of religious studies tends "to

separate religion from power, obscure the interrelationship of religion and power, and even mystify the effects of power." Richard A. Horsley, "Religion and Other Products of Empire," *Journal of the American Academy of Religion* 71, no. 1 (2003): 15.

19. For example, see Talal Asad, *Genealogies of Religion: Disciplines and Reasons of Power in Christianity and Islam* (Baltimore: Johns Hopkins University Press, 1993), 45. As Horsley summarizes: "Several historical forces, such as the European colonial encounter with other peoples and their religions, the development of the sciences, the triumphant rise of capitalist relations of production, and the corresponding emergence of the modern secular state, conspired in the peculiar modern western separation of religion from political-economic life and institutions." Horsley, "Religion and Other Products," 17.
20. Brent Nongbri, *Before Religion: A History of a Modern Concept* (New Haven, CT: Yale University Press, 2013), 95–96.
21. Wilfred Cantwell Smith, *Faith and Belief: The Difference between Them* (Oxford: Oneworld Publications, 1998), 122.
22. Asad, *Genealogies*, 46.
23. Ibid., 46–47.
24. See Edward William Lane, *An Arabic-English Lexicon* (1877; reprint, New Delhi: J. Jetley, 1985), 2104.
25. See Ibn al-ʿArabī, *Fuṣūṣ al-ḥikam*, ed. Abul Ela Affifi (Beirut: Dār al-Kitāb al-ʿArabī, 1966), 178, 113; and also: *al-ilāh al-muʿtaqad* (ibid., 225).
26. Ibid., 121.
27. While Ibn 'Arabi's discourse on belief retains its theological underpinnings of the term *iʿtiqād* in relation to its derivation of *aqīda* (meaning tenet or article of belief), it is strongly tied to its philosophical usage of "convictions rationally acquired" as used in *Kitāb al-amānāt wa'l-iʿtiqādāt* of the Jewish theologian Saʿadyā Gaon (d. 942). See L. Gardet, "Iʿtiḳād," in *The Encyclopaedia of Islam*, 2nd ed., vol. 4 (Leiden: E. J. Brill, 1997), 279. Yet, as Wilfred Cantwell Smith notes, the classical sense should be understood less as "belief" and "more literally [as] to bind oneself, to commit or to pledge oneself to, to take on the engagement of living in accord with a given position." Smith, *Faith and Belief*, 196n9.
28. Lane, *An Arabic-English Lexicon*, 2104.
29. Muḥyī al-Dīn Ibn ʿArabī, *al-Futūḥāt al-makkiyya*, vol. 7 (Beirut: Dār Ṣādir, 2004), 162–63 (Fut. IV, 143).
30. For example, Bukhārī, *al-Tawḥīd*, 34, 130; Muslim, *al-Dhikr*, 1, 25, 28. See Ibn al-ʿArabī, *Fuṣūṣ al-ḥikam*, 225.
31. Jalāl ad-Dīn Rūmī, *Signs of the Unseen: The Discourses of Jalaluddin Rumi*, trans. W. M. Thackston Jr. (New York: Shambhala Publications, 1994), 51.
32. Ibn ʿArabī, *al-Futūḥāt*, vol. 3, 361 (Fut. II, 311).
33. Ibid., vol. 5, 229 (Fut. III, 198).
34. Nicholson, "Preface to the 1911 Edition," x.
35. Ibid (emphasis mine). See Ibn al-ʿArabī, *Fuṣūṣ al-ḥikam*, 113.
36. Nicholson, "Preface to the 1911 Edition," x.

37. Ibid. See Ibn al-ʿArabī, *Fuṣūṣ al-ḥikam*, 226.
38. See p. 5.
39. Éric Geoffroy, *Introduction to Sufism: The Inner Path of Islam* (Bloomington, IN: World Wisdom, 2010), 184.
40. René Guénon, *The Reign of Quantity and the Signs of the Times*, trans. Lord Northbourne, 4th ed. (Hillsdale, NY: Sophia Perennis, 2004), 62–63, 63n1 (emphasis mine). First published *Le Règne de la Quantité et les Signes des Temps* (Gallimard, 1945).
41. A. E. Affifi, *The Mystical Philosophy of Muḥyid Dīn-ibnul ʿArabī* (Cambridge: Cambridge University Press, 1939), 151 (emphasis original).
42. Ibid. (emphasis original).
43. Ibn ʿArabi quoted in Affifi, *The Mystical Philosophy*, 151 (emphasis original).
44. Affifi, *The Mystical Philosophy*, 151.
45. See Henry Corbin, *Alone with the Alone: Creative Imagination in the Sūfism of Ibn ʿArabī*, trans. Ralph Manheim (Princeton, NJ: Princeton University Press, 1998), 124, 195–200, 268, 269
46. Ibid., 198; Henry Corbin, *L'Imagination créatrice dans le Soufisme d'Ibn ʿArabî*, 2nd ed. (Paris: Flammarion, 1977), 153.
47. Corbin, *Alone with the Alone*, 232 (emphasis mine); *L'Imagination créatrice*, 179.
48. Toshihiko Izutsu, *Sufism and Taoism: A Comparative Study of Key Philosophical Concepts* (Berkeley: University of California Press, 1984), 469.
49. As William Chittick notes, like the work of Henry Corbin, Izutsu's personal interests led him to neglect "the practical sides to Ibn al-ʿArabī's teachings and his insistence on weighing all knowledge in the 'Scale of the Law,' the norms revealed through the Koran and the Sunna of the Prophet." William C. Chittick, *The Sufi Path of Knowledge: Ibn al-ʿArabi's Metaphysics of Imagination* (Albany: State University of New York Press, 1989), xix.
50. Ibn al-ʿArabī, *Fuṣūṣ al-ḥikam*, 72.
51. Paul Tillich, *Dynamics of Faith* (New York: Harper & Row, 1957), 1 (emphasis mine).
52. Leonard Lewisohn, "The Transcendental Unity of Polytheism and Monotheism in the Sufism of Shabistarī," in *The Heritage of Sufism, vol. 2: The Legacy of Medieval Persian Sufism (1150–1500)*, ed. Leonard Lewisohn (Oxford: Oneworld, 1999), 382.
53. For example, Ibn ʿArabī, *al-Futūḥāt*, vol. 5, 136 (Fut. III, 117).
54. This position is strikingly similar to the explanation of "heathen" worship according to the early modern "father of Deism," Edward Lord Herbert of Cherbury (d. 1648). As Herbert states in *The Antient Religion*: "The *Sun* was only a kind of sensible Representation of the *Supreme God* under which consideration only the most Wise amongst the *Heathens* worshipped him; knowing very well that GOD himself could not be discerned in any one thing; Universal Nature it self being insufficient to represent him according to his excellent Dignity." Edward Lord Herbert of

Cherbury, *The Antient Religion of the Gentiles and Causes of Their Errors Consider'd* (London: John Nutt, 1705), 33.

55. That is, the divine name of Allāh. See Chittick, *The Sufi Path of Knowledge*, 49.
56. Ibn al-ʿArabī, *Fuṣūṣ al-ḥikam*, 195.
57. While this definition is my own, the term "Theomonism" was popularized by Frank Ballard in his 1906 work *Theomonism True: God and the Universe in Modern Light*. Ballard, following Isaak Rülf's 1903 work *Wissenschaft der Gotteseinheit (Theo-Monismus)*, defines Theomonism as the synthesis of the following three purported antitheses: (1) "The oneness of God in the *inner* and the *outer* world subjectively and objectively," (2) "The oneness of God as the *All* and the *Personal*," and (3) "The oneness of God as presented in *religion* and in *philosophy*." Frank Ballard, *Theomonism True: God and the Universe in Modern Light* (London: Charles H. Kelly, 1906), 458 (emphasis original).
58. Izutsu, *Sufism and Taoism*, 254.
59. Ibid.
60. Ibn 'Arabi quoted in Izutsu, *Sufism and Taoism*, 254.
61. Lane, *An Arabic-English Lexicon*, 2107.
62. Here, Chittick argues that Ibn 'Arabi's assertion that he has submitted to the "religion of love" is an acquiescence "to the Sunna of the Prophet." William Chittick, "The Religion of Love Revisited," *Journal of the Muhyiddin Ibn 'Arabi Society* 54 (2013): 53. See also p. 42.
63. William T. Cavanaugh, *The Myth of Religious Violence: Secular Ideology and the Roots of Modern Conflict* (Oxford: Oxford University Press, 2009), 73. As Brent Nongbri has similarly noted, by the eighteenth century, the idea "of religion as a set of beliefs that could be either true or false" had become naturalized in Western discourse. Nongbri, *Before Religion*, 96.
64. "Obedience" (*inqiyād* and *ṭāʿa*) is indeed the primary classical Arabic definition of *dīn*. See Ibn Fāris al-Lughawī, *Maqayīs al-lugha, d-y-n*, and Lane, *An Arabic-English Lexicon*, 944. This also parallels the original Latin term *religio* and its notion of being bound (from *religare*) to God in terms of obligation or duty. See Wilfred Cantwell Smith, *The Meaning and End of Religion* (Minneapolis: Fortress Press, 1991), 20, 102, 204n5.
65. My translation of "way" for *sharʿ* is not without analogous Arabic usage in the *Fuṣūṣ*, as in the chapter of Moses where Ibn 'Arabi specifically glosses *shirʿa* as "way" (*ṭarīqa*). See Ibn al-ʿArabī, *Fuṣūṣ al-ḥikam*, 201.
66. Ibid., 94
67. See Louis Gardet, "Dīn," in *The Encyclopaedia of Islam,* 2nd ed., vol. 2 (Leiden: E. J. Brill, 1991), 294. See also n. 64 above.
68. Ibn al-ʿArabī, *Fuṣūṣ al-ḥikam*, 95.
69. Ibid.
70. Ibid., 96.

71. Ibid.
72. Here "essence" (*dhāt*) is analogous to the "immutable essence" (*ʿayn thābita*) of each person, which according to Ibn ʿArabi is in relationship with God as a distinct intelligible entity or form (*ṣūra*) within God's knowledge. Ibn al-ʿArabī, *Fuṣūṣ al-ḥikam*, 96.
73. Ibid., 96.
74. Ibid., 94.
75. Ibid., 96.
76. However, talk of salvation and damnation is ultimately relative when it comes to Ibn ʿArabi's radical conception of hell. See discussion, p. 7.
77. Ibn ʿArabī, *al-Futūḥāt*, vol. 2, 36 (Fut. 1, 405).
78. Ibn ʿArabī, *Dhakhāʾir al-aʿlāq: sharḥ tarjumān al-ashwāq*, ed. Muhammad ʿAbd al-Raḥmān al-Kurdī (Paris: Dar Byblion, 2005), 64. The verse that Ibn ʿArabi here comments on is the final line of the thirteenth poem that reads: "There is no one who blames me for passionately desiring her, for she is beloved (*maʿshūqa*)—intrinsically beautiful wherever she is." The feminine subject of the commentary for this line is the feminine noun "beloved" (*maʿshūqa*), which in this passage transitions to the abstract noun, also feminine, "salvation" (*najāh*). However, this poem's first line highlights a different, but perhaps related in Ibn ʿArabi's mind, feminine subject, that is, a "ringdove" (*muṭawwaqa*), and Ibn ʿArabi states in his commentary that he means by it the ambiguous "spirit" (*rūḥ*) breathed into Adam (Qur'an 15:29). Moreover, "she" is also the "subtle human substance" (*al-laṭīfa al-insāniyya*). Ibn ʿArabī, *Dhakhāʾir al-aʿlāq*, 55. Qāshānī calls the *laṭīfa al-insāniyya* the rational soul and the heart. See "The Human Subtlety" in ʿAbd al-Razzāq Qāshānī, *Sufi Technical Terms*, trans. Nabil Safwat, ed. David Pendlebury (London: Octagon Press, 1991), 36.
79. Another classical definition of *dīn* is a particular law or ruling (*ḥukm*). See Lane, *An Arabic-English Lexicon*, 944. The accordance between the English idea of "law" and the Arabic *dīn* is in fact quite old. As Nongbri points out, the first French translation of the Qur'an by André du Ryer published in 1647 translated *dīn* as "loy," which was followed by the first English translation by Alexander Ross published in 1649, who used "law." See Nongbri, *Before Religion*, 40–41.
80. Ibn ʿArabi was aware of this plural and did use it in rare circumstances. In the *Futūḥāt*, Ibn ʿArabi only uses *adyān* to refer to religions in the plural in one particular passage, that is, Ibn ʿArabī, *al-Futūḥāt*, vol. 1, 182 (Fut. I, 145). See p. 71.
81. For example, see Ibn ʿArabī, *al-Futūḥāt*, vol. 1, 182 (Fut. I, 145). See p. 72.
82. When mentioned in Ibn ʿArabi's discussions on belief, the Ashʿarīs and Muʿtazilīs are symbolic of two opposing positions regarding the nature of God: "similarity" (*tashbīh*), or anthropomorphism, and "incomparability" (*tanzīh*), or transcendence, respectively. While each group tends to emphasize one of these positions regarding God's nature over the other, Ibn ʿArabi insists that both aspects are true.

For example, see Ibn al-ʿArabī, *Fuṣūṣ al-ḥikam*, 123; *al-Futūḥāt*, vol. 3, 135, 371 (Fut. II, 116, 319); *al-Futūḥāt*, vol. 6, 103 (Fut. III, 384). Compared to the lengthy literature perpetuating the universalist appropriation of Ibn 'Arabi's discourse on belief, this point has not been given its due. For a nonuniversalist treatment of this topic as intrareligious critique see Alexander Knysh, "'Orthodoxy' and 'Heresy' in Medieval Islam: An Essay in Reassessment," *Muslim World* 83, no. 1 (1993): 58–59; and Ian Almond, *Sufism and Deconstruction: A Comparative Study of Derrida and Ibn 'Arabi* (London: Routledge, 2004), 15–20.

83. Ghazali additionally notes that only through assiduous religious observance and remembrance of God (*dhikr*) is such "untying" accomplished. Abū Ḥāmid al-Ghazālī, *Fayṣal al-tafriqa bayna al-islām wa al-zandaqa* (Beirut: Dar al-Fikr al-Lubnani, 1993), 79–80.
84. In the *Futūḥāt*, Ibn 'Arabi refers to this hadith as the "hadith of self-manifestation" or "hadith of theophany" (*ḥadīth al-tajallī*). Elsewhere, he refers to its main concepts such as *tajallī* or *taḥawwul* and then mentions *Ṣaḥīḥ Muslim*. For example, see Ibn ʿArabī, *al-Futūḥāt*, vol. 5, 52 (Fut. III, 44), and Ibn ʿArabī, *al-Futūḥāt*, vol. 5, 229 (Fut. III, 198).
85. "*wa qad taḥawwala fī sūratihi allatī ra'awhu fīhā awwal marra.*" Muslim, *al-Īmān*, 352.
86. This line is a direct reference to Qur'an 9:30: "*The Jews call 'Uzayr son of God, and the Christians call the Messiah son of God. This is what they speak from their own mouths, imitating what the unbelievers of old used to say. God has damned them (qātalahumu allāh)—how deluded they are!*" While most commenters identify ʿUzayr with the Jewish scribe and high priest Ezra, the Arabist Moshe Sharon posits that the term ʿUzayr represents "the transliteration of the Hebrew ʿOzēr into Arabic," and thus means "helper" or "savior." As such, Moshe argues that rather than referring to a group of Jews who believed Ezra was the son of God, the Qur'an is identifying a group of Jews who, just like their Christian counterparts, believed "in the son of God as the savior." See M. Sharon, "People of the Book," in *Encyclopaedia of the Qur'ān*, vol. 4 (Leiden: Brill, 2004), 36. Gordon Newby, however, speculates that Qur'an 9:30 may equate "Ezra the Scribe with Enoch the Scribe." As Newby notes, in apocryphal works such as *3 Enoch*, Enoch is "translated into heaven . . . and transformed into the powerful angel, Metatron, who was taught by God all the secrets . . . and became a lesser God." Gordon Darnell Newby, *A History of the Jews of Arabia: From Ancient Times to Their Eclipse in Islam* (Columbia: University of South Carolina Press, 1988), 60
87. Muslim, *al-Īmān*, 352.
88. See Ibn ʿArabī, *al-Futūḥāt*, vol. 5, 52–53 (Fut. III, 44–45).
89. Ibid., vol. 1, 235 (Fut. I, 191).
90. Ibid., vol. 5, 187 (Fut. III, 162). Like Ibn 'Arabi's critique of the doctrine of incarnation (*ḥulūl*) in the *Fuṣūṣ* mentioned below, here the mistake of particularization can additionally be understood as restricting full access to God's attributes to only

one specific group rather than an acknowledgment of the truth, as Ibn 'Arabi sees it, that humanity shares in God's attributes universally through the Muhammadan Reality qua *Logos*.

91. Ibn al-ʿArabī, *Fuṣūṣ al-ḥikam*, 141. Here, it should be noted that Ibn 'Arabi's critique is uniquely colored by his particular "monistic" view. As Tim Winter notes, Ibn 'Arabi "condemns the idea that Jesus represents a divine incarnation (*ḥulūl*) rather than a manifestation (*tajallī*) of divine qualities . . . [M]oreover, he finds it unacceptable that God's self-manifestation should have been restricted to only one entity." Tim Winter, "Realism and the Real: Islamic Theology and the Problem of Alternative Expressions of God," in *Between Heaven and Hell: Islam, Salvation, and the Fate of Others*, ed. Mohammad Hassan Khalil (New York: Oxford University Press, 2013), 135. For Ibn 'Arabi's inverted use of "disbelief" or "infidelity" (*kufr*) in the positive sense see n. 187 below.
92. For example, in the *Futūḥāt* Ibn 'Arabi claims that "People of Oneness" (*ahl tawhīd*) are those who inhabit paradise since they have the attribute of oneness, while "the dualists" (*al-thanawiyya*) inhabit hell since they do not have such an attribute and are thus "people of associationism" (*ahl shirk*). However, the "People of the Trinity" (*ahl al-tathlīth*), according to Ibn 'Arabi, are located between the former and the latter. Ibn 'Arabi then asserts that it is hoped that they will be saved since although they are called "disbelievers" (*kuffār*), in actuality their theology is indistinguishable from monotheism, because the Trinity is an aspect of singularity (*fardiyya*) because it is of an odd (*fard*) number, and the odd is a quality of the One (*al-wāḥid*). See Ibn ʿArabī, *al-Futūḥāt*, vol. 5, 199 (Fut. III, 172). Similarly, in the fourth line of the twelfth poem of the *Tarjumān al-ashwāq*, Ibn 'Arabi states as translated by Nicholson: "My Beloved is three although He is One, even as the (three) Persons (of the Trinity) are made one Person in essence." In his commentary, Ibn 'Arabi asserts that "number does not spawn multiplicity in the divine essence (*al-'ayn*)," and then relates that just as in Christianity, where the three hypostases ultimately amount to one God, the Qur'an claims: "*Say, 'Call on God, or on the most Compassionate—whatever way you call, His are the most beautiful names.'*" (17:110). Ibn 'Arabi then claims that, analogously, all of the Qur'anic teachings can be reduced to the three names of God (*allāh*), the Lord (*al-rabb*), and the Compassionate (*al-raḥmān*). Still, Ibn 'Arabi notes, the intention is similarly one God. Ibn ʿArabī, *Dhakhā'ir al-aʿlāq*, 53–54; and Ibn Al-ʿArabī, *The Tarjumán al-Ashwáq*, 70–71. For a discussion on Ibn 'Arabi's metaphysics of "triplicity" see Mohamed Haj Yousef, *Ibn 'Arabī—Time and Cosmology* (New York: Routledge, 2008), 128–130.
93. Winter, "Realism and the Real," 136.
94. Sells, "Ibn ʿArabī's Garden," 311n37.
95. Shah-Kazemi writes overtly from within the Schuonian school, and his two full-length works that argue for an authentic Islamic mode of religious universalism

are dedicated to Frithjof Schuon and Martin Lings (one of Schuon's authorized spiritual successors). See dedication in Reza Shah-Kazemi, *Paths to Transcendence: According to Shankara, Ibn Arabi, and Meister Eckhart* (Bloomington, IN: World Wisdom, 2006); and *The Other in the Light of the One: The Universality of the Qur'ān and Interfaith Dialogue* (Cambridge: Islamic Texts Society, 2006).

96. In addition to n. 97 below, see, for example, Shah-Kazemi, *The Other in the Light*, 52; and "Beyond Polemics and Pluralism: The Universal Message of the Qur'an," in *Between Heaven and Hell: Islam, Salvation, and the Fate of Others*, ed. Mohammad Hassan Khalil (New York: Oxford University Press, 2013), 99.
97. Shah-Kazemi, *Paths to Transcendence*, 124 (emphasis mine).
98. Ibid.
99. Reza Shah-Kazemi, *The Spirit of Tolerance in Islam* (London: I. B. Tauris, 2012), 58.
100. Ibid.
101. Ibn ʿArabī, *al-Futūḥāt*, vol. 6, 65 (Fut. III, 350).
102. Shah-Kazemi, *Paths to Transcendence*, 81.
103. Ibid., 81–82 (emphasis mine). See also p. 102.
104. As James Morris notes, the phrase *muḥammadī al-maqām* literally means "I was 'Muhammad-like in (my spiritual) station.'" James Winston Morris, "The Spiritual Ascension: Ibn ʿArabī and the Miʿrāj Part II," *Journal of the American Oriental Society* 108, no. 1 (1988): 72n186. Ibn 'Arabi does use the more readily translatable *maqām muḥammadī* ("Muhammadan Station") twice in the *Futūḥāt*. See Ibn ʿArabī, *al-Futūḥāt*, vol. 2, 292 (Fut. I, 625), and vol. 6, 199 (Fut. III, 475).
105. This is a reference to a hadith in *Ṣaḥīḥ Muslim* transmitted by Abū Hurayra: "I was preferred over the prophets in six things: (1) I was given the comprehensive words (*ūtītu jawāmiʿ al-kalim*), (2) I was given victory by (filling my enemies with) terror, (3) booty was made lawful for me, (4) the entire earth was made pure for me as a place of worship (*masjid*), (5) I was sent to all creation (universally), (6) and the line of prophets was sealed with me." Muslim, *al-Masājid*, 7. In his *Tafsīr* where he comments on the night journey verse (Qur'an 17:1), Tabarī records a similar hadith by Abu Hurayra. See Frederick S. Colby, *Narrating Muḥammad's Night Journey: Tracing the Development of the Ibn ʿAbbās Ascension Discourse* (Albany: State University of New York Press, 2008), 99, 264n22.
106. Ibn ʿArabī, *al-Futūḥāt*, vol. 6, 65 (Fut. III, 350).
107. According to Brown, "the apocalyptic style" is exemplified by the Qur'an, Joyce's *Finnegans Wake*, and "what Umberto Eco called 'The Poetics of the Open Work.'" Norman O. Brown, "The Apocalypse of Islam," *Social Text*, no. 8 (1983–84): 167.
108. See n. 105 above.
109. Bukhārī, *al-Taʿbīr*, 22.
110. Ibn 'Arabi here slightly rewords the final locution of Qur'an 31:27: "*And if all the trees on the earth were pens and the ocean (was ink), with seven more oceans as well, the words of God would not be exhausted*" (mā nafidat kalimāt allāh).
111. Ibn ʿArabī, *al-Futūḥāt*, vol. 5, 165 (Fut. III, 143).

112. As James Morris notes, hadith referring to Muhammad's *jawāmiʿ al-kalim* are "cited repeatedly by Ibn ʿArabî to summarize the totality of spiritual knowledge or divine 'forms of wisdom' (*hikam*) making up the 'Muhammadan Reality.'" James W. Morris, "Ibn ʿArabî's Spiritual Ascension," in *The Meccan Revelations*, vol. 1, ed. Michel Chodkiewicz (New York: Pir Press, 2002), 352n188.
113. Ibn al-ʿArabī, *Fuṣūṣ al-ḥikam*, 63–64.
114. "*kuntu nabī wa ādam bayna al-māʾ wa al-ṭīn.*" Regarding this alleged hadith, see intro., n. 101.
115. Ibn ʿArabī, *al-Futūḥāt*, vol. 3, 104 (Fut. II, 88).
116. Qur'an 33:40.
117. See Michel Chodkiewicz, *Seal of the Saints: Prophethood and Sainthood in the Doctrine of Ibn ʿArabī*, trans. Liadain Sherrard (Cambridge: Islamic Texts Society, 1993), 71, and Affifi, *The Mystical Philosophy*, 71–73.
118. Affifi, *The Mystical Philosophy*, 86.
119. Ibid., 70, 72.
120. See Aḥmad ibn Ḥanbal, *al-Musnad*, ed. Hamza A. al-Zayn, vol. 17 (Cairo: Dār al-Ḥadīth, 1995), 379 (no. 24482).
121. That is, Qur'an 68:4 and15:87, respectively.
122. Regarding the Ḥanbalī (and qualified Ashʿarī) conception of the Qur'an as equivalent to the attribute of God's speech, see Nader El-Bizri, "God: Essence and Attributes," in *The Cambridge Companion to Classical Islamic Theology*, ed. Tim Winter (Cambridge: Cambridge University Press, 2008), 122–31. See also Margaretha T. Heemskerk, "Speech," in *Encyclopedia of the Qur'ān*, vol. 5 (Leiden: Brill, 2001), 112; and Harry A. Wolfson, *The Philosophy of the Kalam* (Cambridge, MA: Harvard University Press, 1976), 235–62.
123. Ibn ʿArabī, *al-Futūḥāt*, vol. 7, 68–69 (Fut. IV, 60–61).
124. Ibid., 69 (Fut. IV, 61).
125. Cyrus Ali Zargar, *Sufi Aesthetics: Beauty, Love, and the Human Form in the Writings of Ibn ʿArabi and ʿIraqi* (Columbia: University of South Carolina Press, 2011), 66–74. Zargar notes that while Ibn ʿArabi clearly categorized the female form as the most perfect locus of divine beauty, he did indeed approve of the famous practice of gazing on "beardless youths" or in Ibn ʿArabi's terminology "recent ones" (*al-aḥdāth*)—as "fresh from their lord"—for "the accomplished gnostic." Thus, as Ibn ʿArabi states: "In their companionship is a recollection of their newness by which one discerns his eternalness—may he be exalted." Yet, Ibn ʿArabi also asserts that for "novice wayfarers [*al-muridun*] and Sufis [*al-sufiyah*], the companionship of recent ones is forbidden to them, because of the predominance of animal desire in them" (ibid., 73–74). Although Claude Addas records Ibn ʿArabi's stern prohibition of this practice for "Sufis" (along with *samāʿ*), she interestingly notes elsewhere that Ibn ʿArabi entrusted the advanced spiritual education of his own stepson and disciple, Ṣadr al-Dīn Qūnāwī (d. 1274), to Awḥad al-Dīn Kirmānī (d. 1238). Significantly, Ibn ʿArabi was aware

that Kirmani was affiliated with the school of Aḥmad Ghazālī (d. 1126) and the practice of both *samāʿ* and *shāhid bāzī*. As Addas notes, "doubtless, he, like Jāmī, considered that in the case of Awḥad al-Dīn it was a question of a genuine mode of spiritual realization." Addas, *Quest for the Red Sulphur*, 163–64, 229.

126. Zargar, *Sufi Aesthetics*, 71.
127. Ibid.
128. Ibid.
129. The *Dhakhāʾir* has thus been commonly interpreted in either of two ways: (1) as a rather transparent attempt to conceal a romantic longing for Niẓām as an earthly beloved, or (2) that Niẓām is purely an allegorical representation of the divine. Yet, as Zargar persuasively shows, Ibn ʿArabi's vision expressed in the *Dhakhāʾir* articulates a profound mystical unity of *both* "the sensual and supersensory." Zargar, *Sufi Aesthetics*, 124.
130. Nicholson, "Preface to the 1911 Edition," 7.
131. Ibid., 9. Yet, as Chittick observes, what Nicholson apparently found to be "interesting and important" was "from within the cognitive blinkers of British rationalism." Thus, "much of what Nicholson no doubt considered as a 'descent to the ridiculous,'" Chittick trenchantly adds, "provides the key to situating the poetry within the context of Islamic thought." William C. Chittick, *Imaginal Worlds: Ibn al-ʿArabi and the Problem of Religious Diversity* (Albany: State University of New York Press, 1994), 68.
132. Chittick tellingly notes that "Nicholson may have been jumping to conclusions" in his above quoted assertion that Ibn ʿArabi's celebrated verses "express the Ṣúfí doctrine that all ways lead to the One God." Chittick, "The Religion of Love Revisited," 38.
133. Ibid., 59 (emphasis mine).
134. Ibn ʿArabī, *Dhakhāʾir al-aʿlāq*, 50.
135. Leonard Lewisohn, "Sufi Symbolism in the Persian Hermeneutic Tradition: Reconstructing the Pagoda of ʿAṭṭār's Esoteric Poetics," in *ʿAṭṭār and the Persian Sufi Tradition: The Art of Spiritual Flight*, ed. Leonard Lewisohn and Christopher Shackle (New York: I. B. Tauris & Co., 2006), 262, 266. See also J. T. P. De Bruijn, "The *Qalandariyyāt* in Persian Mystical Poetry, from Sanāʾī Onwards," in *The Heritage of Sufism Volume,* vol. 2, ed. Leonard Lewisohn (Oxford: Oneworld Publications, 1999), 85.
136. See Qāshānī, *Sufi Technical Terms*, 27–28.
137. See also Chittick, "The Religion of Love," 58.
138. Ibn ʿArabī, *al-Futūḥāt al-makkiyya*, vol. 8, 117 (Fut. IV, 386).
139. Chittick, "The Religion of Love," 58 (emphasis mine).
140. Ibn ʿArabī, *Dhakhāʾir al-aʿlāq*, 50.
141. Ibn Al-ʿArabī, *The Tarjumán al-Ashwáq*, 69.
142. Muslim, *al-Masājid*, 7; see n. 105 above.
143. Ibn ʿArabī, *Dhakhāʾir al-aʿlāq*, 50.

144. ʿAlī ibn Aḥmad al-Wāhidī (d. 1075) notes in his *Asbāb al-nuzūl* (*Occasions of Revelation*) that Ibn ʿAbbās reported that this verse was revealed when Muhammad witnessed some of the Quraysh worshiping idols in the Kaʿba and called on them to follow him instead. Al-Wahidi also narrates another report from Ibn 'Abbas that this verse was revealed to the Jews, while he additionally mentions that Ibn Isḥaq reported from a different source that it was addressed to the Christians. See ʿAlī ibn Aḥmad al-Wāhidī, *Asbāb al-nuzūl* (Dammam: Dar al-Islah, 1992), 103–4. As a scholar with formidable training and transmission in hadith and tafsir, Ibn 'Arabi would have certainly been aware of these traditions and may have been making an allusion to them through his commentary on this verse via the previous two famous verses that reveal his "heart capable of every form" including the sites of worship for idolaters, Jews, and Christians. See Addas, *Quest for the Red Sulphur*, 97–98.
145. Ibn ʿArabī, *Dhakhāʾir al-aʿlāq*, 50.
146. Ibid., 50–51.
147. Sells, "Ibn ʿArabī's Garden," 311n37. While in this instance Nicholson's translation of "Moslems" for *al-muḥammadiyyīn* is too restrictive, *al-muḥammadiyyīn* may still, for Ibn 'Arabi, denote "Muslims" in a general sense. Proof for this is found in the writing of ʿAbd al-Razzāq al-Qāshāni (d. 1329), who was an important, early interpreter of Ibn 'Arabi. When Qashani comments on Qur'an 5:49 in his well-known exegesis, he uses *al-muḥammadiyyīn* for "Muslims" in comparison to Jews (*al-yahūd*) and Christians (*al-naṣārā*) and the particular metaphysical "transgression" (*fisq*) that is manifested within each group: "The transgression of the Muhammadans is turning towards their own selves and the departure from the dominion of essential unity." ʿAbd al-Razzāq al-Qāshāni, *Tafsīr Ibn 'Arabī*, vol. 1 (Beirut: Dar Sader, 2002), 151. Similarly, Caner Dagli notes, "When Ibn al-'Arabi speaks of the Muhammadans, he is referring not only to the members of the community of Muhammad but also to a certain kind of soul that has been formed or manifests the particular characteristics of the Islamic revelation." Dagli, *The Ringstones of Wisdom*, 44n39.
148. Chittick, "The Religion of Love," 54 (emphasis mine).
149. See Chittick, *The Sufi Path of Knowledge*, 375–81.
150. Sells, "Ibn ʿArabī's Garden," 311n37–312n37 (emphasis mine).
151. Ibid., 312n37 (emphasis mine).
152. As found in a hadith in Tirmidhī, *al-Manāqib*, 13. However, instead of the adjectival form *ṣafī* used by Ibn 'Arabi, Tirmidhī records the eighth form perfect verb *iṣṭafā*: "Adam is the one whom God chose" (*ādam iṣṭafāhu allāh*).
153. Regarding Ibn 'Arabi's technical usage of "meaning" (*maʿnā*) as "innermost reality," see Chittick, *The Sufi Path of Knowledge*, 28.
154. See Ibn al-ʿArabī, *Fuṣūṣ al-ḥikam*, 64. See also Chodkiewicz, *Seal of the Saints*, 170, 128–46, passim.

155. See Ibn al-ʿArabī, *Fuṣūṣ al-ḥikam*, 64.
156. Ibid. Ibn ʿArabi has been criticized for ranking the perfected saint over that of the prophet. This position is often explained away as simply Ibn ʿArabi's assertion that sainthood (*walāya*) as conceived of here is simply the hidden (and divine) attribute of outward prophethood (*nubuwwa*), and as such Muhammad is himself the "real" Seal of Sainthood. Yet, according to Ibn ʿArabi, since he is the historical Seal of Sainthood, when Jesus descends he will be under the "authority" of Ibn ʿArabi himself. See Chodkiewicz, *Seal of the Saints*, 125.
157. As William Chittick notes, "In its primordial nature (*fiṭra*) every human microcosm is the outward form (*ṣūra*) of an inward meaning (*maʿna*) that is named 'Allah.'" Chittick, *The Sufi Path of Knowledge*, 20.
158. Ibid., 375 (emphasis mine).
159. Ibid., 376 (emphasis mine).
160. See discussion, pp. 15–16.
161. Ibn ʿArabī, *Dhakhāʾir al-aʿlāq*, 49.
162. This is especially the case for the *Fuṣūṣ* and the *Futūḥāt*. According to Ibn ʿArabi's own references, the *Tarjumān* and the *Dhakhāʾir* were written around 1215 CE. The *Fuṣūṣ* was written in 1229 CE, while the *Futūḥāt* went through two major drafts; the first was finished in 1231 and the second in 1238 CE, two years prior to his death. See Claude Addas, *Quest for the Red Sulphur: The Life of Ibn ʿArabī* (Cambridge: Islamic Texts Society, 1993), 306–10.
163. Ibn ʿArabī, *al-Futūḥāt*, vol. 3, 133 (Fut. II, 113–114).
164. Ibn ʿArabī, *Dhakhāʾir al-aʿlāq*, 49.
165. Michael Sells duly notes this fact. As he states: "The reference to 'tradition' . . . is a reference to the 'hadith of the transformations,' which describes the various forms in which the divine *appears to Muslims* in the afterlife, forms often in contrast with the forms they had expected." Michael A. Sells, *Mystical Languages of Unsaying* (Chicago: University of Chicago Press, 1994), 110–11 (emphasis mine).
166. Ibn al-ʿArabī, *Fuṣūṣ al-ḥikam*, 121.
167. Ibid.
168. Ibid.
169. Ibid., 114, 226.
170. Ibid., 113.
171. Izutsu, *Sufism and Taoism*, 254. See also p. 31.
172. Izutsu, *Sufism and Taoism*, 254 (emphasis mine).
173. Seyyed Hossein Nasr, introduction to *The Essential Writings of Frithjof Schuon*, by Frithjof Schuon, ed. Seyyed Hossein Nasr (Amity: Amity House, 1986), 16. See discussion, pp. 148–49.
174. Shah-Kazemi, *Paths to Transcendence*, 126.
175. Reza Shah-Kazemi, "The Metaphysics of Interfaith Dialogue: Sufi Perspectives on the Universality of the Quranic Message," in *Paths to the Heart: Sufism and*

the Christian East, ed. James S. Cutsinger (Bloomington, IN: World Wisdom, 2004), 180.

176. Ibid., 180n78 (emphasis mine).
177. Frithjof Schuon, *Gnosis: Divine Wisdom*, ed. James S. Cutsinger, trans. Mark Perry, Jean-Pierre Lafouge, and James Cutsinger (Bloomington, IN: World Wisdom, 2006), 17. For a discussion of this aspect of Schuon's thought compared to Ibn 'Arabi, see pp. 141–44.
178. The idea that the human being was created by God as the comprehensive configuration of the divine names—and thus reflective of God's "form"—for God to witness Himself is the initial subject of Ibn 'Arabi's first chapter of Adam in the *Fuṣūṣ*. See Ibn al-ʿArabī, *Fuṣūṣ al-ḥikam*, 48–50. As Zargar notes, according to Ibn 'Arabi, "the gnostic heart, on account of the superiority of human knowledge and the comprehensiveness of human existence, is transformed to reflect the divine self-disclosures in a manner more accurate than the cosmos." Zargar, *Sufi Aesthetics*, 35. See also Zargar's specific discussion of Adam in terms of Ibn 'Arabi's concept in the *Fuṣūṣ* above (ibid., 71–72, 183n50).
179. Corbin, *Alone with the Alone*, 386–87n19 (emphasis original).
180. Ibid., 386n19 (emphasis mine).
181. Schimmel, *Mystical Dimensions of Islam*, 272.
182. For example, Bukhārī, *al-Isti'dhān*, 1.
183. The full title *al-Tanazzulāt al-mawṣiliyya fī asrār al-ṭahārāt wa al-ṣalawāt wa al-ayyām al-aṣliyya* has various alternatives in use, such as *Laṭā'if al-asrār* and *Tanazzul al-amlāk*, the latter being the published title cited here. The *Tanazzulāt* was written several years after the *Tarjumān* in 1204–5. See Addas, *Quest for the Red Sulphur*, 220–21, 304.
184. This verse, and the one that follows, appears to refer to Qur'an 57:13, which describes a wall and a door, outside of which is torment, while inside is mercy. I am indebted to Cyrus Zargar's keen insight here.
185. Ibn ʿArabī, *Tanazzul al-amlāk min 'ālam al-arwāḥ ilā 'ālam al-aflāk* (Cairo: Dār al-Fikr al-ʿArabī, 1961), 61.
186. Ibid.
187. Ibid. Here, Ibn 'Arabi alludes to the idea of "infidelity" (*kufr*) in the positive sense of "covering," although he does not specifically use the term *kafara*. In the *Futūḥāt*, Ibn 'Arabi uses the term for "infidels" (i.e., *kāfirūn* and *kuffār*, etc.) to describe the highest category of saints known as the "people of blame" (*malāmiyya*) who hide themselves from the public, since "they are those who cover their spiritual station" (*wa hum al-sātirūn maqāmahum*) and are thus like "farmers because they cover seed in the earth" (*yasturūn al-badhr fī al-arḍ*). See Ibn ʿArabī, *al-Futūḥāt*, vol. 3, 158 (Fut. II, 136).
188. Ibn ʿArabī, *Tanazzul al-amlāk*, 61.
189. Carl W. Ernst, *Words of Ecstasy in Sufism* (Albany: State University of New York Press, 1985), 71.

190. Ibid.
191. As Ibn ʿArabi says in the *Futūḥāt*, "The essence of the sharia is the essence of ultimate reality (*al-ḥaqīqa*)" and "the sharia is itself ultimate reality." Ibn ʿArabī, *al-Futūḥāt*, vol. 4, 219 (Fut. II, 563).
192. Ibn ʿArabī, *Tanazzul al-amlāk*, 62.
193. Ibn al-ʿArabī, *Fuṣūṣ al-ḥikam*, 64.
194. Ibid., 226.
195. See my brief discussion on this terminology in relation to the literary theory of Harold Bloom in the introduction, p. 20 and intro., n. 137.
196. Ibn ʿArabī, *al-Futūḥāt*, vol. 3, 256 (Fut. II, 219–20).
197. As Horsley states, "It would appear that as often as not religion and other forms of cultural practice are embedded in political-economic power relations and—far from being reducible to them—reflect, express, resist, and even constitute those relations of power." Horsley, "Religion and Other Products," 38.

CHAPTER 2

1. Ernst H. Kantorowicz, *The King's Two Bodies* (Princeton, NJ: Princeton University Press, 1957), 3.
2. See Muḥyī al-Dīn Ibn ʿArabī, *al-Futūḥāt al-makkiyya*, vol. 8 (Beirut: Dār Ṣādir, 2004), 296–97 (Fut. IV, 547–48). As Claude Addas notes, Ibn ʿArabi was most likely introduced to Kayka'us by his friend Majd al-Dīn Isḥāq b. Yūsuf al-Rūmī, who was the father of Ṣadr al-Dīn Qūnawī, perhaps as early as 1205 when Kayka'us's father, Kaykhusraw (r. 1192–96 and 1205–11) was king. Regardless, Ibn ʿArabi seems to have developed a friendship with Kayka'us and served as an advisor in some capacity. See Claude Addas, *Quest for the Red Sulphur: The Life of Ibn ʿArabī* (Cambridge: Islamic Texts Society, 1993), 225–34.
3. The "Protected People" (*ahl al-dhimma*) were originally Jews and Christians—that is, "the People of the Book" (*ahl al-kitāb*)—and later other historically designated religious groups who were theoretically to be given protection and a limited set of rights by Muslim polities in exchange for their payment of an indemnity tax (*jizya*) stipulated in verse 9:29 of the Qur'an.
4. Ibn ʿArabī, *al-Futūḥāt*, vol. 8, 296 (Fut. IV, 547).
5. Ibid.
6. Ibid.
7. Elsewhere in the *Futūḥāt*, Ibn ʿArabi states that God made *shirk* "from among the grave offenses (*al-kabā'ir*) that are not forgiven." Ibn ʿArabī, *al-Futūḥāt*, vol. 2, 429 (Fut. I, 749).
8. The claim that this accord was originally issued by the second caliph, ʿUmar ibn al-Khattab (r. 634–44), as Ibn ʿArabi does here, was rejected by late nineteenth and early twentieth-century European Orientalists like William Muir (d. 1905) and Thomas Walker Arnold (d. 1930), and most forcefully argued against

by Arthur Stanley Tritton (d. 1973). Rather, Tritton speculated it more likely that the Umayyad caliph ʿUmar II (ʿUmar ibn ʿAbd al-ʿAzīz [r. 717–20]) was linked to the origins of the so-called pact. Mark R. Cohen, "What Was the Pact of ʿUmar? A Literary-Historical Study," *Jerusalem Studies in Arabic and Islam* 23 (1999): 100n1, 101. Yet, as Milka Levy-Rubin notes, "Although it has been claimed (without due evidence) that some of these prohibitions may have been ascribed to ʿUmar b. ʿAbd al-ʿAziz anachronistically, it seems quite unmistakable that the regulations of the *ghiyār* [distinguishing marks] were a product of his policy and ideology." Milka Levy-Rubin, "*Shurūṭ ʿUmar*: From Early Harbingers to Systematic Enforcement," in *Beyond Religious Borders: Interaction and Intellectual Exchange in the Medieval Islamic World*, ed. David M. Freidenreich and Miriam Goldstein (Philadelphia: University of Pennsylvania Press, 2012), 33. Regardless of their origins, Levy-Rubin argues that by the second half of the ninth century, these restrictions had become the norm rather than the exception in the treatment of *dhimmīs* (ibid., 32). See also Milka Levy-Rubin, *Non-Muslims in the Early Islamic Empire: From Surrender to Coexistence* (Cambridge: Cambridge University Press, 2011), 88–98. Although Ibn 'Arabi's letter is faithful (almost verbatim) to the prohibitions within what is referred to as "the authentic Pact of ʿUmar," it nevertheless lacks what Cohen has described as its "literary frame," which embodies its most characteristic elements—that is, the articulation of the prohibitions in the first-person voice of the Christians of Syria in a letter addressed to 'Umar, as well as 'Umar's confirmative response. Rather, somewhat like Ibn Ḥazm's (d. 1064) version in his *Marātib al-ijmāʿ* (but more faithful to the content of "the authentic Pact"), Ibn 'Arabi renders the stipulations in the third person. See Ibn Ḥazm, *Marātib al-ijmāʿ fī al-ʿibādāt wa al-muʿāmalāt wa al-iʿtiqādāt (Cairo: Maktabat al-Qudsī, 1938), 115. See also Cohen, "What Was the Pact of ʿUmar?," 103, 121; Jacob Rader Marcus, The Jew in the Medieval World: A Source Book, 315–1791, rev ed. (1938; Cincinnati: Hebrew Union College Press, 1999), 14–16; and Giuseppe Scattolin, "Sufism and Law in Islam: A Text of Ibn 'Arabi (560/ 1165–638/ 1240) on 'Protected People' (Ahl al-Dhimma)," Islamochristiana 24 (1998): 37–55.*

9. Ibn ʿArabī, *al-Futūḥāt*, vol. 8, 296–97 (Fut. IV, 547–48).
10. Ibid., 297 (Fut. IV, 547).
11. The idea that the People of the Book could be counted as associationists (*mushrikūn*) was in fact common in Ibn 'Arabi's day. For example, Abū Ḥāmid al-Ghazālī (d. 1111), perhaps the most authoritative of his scholarly and mystical predecessors, asserted that the Jews and Christians—along with prophecy denying rationalists (*al-barāhima*), dualists (*al-thanawīyya*), and heretical philosophers (*al-zanādiqa*)—are "associationists (*mushrikūn*) in that they all deny the Messenger; indeed, every disbeliever (*kāfir*) denies the Messenger." Abū Ḥāmid al-Ghazālī, *Fayṣal al-tafriqa bayna al-islām wa al-zandaqa* (Beirut: Dar al-Fikr al-Lubnani, 1993), 26. This view was also shared by the famous exegete and philosopher Fakhr al-Dīn al-Rāzī (d. 1209) among others. See D.

Gimaret, "S͟hirk," in *The Encyclopaedia of Islam*, 2nd ed., vol. 9 (Leiden: E. J. Brill, 1997), 485.

12. Ibn ʿArabī, *al-Futūḥāt*, vol. 8, 297 (Fut. IV, 547). As Levy-Rubin notes, the *ghiyār* edict provided by the Pact of ʿUmar was not merely intended to distinguish Muslim from non-Muslim, but to additionally humiliate those guilty of unbelief. See Levy-Rubin, *Non-Muslims in the Early Islamic Empire*, 95.
13. Ibn ʿArabī, *al-Futūḥāt*, vol. 8, 297 (Fut. IV, 547).
14. "*lā tubnā kanīsa fī al-islām wa lā yujaddad mā khariba minhā.*" Ibn ʿArabī, *al-Futūḥāt*, vol. 8, 297 (Fut. IV, 548). This hadith is not found in the sound collections, but can be found in collections of disputed hadith. For example, Ibn al-Jawzī (d. 1200) includes it in his *al-Taḥqīq fī masāʾil al-khilāf* and states that it is not considered sound. Ibn al-Jawzī, *al-Taḥqīq fī masāʾil al-khilāf*, ed. ʿAbd al-Muʿṭī Amīn Qalʿajī, vol. 10 (Aleppo: Dār al-Waʿī al-ʿArabī, 1998), 226.
15. R. W. J. Austin, introduction to *The Bezels of Wisdom*, by Ibn al-ʿArabi, trans. R. W. J. Austin (Mahwah: Paulist Press, 1980), 10 (emphasis mine). For my choice to translate the *Fuṣūṣ al-ḥikam* as *The Ring Stones of Wisdom* see intro., n. 68.
16. Claude Addas, *Ibn ʿArabi: The Voyage of No Return*, trans. David Streight (Cambridge: Islamic Texts Society, 2000), 108.
17. Alexander D. Knysh, *Ibn ʿArabi in the Later Islamic Tradition: The Making of a Polemical Image in Medieval Islam* (Albany: State University of New York Press, 1999), 20.
18. A not-so-different approach is often found among Orientalists and Muslim modernists who suspect Ibn ʿArabi of bad faith. For example, A. E. Affifi decidedly called Ibn ʿArabi's use of "Islamic dogma" and "orthodox garb" a "sham." See A. E. Affifi, *The Mystical Philosophy of Muḥyid Dīn-ibnul ʿArabī* (Cambridge: Cambridge University Press, 1939), xi, 151. Similarly, Rom Landau noted: "Conscious of the dangers threatening an unorthodox thinker setting his views against those of the theologians representing authority, Ibn ʿArabi deliberately complicated his style. He would try to make an outrageously heterodox piece of argumentation look irreproachable by expressing it in the language or imagery of orthodoxy." Rom Landau, *The Philosophy of Ibn ʿArabi* (London: George Allen and Unwin, 1959), 24. Fazlur Rahman likewise claimed that the Sufi "lack of integration, indeed positive dislocation, between the Inner and the Outer leads to the suspicion that their insistence on the *S͟harīʿah* is formal and even hypocritical. This dislocative attitude . . . found its authoritative formulation in Ibn al-ʿArabī and his followers." Fazlur Rahman, introduction to *Intik͟hāb-i Maktūbāt-i Shayk͟h Aḥmad Sirhindī*, by Ahmad Sirhindī (Karachi: Iqbal Akadami, 1968), 51. Finally, and perhaps most relevant to the present discussion, Frithjof Schuon argued that although Ibn ʿArabi specified that the "religion of Love" is "Islam," he was "doubtless obliged to do so in order to avoid a charge of heresy, and he could do so in good conscience by understanding the term *islâm* in its direct and universal meaning." Frithjof Schuon, *Form and Substance in the Religions*,

trans. Mark Perry and Jean-Pierre LaFouge (Bloomington, IN: World Wisdom, 2002), 118n16.

19. William C. Chittick, *Imaginal Worlds: Ibn al-'Arabī and the Problem of Religious Diversity* (Albany: State University of New York Press, 1994), 125 (emphasis mine).
20. Yet, Chittick has been taken to task for not even mentioning the Andalusian Sufi's letter to the Seljuk sultan in his study on Ibn 'Arabi and religious diversity, *Imaginal Worlds*, quoted above. According to Carl-A. Keller, such an omission makes his "otherwise very penetrating observations . . . rather one-sided." Carl-A. Keller, "Perceptions of Other Religions in Sufism," in *Muslim Perceptions of Other Religions: A Historical Survey*, ed. Jacques Waardenburg (New York: Oxford University Press, 1999), 189.
21. Chittick, *Imaginal Worlds*, 125.
22. Asín Palacios quoted in Addas, *Quest for the Red Sulphur*, 234. See Miguel Asín Palacios, *El Islam cristianizado: estudio del "sufismo" a través de las obras de Abenarabi de Murcia* (Madrid: Editorial Plutarco, 1931), 94.
23. Keller, "Perceptions of Other Religions," 189 (emphasis mine).
24. Scattolin, "Sufism and Law in Islam," 51.
25. This is how Paul Heck situates the historical legacy of Sufism in his edited volume specifically "devoted to the political dimension of Sufism." Here, Sufism *proper* is still claimed to be "primarily [a] spiritual venture." *Sufism and Politics: The Power of Spirituality*, ed. Paul L. Heck (Princeton, NJ: Markus Wiener Publishers, 2007), 1 (emphasis mine).
26. For example, Reza Shah-Kazemi, "The Metaphysics of Interfaith Dialogue: Sufi Perspectives on the Universality of the Quranic Message," in *Paths to the Heart: Sufism and the Christian East*, ed. James S. Cutsinger (Bloomington, IN: World Wisdom, 2002), 181.
27. Ibn 'Arabi scholar Eric Winkel is currently undertaking this translation project in English.
28. Michel Chodkiewicz, "Toward Reading the *Futûhât Makkiyya*," in *The Meccan Revelations*, vol. 2, ed. Michel Chodkiewicz (New York: Pir Press, 2004), 7.
29. As R. Kevin Jaques observes, "For several generations of scholars of Islam, Hodgson's work has been the staple of doctoral exams and generally required reading." R. Kevin Jaques, "Belief," in *Key Themes for the Study of Islam*, ed. Jamal J. Elias (London: Oneworld, 2014), 383n2.
30. Omid Safi, "Bargaining with *Baraka:* Persian Sufism, 'Mysticism,' and Pre-modern Politics," *Muslim World* 90 (2000): 283n28.
31. As Hodgson notes, "many speak of the 'impact of the West'—not of technicalism—on Islamdom, as if it were two societies, not two ages, that met; as if it were that Western progress had finally reached the point where Muslims could no longer escape it, rather than that something new had happened to Western culture which thereby was happening to Islamdom and the whole world as well. It is symptomatic

of this attitude when the new age is dated from 1500, from the first larger contacts between the West and the other civilizations, rather than a century later, when actual technicalism supervened; as if what was decisive were not the *new level* of social process in the world, which happened to have emerged in the West, but rather the *new outreach* of the *West*, which happened soon to be going on to new levels." Marshall G. S. Hodgson, *The Venture of Islam: Conscience and History in a World Civilization*, vol. 3 (Chicago: University of Chicago Press, 1974), 204–5 (emphasis original).

32. Ibid., 205.
33. As I explore below, Hodgson leaned toward a type of essentialism regarding religious experience common in his day. He cited Orientalist and universalist scholars who submitted to varying degrees of this view of mysticism such as Rudolph Otto, Evelyn Underhill, Margaret Smith, Reynold A. Nicholson, A. J. Arberry, Louis Massignon, Henry Corbin, Mircea Eliade, Titus Burckhardt, and Wilfred C. Smith.
34. Hodgson, *The Venture of Islam*, vol. 2, 228–29.
35. As Hodgson notes in the first volume, "Ṣûfîs *increasingly tended to minimize differences among religious beliefs*. In contrast to the communalist exclusivity of most of the Piety-minded, *they readily tended toward a universalistic viewpoint*." Hodgson, *The Venture of Islam*, vol. 1, 401 (emphasis mine).
36. Ibid., 362.
37. Ibid., 363.
38. Ibid., 365.
39. Ibid., 365–66.
40. Ibid., 393.
41. Ibid.
42. Ibid. (emphasis mine).
43. Ibid.
44. Hodgson, *The Venture of Islam*, vol. 2, 185 (emphasis mine).
45. Ibid., 243.
46. Ibid., 232–33.
47. Hodgson, *The Venture of Islam*, vol. 1, 396.
48. Jeremy Carrette and Richard King, *Selling Spirituality: The Silent Takeover of Religion* (New York: Routledge, 2005), 38.
49. William T. Cavanaugh, *The Myth of Religious Violence: Secular Ideology and the Roots of Modern Conflict* (Oxford: Oxford University Press, 2009), 162
50. Ibid., 166, 177.
51. Ibid., 123–24.
52. Kenneth Cracknell, "Introductory Essay," in *Wilfred Cantwell Smith: A Reader*, ed. Kenneth Cracknell (Oxford: Oneworld, 2001), 6, 20.
53. Wilfred Cantwell Smith, *Islam in Modern History* (Princeton, NJ: Princeton University Press, 1957), 37.

54. Omid Safi, *The Politics of Knowledge in Premodern Islam: Negotiating Ideology and Religious Inquiry* (Chapel Hill: University of North Carolina Press, 2006), 127. See also Safi, "Bargaining with Baraka," 259–88.
55. Safi, *The Politics of Knowledge*, 128.
56. Ibid., xxxi.
57. Besides his aforementioned letter to Kayka'us, Ibn 'Arabi reports his successful intercession with a ruler on behalf of man who requested his help to regain authority (*mulk*). The point of this particular anecdote, however, is that Ibn 'Arabi refused to accept the gifts that were offered to him in return. As such, Ibn 'Arabi relates that acceptance of any gift for such an act of intercession was likened to an act of usury (*al-ribā*) by the Prophet and is thus prohibited. Ibn ʿArabī, *al-Futūḥāt*, vol. 8, 232 (Fut. IV, 489).
58. Addas, *Quest for the Red Sulphur*, 276.
59. Ibid., 277.
60. Chantal Mouffe, *The Return of the Political* (London: Verso, 1993), 3.
61. Ibid., 2 (emphasis mine).
62. Ibid.
63. As Schmitt notes: "A world in which the possibility of war is utterly eliminated, a completely pacified globe, would be a world without the distinction of friend and enemy and hence a world without politics." Carl Schmitt, *The Concept of the Political,* trans. George Schwab (Chicago: University of Chicago Press, 2007), 35.
64. Hugh Nicholson, *Comparative Theology and the Problem of Religious Rivalry* (New York: Oxford University Press, 2011), 9 (emphasis mine).
65. Shah-Kazemi, "The Metaphysics of Interfaith Dialogue," 181 (emphasis mine).
66. John Burton, "Abrogation," in *Encyclopedia of the Qur'ān*, vol. 1 (Leiden: Brill, 2001), 11–12.
67. al-Ghazālī, *al-Mustaṣfā min ʿilm al-uṣūl,* cited in Burton, "Abrogation," 11.
68. Bruce Lawrence, "Shahrastānī, Al-," *Encyclopedia of Religion*, 2nd ed., vol. 12 (Detroit: Macmillan Reference USA, 2005), 8267.
69. Muḥammad ibn ʿAbd al-Karīm al-Shahrastānī, *Kitāb nihāyat al-aqdām fī ʿilm al-kalām*, ed. Alfred Guillaume (Baghdad: Maktabat al-Muthanna, 1964), 499. As Jacques Waardenburg notes, "The principal argument used specifically against Judaism concerned the doctrine of *naskh* (abrogation). . . . Jewish theologians, by contrast, held that it is impossible for God to change his mind, as God does not change his decree and dispensation." Jacques Waardenburg, "The Medieval Period 650–1500," in *Muslim Perceptions of Other Religions: A Historical Survey*, ed. Jacques Waardenburg (New York: Oxford University Press, 1999), 52.
70. Bukhārī, *al-Riqāq*, 98.
71. al-Shahrastānī, *Kitāb nihāyat al-aqdām*, 503.

72. As Addas notes, Ibn 'Arabi was familiar with Ibn Barrajan's work and had formally studied his *Kitāb al-ḥikma* (i.e., *K. Īḍāḥ al-ḥikma bi-aḥkām al-ʿibra*). Addas, *Quest for the Red Sulphur*, 55. See also Claude Addas, "Andalusī Mysticism and the Rise of Ibn ʿArabī," in *The Legacy of Muslim Spain*, ed. Salma Khadra Jayyusi, vol. 2 (Leiden: E. J. Brill, 1992), 925–26; and Yousef Casewit, *The Mystics of al-Andalus: Ibn Barrajān and Islamic Thought in the Twelfth Century* (Cambridge: Cambridge University Press, 2017), 163–64.
73. Casewit, *The Mystics of al-Andalus*, 258.
74. Ibid. (emphasis mine).
75. See p. 57.
76. A similar argument for the particularism of the Qur'anic critique of the People of the Book has been recently made by Fred Donner in *Muhammad and the Believers: At the Origins of Islam* (Cambridge, MA: Harvard University Press, 2010), see esp. 68–71. See also Vajda, "Ahl al-Kitāb," in *The Encyclopaedia of Islam*, 2nd ed., vol. 1 (Leiden: E. J. Brill, 1986), 264.
77. Chittick, *Imaginal Worlds*, 124.
78. Ibid. (emphasis mine).
79. Ibid.
80. See my discussion on Qur'an 3:84 and Ibn 'Arabi's attainment of the Muhammadan Station, pp. 37–39.
81. William C. Chittick, *The Sufi Path of Knowledge: Ibn al-'Arabi's Metaphysics of Imagination* (Albany: State University of New York Press, 1989), 171 (emphasis mine).
82. Ibn ʿArabī, *al-Futūḥāt*, vol. 3, 192 (Fut. II, 165).
83. For example, Qur'an 2:4–5, 2:136, 2:285, 3:3, 3:84, 4:162, 29:46, and 35:31.
84. Ṣadr al-Dīn Qūnawī was also the guardian of Ibn 'Arabi's handwritten, revised manuscript of the *Futūḥāt*. See Chodkiewicz, "Toward Reading the *Futûhât*," 5.
85. William C. Chittick, *Faith and Practice of Islam: Three Thirteenth Century Sufi Texts* (Albany: State University of New York Press, 1992), xi.
86. Ibid., 37 (emphasis mine).
87. See n. 83 above.
88. Chittick, *Faith and Practice of Islam*, 183.
89. Ibid., 183–84.
90. Ibn 'Arabi quoted in Chittick, *Faith and Practice of Islam*, 184.
91. Chittick, *Imaginal Worlds*, 125; and William C. Chittick, "Religious Diversity: A Myth of Origins," in *The Religious Other: Towards a Muslim Theology of Other Religions in a Post-Prophetic Age*, ed. Muhammad Suhail Umar (Lahore: Iqbal Academy, 2008), 280.
92. Chittick, *Imaginal Worlds*, 125 (emphasis mine).
93. Ibid. (emphasis mine).

94. See the following by chronological order of publishing date: Mona Siddiqui, *My Way: A Muslim Woman's Journey* (London: I. B. Tauris, 2014), 129–30; Jerusha Tanner Lamptey, *Never Wholly Other: A Muslima Theology of Religious Pluralism* (New York: Oxford University Press, 2014), 42, 46; Reza Shah-Kazemi, "Beyond Polemics and Pluralism: The Universal Message of the Qur'an," in *Between Heaven and Hell: Islam, Salvation, and the Fate of Others*, ed. Mohammad Hassan Khalil (New York: Oxford University Press, 2013), 95; Reza Shah-Kazemi, *The Spirit of Tolerance in Islam* (London: I. B. Tauris, 2012), 88; Sayafaatun Almirzanah, *When Mystic Masters Meet: Towards a New Matrix for Christian-Muslim Dialogue* (New York: Blue Dome, 2011), 218; Reza Shah-Kazemi, *The Other in the Light of the One: The Universality of the Qur'ān and Interfaith Dialogue* (Cambridge: Islamic Texts Society, 2006), 241; Reza Shah-Kazemi, *Paths to Transcendence: According to Shankara, Ibn Arabi, and Meister Eckhart* (Bloomington, IN: World Wisdom, 2006), 121; Reza Shah-Kazemi, "The Metaphysics of Interfaith Dialogue," 182. Reference to the passage that Chittick has translated in support of his same argument are also made by Éric Geoffroy, "Pluralism or the Consciousness of Alterity in Islam," in *Universal Dimensions of Islam: Studies in Comparative Religion*, ed. Patrick Laude (Bloomington, IN: World Wisdom, 2011), 102; and Abd ar-Razzâq Yahya (Charles-André Gilis), *L'Esprit universel de L'Islam* (Algiers: La Maison des Livres, 1989), 119.
95. See Nuh Ha Mim Keller, *Sea without Shore: A Manual of the Sufi Path* (Amman: Sunna Books, 2011), 325. Keller is the head of the Hāshimī-Darqāwī *ṭarīqa* (in the Shādhilī ʿAlāwiyya line), and his shaykh, 'Abd al-Rahman al-Shaghouri (d. 2004), was also a public defender of Ibn 'Arabi in Syria (ibid., 7). For a brief biography of Keller and the history of his order see Marcia Hermansen, "The 'Other' Shadhilis of the West," in *Une voie soufie dans le monde: la Shâdhiliyya*, ed. Éric Geoffroy (Paris: Maisonneuve & Larose, 2005), 493–94.
96. Ibn ʿArabī, *al-Futūḥāt*, vol. 5, 177 (Fut. III, 153), translated by Nuh Ha Mim Keller in "On the Validity of All Religions in the Thought of ibn Al-'Arabi and Emir 'Abd al-Qadir: A Letter to 'Abd al-Matin," 1996, accessed July 8, 2016, www.masud.co.uk/ISLAM/nuh/amat.htm. See published version in Keller, *Sea without Shore*, 323–24.
97. Ibn ʿArabī, *al-Futūḥāt*, vol. 1, 180 (Fut. I, 143).
98. "*al-zamān qad istadāra ka-haya'atihi yawm khalaqa al-samawāt wa al-arḍ.*" Bukhārī, *Badaʾ al-khalq*, 8).
99. See A. Moberg, "Nasīʾ," in *The Encyclopaedia of Islam*, 2nd ed., vol. 7 (Leiden: E. J. Brill, 1993), 977. This practice was subsequently prohibited in verse 9:37 of the Qur'an.
100. Ibn ʿArabī, *al-Futūḥāt*, vol. 1, 180 (Fut. I, 143).
101. Ibid., vol. 1, 181 (Fut. I, 144).
102. According to Lane, the infinitive *ẓuhūr* with the prep. *ʿalā/bi* is rendered in its first form perfect *ẓahara ʿalayhi*: "*He overcame, conquered, subdued, overpowered,*

or mastered, him; gained the mastery or victory, or prevailed, over him." See Edward William Lane, *An Arabic-English Lexicon* (1877; reprint, New Delhi: J. Jetley, 1985), 1926. This is the same sense of the fourth form verb *yuẓhir* in Qur'an 9:33, which Ibn 'Arabi seems to refer to here: "*It is He who sent His Messenger with guidance and the Religion of Truth to triumph over every religion, though the associationists are averse.*"

103. Ibn ʿArabī, *al-Futūḥāt*, vol. 1, 182 (Fut. I, 145).
104. In all other cases, Ibn 'Arabi importantly prefers to refer to previous "religions" as "revealed laws" (*sharāʾiʿ*), thus emphasizing in Ibn 'Arabi's normative conception how the "true" religion of God is perpetual, while the rulings are what change according to the particular prophetic messenger and the times and conditions of the age they manifest within.
105. Although the pronoun here can grammatically refer to God, it is perhaps better read as referring to Muhammad since in legal discourse the verb *taqrīr* refers to Muhammad's approval of an action as the determination of permissibility in legal rulings. See "Sources of Law," in *Encyclopaedia of Islamic Law*, vol. 1, ed. Arif Ali Khan and Tauqir Mohammad Khan (New Delhi: Pentagon Press, 2006), 76.
106. That is, they can use their own rulings.
107. Ibn ʿArabī, *al-Futūḥāt*, vol. 1, 182 (Fut. I, 145).
108. While this line connotes the idea of the People of the Book's rulings bearing "witness" against them on the Day of Judgment, given Ibn 'Arabi's assertion that the People of the Book will gain "felicity" by following such laws, the prepositional binary "against/for" (*'alā/li*) is perhaps best understood as "in spite of." In other words, although the People of the Book are an exception to the general rule of abrogation, their relative "success" as adopted members within the Muslim *umma* is afforded to them *in spite of* their own laws, not *because of them*. Regarding Ibn 'Arabi's acknowledgment of the People of the Book's "success" or "felicity" (*sa'āda*) see discussion, pp. 114–15.
109. al-Nābigha al-Dhubyānī (d. 604), one of the six preeminent pre-Islamic Arabic poets famous for his *Dīwān*. See Wilhelm Ahlwardt, *The Divans of the Six Ancient Arabic Poets Ennabiga, 'Antara, Tharafa, Zuhair, 'Alqama and Imruulqais: Chiefly According to the Mss. of Paris, Gotha, and Leyden; and the Collection of Their Fragments with a List of the Various Readings of the Text* (London: Trübner and Company, 1870); and A. Arazi, "al-Nābigha al-Dhubyānī," in *The Encyclopaedia of Islam*, 2nd ed., vol. 7 (Leiden: E. J. Brill, 1993), 840–42.
110. From al-Nabigha's *Dīwān* and composed for Nuʿmān b. Mundhīr, the king of Ḥīra. See Al-Nābigha al-Dhubyānī, *Le Dîwân de Nâbiga Dhobyânî*, ed. and trans. Hartwig Derenbourg (Paris: Imprimerie nationale, 1869), 83 (Arabic), 126 (French translation).
111. Ibn ʿArabī, *al-Futūḥāt*, vol. 1, 182 (Fut. I, 145).

112. See n. 67 above.
113. Ibn ʿArabī, *al-Futūḥāt*, vol. 1, 274 (Fut. I, 225).
114. "*law kāna mūsā ḥayy ma wasiʿahu illā an yatbaʿanī.*" A variation of this hadith can be found in the Musnad of Ibn Ḥanbal. See Aḥmad ibn Ḥanbal, *al-Musnad*, ed. Hamza A. al-Zayn vol. 11 (Cairo: Dār al-Ḥadīth, 1995), 500 (no. 14565).
115. Ibn ʿArabī, *al-Futūḥāt*, vol. 1, 273 (Fut. I, 224).
116. There are several hadith that assert Jesus will, upon his return, "break the cross and kill the pig." For example, see Bukhārī, *al-Buyūʿ*, 177.
117. Ibn ʿArabī, *al-Futūḥāt*, vol. 1, 274 (Fut. I, 225).
118. See n. 114 above. For examples of this hadith in the *Futūḥāt* see Ibn ʿArabī, *al-Futūḥāt*, vol. 1, 273 (Fut. I, 224). See also Ibn ʿArabī, *al-Futūḥāt*, vol. 1, 170 (Fut. I, 135); vol. 1, 181 (Fut. I, 144); vol. 1, 244 (Fut. I, 198); vol. 1, 295 (Fut. I, 244); vol. 2, 172 (Fut. I, 522); vol. 3, 157 (Fut. II, 134); and vol. 3, 163 (Fut. III, 141).
119. Ibn ʿArabi here refers to a version of the hadith noted in n. 116 above claiming that after Jesus's return, but still "during his lifetime, God will bring to naught all of the religions except Islam" (*yuhliku allāh fī zamānihi al-milal kullahā illā al-islām*). See Abū Dāwūd, *al-Malāḥim*, 34.
120. Ibn ʿArabī, *al-Futūḥāt*, vol. 1, 274 (Fut. I, 225).
121. Ibid.
122. See n. 11 above.
123. Ibn ʿArabī, *al-Futūḥāt*, vol. 1, 274 (Fut. I, 225).
124. Ibid.
125. Ibn ʿArabi's treatment of Ibn Barthamla is briefly discussed by Michel Chodkiewicz, *Seal of the Saints: Prophethood and Sainthood in the Doctrine of Ibn ʿArabī*, trans. Liadain Sherrard (Cambridge: Islamic Texts Society, 1993), 78–79. Chodkiewicz concludes by noting that Ibn ʿArabi's final recourse to the *jizya* serves as an exoteric way out for saints like Ibn Barthamla who belonged to previous revelations abrogated by the advent of Muhammad. According to Chodkiewicz, through the payment of the *jizya*, the People of the Book "are integrated into the Islamic order of things, and by this very fact their own Law, which theoretically has been invalidated by the coming of Islam, re-acquires for them a validity which is so to speak derivative. Nevertheless, as we may gather from the reference to the *jizya*, we are no longer speaking of anchorites, who by definition are outside the norms of a community, but of individuals who are, technically, 'infidels.'" Chodkiewicz, *Seal of the Saints*, 79.
126. Ibn ʿArabī, *al-Futūḥāt*, vol. 1, 170 (Fut. I, 135).
127. Ibid. (Fut. I, 134). The latter quote is a reference to the non-canonical hadith "*kuntu nabī wa ādam bayna al-māʾ wa al-ṭīn*." For its meaning in relation to the divine names, see discussion p. 40. See also intro., n. 101.
128. Ibn ʿArabī, *al-Futūḥāt*, vol. 1, 170 (Fut. I, 135).
129. Ibid.

130. Ibid.
131. Ibid.
132. Ibid.
133. Ibid.
134. Ibid.
135. Eckart Frahm, "Rising Suns and Falling Stars: Assyrian Kings and the Cosmos," in *Experiencing Power, Generating Authority: Cosmos, Politics, and the Ideology of Kingship in Ancient Egypt and Mesopotamia*, ed. Jane A. Hill, Philip Jones, and Antonio J. Morales (Philadelphia: University of Pennsylvania Museum of Archaeology and Anthropology, 2013), 99.
136. Franz Cumont, *Astrology and Religion among the Greeks and Romans* (New York: Knickerbocker Press, 1912), 127–28.
137. Ibn ʿArabī, *al-Futūḥāt*, vol. 4, 84 (Fut. II, 445).
138. Ibn al-ʿArabī, *Fuṣūṣ al-ḥikam*, 75.
139. Ibid.
140. Ibid. For a brief discussion on the nature of "the Muhammadans" (*al-muḥammadiyyīn*), see pp. 45–47 and chap. 1, n. 147.
141. Chodkiewicz, *Seal of the Saints*, 170.
142. That is, "the Seal of Muhammadan Sainthood" (*khātam al-walāya al-muḥammadiyya*). See Ibn ʿArabī, *al-Futūḥāt*, vol. 6, 243 (Fut. III, 514), and Ibn al-ʿArabī, *Fuṣūṣ al-ḥikam*, 64.
143. In chapter 1, I discuss Ibn ʿArabi's attainment of the "Muhammadan Station" (*muḥammadī al-maqām*) as he describes it in the "attainment passage" of the *Futūḥāt* (i.e., Fut. III, 350) and its relationship to the theme of "comprehensiveness" within Ibn ʿArabi's *logos* orientation. See pp. 38–41.
144. Ibn ʿArabī, *al-Futūḥāt*, vol. 1, 189 (Fut. I, 151).
145. Ibid., vol. 5, 164 (Fut. III, 142).
146. Ibid. Here, the dual form of "configuration" (*nashaʾ*) denotes his spiritual and physical forms.
147. Ibid.
148. That is, that of the *jinn*.
149. Ibn ʿArabī, *al-Futūḥāt*, vol. 5, 164 (Fut. III, 142). This passage ends by alluding to the hadith "the scholars of my community are like the prophets preceding me." This saying and its like (i.e., "the scholars of my community are like the prophets of the Children of Israel") are a favorite among Sufis, but are not considered to be authentic within normative scholarship. See Michael M. J. Fischer and Mehdi Abedi, *Debating Muslims: Cultural Dialogues in Postmodernity and Tradition* (Madison: University of Wisconsin Press, 1990), 142.
150. See p. 68 and n. 94 above.
151. Shah-Kazemi quoted by Caner Dagli, "The Quran and the Perennial Philosophy" (Conference: Intellectuality and Spirituality in the Islamic Tradition: A Prelude

to the Perennial Philosophy, May 21–22, 2016, at The George Washington University, Washington, DC), accessed July 19, 2017, https://www.youtube.com/watch?v=Vs3Vj1LYPvI [beginning at the 46:15 min. mark]. See also Shah-Kazemi, *The Other in the Light of the One*, 242–43.

152. Shah-Kazemi quoted by Dagli, "The Quran and the Perennial Philosophy," accessed July 19, 2017, https://www.youtube.com/watch?v=Vs3Vj1LYPvI [beginning at the 46:37 min. mark]. See also Shah-Kazemi, "Beyond Polemics and Pluralism," 95.
153. Dagli, "The Quran and the Perennial Philosophy," https://www.youtube.com/watch?v=Vs3Vj1LYPvI [beginning at the 47:55 min. mark] (emphasis mine).
154. For a brief discussion on the notion of "strong misreading" in relation to the literary theory of Harold Bloom see p. 20 and intro., n. 137.
155. Ibn ʿArabī, *al-Futūḥāt*, vol. 5, 168 (Fut. III, 145).
156. Peter Fibiger Bang with Dariusz Kołodziejczyk, "'Elephant of India': Universal Empire through Time and across Cultures," in *Universal Empire: A Comparative Approach to Imperial Culture and Representation in Eurasian History*, ed. Peter Fibiger Bang and Dariusz Kołodziejczyk (Cambridge: Cambridge University Press, 2012), 27–28 (emphasis mine).
157. Cohen, "What Was The Pact of ʿUmar?," 129.
158. Indeed, as Richard Horsley notes, the idea that religion is "*something in itself* may simply stand in the way of recognizing the various ways in which what may appear as 'religious' expressions are inseparably related to other aspects of life. *The various meanings and practices that we refer to as religious are always already in a context of political-economic and other relations.*" Richard A. Horsley, "Religion and Other Products of Empire," *Journal of the American Academy of Religion* 71, no. 1 (2003): 39 (emphasis mine).

CHAPTER 3

1. Friedrich Schleiermacher, *On Religion: Speeches to Its Cultured Despisers*, trans. John Oman (London: K. Paul, Trench, Trübner & Co., 1893), 216.
2. Frithjof Schuon, *Logic and Transcendence: A New Translation with Selected Letters*, trans. Mark Perry, Jean-Pierre Lafouge, and James S. Cutsinger, ed. James S. Cutsinger (Bloomington, IN: World Wisdom, 2009), 4.
3. Bruno Latour, *We Have Never Been Modern*, trans. Catherine Porter (Cambridge, MA: Harvard University Press, 1993), 76.
4. Guénon assumed the name Palingénius while serving as the holy bishop for the Gnostic Church in Paris. See William Quinn, "Guénon, René Jean Marie Joseph," *Dictionary of Gnosis and Western Esotericism*, ed. Wouter J. Hanegraaff (Leiden: Brill, 2006), 442. On Guénon's influence see ibid., 444–45.
5. Palingénius (R. Guénon), "La Gnose et les écoles spiritualistes," *La Gnose*, no. 2 (1909): 20, 21.

6. Ibid., 20.
7. Ibid., 21.
8. Ibid.
9. Martin Lings notes that Guénon's particular spiritual "function" was "to remind twentieth century man of the need for orthodoxy." According to Lings, Guénon restored to the world the "original meaning" of orthodoxy as a "rectitude of opinion . . . which compels the intelligent man not merely to reject heresy, but also to recognize the validity of all those faiths which conform to those criteria on which his own faith depends for its orthodoxy." Martin Lings, introduction to *The Essential René Guénon: Metaphysics, Tradition, and the Crisis of Modernity*, by René Guénon, ed. John Herlihy (Bloomington, IN: World Wisdom, 2009), xxvi–vii.
10. Regarding the origins of the "Perennial Philosophy" (*philosophia perennis*) see prol., n. 5.
11. William Stoddart, foreword to *René Guénon: Some Observations*, by Frithjof Schuon, ed. William Stoddart (Hillsdale, NY: Sophia Perennis, 2004), xi.
12. See prol., n. 5.
13. Stoddart, foreword to *René Guénon*, xi.
14. Jean-Baptiste Aymard and Patrick Laude, *Frithjof Schuon: Life and Teachings* (Albany: State University of New York Press, 2004), 23; see also intro., n. 28.
15. For a nonhagiographical, albeit tendentious, biography of Schuon's role as Sufi shaykh and leader of a universalist religious movement see Mark J. Sedgwick, *Against the Modern World: Traditionalism and the Secret Intellectual History of the Twentieth Century* (New York: Oxford University Press, 2004), 73–94, 147–77.
16. William Quinn, "Schuon, Frithjof (Also Known as Shaykh ʿIsâ Nur al-Dîn Ahmad al-Shâdhilî al-Darqâwî al-ʿAlawî al-Maryamî)," *Dictionary of Gnosis and Western Esotericism*, ed. Wouter J. Hanegraaff (Leiden: Brill, 2006), 1044.
17. Aymard and Laude, *Frithjof Schuon*, 5, 7, 10.
18. Excepting some forms of Freemasonry, Guénon saw the West as entirely devoid of initiatic traditions. For Schuon's criticisms on Guénon, see Frithjof Schuon, *René Guénon: Some Observations*, ed. William Stoddart (Hillsdale, NY: Sophia Perennis, 2004). In regards to Christianity as a valid initiatic path see ibid., 37–47.
19. Frithjof Schuon, *Christianity/Islam: Perspectives on Esoteric Ecumenism*, ed. James S. Cutsinger (Bloomington, IN: World Wisdom, 2008), 23.
20. Frithjof Schuon quoted in Aymard and Laude, *Frithjof Schuon*, 7.
21. Paul Sérant, "Frithjof Schuon and René Guénon," in *René Guénon: Some Observations*, by Frithjof Schuon, ed. William Stoddart (Hillsdale, NY: Sophia Perennis, 2004), 59.
22. Indeed, Schuon saw his own "initiatic function" as a shaykh to be "the 'providential complement' of the Guénonian message," since "Guénon had never been conferred with an initiatic function." Aymard and Laude, *Frithjof Schuon*, 67, 161n70.

23. John Herlihy, preface to *The Essential René Guénon: Metaphysics, Tradition, and the Crisis of Modernity*, by René Guénon, ed. John Herlihy (Bloomington, IN: World Wisdom, 2009), xi.
24. See Eric Geoffroy, *Introduction to Sufism: The Inner Path of Islam* (Bloomington, IN: World Wisdom, 2010), 187.
25. As Nasr himself notes, towards the end of the 1950s he "embraced Sufism not only intellectually but also existentially in a form linked to the Maghrib and more particularly to the spiritual lineage of the great Algerian master Shaykh Aḥmad al-ʿAlawī and Shaykh ʿĪsā Nūr al-Dīn Aḥmad [i.e., Frithjof Schuon]." Seyyed Hossein Nasr, "Intellectual Autobiography," in *The Philosophy of Seyyed Hossein Nasr*, ed. Lewis Edwin Hahn, Randall E. Auxier, and Lucian W. Stone, Jr. (Chicago: Open Court, 2001), 27. For Schuon's full Muslim name (including his assumed Sufi pedigree) see n. 16 above. See also William C. Chittick, introduction to *The Essential Seyyed Hossein Nasr*, by Seyyed Hossein Nasr (Bloomington, IN: World Wisdom, 2007), xi.
26. Seyyed Hossein Nasr, *Sufi Essays* (Albany: State University of New York Press, 1991), 146–47 (emphasis mine).
27. First published *Comprendre l'Islam* (Gallimard, 1961).
28. Frithjof Schuon, *Understanding Islam* (Bloomington, IN: World Wisdom Books, 1998), 36.
29. Ibid., 36–37 (emphasis mine).
30. See Pietro Nutrizio, "Rene Guenon: A Biographical Note," in René Guénon, *The Lord of the World: Le Roi du monde* (Ripon: Coombe Springs Press, 1983), 68; and Aymard and Laude, *Frithjof Schuon*, 72.
31. In the wake of 9/11 there has been a spate of Perennialist-leaning articles and books that focus on the thought of Ibn ʿArabi and its usefulness in the context of contemporary religious pluralism and interfaith dialogue. Many of these books specifically compare Ibn ʿArabi with supposed premodern universalists of other faiths—most typically his assumed medieval Christian counterpart the Dominican theologian Meister Eckhart (d. 1327). Such material has been generally published under similar titles, which often share the same translated passages of Ibn ʿArabi; for example, Reza Shah-Kazemi, *Paths to Transcendence: According to Shankara, Ibn Arabi, and Meister Eckhart* (Bloomington, IN: World Wisdom, 2006); Ghasem Kakaie, "Interreligious Dialogue: Ibn ʿArabi and Meister Eckhart," *Journal of the Muhyiddin Ibn ʿArabi Society* 45 (2009): 45–63; Robert J. Dobie, *Logos and Revelation: Ibn ʿArabi, Meister Eckhart, and Mystical Hermeneutics* (Washington, DC: Catholic University of America Press, 2010); and Sayafaatun Almirzanah, *When Mystic Masters Meet: Towards a New Matrix for Christian-Muslim Dialogue* (New York: Blue Dome, 2011). Added to this list should be Shah-Kazemi's *The Other in the Light of the One*, where Ibn ʿArabi's ideas as interpreted from within a Perennialist framework play a central role. See Reza Shah-Kazemi, *The Other*

in the Light of the One: The Universality of the Qur'ān and Interfaith Dialogue (Cambridge: Islamic Texts Society, 2006).

32. Chittick, introduction to *The Essential Seyyed Hossein Nasr*, xiii. Sedgwick has noted the ubiquitous presence of Schuonian Perennialism within Western publishing houses since 1950: "In the period 1950–99 Schuon and 23 other identified followers published some 220 books. Eighty of these were well enough received to be translated into other languages (135 translations in total) or to go into new editions. Thirty were major works." Sedgwick, *Against the Modern World*, 167.
33. Seyyed Hossein Nasr, *Three Muslim Sages: Avicenna, Suhrawardī, Ibn 'Arabī* (Cambridge, MA: Harvard University Press, 1964), 117 (emphasis mine).
34. James W Morris, "Ibn ʿArabī and His Interpreters. Part I: Recent French Translations," *Journal of the American Oriental Society* 106, no. 3 (1986): 541n8.
35. Ibid. (emphasis mine).
36. James Winston Morris, "Ibn 'Arabi in the 'Far West,'" *Journal of the Muhyiddin Ibn 'Arabi Society* 24 (2001): 105–106.
37. Ibid., 106.
38. Ibid. (emphasis mine).
39. William C. Chittick, "A Sufi Approach to Religious Diversity: Ibn al-ʿArabī on the Metaphysics of Revelation," in *Religion of the Heart: Essays Presented to Frithjof Schuon on His Eightieth Birthday*, ed. Seyyed Hossein Nasr and William Stoddart (Washington, DC: Foundation for Traditional Studies, 1991), 51.
40. William C. Chittick, "Response to the Questions of Ahmet Faruk Çağlar (unpublished in English; originally published in Turkish)," posted on Chittick's academia.edu page, accessed May 12, 2016, https://www.academia.edu/7371820/Responses_to_Questions_Posed_by_Ahmet_Faruk_%C3%87a%C4%9Flar_unpublished_in_English_originally_published_in_Turkish_, 1.
41. William C. Chittick, "Interview with Mohamed Omar (unpublished in English; originally published online in Swedish)": posted on Chittick's academia.edu page, accessed May 12, 2016, https://www.academia.edu/7371849/Interview_with_Mohamed_Omar_unpublished_in_English_originally_published_online_in_Swedish_, 6.
42. Ibid., 6–7 (emphasis mine).
43. Ibid. (emphasis mine).
44. Huston Smith, "Is There a Perennial Philosophy?," *Journal of the American Academy of Religion* 55, no. 3 (1987): 562 (emphasis mine). Smith here claims "to present the position . . . of Rene Guenon, A. K. Coomaraswamy, Titus Burckhardt, Frithjof Schuon, Martin Lings, S. H. Nasr, and their like" (ibid., 560n11).
45. Seyyed Hossein Nasr, "Frithjof Schuon and the Islamic Tradition," in *The Essential Sophia*, ed. Seyyed Hossein Nasr and Katherine O'Brien (Bloomington, IN: World Wisdom, 2006), 268.
46. See chap. 1, n. 95.

47. Nasr, *Sufi Essays*, 127 (emphasis mine).
48. Chittick, introduction to *The Essential Seyyed Hossein Nasr*, ix.
49. Shah-Kazemi, *The Other in the Light*, xvii.
50. Ibid., 250.
51. Adnan Aslan, *Religious Pluralism in Christian and Islamic Philosophy: The Thought of John Hick and Seyyed Hossein Nasr* (Richmond: Curzon, 1998), 77 (emphasis mine).
52. Ibid., 129.
53. Ibid.
54. Ibid.
55. As Hick states: "The needed Copernican revolution in theology involves . . . a shift from the dogma that Christianity is at the centre to the realisation that it is God who is at the centre, and that all the religions of mankind, including our own, serve and revolve around him." John Hick, *God and the Universe of Faiths: Essays in the Philosophy of Religion* (Oxford: Oneworld Publications, 1993), 131. See also Philip Almond, "John Hick's Copernican Theology," *Theology* 86, no. 709 (1983): 36–41.
56. Gavin D'Costa has noted how Hick's recourse to the Kantian typologies of *noumenal* Real and *phenomenal* religious responses forces the distinctive truth claims of each religion "into agnosticism." See Gavin D'Costa, "John Hick and Religious Pluralism: Yet Another Revolution," in *Problems in the Philosophy of Religion: Critical Studies of the Work of John Hick*, ed. Harold Hewitt Jr. (Houndmills: Macmillan Press, 1991), 7. See also John Hick, *God Has Many Names* (Philadelphia: Westminster Press, 1982), 105.
57. Here, the idea of "antireductionist" is *essentialist* in that it posits a nonreducible, *sui generis*, or essential "religious reality," which, in the words of Steven Wasserstrom, exists "somehow beyond aesthetics, ethics and logic, inhabiting the domains of neither law, nor art, nor science." As Wasserstrom notes, Schleiermacher was a strong influence in antireductionist approaches to religion such as Henry Corbin and Jung, as well as the Chicago School of History of Religions such as Mircea Eliade. "The Schleiermacherian *gefühl* (feeling) became, for the Historians of Religions, one of inward 'experience.' Following Otto and Jung, as well as many esoteric thinkers, Eliade called such experience 'numinous.' The experience of the 'sacred,' 'numinous,' or 'holy,' in short, was asserted to be the foundational constituent of religion." Steven M. Wasserstrom, *Religion after Religion: Gershom Scholem, Mircea Eliade, and Henry Corbin at Eranos* (Princeton, NJ: Princeton University Press, 1999), 29.
58. For example, René Guénon, *The Crisis of the Modern World* (Hillsdale, NY: Sophia Perennis, 2004), 61–62; and Schuon, *Christianity/Islam*, 23, 32n11.
59. Indeed, much like Schuonian Perennialism, Schleiermacher's notion of God consciousness is based upon a Neoplatonic notion that all things are reflective of a transcendent reality grounded within a unified cosmos. Where Schleiermacher most differs from the Perennialists, however, is his "modern" turn toward an immanent

progressivism. Following a Hegelian-like historical teleology, Schleiermacher sees the divine Spirit (*heiliger Geist*) working through human culture and religion in a melioristic fashion. As Jens Zimmermann notes, for Schleiermacher, "the assumption of an organic teleology intrinsic to human nature tends to blur the distinction between culture and Spirit." Jens Zimmermann, *Humanism and Religion: A Call for the Renewal of Western Culture* (Oxford: Oxford University Press, 2012), 148. For Schuon, however, true religion qua esoterism understands "Reality" in starkly Neoplatonic terms as the necessary source of all contingent realities. Its unity is that which is expressed by all religions, but as such is hidden from the slumbering consciousness of humanity and is, in general, negatively related to human culture, which is in this more pessimistic view progressively degenerative. See Aymard and Laude, *Frithjof Schuon*, 84.

60. As Schleiermacher states, "Every sacred writing is in itself a glorious production, a speaking monument from the heroic time of religion." Although Schleiermacher provisionally accepts the possibility of "producing" a new religion for the person for whom the existing forms are not adequate, he qualifies this notion by asserting that "most men, following their nature, will belong to an existing form." Schleiermacher, *On Religion*, 91, 225.
61. As I discuss below, both Schleiermacher and Schuon ultimately reject rational epistemology and morality as a basis of religious "truth" and would agree that since religious forms are diverse and conflictive, the essence of religion can only be directly accessed through various suprarational modalities—that is, intuition and feeling (for Schleiermacher) or gnosis (for Schuon).
62. For example: "In understanding religion, not only in a particular form or in a word-for-word way, but in its formless essence, we also understand the religions, that is to say, the meaning of their plurality and diversity; this is the plane of *gnosis*, of the *religio perennis*." Frithjof Schuon, *Light on the Ancient Worlds* (Bloomington, IN: World Wisdom, 2006), 125.
63. For example: "Religion is a 'supernaturally natural' fact, which proves its truth—from the point of view of extrinsic proofs—by its human universality, so that the plurality and ubiquity of the religious phenomenon constitute a powerful argument in favor of *religion as such*." Frithjof Schuon, *Gnosis: Divine Wisdom*, ed. James S. Cutsinger, trans. Mark Perry, Jean-Pierre Lafouge, and James Cutsinger (Bloomington, IN: World Wisdom, 2006), 21 (emphasis mine).
64. Harry Oldmeadow, *Frithjof Schuon and the Perennial Philosophy* (Bloomington, IN: World Wisdom, 2010), 83 (emphasis mine).
65. Wilfred Cantwell Smith, *The Meaning and End of Religion* (Minneapolis: Fortress Press, 1991), 45 (emphasis mine).
66. Russell T. McCutcheon, *Manufacturing Religion: The Discourse on Sui Generis Religion and the Politics of Nostalgia* (New York: Oxford University Press, 1997), 60.

67. Zimmermann, *Humanism and Religion*, 136; and David E. Klemm, "Culture, Arts, and Religion," in *The Cambridge Companion to Friedrich Schleiermacher*, ed. Jacqueline Mariña (Cambridge: Cambridge University Press, 2005), 253–54.
68. Schleiermacher, *On Religion*, 216.
69. Ibid., 217 (emphasis mine).
70. William A. Johnson, *On Religion: A Study of Theological Method in Schleiermacher and Nygren* (Leiden: E. J. Brill, 1964), 37 (emphasis mine).
71. Ibid., 36.
72. Seyyed Hossein Nasr, introduction to *The Essential Writings of Frithjof Schuon*, by Frithjof Schuon, ed. Seyyed Hossein Nasr (Amity: Amity House, 1986), 9.
73. A. N. Williams, *The Architecture of Theology: Structure, System, and Ratio* (Oxford: Oxford University Press, 2011), 24.
74. Schuon, *Gnosis*, 17 (emphasis mine).
75. Schleiermacher, *On Religion*, 217 (emphasis mine).
76. Bernard A. Lonergan quoted in George Lindbeck, *The Nature of Doctrine: Religion and Theology in a Postliberal Age* (Louisville, KY: Westminster John Knox Press, 2009), 31.
77. Patrick Laude, *Pathways to an Inner Islam: Massignon, Corbin, Guénon, and Schuon* (Albany: State University of New York Press, 2010), 14.
78. Aymard and Laude, *Frithjof Schuon*, 91.
79. As Robert M. Adams notes, intuition (*Anschauung*) as "a sort of mental seeing, distinct from any systematic theory" is the dominant mode of religious consciousness in the first edition of *On Religion*, with "feeling" as secondary. In the second edition, however, feeling becomes dominant over intuition. See Robert Merrihew Adams, "Faith and Religious Knowledge," in *The Cambridge Companion to Friedrich Schleiermacher*, ed. Jacqueline Mariña (Cambridge: Cambridge University Press, 2005), 36. Yet, Theodore Vial points out that intuition and feeling are two sides of the same coin for Schleiermacher: while intuition is the objective side of experience (i.e., the action of the world upon us), feeling is the subjective side (i.e., the change within us that occurs as a result of such action). See Theodore Vial, "Anschauung and Intuition, Again (Or, 'We Remain Bound to the Earth')," in *Schleiermacher, the Study of Religion, and the Future of Theology: A Transatlantic Dialogue*, ed. Brent W. Sockness and Wilhelm Gräb (Berlin: Walter De Gruyter, 2010), 46. For example, in the first edition, Schleiermacher states: "On intuition of the Universe my whole Speech hinges. It is the highest formula of religion, determining its nature and fixing its boundaries. 'All intuition proceeds from the influence of the thing perceived on the person perceiving. The former acts originally and independently, and the latter receives, combines and apprehends in accordance with its nature.'" Schleiermacher, *On Religion*, 278.
80. John Oman, preface to *On Religion*, vii. It should also be noted that John Laughland connects the use of the term *Anschauung* in the philosophy of

Schelling, who was an important influence upon Schleiermacher, with the concept of gnosis in Schelling's notion of "intellectual contemplation" (*intellektuelle Anschauung*): "Intellectual contemplation was the self-knowledge of the absolute I: I know myself to be an I by intellectual contemplation, and that contemplation affords access to the Absolute itself, the absolute I." John Laughland, *Schelling versus Hegel: From German Idealism to Christian Metaphysics* (Aldershot: Ashgate Publishing, 2007), 44.

81. Robert Merrihew Adams, "Faith and Religious Knowledge," in *The Cambridge Companion to Friedrich Schleiermacher*, ed. Jacqueline Mariña (Cambridge: Cambridge University Press, 2005), 36–37.
82. Schleiermacher, *On Religion*, 40.
83. Ibid., 278, 282.
84. Ibid., 52–53.
85. Ibid., 107n7 (emphasis mine).
86. Jacqueline Mariña, *Transformation of the Self in the Thought of Friedrich Schleiermacher* (Oxford: Oxford University Press, 2008), 230 (emphasis mine).
87. Schuon, *Gnosis*, 18 (emphasis mine).
88. Ibid., 10, 12 (emphasis mine).
89. Talal Asad, *Genealogies of Religion: Discipline and Reasons of Power in Christianity and Islam* (Baltimore: Johns Hopkins University Press, 1993), 34.
90. Ibid., 35 (emphasis mine).
91. For a discussion regarding the primary role of mystical experience over language and concepts in Sufism see Carl W. Ernst, "Mystical Language and the Teaching Context in the Early Lexicons of Sufism," in *Mysticism and Language*, ed. Steven T. Katz (New York: Oxford University Press, 1992), 181–201.
92. Asad, *Genealogies of Religion*, 35 (emphasis mine).
93. William C. Chittick, *Imaginal Worlds: Ibn al-ʿArabī and the Problem of Religious Diversity* (Albany: State University of New York Press, 1994), 125 (emphasis mine).
94. Ibid. (emphasis mine).
95. Ibid. (emphasis mine).
96. Although Ibn ʿArabi's cosmology did follow the classical Ptolemaic system of seven heavens, it was not entirely geocentric because, as noted in chapter 2, Ibn ʿArabi understood that the sun (and its sphere of the fourth heaven) was the cosmic hub around which the entire firmament turns. Thus, as Mohamed Haj Yousef notes, Ibn ʿArabi's "actual view of the (local) world is therefore in some sense 'heliocentric,' at least in relation to the unique central status or 'rank' (*makâna*) of the Sun." Mohamed Haj Yousef, *Ibn ʿArabī—Time and Cosmology* (New York: Routledge, 2008), 14. Here, it should be noted that the beginnings of Heliocentrism can be traced to Philolaus of Croton (d. c. 385 BCE), a Pythagorean philosopher, who "gave the earth, moon, sun, and planets an orbital motion about a central fire, which he called 'the hearth of the universe.'" It was, however, Aristarchus of

Samos (d. c. 230 BCE) who can properly be called the first to have proposed a true heliocentric theory, positing the orbit of the earth around the sun. William H. Stahl, "Aristarchus of Samos," in *Complete Dictionary of Scientific Biography*, vol. 1 (Detroit: Charles Scribner's Sons, 2008), 246–48.

97. Like Heliocentrism (as discussed in n. 96 above), the idea of a pluralistic cosmos also has its roots in pre-Socratic philosophy and was taken up by the Muslim philosopher Fakhr al-Dīn al-Rāzī (d. 1209), who argued for a cosmos of multiple worlds. However, these ideas only served philosophical and theological arguments. As Priyamvada Natarajan notes, such contentions were "entirely theoretical" and "not about the existence of other worlds—what we think of as solar systems today—or specifically life-bearing planets but rather centered on grappling with the notions of infinity and the edge of the cosmos." Priyamvada Natarajan, *Mapping the Heavens: The Radical Scientific Ideas That Reveal the Cosmos* (New Haven, CT: Yale University Press, 2016), 204.
98. Much like modern Perennialist thinkers, Bruno was a metaphysical universalist. His cosmology expanded upon Copernicus's heliocentric model and argued for an interconnected and interdependent reality where our sun was merely a star in an infinite universe: "There are countless suns and an infinity of planets which circle round their suns as our seven planets circle round ours." Giordano Bruno quoted in Michael White, *The Pope and the Heretic: The True Story of Giordano Bruno, the Man Who Dared to Defy the Roman Inquisition* (New York: William Morrow, 2002), 71–72.
99. Nasr, introduction to *The Essential Writings*, 5 (emphasis mine).
100. Originally published in French as *Sentiers de gnose* (Paris: La Colombe, 1957).
101. Schuon, *Gnosis*, 19–20 (emphasis mine).
102. This translation has been quoted extensively by Reza Shah-Kazemi; for example, see Shah-Kazemi, *The Other in the Light*, 241; *Paths to Transcendence*, 121; *The Spirit of Tolerance in Islam* (London: I. B. Tauris, 2012), 88; "Beyond Polemics and Pluralism: The Universal Message of the Qur'an," in *Between Heaven and Hell: Islam, Salvation, and the Fate of Others*, ed. Mohammad Hassan Khalil (New York: Oxford University Press, 2013), 95; "The Metaphysics of Interfaith Dialogue: Sufi Perspectives on the Universality of the Quranic Message," in *Paths to the Heart: Sufism and the Christian East*, ed. James S. Cutsinger (Bloomington, IN: World Wisdom, 2004), 182.
103. Shah-Kazemi, *Paths to Transcendence*, 121 (emphasis mine).
104. Ibid. (emphasis mine).
105. Ibid., 121–22 (emphasis mine).
106. Schuon, *Christianity/Islam*, 92 (emphasis mine).
107. Shah-Kazemi, *Paths to Transcendence*, 200 (emphasis mine).
108. For a list of examples, see chap. 2, n. 94.

109. Muḥyī al-Dīn Ibn ʿArabī, *al-Futūḥāt al-makkiyya*, vol. 1 (Beirut: Dār Ṣādir, 2004), 274 (Fut. I, 225). See discussion, pp. 73, 75–76.
110. Ibid., 182 (Fut. I, 145). See discussion, pp. 72–73.
111. Shah-Kazemi, *Paths to Transcendence*, 119.
112. See pp. 37–39; I translate 3:84 as follows: "*Say: we have faith in God and what has been sent down upon us, and in what was sent down upon Abraham, Ishmael, Isaac, Jacob, and the tribes (of Israel), and in what was given to Moses, Jesus, and the prophets from their Lord; we do not distinguish between any of them, and to Him we are of those who submit* (muslimūn)."
113. Shah-Kazemi, *Paths to Transcendence*, 81–82 (emphasis mine). See also p. 38.
114. Ibid., 118 (emphasis mine).
115. Ibn ʿArabī, *al-Futūḥāt*, vol. 6, 65 (Fut. III, 350). See pp. 38–39.
116. See discussion, pp. 71–77, 282. See also Ibn ʿArabī, *al-Futūḥāt*, vol. 1, 170 (Fut. I, 135); *al-Futūḥāt*, vol. 5, 287–88 (Fut. III, 251).
117. See discussion, pp. 15–16.
118. Norman O. Brown, *Apocalypse and/or Metamorphosis* (Berkeley: University of California Press, 1991), 51.
119. Jane McAuliffe, *Qur'ānic Christians: An Analysis of Classical and Modern Exegesis* (Cambridge: Cambridge University Press, 1991), 289.
120. Qur'an 13:39 and 43:4. See Daniel A. Madigan, "Preserved Tablet," in *Encyclopaedia of the Qur'ān*, vol. 4 (Leiden: Brill, 2004), 261–63.
121. Qur'an 2:75, 4:46, 5:13, and 5:41.
122. Qur'an 2:59 and 7:162.
123. Shah-Kazemi, *The Other in the Light*, 237.
124. This is a rather misleading statement, as there are actually four different Qur'anic verses that accuse the Jews of altering their scripture, which include (as mentioned in n. 121 above) 2:75, 4:46, 5:13, and 5:41. However, 4:46 is the only verse that actually gives an example of such alteration.
125. That is, Qur'an 5:44 and 5:46. Shah-Kazemi, *The Other in the Light*, 237.
126. Shah-Kazemi, *The Other in the Light*, 238 (emphasis mine).
127. Ibid., 237.
128. Hava Lazarus-Yafeh, "Taḥrīf," in *The Encyclopaedia of Islam*, 2nd ed., vol. 10 (Leiden: E. J. Brill, 2000), 111–12. See also Camilla Adang, *Muslim Writers on Judaism and the Hebrew Bible from Ibn Rabban to Ibn Hazm* (Leiden: E. J Brill, 1996), 223.
129. See Adang, *Muslim Writers on Judaism*, 223.
130. Shah-Kazemi briefly mentions the two different arguments in a footnote. See Shah-Kazemi, *The Other in the Light*, 237n49.
131. Chittick, *Imaginal Worlds*, 125.
132. Ibid. (emphasis mine).
133. Ibid., 125–26 (emphasis mine).

134. Smith, "Is There a Perennial Philosophy?," 562.
135. That is, chapter 267; the other ascension narrative is recounted in chapter 367 of the *Futūḥāt*. See pp. 37–38.
136. Ibn ʿArabī, *al-Futūḥāt*, vol. 3, 325 (Fut. II, 279–80). Several hadith contain a similar image of four rivers of paradise without the scriptural references—typically including the "two manifest" (*ẓāhirāni*) rivers of the Nile and the Euphrates, as well as "two hidden" (*bāṭināni*) rivers (e.g., Bukhārī, *al-Ashriba*, 36, *Bad' al-khalq*, 18; Muslim, *al-Imān*, 323). This tradition closely follows a version found in the Hebrew Bible, which similarly includes the Euphrates, but has the Tigris instead of the Nile while also including the names of the two other rivers, Pishon and Gihon (Genesis 2:10–15).
137. Ibn ʿArabī, *al-Futūḥāt*, vol. 3, 325 (Fut., II, 280).
138. Here the imperative of *sharaʿa* denotes to begin or commence, but also to prescribe.
139. Ibn ʿArabī, *al-Futūḥāt*, vol. 3, 325 (Fut. II, 280).
140. "*al-ʿulamāʾ warathatu al-anbiyāʾ*." Abū Dāwūd, *al-ʿIlm*, 1.
141. Ibn al-ʿArabī, *Fuṣūṣ al-ḥikam*, ed. Abul Ela Affifi (Beirut: Dār al-Kitāb al-ʿArabī, 1966), 134–35.
142. As Ibn ʿArabi states, "Do you think that monk remained on the rulings of the Christians? No, by God, the sacred law (*sharīʿa*) of Muhammad, may God bless him and grant him peace, is abrogative (*nāsikha*)!" Ibn ʿArabī, *al-Futūḥāt*, vol. 1, 273 (Fut. I, 224). See p. 74.
143. James Morris, "Ibn ʿArabi's 'Esotericism': The Problem of Spiritual Authority," *Studia Islamica* 71 (1990): 45.
144. Itzchak Weismann, *Taste of Modernity: Sufism, Salafiyya, and Arabism in Late Ottoman Damascus* (Leiden: Brill, 2001), 144 (emphasis mine).
145. Ibn ʿArabi recounts this dream in the introduction to his transcription of Ibn Hazm's *Ibṭal al-qiyās wa al-raʾy wa al-istiḥsān wa al-taqlīd wa al-taʿlīl*, as was first noted in the West by Goldziher in *Die Ẓâhiriten* in 1884. See Ignaz Goldziher, *The Ẓāhirīs: Their Doctrine and Their History*, trans. and ed. Wolfgang Behn (Leiden: Brill, 2008), 170. This incident is also recorded in the *Futūḥāt*, see Ibn ʿArabī, *al-Futūḥāt*, vol. 4, 169 (Fut. II, 519).
146. Not only did Ibn ʿArabi personally transcribe Ibn Hazm's treatise attacking analogical and discretional reasoning, *Ibṭal al-qiyās wa al-raʾy*, which were legal methodologies Ibn ʿArabi also disavowed, he also wrote an abridgement of Ibn Hazm's thirty-volume treatise on legal theory, *al-Muḥallā bi al-āthār*. See Gerald T. Elmore, *Islamic Sainthood in the Fullness of Time: Ibn al-ʿsArabī's Book of the Fabulous Gryphon* (Leiden: Brill, 1999), 42; and Cyrille Chodkiewicz, "The Law and the Way," in *The Meccan Revelations,* vol. 2, ed. Michel Chodkiewicz (New York: Pir Press, 2004), 61. See also n. 147 and n. 148 below.

147. Since Goldziher claimed that Ibn 'Arabi "followed the Ẓāhirīs in matters of jurisprudence" (Goldziher, *The Ẓāhirīs*, 171), there has been an ongoing discussion whether or not he can really be classified as a Ẓāhirī. For example, see Michel Chodkiewicz, *An Ocean without Shore: Ibn 'Arabî, the Book, and the Law*, trans. David Streight (Albany: State University of New York Press, 1993), 55; Morris, "Ibn 'Arabi's 'Esotericism,'" 61n52; Elmore, *Islamic Sainthood*, 43n161. However, a recent dissertation by Samer Dajani conclusively shows that Ibn 'Arabi cannot technically be considered a follower of this school. As Dajani notes: "Though it shared much with the Ẓāhirī school, and indeed benefited greatly from it, Ibn ʿArabī's approach could not truly be described as Ẓāhirī. Ibn ʿArabī had his own reasons for adopting many of the key positions of the Ẓāhirī school that were very different from the reasons that led the Ẓāhirīs to adopt their own positions." Samer M. K. Dajani, "Ibn ʿArabī's Conception of Ijtihād: Its Origins and Later Reception" (PhD thesis, SOAS, University of London, 2015), 148.
148. As Dajani notes, "Ibn ʿArabī chose those principles of the Ẓāhirī school that preserved people's right to act freely outside the limited set of divine prescriptions, and rejected those that placed certainty—which could be attained through sainthood—above leniency." Dajani, "Ibn ʿArabī's Conception of Ijtihād," 149–50. For example, in order to provide people with the path of least hardship, Ibn 'Arabi agreed with the Ẓāhirīs in prohibiting additions to divinely-revealed prescriptions and proscriptions, in the rejection of confining laypeople to a single school of law, and in the rejection of analogical reasoning (*qiyās*) "because God, with His mercy, had pardoned all that was not explicitly stated in the revealed sources" (ibid., 149). Yet in spite of this, Ibn 'Arabi did accept analogical reasoning from those who believed in it, which as Dajani notes, "would have been anathema to the Ẓāhirīs" (ibid., 114).
149. Adam Sabra, "Ibn Ḥazm's Literalism: A Critique of Islamic Legal Theory (I)," *Al-Qantara* 28, no. 1 (2007): 16.
150. Ibid., 20.
151. Dajani, "Ibn ʿArabī's Conception of Ijtihād," 150.
152. Sabra, "Ibn Ḥazm's Literalism," 17.
153. Ibid. (emphasis mine).
154. Chodkiewicz, *An Ocean without Shore*, 30 (emphasis mine).
155. As Shahab Ahmed argues, Ibn 'Arabi reads the Qur'an (as well as the hadith corpus) "in a manner in which the text of the revelation is made subject to the demands of a cosmology so apparently counter-intuitive to the text as to make the meaning of the text of the Qur'ān appear dependent on that cosmology—rather than that cosmology dependent on the text of the Qur'ān. It is not that this hermeneutic ignores Divine and Prophetic texts, but rather that it appropriates them by reading them against the apparent Divine grain." Shahab Ahmed, *What Is Islam? The Importance of Being Islamic* (Princeton, NJ: Princeton University

Press, 2016), 98. See also Ata Anzali in "The Primordial Tension of *Bāṭin* (the Hidden) versus *Ẓāhir* (the Manifest): The Case of Ibn ʿArabī and His Quranic Hermeneutics," *Journal of the Muhyiddin Ibn ʿArabi Society* 53 (2014): 69–87.

156. Elmore also notes that Ibn ʿArabi was indeed labeled a Ẓāhirī "propagandist" by the biographical historian Aḥmad b. Muhammad Ibn Khallikān (d. 1282). Elmore, *Islamic Sainthood*, 42–44, 45.

157. For a detailed overview of Ibn Hazm's position on the abrogation of Mosaic law see Adang, *Muslim Writers on Judaism*, 216–22.

158. Ibid., 221.

159. While Ibn Hazm was above all a rationalist and dialectician—and not a Sufi in any "normative" sense—it is certainly the case that many aspects of his literalist approach to religion were conducive to Sufism. As Elmore notes, this is particularly true with "the uncompromising, *monistic* variety of Ibn al-ʿArabī, for whom the obvious 'Outer' was ever the inalienable manifestation of the unseen 'Inner.'" Elmore, *Islamic Sainthood*, 44. Indeed, Goldziher had himself noted how "exponents of Ṣūfism were so easily accommodated within the frame of the Ẓāhirite school." Ignaz Goldziher, *The Ẓāhirīs*, 165.

160. James W. Morris, "Ibn ʿArabi's 'Esotericism': The Problem of Spiritual Authority," *Studia Islamica* 71 (1990): 38.

161. As Marshall Hodgson notes, Ghazali denied that theology (*kalām*) "led to any positive truth in itself. It was no use at all to the ordinary person whose faith was still sound (and such a person should be protected from exposure to its doubt-engendering argumentation)." Marshall G. S. Hodgson, *The Venture of Islam: Conscience and History in a World Civilization*, vol. 2 (Chicago: University of Chicago Press, 1974), 181. For the similarities between Ghazali and Ibn Hazm regarding theology see Anwar G. Chejne, *Ibn Hazm* (Chicago: Kazi Publications, 1982), 80.

162. Ibn ʿArabī, *al-Futūḥāt*, vol. 1, 54 (Fut. I, 35).

163. Even though Ibn ʿArabi has no sustained polemic against the People of the Book, as does Ibn Hazm in several of his major works, his mention of them in the passages examined here echo the vitriol for which Ibn Hazm was infamous. For a brief survey of Ibn Hazm's polemical works against Judaism and Christianity see Adang, *Muslim Writers on Judaism*, 64–69. Moreover, Ibn Hazm also claimed that out of all previously revealed laws, Muhammad's law is the only one remaining that contains the complete truth "that should be known and followed without the slightest deviation." Anwar G. Chejne, *Ibn Hazm* (Chicago: Kazi Publications, 1982), 109.

164. Gordon D. Newby, *A History of the Jews of Arabia: From Ancient Times to Their Eclipse under Islam* (Columbia: University of South Carolina Press, 1988), 66.

165. See G. Vajda, "Isrāʾīliyyāt," in *The Encyclopaedia of Islam*, 2nd ed., vol. 4 (Leiden: E. J. Brill, 1997), 212.

166. Ibid.

167. Indeed, al-Makkī distinguished between the disciplined Sufi "assemblies of remembrance" (*majālis al-dhikr*) and the inferior meetings of the storytellers (*majālis al-quṣṣāṣ*), which he felt were merely gatherings for the hoi polloi. Moreover, he "also objected to the storytellers' recitation of false traditions." Jonathan P. Berkey, *Popular Preaching and Religious Authority in the Medieval Islamic Near East* (Seattle: University of Washington Press, 2001), 27, 103n30.
168. As Massignon notes, such *majālis al-dhikr* were originally sessions in which practitioners "recited sections of the Qur'ān, as well as prose and verse on related themes for meditation." Louis Massignon, *Essay on the Origins of the Technical Language of Islamic Mysticism*, trans. Benjamin Clark (Notre Dame: University of Notre Dame Press, 1997), 73.
169. That is, the Qur'anic accusation that the Jews were guilty of scriptural *taḥrīf* (2:75, 4:46, 5:13, and 5:41) and *tabdīl* (2:59 and 7:162).
170. Ibn ʿArabī, *al-Futūḥāt*, vol. 3, 298 (Fut. II, 256).
171. See pp. 35–36, 55–56.
172. Indeed, Ibn Hazm liked to curse the Jews so much he even included such an imprecation in the title of one of his major works: *Refutation of Ibn al-Naghrīla the Jew, May God Curse Him* (*al-Radd ʿalā' ibn al-naghrīla al-yahūdī, laʿanahu' llāh*). See Adang, *Muslim Writers on Judaism*, 67.
173. Theodore Pulcini, *Exegesis as Polemical Discourse: Ibn Ḥazm on Jewish and Christian Scriptures* (Atlanta: Scholars Press, 1998), 59–60. See also Adang, *Muslim Writers on Judaism*, 239–40.
174. Ibn Hazm quoted in Adang, *Muslim Writers on Judaism*, 240.
175. Lazarus-Yafeh, "Taḥrīf," 112. See also Adang, *Muslim Writers on Judaism*, 246–48, 251.
176. Adang, *Muslim Writers on Judaism*, 251.
177. As Yousef Casewit notes, not only was Ibn Barrajan a staunch supersessionist, but also he believed "that the Torah and Gospels suffered severe distortions either by way of false interpretations (*taḥrīf al-maʿnā*) or textual forgery (*taḥrīf al-naṣṣ*)." Yet, it should also be mentioned that Ibn Barrajan did not engage in the polemical attacks against the Hebrew Bible and New Testament that Ibn Hazm specialized in. Rather, as Casewit points out, Ibn Barrajan "tried to incorporate Biblical material into his exegetical works to deepen his understanding of the Qur'ān." Yousef Casewit, *The Mystics of al-Andalus: Ibn Barrajān and Islamic Thought in the Twelfth Century* (Cambridge: Cambridge University Press, 2017), 258, 263.
178. For example, "addition" (*al-ziyāda*) and "substitution" (*tabdīl*).
179. Ibn ʿArabī, *al-Futūḥāt*, vol. 6, 76 (Fut. III, 360). See also ibid., vol. 8, 153 (Fut. IV, 417).
180. Except for the difference of the attached third-person plural pronoun on *aḍalla*, instead of third-person singular, this is taken from Qur'an 45:23: "*God misguided him* (aḍallahu) *in full knowledge (of his true state).*" To understand the meaning

of "*in full knowledge*," the following comment of Muhammad Asad is useful: "All Qur'anic references to God's 'letting man go astray' must be understood against the background of 2:26–27 'none does He cause to go astray save the iniquitous, who break their bond with God': that is to say, man's 'going astray' is a consequence of his own attitudes and inclinations and not a result of an arbitrary 'predestination' in the popular sense of this word." Muhammad Asad, *The Message of the Qur'ān: The Full Account of the Revealed Arabic Text* (London: Book Foundation, 2012), 414n4.

181. This is a direct reference to the famous *ḥadīth qudsī*: "My servant approaches Me through nothing I love more than what I have made obligatory for him. My servant continues to come close to Me through supererogatory works until I love him. When I love him, I am his hearing by which he hears, his sight by which he sees, his hand by which he grasps, and his foot by which he walks." Bukhārī, *al-Riqāq*, 91.
182. Ibn ʿArabī, *al-Futūḥāt*, vol. 1, 181 (Fut. I, 145).
183. Ibid., vol. 6, 54–70 (Fut., III, 340–54).
184. Ibid., 65 (Fut. III, 350). See pp. 37–38.
185. There are a total of six sections within the *Futūḥāt*, the *faṣl al-manāzil* being the fourth and includes chapters 270 through 383 (Fut. II, 571-III, 523). For a brief overview of each section of the *Futūḥāt* see Michel Chodkiewicz, "Toward Reading the *Futûhât Makkiyya*," in *The Meccan Revelations*, vol. 2, ed. Michel Chodkiewicz (New York: Pir Press, 2004), 7–11.
186. James W. Morris, "Ibn 'Arabî's Spiritual Ascension," in *The Meccan Revelations*, vol. 1, ed. Michel Chodkiewicz (New York: Pir Press, 2002), 229.
187. Ibn 'Arabi holds to the traditional view that Satan was a jinn. As such, Satan's elemental makeup is predominantly the elements of fire and air, whereas Adam's is water and earth. However, Ibn 'Arabi acknowledges that as created beings, they each have something of all four elements. See William C. Chittick, "Iblīs and the Jinn in *al-Futūḥāt al-Makkiyya*," in *Classical Arabic Humanities in Their Own Terms: Festschrift for Wolfhart Heinrichs on His 65th Birthday Presented by His Students and Colleagues*, ed. Beatrice Gruendler (Leiden: Brill, 2008), 104.
188. Ibn ʿArabī, *al-Futūḥāt*, vol. 6, 66 (Fut. III, 351).
189. Al-Tabari builds on the story of Ezra as one of the pious captives in Babylon who returned to Palestine and grieved over the loss of the Torah. An angel came to him and gave him a drink, which allowed him to write down the entire Torah, thus restoring it and establishing it among the Jews in Palestine. After his death, however, the Jews considered Ezra to be the son of God as mentioned in the Qur'an 9:30: "*The Jews call 'Uzayr son of God, and the Christians call the Messiah son of God.*" See Adang, *Muslim Writers on Judaism*, 230–31. Regarding the identification of "*'Uzayr*" as Ezra see chap. 1, n. 86.
190. Adang, *Muslim Writers on Judaism*, 231.

191. Ibid., 246.
192. Thus, according to Ibn Hazm, the only way that Jews and Christians can fulfill the injunctions of their divine revelations and attain to salvation is by embracing Islam and following the sharia of Muhammad. See Adang, *Muslim Writers on Judaism*, 248.
193. That is, under the conditions of Qur'an 9:29. See p. 73.
194. Ibn ʿArabī, *al-Futūḥāt*, vol. 5, 168 (Fut. III, 145).
195. See pp. 35–36, 55–56.
196. The term *yasʿadūn* ("they attain to a state of felicity") here is the imperfect, third-person plural form of the perfect verb *saʿida*, meaning to be happy or in a state of felicity. As Chittick notes, the infinitive noun of the same form, *saʿāda*, is "most commonly employed for salvation in Islamic texts." As such, its meaning denotes a happiness that "pertains fundamentally to life after death" and thus is often translated as "felicity." William C. Chittick, *Faith and Practice of Islam: Three Thirteenth Century Sufi Texts* (Albany: State University of New York Press, 1992), 13. Yet Ibn 'Arabi's famous Syrian commentator ʿAbd al-Ghanī al-Nābulusī (d. 1731) acknowledged that in the above passage both worldly and eternal happiness could be possible meanings for *saʿāda*. Regarding the latter, he states: "These *d̠immīs* would be those about whom it is said that they gained the happiness which is free from all misery, just by giving the *ǧizya*." Al-Nābulusī quoted in Michael Winter, "A Polemical Treatise by ʿAbd al-Ġanī al-Nābulusī against a Turkish Scholar on the Religious Status of the D̠immīs," *Arabica* 35, no. 1 (1988): 97, 99. See also Elizabeth Sirriyeh, *Sufi Visionary of Ottoman Damascus: 'Abd al-Ghanī al-Nābulusī, 1641–1731* (New York: RoutledgeCurzon, 2005), 92–93.
197. Asad, *Genealogies of Religion*, 42.
198. See pp. 32–34.
199. The identification of the technical term *islām* with obedience to Muhammad's particular revealed message and law is reflected in early theological writing such as the so-called *Fiqh Akbar II* (circa tenth century CE), where "*islām* is indeed . . . a surrender (*taslīm*) to the divine Will as *expressed* by the ḳurʾānic teaching, and an obedience (*inḳiyād*) to His commandments; and, by this very means, admission to the Community. . . . Quite soon, admission to the Community was to be the aspect preferred. If the requisite inner attitude does not correspond to it, there is some grave individual failing (*fisḳ*), there is no abandonment of *islām*." L. Gardet, "Islām," in *The Encyclopaedia of Islam*, 2nd ed., vol. 4 (Leiden: E. J. Brill, 1997), 174.
200. Jacques Waardenburg, "The Medieval Period 650–1500," in *Muslim Perceptions of Other Religions: A Historical Survey*, ed. Jacques Waardenburg (New York: Oxford University Press, 1999), 44.
201. Of course, for Ibn 'Arabi the primary element of this triad is *prophethood*.
202. See p. 57, and chap. 2, n. 22.

203. Nicholson's analysis of Jili is commended by Schimmel. See Annemarie Schimmel, *Mystical Dimensions of Islam* (Chapel Hill: University of North Carolina Press, 1975), 281.
204. Reynold A. Nicholson, *Studies in Islamic Mysticism* (Cambridge: Cambridge University Press, 1921), 139 (emphasis mine).
205. Ibid., 138, 141.
206. Ibid., 133 (emphasis mine).
207. That is, the 'Arabiyya Shādhiliyya (or Shādhiliyya 'Arabiyya); see Meir Hatina, "Where East Meets West: Sufism, Cultural Rapprochement, and Politics," *International Journal of Middle East Studies* 39 (2007): 390.
208. Weismann, *Taste of Modernity*, 6. It should be noted here that Perennialists often point out as evidence for 'Abd al-Qadir's religious universalism his compassionate treatment of French prisoners during the Algerian resistance and his famous 1860 defense of Damascene Christians against a pogrom initiated by Druze leaders. However, as Weismann notes, "ʿAbd al-Qādir does not deny the duty of jihad against the opponents of Islam, *until they pay the poll tax and are humiliated*, although he describes it as the most difficult commandment for the sufis to endure." Importantly, however, his compassionate attitude toward the Christians did cause a significant spiritual rift with Ibn 'Arabi, who supposedly came to 'Abd al-Qadir in a dream and reprimanded him for giving some of them the traditional Muslim greeting of *taslīm*. Ibid., 190 (emphasis mine). For a Perennialist treatment of 'Abd al-Qadir see Reza Shah-Kazemi, "From the Spirituality of *Jihād* to the Ideology of Jihadism," in *Islam, Fundamentalism, and the Betrayal of Tradition, Revised and Expanded: Essays by Western Muslim Scholars*, ed. Joseph E. B. Lumbard (Bloomington, IN: World Wisdom, 2009), 130–36.
209. Sedgwick, *Against the Modern World*, 61, 62. See also Hülya Küçük, "A Brief History of Western Sufism," *Asian Journal of Social Science* 36, no. 2 (2008): 296.
210. In 1919, Nyberg published a critical edition of three of Ibn 'Arabi's smaller works: *Inshāʾ al-dawāʾir* (*The Book of Circles*), *ʿUqlat al-mustawfiz* (*The Knot of Preparedness*), and *Tadbīrāt al-ilāhiyya* (*The Divine Dispositions*). See H. S. Nyberg, *Kleinere Schriften des Ibn al-'Arabî* (Leiden: E. J. Brill, 1919).
211. H. S. Nyberg quoted in Paul Chacornac, *The Simple Life of René Guénon* (Hillsdale, NY: Sophia Perennis, 2004), 36.
212. See 'Abdul-Hâdî (John Gustav Agelii, dit Ivan Aguéli), *Ecrits pour La Gnose: comprenant la traduction de l'arabe du Traité de l'Unité* (Milano: Archè, 1988). See also Sedgwick, *Against the Modern World*, 59–60.
213. 'Abdul-Hâdî, "Pages dédiées à Mercure," in *Ecrits pour La Gnose*, 30. Schuon seems to have literally claimed this initiation for himself in response to repeated experiences and visions of the Virgin Mary. He states: "It is not I who have chosen the Virgin, it is she who has chosen me." Schuon quoted in Aymard and Laude, *Frithjof Schuon*, 75. Schuon eventually changed the name of his *ṭarīqa* to the

ʿAlāwiyya Maryamiyya in the mid-1960s as a result of what Aymard and Laude have called "the Marial grace" (Ibid., 75, 76).

214. Hatina, "Where East Meets West," 396.
215. 'Abdul-Hâdî, "Pages dédiées à Mercure," 28.
216. 'Abd al-Hadi quoted in Meir Hatina, "Where East Meets West," 396, 407n47.
217. 'Abdul-Hâdî, "L'universalité en l'Islam," in *Ecrits pour La Gnose*, 101.
218. Ibid., 100.
219. Ibid., 88 (emphasis original).
220. Such a shift began with the 1948 publication of *The Transcendent Unity of Religions*. See p. 140.
221. Schuon, *Christianity/Islam*, 92, 93.
222. Ibid., 98.
223. Frithjof Schuon, *Sufism: Veil and Quintessence: A New Translation with Selected Letters*, trans. Mark Perry, Jean-Pierre Lafouge, and James S. Cutsinger, ed. James S. Cutsinger (Bloomington, IN: World Wisdom, 2006), 33.
224. See Schuon, *Sufism*, 33, 65. The following chapter deals with Schuon's discursive usage of the nineteenth-century terminological binary of Aryan/Semitic.
225. Letter quoted in Aymard and Laude, *Frithjof Schuon*, 46.

CHAPTER 4

1. Daniel Dubuisson, *The Western Construction of Religion: Myths, Knowledge, and Ideology* (Baltimore: Johns Hopkins University Press, 2003), 196.
2. Frithjof Schuon, *Songs without Names, Volumes I-VI* (Bloomington, IN: World Wisdom, 2006), 99.
3. Schuonian Perennialism uses the terms *philosophia perennis, sophia perennis,* and *religio perennis* more or less interchangeably. As I mentioned in the prologue, the concept of the *philosophia perennis* was coined by Agostino Steuco (d. 1548) in his work *De perenni philosophia* (1540). See prol., n. 5. As Hanegraaff notes, since Leibniz made reference to the term *perennis philosophia* without attributing it to Steuco, it was loosened from its original Catholic moorings in the Renaissance and entered into more generalized usage. Schuon's particular lineage originates within the "Traditionalist" school of René Guénon (d. 1951) and should not be confused with Aldous Huxley's independent popularization expressed in his 1944 work *The Perennial Philosophy*. See Wouter J. Hanegraaff, "Tradition," *Dictionary of Gnosis and Western Esotericism*, ed. Wouter J. Hanegraaff (Leiden: Brill, 2006), 1130–34.
4. As Jean-Baptiste Aymard and Patrick Laude recently asserted: "Schuon ranks amongst the Neoplatonist line of the greatest Sufi masters, such as Ibn 'Arabî." Jean-Baptiste Aymard and Patrick Laude, *Frithjof Schuon: Life and Teachings* (Albany: State University of New York Press, 2004), 72.

5. Schuon embraced Islam in 1932 and was initiated into Sufism by the famous Algerian shaykh Ahmad al-ʿAlāwī in Mostaganem, Algeria. Seyyed Hossein Nasr, "Frithjof Schuon and the Islamic Tradition," in *The Essential Sophia*, ed. Seyyed Hossein Nasr and Katherine O'Brien (Bloomington, IN: World Wisdom, 2006), 259; and Mark J. Sedgwick, "The 'Traditionalist' Shâdhiliyya in the West: Guénonians and Schuonians," in *Une voie soufie dans le monde: la Shâdhiliyya*, ed. Éric Geoffroy (Paris: Maisonneuve & Larose, 2005), 461.
6. William Quinn, "Schuon, Frithjof (Also Known as Shaykh ʿIsâ Nur al-Dîn Ahmad al-Shâdhilî al-Darqâwî al-ʿAlawî al-Maryamî)," *Dictionary of Gnosis and Western Esotericism*, ed. Wouter J. Hanegraaff (Leiden: Brill, 2006), 1043.
7. For example, see Éric Geoffroy, *Introduction to Sufism: The Inner Path of Islam* (Bloomington, IN: World Wisdom, 2010), 184, 187. See also Thierry Zarcone, "Rereadings and Transformations of Sufism in the West," *Diogenes* 47, no. 187 (1999): 116; and Setareh Houman, *From the* Philosophia Perennis *to American Perennialism*, trans. Edin Q. Lohja (Chicago: Kazi Publications, 2014), 215. While the term *waḥdat al-wujūd* was never explicitly used by Ibn 'Arabi himself, it has come to emblematically represent his unitive metaphysics, signifying God as the ontological reality of all things. See William Chittick, "Rūmī and *waḥdat al-wujūd*," in *Poetry and Mysticism in Islam: The Heritage of Rūmī*, ed. Amin Banani, Richard Hovannisian, and Georges Sabagh (New York: Cambridge University Press, 1994), 71, 75, 87, passim.
8. See pp. 86–88.
9. In 1936, Schuon "received [an] unexpected grace" giving him "the dazzling and intrinsic certitude that he had been invested with the function of *Shaykh*" for the European branch of the ʿAlāwiyya Sufi order, which he maintained until his death. Aymard and Laude, *Frithjof Schuon*, 23. See also n. 5 above.
10. Michael Oren Fitzgerald, "Frithjof Schuon: Providence without Paradox," *Sacred Web* 8 (2001): 30.
11. Quinn, "Schuon, Frithjof," 1044.
12. Reza Shah-Kazemi, "The Metaphysics of Interfaith Dialogue: Sufi Perspectives on the Universality of the Quranic Message," in *Paths to the Heart: Sufism and the Christian East*, ed. James S. Cutsinger (Bloomington, IN: World Wisdom, 2002), 141. See also Reza Shah-Kazemi, *Paths to Transcendence: According to Shankara, Ibn Arabi, and Meister Eckhart* (Bloomington, IN: World Wisdom, 2006); Reza Shah-Kazemi, *The Other in the Light of the One: The Universality of the Qur'ān and Interfaith Dialogue* (Cambridge: Islamic Texts Society, 2006); Reza Shah-Kazemi, "Beyond Polemics and Pluralism: The Universal Message of the Qur'an" (paper presented at the conference "Al-Azhar and the West: Bridges of Dialogue," Cairo, January 5, 2009); Reza Shah-Kazemi, *The Spirit of Tolerance in Islam* (London: I. B. Tauris, 2012); Reza Shah-Kazemi, "Beyond Polemics and Pluralism: The Universal Message of the Qur'an," in *Between Heaven and*

Hell: Islam, Salvation, and the Fate of Others, ed. Mohammad Hassan Khalil (New York: Oxford University Press, 2013), passim.

13. Shah-Kazemi, *Paths to Transcendence*, 193, 193n1.
14. Schuon quoted in Aymard and Laude, *Frithjof Schuon*, 46.
15. James S. Cutsinger, introduction to *Frithjof Schuon, Splendor of the True: A Frithjof Schuon Reader*, ed. and trans. James S. Cutsinger (Albany: State University of New York Press, 2013), xxx.
16. One such Perennialist apologetic explanation of Schuon's religio-racial typology can be found in William Stoddart's *Remembering in a World of Forgetting*, where under the heading "The Meaning of Race," the author notes: "Schuon's view envisages that each of the great religions corresponds to the need of a particular human 'receptacle,' this being either a particular race or else a particular mentality." While Stoddart's description of Schuon's racial typology faithfully includes a tripartite chart of the world's three races (white, yellow, and black)—which follows the racial schema famously set forth by Arthur de Gobineau (see n. 149 below)—he circumvents further discussion by stating: "this issue is too complex to elaborate here." William Stoddart, *Remembering in a World of Forgetting: Thoughts on Tradition and Postmodernism*, ed. Mateus Soares de Azevedo and Alberto Vasconcellos Queiroz (Bloomington, IN: World Wisdom, 2008), 66.
17. For example, Aymard and Laude, *Frithjof Schuon*; Harry Oldmeadow, *Frithjof Schuon and the Perennial Philosophy* (Bloomington, IN: World Wisdom, 2010); and Michael Oren Fitzgerald, *Frithjof Schuon: Messenger of the Perennial Philosophy* (Bloomington, IN: World Wisdom, 2010).
18. Huston Smith, foreword to *Frithjof Schuon, Splendor of the True: A Frithjof Schuon Reader*, ed. and trans. James S. Cutsinger (Albany: State University of New York Press, 2013), xiii.
19. James S. Cutsinger, introduction to *Frithjof Schuon, Splendor of the True: A Frithjof Schuon Reader*, ed. and trans. James S. Cutsinger (Albany: State University of New York Press, 2013), xv. As just one small example of the prestige Schuon enjoyed within the academy during his lifetime, on the back cover of my copy of *Survey of Metaphysics and Esoterism* (1986 paperback), there are no less than six *extremely* effusive, signed blurbs, all written by professors at top research universities (all American excepting one Canadian) from religious studies departments (and one philosophy department), including a departmental chair. Indeed, one of these blurbs was tellingly penned by Cutsinger himself as follows: "A magnificent book, which exceeds what even this master's most faithful readers have been led to expect. Schuon proves anew, by an even greater compression and irradiation of his Wisdom, how inexhaustibly beautiful is the Truth." James S. Cutsinger quoted in *Survey of Metaphysics and Esoterism*, by Frithjof Schuon, trans. Gustavo Polit (Bloomington, IN: World Wisdom Books, 1986), back cover (capitalization original).

20. Ibid., xvii (emphasis mine).
21. Ibid., xxxii (emphasis mine).
22. Ibid., xxxiv.
23. As Huston Smith has noted, Nasr is the only scholar ever to have the dual honor of inclusion in the Library of Living Philosophers and having delivered the Gifford Lectures in Glasgow, Scotland, published as *Knowledge and the Sacred* in 1981. Smith, foreword to *Frithjof Schuon,* vii.
24. Seyyed Hossein Nasr, *Knowledge and the Sacred* (Albany: State University of New York Press, 1989), 107. Nasr has continued to extol Schuon since his death in 1998, more recently dubbing him "one of the most remarkable intellectual and spiritual luminaries of the past century." Seyyed Hossein Nasr, foreword to *Frithjof Schuon: Life and Teachings,* by Jean-Baptiste Aymard and Patrick Laude (Albany: State University of New York Press, 2004), xii.
25. Cutsinger, introduction to *Frithjof Schuon,* xxxv (emphasis mine).
26. Ibid. (emphasis mine).
27. The accounts and supposed evidence used for the critical analyses of Schuon's discourse in relation to the scandal, however, are problematic since much of it comes from a disgruntled disciple, Mark Koslow. As Urban himself notes, "Of course, coming as they do from a former disciple, Koslow's accounts must be regarded with a certain amount of suspicion." Yet, Urban defends his use of Koslow's accounts since "it would seem . . . that there is more than enough corroborating evidence—including a huge number of photographs, texts written by present and former disciples, court documents, and other firsthand testimonies—to support most of his descriptions of the Schuon group." Hugh Urban, "A Dance of Masks: The Esoteric Ethics of Frithjof Schuon," in *Crossing Boundaries: Essays on the Ethical Status of Mysticism,* ed. G. William Barnard and Jeffrey J. Kripal (New York: Seven Bridges Press, 2002), 407. For a summary of Koslow's claims and corroborating evidence, as well as the details of the charges and terminated investigation, see ibid., 438–40 (appendices A and B). See also Mark J. Sedgwick, *Against the Modern World: Traditionalism and the Secret Intellectual History of the Twentieth Century* (New York: Oxford University Press, 2004), 175–77; Arthur Versluis, *American Gurus: From Transcendentalism to New Age Religion* (New York: Oxford University Press, 2014), 167–73; and Ziauddin Sardar, "A Man for All Seasons?," *Impact international* 23 (1993): 33–36.
28. Nasr, foreword to *Frithjof Schuon,* ix.
29. Cutsinger, introduction to *Frithjof Schuon,* xvi.
30. In his article "A Dance of Masks"—one of *the only* sustained critical analyses of Schuon besides Sedgwick's *Against the Modern World*—Urban interrogates the ethical validity of Schuon's discourse in comparison with the alleged antinomian practices performed by Schuon and his disciples in Bloomington. Here, Urban's concern with Schuon's "personal cult" and the apparently "disturbing" complex association it presents "between esotericism and ethics" appears to divert his

analysis into reducing Schuon's discourse to that of its author, whom Urban concludes to be "Janus-faced, even schizoid." Urban, "A Dance of Masks," 430. Yet, such a reductive slide forgoes a deeper inquiry into Schuon's discourse itself, a discourse whose rules from the very beginning were quite upfront and consistent in their antinomian epistemology and cosmology, as I discuss at the end of the chapter.

31. Russell T. McCutcheon, *Manufacturing Religion: The Discourse on Sui Generis Religion and the Politics of Nostalgia* (New York: Oxford University Press, 1997), 34.
32. Ibid., 27, 92 (emphasis mine).
33. As Maurice Olender notes, "The plain truth of the matter is that, in the heart of Europe in the middle of the twentieth century, the words Aryan and Semite became labels of life and death for millions of men, women, and children classed as one or the other." Olender, *The Languages of Paradise: Aryans and Semites, a Match Made in Heaven*, trans. Arthur Goldhammer (New York: Other Press 2002), 19.
34. The British historian Robert Irwin has rather sardonically asserted that "Schuon . . . deplored the Allied victory in 1945 as the victory of the profane over something more ancient." Robert Irwin, *Memoirs of a Dervish: Sufis, Mystics and the Sixties* (London: Profile Books, 2011), 89. Yet, the Perennialist author Michael Fitzgerald apologetically claims that "Perennialists actively resisted both Fascism and Nazism during World War II," and specifically notes how Schuon "fought against the Nazis, was captured, escaped from a Nazi prison camp and fled into Switzerland." Michael Fitzgerald, "Book Reviews against Tradition: Mark Sedgwick, *Against the Modern World*," *Sacred Web* 13 (2004): 145, 145n19. For a detailed account of Schuon's so-called escape—which happened after he was actually *released* by the Nazis since, as a resident of Alsace, they considered him German—see Aymard and Laude, *Frithjof Schuon*, 26. For his part, Urban asserts that "Schuon's political views are strikingly similar to those of the Fascist metaphysician and representative of 'Traditionalism,' Julius Evola." Urban, "A Dance of Masks," 432n10. Yet, given Schuon's almost total silence on political affairs and attendant political quietism (unlike Evola or Mircea Eliade), there is little historical evidence for such an assertion. That being said, there are definite places in Schuon's discourse that strikingly echo classic fascist motifs. The most obvious example is Schuon's 1957 monograph *Castes and Races* (*Castes et Races*), which is divided into three chapters, the first two dealing with the "Meaning of Caste" and "Meaning of Race," respectively, and the final with that of the "Principles and Criteria of Art." As Roger Griffin notes, the idea of art as an expression of the soul of the people was one of the few common motifs within the diverse manifestation of fascism: "For the cultural theorists of Fascism, Nazism, the British Union of Fascists, the Falange, the Iron Guard, or the AIB, whatever their stance on modernism, realism, or the celebration of rural life, art was meant to express

the uncorrupted soul of the people, and made manifest the health or decadence of the entire culture." Roger Griffin, "Fascism," *New Dictionary of the History of Ideas*, vol. 2, ed. Maryanne Cline Horowitz (Detroit: Charles Scribner's Sons, 2005), 800. In his final section on art in *Castes and Races*, Schuon thus notes that "Sacred art represents above all the spirit, and profane art the collective soul or genius," where the genius is "*spiritual and racial*." Thus, "taken together spiritual genius and collective genius make up traditional genius which gives its imprint to the whole civilization." Frithjof Schuon, *Castes and Races*, trans. Marco Pallis and Macleod Matheson (Bedfont: Perennial Books, 1982), 64 (emphasis mine).

35. McCutcheon, *Manufacturing Religion*, 89.
36. The Perennialist perspective of René Guénon is commonly labeled "Traditionalist"—so named after the "primordial tradition," which is the Guénonian equivalent of so-called perennial truth (i.e., the *philosophia perennis, sophia perennis,* and *religio perennis*). For example, see René Guénon, *Introduction to the Study of the Hindu Doctrines*, trans. Marco Pallis (Hillsdale, NY: Sophia Perennis, 2004), 51. See also pp. 84–85.
37. Nasr, "Frithjof Schuon," 258.
38. Frithjof Schuon, *The Transcendent Unity of Religions* (Wheaton, IL: Quest Books), 18 (emphasis mine).
39. Ibid., 19 (emphasis mine).
40. Schuon's argument is an example of a fallacy of equivocation. It equivocates by using the term "unique" in two different senses articulated in the following syllogism: (a) "unicity alone [is] unique," (b) "no fact [is] unicity," therefore (c) "there is no such thing in existence as a unique fact." Earlier in the same passage, Schuon further enunciates the details of this equivocation: "a form, by definition, cannot be unique and exclusive, that is to say, it cannot be the only possible expression of what it expresses. Form implies specifications or distinction, and the specific is only conceivable as a modality of a 'species,' that is to say, of a category that includes a combination of analogous modalities." Schuon, *The Transcendent Unity*, 18. Thus, when Schuon makes the theological—*and tautological*—claim that the essence of divine "unicity" is absolutely unique, he means to say that divine Truth is beyond categorization, since *by definition* it is without any limitation. To claim, however, that there is "no fact" that is unique—because facts are comparable to other "analogous modalities"—is to use the term "unique" only in relation to Platonic essences or *kinds* of things. Yet, this essentialist conception of "facts" as so many universal categories disregards their uniqueness in and of themselves, that is, as independent phenomena occurring in time and space. As such, *it does not follow* that because the divine is beyond categorical limitation there are consequently no unique facts, since in this syllogism the uniqueness of the divine specifically applies to its categorical uniqueness as absolute necessary essence, while the uniqueness of facts must *also* (and perhaps *only*) apply to their accidental uniqueness in time and space.

41. Schuon, *The Transcendent Unity*, 20.
42. Ibid., xxix (emphasis mine).
43. Ibid., xxx (emphasis mine).
44. Frithjof Schuon, *From the Divine to the Human: Survey of Metaphysics and Epistemology: A New Translation with Selected Letters*, trans. Mark Perry and Jean-Pierre Lafouge, ed. Patrick Laude (Bloomington, IN: World Wisdom, 2013), xi (emphasis mine).
45. Schuon, *Castes and Races*, 53 (emphasis mine).
46. Ibid. (emphasis mine).
47. See n. 5 above. The ʿAlāwiyya Sufi order became the ʿAlāwiyya Maryamiyya in the mid-1960s due to Schuon's special devotion to the Virgin Mary as discussed below. See Sedgwick, *Against the Modern World*, 147; Sedgwick, "The 'Traditionalist' Shâdhiliyya," 468; and Nasr, "Frithjof Schuon," 258–59, 260n2.
48. Schuon, *Sufism*, 24 (emphasis mine).
49. Ibid., 28 (emphasis mine). Schuon uses the term "subjectivist" (*subjectiviste*) here to refer to an attitude attributable to "Semitic" ontology as passionately visceral, but denying "objective" reality. For the original wording in French, see Frithjof Schuon, *Le Soufisme: voile et quintessence* (Paris: Dervy-Livres, 1980), 38. Regarding the same language in Aryanist discourse, see p. 134 and n. 146 below.
50. Schuon, *Sufism*, 28 (emphasis mine).
51. Ibid.
52. Although Guénon defended the Indian caste system in spirituo-racial terms, he dismissed the idea of an "Aryan race" as an Orientalist invention and thus "devoid of meaning." René Guénon, *Introduction to the Study of the Hindu Doctrines*, trans. Marco Pallis (Hillsdale, NY: Sophia Perennis, 2004), 51, 123. See also René Guénon, *Symbols of Sacred Science*, trans. Henry D. Fohr, ed. Samuel D. Fohr (Hillsdale, NY: Sophia Perennis, 2001), 65n12.
53. Sedgwick observes that one of the most important precursors to Guénonian Traditionalism—and thus later Schuonian Perennialism—was the "Vedanta-Perennialism" of the Theosophical Society. Sedgwick, *Against the Modern World*, 40. Although the discourse of theosophy is shot through with the racialist conceptions of its nineteenth-century milieu, H. P. Blavatsky's narrative of "anthropogenesis" and her particular conception of the Aryan race was a significant departure from the academic Aryanism of her day. Indeed, Blavatsky specifically distinguished herself from "Max Müller and the other *Aryanists.*" See H. P. Blavatsky, *The Secret Doctrine: The Synthesis of Science, Religion, and Philosophy*, vol. 2 (1888; reprint, Los Angeles: The Theosophy Co., 1947), 425. See also Colin Kidd, *The Forging of Races: Race and Scripture in the Protestant Atlantic World, 1600–2000* (Cambridge: Cambridge University Press, 2006), 244. Yet, it should also be noted that Blavatsky's work directly influenced the metaphysical views of the Austrian mystagogue Guido von List (d. 1919) and his subsequent Aryanist esotericism known as Armanism. List's ideas were further developed by Jörg Lanz

von Liebenfels (d. 1954) and popularized in his Aryan supremacist journal *Ostara*, which most probably played a role in the development Hitler's anti-Semitic ideology. Goodrick-Clarke, *The Occult Roots of Nazism: Secret Aryan Cults and Their Influence on Nazi Ideology* (New York: New York University Press, 2004), 52–54, 192–200.

54. Léon Poliakov, *The Aryan Myth: A History of Racist and Nationalist Ideas in Europe*, trans. Edmund Howard (New York: Barnes and Noble Books, 1996).
55. As Poliakov notes, it was Schlegel who first gave the discipline of comparative philology "an anthropological twist by deducing from the relationship of language a relationship of race." Poliakov, *The Aryan Myth*, 190.
56. Born and raised in Switzerland within a family of Germanic origin, Schuon self-identified as a "South German" who was, in his own words, "deeply rooted in poetic and mystical romanticism—having grown up with the German fairy-tale and German song." Frithjof Schuon, "Excerpts from Letters of the Shaykh," in *Shari'ah 2* [Maryamiyya handbook] (privately circulated photocopied typescript, 1995), 2. For a longer quotation of this same letter, see Patrick Ringgenberg, *Diversité et unité des religions chez René Guénon et Frithjof Schuon* (Paris: L'Harmattan, 2010), 303n554. While Aymard and Laude note that the young Schuon read "Goethe and Schiller, then later Heine" (Aymard and Laude, *Frithjof Schuon*, 7), it is open to speculation how much the neo-Romantic movement of *völkisch* mysticism may have influenced Schuon's Aryanist discursive formations. Indeed, a romantic nostalgia for an idyllic medieval past found within German folklore and folk songs was formative for the *völkisch* movement and later the Third Reich. As George Mosse notes, "the fairy tale, so the Nazi Party held, can show us the constant component of the Volk, its idealism and will to survive." George L. Mosse, *Masses and Man: Nationalist and Fascist Perceptions of Reality* (New York: Howard Fertig, 1980), 77. See also Goodrick-Clarke, *The Occult Roots of Nazism*, 3, 30, 34, 36, 44, 66–77; and George L. Mosse, *The Crisis of German Ideology: Intellectual Origins of the Third Reich* (New York: Grosset and Dunlap, 1964).
57. Tomoko Masuzawa, *The Invention of World Religions: Or, How European Universalism Was Preserved in the Language of Pluralism* (Chicago: University of Chicago Press, 2005), 151–52; and Mosse, *The Crisis of German Ideology*, 42.
58. Friedrich Schlegel, *On the Language and Wisdom of the Indians*, in *Aesthetic and Miscellaneous Works of Friedrich von Schlegel*, trans. E. J. Millington (London: George Bell & Sons, 1900), 428–29. See also Dorothy M. Figueira, *Aryans, Jews, Brahmins: Theorizing Authority through Myths of Identity* (Albany: State University of New York Press, 2002), 29–30.
59. Schlegel, *On the Language*, 457 (emphasis mine).
60. Ibid., 462.
61. Mosse, *The Crisis of German Ideology*, 41.

62. Arthur de Gobineau, *The Inequality of Human Races*, trans. Adrian Collins (New York: G. P. Putnam's Sons, 1915), 189 (emphasis mine).
63. Ernest Renan, *Mélanges religieux et historiques* (Paris: Calmann-Lévy, 1904), 242.
64. Ernest Renan, *History of the People of Israel: Till the Time of King David*, vol. 1, trans. C. B. Pitman and D. Bingam (Boston: Little, Brown, and Company, 1905), 3 (emphasis mine).
65. Ibid., 7–8 (emphasis mine).
66. Renan quoted in Poliakov, *The Aryan Myth*, 208.
67. Schuon, *Castes and Races*, 37 (emphasis mine). See also n. 219 and n. 229 below.
68. Schuon, *Sufism*, 20 (emphasis mine).
69. Ibid., 26 (emphasis mine).
70. That is, the *Upanishads*, the ultimate teaching of the Veda. The popular Western reduction of Hinduism to the Vedanta is in large part due to the popularity of Anquetil-Duperron's Latin translation of the *Oupnek'hat* (sections of the *Upanisads* taken from Dara-Shukoh's Persian translation) at the turn of the nineteenth century. See Richard King, *Orientalism and Religion: Postcolonial Theory, India and "The Mystic East"* (London: Routledge, 2002), 119–20. In European Romantic usage, "Vedanta" became synonymous with *Advaita Vedānta,* the nondualistic philosophy developed and popularized by the Indian philosopher Shankara (d. 820). J. J. Clarke, *Oriental Enlightenment: The Encounter between Asian and Western Thought* (London: Routledge, 1997), 56, 229n3.
71. Poliakov, *The Aryan Myth*, 197.
72. Roderick Stackelberg, "*Völkisch* Movement and Ideology," in *Antisemitism: A Historical Encyclopedia of Prejudice and Persecution*, ed. Richard S. Levy (Santa Barbara, CA: ABC-CLIO, 2005), 113. Chamberlain's 1899 work *Foundations of the Nineteenth Century* (*Die Grundlagen des neunzehnten Jahrhunderts*) became "the Bible" of racial truth for the *völkisch* movement in Germany and served as an important intellectual and ideological precursor for the theorists of the Third Reich. For example, Alfred Rosenberg's *Foundations of the Twentieth Century.* See Mosse, *The Crisis of German Ideology*, 97; and John P. Jackson Jr. and Nadine M. Weidman, *Race, Racism, and Science: Social Impact and Interaction* (Santa Barbara, CA: ABC-CLIO Inc., 2004), 124. See also Poliakov, *The Aryan Myth*, 318–20.
73. Houston Stewart Chamberlain, *Foundations of the Nineteenth Century*, vol. 1, trans. John Lees (New York: Howard Fertig, 1968), 338n†.
74. Ibid., 6, 435 (emphasis mine).
75. Chamberlain, *Foundations*, vol. 2, 411.
76. Frithjof Schuon, "The Perennial Philosophy," in *The Underlying Religion: An Introduction to the Perennial Philosophy*, ed. Martin Lings and Clinton Minnaar (Bloomington, IN: World Wisdom, 2007), 244.
77. Schuon, *Sufism*, 21.

78. Ibid. (emphasis mine).
79. Frithjof Schuon, *Gnosis: Divine Wisdom*, ed. James S. Cutsinger, trans. Mark Perry, Jean-Pierre Lafouge, and James Cutsinger (Bloomington, IN: World Wisdom, 2006), 17 (emphasis mine).
80. Ibid.
81. Schuon, *Castes and Races*, 42n30 (emphasis mine).
82. Schuon, *Gnosis*, 17 (emphasis mine).
83. Schuon, *Sufism*, 27–28 (emphasis mine).
84. For example, Frithjof Schuon, *Spiritual Perspectives and Human Facts*, ed. James S. Cutsinger (Bloomington, IN: World Wisdom, 2007), 118; Ernest Renan, *Histoire générale et système comparé des langues sémitiques*, 2nd ed. (Paris: A l'Imprimerie Impériale, 1858), 8; and Ernest Renan, *The Life of Jesus*, trans. Charles Edwin Wilbour (London: Trübner and Co., 1864), 64.
85. Renan, *Histoire générale*, 8.
86. Frithjof Schuon, *Christianity/Islam: Perspectives on Esoteric Ecumenism*, ed. James S. Cutsinger (Bloomington, IN: World Wisdom, 2008), 71.
87. Ibid. (emphasis mine). It should be noted that Schuon here clearly qualifies an earlier statement made in *Castes and Races* that ostensibly implies a straight equivalence between avatars and prophets: "The Hindus may surpass every other human group by their contemplativity and the metaphysical genius resulting from this; but the yellow race is in its turn far more contemplative than the Western branch of the white race, and this makes it possible, looking at things as a whole, to speak of spiritual superiority in the traditional East, whether white or yellow; also including in this superiority the Messianic and Prophetic outlook of the Semites, which runs parallel with the Aryan *avataric* outlook." Schuon, *Castes and Races*, 53.
88. Olender, *The Languages of Paradise*, 66 (emphasis mine).
89. Frithjof Schuon, *Form and Substance in the Religions*, trans. Mark Perry and Jean-Pierre LaFouge (Bloomington, IN: World Wisdom, 2002), 24 (emphasis mine).
90. See Arne Grøn, "Idealism," in *Encyclopedia of Science and Religion*, vol. 1, ed. J. Wentzel Vrede van Huyssteen (New York: Macmillan Reference USA, 2003), 446.
91. Chamberlain, *Foundations*, vol. 1, 420.
92. Schuon, *Form and Substance*, 24n19 (emphasis mine).
93. Frithjof Schuon, *Survey of Metaphysics and Esoterism*, trans. Gustavo Polit (Bloomington, IN: World Wisdom Books, 1986), 176 (emphasis mine).
94. Stefan Arvidsson, *Aryan Idols: Indo-European Mythology as Ideology and Science* (Chicago: University of Chicago Press, 2006), 117.
95. Olender, *The Languages of Paradise*, 71.
96. Renan, *The Life of Jesus*, 141.
97. Ibid., 159 (emphasis mine).
98. See n. 72 above.

99. Chamberlain, *Foundations*, vol. 1, 221.
100. Ibid.
101. Ibid., 202.
102. Chamberlain, *Foundations*, vol. 2, 411.
103. Renan, *The Life of Jesus*, 94, 95 (emphasis original).
104. Schuon, *Form and Substance*, 228 (emphasis mine).
105. Guénon claimed that the *Sanātana Dharma* was the only "fully integral" tradition, that is, the "primordial tradition." René Guénon, *Studies in Hinduism*, trans. Henry D. Fohr, ed. Samuel D. Fohr (Hillsdale, NY: Sophia Perennis, 2001), 81–82. For the Guénonian idea of "primordial tradition," see pp. 84–85.
106. In an article originally published in 1985, Schuon states that "Guénon was entirely right in specifying that *Vedānta* is the most direct and, in a certain respect, the most assimilable expression of pure metaphysics; no attachment to any non-Hindu tradition obliges us not to know this, or to pretend not to know it." Frithjof Schuon, "René Guénon: A Note," in *René Guénon: Some Observations*, ed. William Stoddart (Hillsdale, NY: Sophia Perennis, 2004), 8.
107. René Guénon, *Man and His Becoming According to the Vedānta*, trans. Richard C. Nicholson (Hillsdale, NY: Sophia Perennis, 2004), 38n12. Here, it should be noted that Guénon bases this opinion on *Risālat al-aḥadiyya*, a work by Awḥad al-Dīn Balyānī (d. 1287) but frequently attributed to Ibn 'Arabi. For a thorough treatment of the doctrinal differences and historical consequences of the misattribution of Balyani's text see Chodkiewicz's introduction and detailed notes in Awḥad al-Dīn Balyānī, *Epître sur l'Unicité Absolue*, trans. Michel Chodkiewicz (Paris: Les Deux Oceans, 1982).
108. See p. 117.
109. Indeed, it was Aguéli who wrongly attributed the aforementioned *Risālat al-aḥadiyya* to Ibn 'Arabi (see n. 107 above). Guénon was introduced to this work through Aguéli's translation, which was originally published in three parts in *La Gnose* magazine in 1911. See 'Abdul-Hâdî (John Gustav Agelii, dit Ivan Aguéli), *Ecrits pour La Gnose: comprenant la traduction de l'arabe du Traité de l'Unité* (Milano: Archè, 1988), 107–33.
110. Mark J. Sedgwick, "Guénonian Traditionalism and European Islam," in *Producing Islamic Knowledge: Transmission and Dissemination in Western Europe*, ed. Martin van Bruinessen and Stefano Allievi (London: Routledge, 2011), 183n4 (emphasis mine).
111. Martin Lings, "Preface to the 1978 Edition," in *The Tarjumán al-Ashwáq: A Collection of Mystical Odes*, by Muḥyiʾddīn Ibn Al-ʿArabī, trans. and ed. Reynold A. Nicholson (1911; reprint, London: Royal Asiatic Society, 1978), xiii.
112. Frithjof Schuon, *Understanding Islam* (Bloomington, IN: World Wisdom Books, 1998), 37.

113. Frithjof Schuon, *Light on the Ancient Worlds* (Bloomington, IN: World Wisdom, 2006), 120.
114. Frithjof Schuon, *Logic and Transcendence: A New Translation with Selected Letters*, trans. Mark Perry, Jean-Pierre Lafouge, and James S. Cutsinger, ed. James S. Cutsinger (Bloomington, IN: World Wisdom, 2009), 125.
115. Schuon, *Sufism*, 33.
116. See Ibn al-ʿArabī, *Fuṣūṣ al-ḥikam*, ed. Abul Ela Affifi (Beirut: Dar al-Kitab al-ʿArabi, 1966), 101.
117. Schuon, *Sufism*, 45 (emphasis mine).
118. Ibn ʿArabi quoted in Schuon, *Sufism*, 40n29; see Muḥyiʾddīn Ibn Al-ʿArabī, *The Tarjumán al-Ashwáq: A Collection of Mystical Odes*, trans. and ed. Reynold A. Nicholson (1911; reprint, London: Royal Asiatic Society, 1978), 69. Most likely relying on Nicholson's translation, Schuon's use of "Muslims" here for *al-muḥammadiyyīn* is admittedly too restrictive for Ibn ʿArabi's intended meaning; here, he *primarily* refers to the "Muhammadan saints" as those adepts who have achieved the closest of all spiritual stations in relation to the Prophet. See discussion, pp. 45–46, and chap. 1, n. 147. Nevertheless, it is Schuon's demurral that is telling.
119. Schuon, *Sufism*, 40n29 (emphasis mine).
120. Ibid. (emphasis mine).
121. Ibid. Schuon's opposition of "facts" against "principles" here refers to a syllogism he first made in *The Transcendent Unity of Religions* regarding the impossibility of any "fact" in the world (i.e., any "formalistic" religious perspective) to fully commune with the divine. As shown in n. 40 above, however, the syllogism itself is flawed.
122. Schuon, *Survey of Metaphysics*, 115–22.
123. Ibid., 115 (emphasis mine).
124. Ibid.
125. Ibid.
126. Ibid.
127. Ibid., 118.
128. Ibid., 118.
129. Schuon, *Sufism*, 31.
130. Ibid.
131. Ibid. Schuon repeatedly denigrates Semitic Ashʿarism as "individualistic," which is analogous to his similarly stated accusation of "subjectivist." See n. 49 above. Elsewhere, Schuon categorizes such "ordinary" theology as "the general style of Islam as a Semitic monotheism," which he similarly defines as "the style of a voluntarist and emotional individualism." He then praises the Arab Sufi al-Niffarī (d. 977) as "a pure adept of *gnosis*" and thus capable of transcending his own Semitic "style." Frithjof Schuon, *Logic and Transcendence: A New Translation with Selected Letters*, trans. Mark Perry, Jean-Pierre Lafouge, and James S. Cutsinger, ed. James

S. Cutsinger (Bloomington, IN: World Wisdom, 2009), 112, 112n14. And again elsewhere, Schuon praises the Arab Sufi Ibn ʿAṭāʾ Allāh (d. 1309) for mixing "the spirit of the Psalms with that of the *Upanishads*"—yet another mapping strategy that Schuon employs to authorize an Arab Sufi's transcendence of their otherwise Semitic mentality. Schuon, *Sufism*, 19.

132. Schuon, *Sufism*, 31.
133. Ibid. Yet, as Caner Dagli notes, in the *Fuṣūṣ* it appears that Ibn ʿArabi himself was critical of voluntarism when he states (as Dagli translates): "Some thinkers, men of feeble intellects, after it having been well established for them that God does as He wills, go on to sanction that things be imputed unto God which contradict wisdom and reality *as it is*." Dagli thus comments: "This sentence is a criticism of the voluntarism of the theologians such as the Ashʿarites who emphasized the Will of God over all other things." Caner K. Dagli, trans., *The Ringstones of Wisdom* (*Fuṣūṣ al-ḥikam*), by Ibn Al-ʿArabī (Chicago: Great Books of the Islamic World, 2004), 34, 34n67. See also Ibn al-ʿArabī, *Fuṣūṣ al-ḥikam*, 67.
134. Schuon, *Logic and Transcendence*, 124. Indeed, elsewhere Schuon claims that "it is from Hanbalism that Asharite *kalām* inherited its most questionable theses." Schuon, *Christianity/Islam*, 164.
135. Schuon, *Logic and Transcendence*, 124 (emphasis mine).
136. Ibid., 124–25 (emphasis mine). It is worthy of note that in a footnote, Schuon asserts that Christianity differs from such Islamic fideism, since "Christianity . . . is founded on the mystery of love and not directly on that of faith" (ibid., 125n29). Elsewhere, Schuon takes Ibn ʿArabi to task for supporting "the excessive fideism of the Hanbalites," a school (*madhhab*) of law and theology known for its populist traditionalism and radical anthropomorphism. See Schuon, *Sufism*, 65.
137. Schuon, *Christianity/Islam*, 150–51 (emphasis mine).
138. Schuon, *Logic and Transcendence*, 78.
139. Ibid.
140. Schuon, *Form and Substance*, 210 (emphasis mine).
141. Schuon, *Christianity/Islam*, 165 (emphasis mine).
142. See Patrick D. Hopkins, "Natural Law," *Encyclopedia of Philosophy*, 2nd ed., vol. 6, ed. Donald M. Borchert (Detroit: Macmillan Reference USA, 2006), 507.
143. Schuon, *Christianity/Islam*, 165 (emphasis mine).
144. Chamberlain, *Foundations*, vol. 1, 419 (emphasis mine).
145. Ibid., 242–43 (emphasis mine).
146. For Lassen, the worldview of the Semite "is subjective and egotistical." Lassen quoted in Arvidsson, *Aryan Idols*, 94. According to Lassen, such extreme subjectivity and egotism had made Semitic religiosity intolerant and exclusivist. Moreover, Semites are so overcome with passion and emotion that they cannot appreciate the higher arts such as sculpture or painting like the Indo-Germans. See Arvidsson, *Aryan Idols*, 94.

147. Chamberlain, *Foundations*, vol. 1, 215 (emphasis mine).
148. Schuon, *Castes and Races*, 43 (emphasis mine).
149. In *Essay on the Inequality of the Human Races*, Gobineau famously posits the division of humanity into three immutable but unequal races of "the black, the yellow, and the white." Gobineau, *The Inequality of Human Races*, 205. Elsewhere Schuon states: "There are three great racial types, the white, the yellow, and the black." Frithjof Schuon, *To Have a Center* (Bloomington, IN: World Wisdom Books, 1990), 44.
150. Schuon, *Castes and Races*, 43 (emphasis mine).
151. Schuon, *Logic and Transcendence*, 128 (emphasis mine).
152. Schuon, *Sufism*, 21 (emphasis mine).
153. Frithjof Schuon, *Echoes of Perennial Wisdom*, trans. Mark Perry and Jean-Pierre Lafouge (Bloomington, IN: World Wisdom, 2003), 60 (emphasis mine).
154. Ibid.
155. Schuon, *Sufism*, 24 (emphasis mine).
156. Schuon, "Excerpts from Letters," 10 (emphasis mine).
157. Ibid., 2.
158. Ibid.
159. Ibid.
160. Ibid.
161. See Aymard and Laude, *Frithjof Schuon*, 76.
162. Schuon, *Christianity/Islam*, 87–88 (emphasis mine).
163. Schuon, "Excerpts from Letters," 2 (emphasis mine).
164. Frithjof Schuon, *The Fullness of God: Frithjof Schuon on Christianity*, trans. Mark Perry, ed. James S. Cutsinger (Bloomington, IN: World Wisdom, 2004), 137.
165. Schuon, *Form and Substance*, 118.
166. Schuon, *Christianity/Islam*, 88.
167. Schuon, "Excerpts from Letters," 2.
168. Ibid., 3. For a longer quotation of this same letter, see Ringgenberg, *Diversité et unité des religions*, 302, 303n554.
169. Schuon, "Excerpts from Letters," 4 (emphasis mine).
170. As Stefan Arvidsson notes: "Out of romanticism's passion for India, and out of the knowledge of the Indo-European languages, a paradigm developed in the mid-nineteenth century that provided the framework for historical research about Indo-European religion. . . . The Indo-European sources were thought to show that Indo-Europeans or Proto-Indo-Europeans perceived God in nature, or that they chose natural phenomena as symbols for God. The sun, the morning, lightning, and clear sky were favorites, according to scholars." Arvidsson, *Aryan Idols*, 122.
171. For a selection of Schuon's naked Virgin paintings, see Frithjof Schuon, *Images of Primordial and Mystic Beauty: Paintings by Frithjof Schuon* (Bloomington,

IN: Abodes, 1992), 231–77. This collection is divided into the following sections: "Red Indian World," "Miscellaneous," "Yogini and Devi," and "Celestial Virgin." Although many of the paintings in this volume are of entirely naked women whose pubic regions have been fully depilated, all of the "Celestial Virgin" images are partially naked, displaying the Virgin's breasts only. For an example of a fully naked Virgin by Schuon (also without pubic hair) see Mark Koslow, "Frithjof Schuon: Child Molestation and Obstruction of Justice," accessed November 27, 2015, http://www.naturesrights.com/knowledge%20power%20book/frithjof_Schuon.asp.

172. Schuon, "Excerpts from Letters," 7.
173. Schuon quoted in Oldmeadow, *Frithjof Schuon*, 190. It is worth noting that a similar esoteric sentiment around nudity permeated *völkisch* ideology. As George Mosse notes, *völkisch* ideologues such as Willibald Hentschel held that external beauty mirrored the beauty of the soul, and as such clothing "alienated man from his body, which was a divine gift, and thus destroyed his inner equilibrium." Mosse, *The Crisis of German Ideology*, 116. This romanticized image of primordial nudity—often depicted in the form of a fully naked, ethereal blond youth with arms outstretched—became an icon of German Aryanism and was a favorite motif of the symbolist illustrator Karl Höppner, better known as Fidus. As Mosse notes, "The love for the nude body which Fidus helped to further, became important in the Youth Movement as representing *the urge for the genuine which required a return to nature*" (ibid., 85, emphasis mine). Indeed, the stylistic similarities among the nude figures found in the paintings of Schuon and those in the symbolist illustrations of Fidus are much more conspicuous than Schuon's ostensible claim to classical Hindu iconography. See also n. 171 above.
174. Schuon, "Excerpts from Letters," 2 (emphasis mine).
175. Frithjof Schuon, *Islam and the Perennial Philosophy* (London: World of Islam Festival Publishing Company, 1976), 146 (emphasis mine).
176. Schuon, "Excerpts from Letters," 5.
177. Ibid.
178. Ibid., 6 (emphasis mine).
179. Ibid. (emphasis mine).
180. Schuon, *Form and Substance*, 118 (emphasis mine).
181. Ibid., 118n16.
182. Ibid., 106 (emphasis mine).
183. Ibid., 115.
184. Schuon, *The Fullness of God*, 170.
185. See Muḥyī al-Dīn Ibn ʿArabī, *al-Futūḥāt al-makkiyya*, vol. 6 (Beirut: Dār Ṣādir, 2004), 243 (Fut. III, 514); Ibn al-ʿArabī, *Fuṣūṣ al-ḥikam*, 64; Michel Chodkiewicz, *Seal of the Saints: Prophethood and Sainthood in the Doctrine of Ibn ʿArabī*, trans. Liadain Sherrard (Cambridge: Islamic Texts Society, 1993), 121, 125; and Claude

Addas, *Quest for the Red Sulphur: The Life of Ibn 'Arabī* (Cambridge: Islamic Texts Society, 1993), 77–78, 200.

186. As Nasr points out, Schuon's article "The Spiritual Significance of the Substance of the Prophet" "reveals a very rare intimacy with *al-haqīqat al-muhammadiyyah.*" Nasr, "Frithjof Schuon," 263. See Frithjof Schuon, "The Spiritual Significance of the Substance of the Prophet," in *Islamic Spirituality: Foundations*, ed. Seyyed Hossein Nasr (New York: Crossroad, 1987), 48–63.
187. See Sedgwick, *Against the Modern World*, 90, 147, 170.
188. Renaud Fabbri, "The Milk of the Virgin: The Prophet, the Saint and the Sage," *Sacred Web* 20 (2007): 265, 239.
189. Schuon, "Excerpts from Letters," 7 (emphasis mine).
190. See Sedgwick, *Against the Modern World*, 170.
191. Schuon, "Excerpts from Letters," 7.
192. This refers to the "Six Themes of Meditation" (i.e., Death and Life, Repose and Action, and Knowledge and Being), which Schuon "received" after he had a vision by which he was convinced of a divine promotion to full shaykh. The themes thus marked Schuon's formal break from the Algerian Alawiyya through the emergence of a distinctive spiritual practice. By the second phase, the Schuonian Alawiyya had *zawiyas* in Basel, Amiens, and Paris. See Sedgwick, *Against the Modern World*, 90–92.
193. Schuon, "Excerpts from Letters," 7.
194. Ibid.
195. Frithjof Schuon quoted in Aymard and Laude, *Frithjof Schuon*, 16 (emphasis mine).
196. Aymard and Laude, *Frithjof Schuon*, 20.
197. Nasr, "Frithjof Schuon," 267.
198. Schuon, *The Transcendent Unity*, 35. Schuon here is most likely referring to Ivan Aguéli's conception of Ibn 'Arabi and Islam. Schuon quotes Aguéli's article entitled "L'universalité en l'Islam" in several places (e.g., Schuon, *The Transcendent Unity*, 157–58; and *Sufism*, 88) and also refers to Balyani's *Risālat al-aḥadiyya* repeatedly, which Aguéli wrongly attributed to Ibn 'Arabi and translated, originally published in three parts in *La Gnose* 6, 7, 8 (1911): 168–74; 199–202; 217–23. See Abdul-Hâdi (John Gustav Agelii, dit Ivan Aguéli), *Ecrits pour La Gnose: comprenant la traduction de l'arabe du Traité de l'Unité* (Milano: Archè, 1988), 107–33. Regarding the misattribution of Balyani's text, see n. 107 above.
199. Schuon, *The Transcendent Unity*, 35–36 (emphasis mine).
200. Ibid. (emphasis mine). Certain verses in the Qur'an attest to the equality of the prophets (e.g., Qur'an 3:84, 42:13, 10:47, 41:43, 5:48, 2:62), while other verses declare that some were superior to others (e.g., Qur'an 2:253, 17:55).
201. Schuon, *The Transcendent Unity*, 36 (emphasis mine).
202. While most likely a preunderstanding of the *Fuṣūṣ* itself and its *logos*-oriented theme of prophetic wisdoms (see p. 40), Schuon's interpretation may alternatively

be based on the commentary of ʿAbd al-Razzaq al-Qāshānī (d. 1329) misattributed to Ibn ʿArabi. Indeed, Nasr notes that Qashani's commentary was a favorite of Schuon's. Nasr, "Frithjof Schuon," 263. Although Qashani does not comment on Qur'an 2:253 or 17:55 directly, he does recognize unique prophetic missions, but only within an overarching hierarchy. For example, he attributed to Moses the mission of the unification of the external and the attribute of "the outer" (*al-ẓāhir*) to the Torah, while to Jesus he acknowledged the mission of the unification of the interior and assigned the attribute of "the inner" (*al-bāṭin*) to the Gospel. However, like Ibn ʿArabi, Qashani maintained what he referred to as the historical "deviations" of Judaism and Christianity, and as such he asserted a traditional prophetic hierarchy with Muhammad at its apex, claiming for him the mission of the unification of the essence and the Qur'anic synthesis of inner and outer through the doctrine of Unity (*al-tawḥīd*). As Pierre Lory notes, for Qashani, although all prophetic religions lead to "a single Reality," Islam—and in particular the practice of Sufism—is the only path that gives "access to complete spiritual realization." See Pierre Lory, *Les Commentaires ésotériques du Coran d'après ʿAbd al-Razzâq al-Qâshânî* (Paris: Les Deux Océans, 1980), 148, 135–53.

203. See my brief discussion on this terminology in relation to the literary theory of Harold Bloom, p. 20 and intro., n. 137.
204. Ibn al-ʿArabī, *Fuṣūṣ al-ḥikam*, 132.
205. See pp. 80–81.
206. Ibn Al-ʿArabī, *The Ringstones of Wisdom* (*Fuṣūṣ al-ḥikam*), trans. Caner K. Dagli (Chicago: Great Books of the Islamic World, 2004), 148.
207. Dagli, trans., *The Ringstones of Wisdom*, 148n5 (emphasis mine).
208. Ibid., 148n6.
209. Indeed, Ibn ʿArabi goes on to quote Qur'an 16:71 (here translated by Dagli): "*God favoreth some of you above others in bounty*." Ibn Al-ʿArabī, *The Ringstones of Wisdom*, 148.
210. Ibid., 148n6.
211. See p. 40.
212. For example, Ibn al-ʿArabī, *Fuṣūṣ al-ḥikam*, 63–64.
213. Ibid., 214.
214. Ibn ʿArabī, *al-Futūḥāt*, vol. 5, 287–88 (Fut. III, 251).
215. Schuon, *Christianity/Islam*, 98–99 (emphasis mine).
216. Schuon, *The Transcendent Unity*, 36.
217. Schuon, *Gnosis*, 17 (emphasis mine).
218. Ibid. (emphasis mine).
219. In *Castes and Races*, Schuon seeks to spiritualize the concept of race in terms of a metaphysical idea of caste based on the spiritual dispositions of ontic typologies rather than blood. Such typologies can be found in "pure" blood groups, but not necessarily. Schuon thus notes: "In order to understand the meaning of races one

must first of all realize that they are derived from fundamental aspects of humanity and not from something fortuitous in nature. If racialism is something to be rejected, so is an anti-racialism which errs in the opposite direction by attributing racial difference to merely accidental causes. . . . What is never understood by those who have a passion for racial purity is that *there is a greater qualitative difference between the psychic heredity of different natural castes*—even if the race be the same—than between that of members of the same caste of differing race; fundamental and personal tendencies have more importance than racial modes, at any rate so far as the major races or healthy branches of these are concerned, though not degenerate groups." Schuon, *Castes and Races*, 39–40. See also n. 229 below.

220. Ibid., 42n30 (emphasis mine).
221. Ibid., 38 (emphasis mine).
222. Ibid., 44 (emphasis mine).
223. For example, in *Castes and Races*, Schuon states: "All these expressions can be no more than approximations, for everything is relative, especially in an order of things as complex as race." Schuon, *Castes and Races*, 43. See also n. 229 below.
224. According to David Theo Goldberg, the idea of "native primitivism" equates "African adults with infantility, and dialogically reduces Africa to the childish." David Theo Goldberg, *The Threat of Race: Reflections on Racial Neoliberalism* (Malden, MA: Wiley-Blackwell, 2008), 173.
225. Kidd, *The Forging of Races*, 171.
226. Ibid. (emphasis mine).
227. Schuon, *Gnosis*, 17 (emphasis mine).
228. See p. 93.
229. Although in one of his essays Schuon refers to Gobineau and Chamberlain as "certain racists," the term "racist" is deployed not as an attack on racial typology itself, but only on its metaphysical *limitations*. Thus, Schuon specifically takes Gobineau and Chamberlain to task for being unaware of the fact that "each race repetition of certain types" is due not simply "to mixtures" of bloodline, but to the repetition of "typological possibilities" consisting of "astrological types, the universality of the temperaments, and other factors." Schuon, *To Have a Center*, 46. Yet, in the same work, Schuon notes: "*If the mixture between races too different from each other is to be avoided, it is precisely because this disparity generally has a consequence that the individual possesses two centers, which means practically speaking that he has none; in other words that he has no identity*" (ibid., 7) (emphasis mine). Here, it is clear that Schuon not only found racial typologies theoretically useful but also understood biological race itself to be representative of ontological "identity" as "center."
230. Frithjof Schuon, *Christianity/Islam*, 28 (emphasis mine).
231. Schuon, *Gnosis*, 20 (emphasis mine).
232. Schuon later notes that " 'outwardly' the religions are 'mythologies' or, more precisely, symbolisms designed for different human receptacles and displaying

by their limitations, not a contradiction *in divinis*, but on the contrary a mercy." Schuon, *Gnosis*, 63.

233. Ibid., 20 (emphasis mine).
234. Schuon, *Logic and Transcendence*, 100.
235. Ibid. (emphasis mine).
236. Schuon cites Max Müller as the originator of the term "henotheism" and notes that while it is still "alive" in Hinduism, "the henotheist mentality is characteristic of the entire East to one degree or another." Schuon, *Logic and Transcendence*, 99, 100. The term "henotheism" was first used by Friedrich Schelling (d. 1854) in his study of mythology to designate a "rudimentary monotheism." It was later popularized by Müller as a "belief in single gods"—a particular form of polytheism characteristic of the gods in the Rigveda. As opposed to the hierarchical polytheism of ancient Greece and Rome, henotheism was characterized by the worship of a plurality of gods, each representing the absolute and thus not constrained by the powers of other gods. Müller theorized that the henotheistic phase was the global precursor to both polytheistic and monotheistic modes of worship. See Michiko Yusa, "Henotheism," in *Encyclopedia of Religion*, 2nd ed., vol. 6 (Detroit: Macmillan Reference USA, 2005), 3913–14.
237. Schuon, *Logic and Transcendence*, 101 (emphasis mine).
238. In the section of the *Fuṣūṣ* that Schuon cites from the chapter of Muhammad, Ibn 'Arabi uses the term "divinity of belief" in the singular: *al-ilāh al-muʿtaqad*. See Ibn al-ʿArabī, *Fuṣūṣ al-ḥikam*, 225–26.
239. Schuon, *Sufism*, 40.
240. Ibn 'Arabi quoted in Schuon, *Sufism*, 40. See Ibn al-ʿArabī, *Fuṣūṣ al-ḥikam*, 226.
241. Schuon, *Sufism*, 41 (emphasis mine).
242. See chap. 1, n. 63.
243. Schuon, *Sufism*, 41 (emphasis mine).
244. What Schuon here refers to as prophetic "synthesis" (see p. 146) refers precisely to Ibn 'Arabi's cosmology of Muhammad's "comprehensiveness" as the "sum total" of all the prophets discussed in chapter 1. See esp. pp. 38–41.
245. Because the *religio perennis* is understood to be the pure and essential "archetype" that unifies the various divine archetypes from which the individual religions manifest, it is, according to such logic, a divine attribute itself. See pp. 30, 50, 53. See also n. 246 below.
246. While I discussed in chapter 3 the genealogical importance of Schleiermacher's systematic treatment of religion as an essence unique to itself, it is with the thought of Schleiermacher's contemporary Georg W. F. Hegel (d. 1831) that we find a similar but more forceful reified notion of religion as a transcendent essence. Thus, Smith notes it was Hegel who first "posited 'religion' as a *Begriff*, a self-subsisting transcendent idea that unfolds itself in dynamic expression in the course of ever-changing history—unfolds itself as 'positive religion' (in the singular)." Wilfred

Cantwell Smith, *The Meaning and End of Religion* (Minneapolis: Fortress Press, 1991), 47.

247. Carl W. Ernst, *Following Muhammad: Rethinking Islam in the Contemporary World* (Chapel Hill: University of North Carolina Press, 2003), 51.
248. Indeed, Ibn 'Arabi stipulated that the "office of the Seal of Muḥammadan Sainthood belongs to an Arab, one of the noblest in lineage and power." Ibn 'Arabi quoted in Chodkiewicz, *Seal of the Saints*, 117–18. For a detailed account of the family lineage that Ibn 'Arabi proudly claimed see Addas, *Quest for the Red Sulphur*, 17–18.
249. Hugh Nicholson, *Comparative Theology and the Problem of Religious Rivalry* (New York: Oxford University Press, 2011), 6.
250. Although Schuon claimed that "one cannot make a 'religion' out of *Advaita Vedânta*," his above statement along with his substitution of Mary for Muhammad qua *Logos* renders such a distinction merely semantic. See Schuon, *The Fullness of God*, 173–74.
251. Russell T. McCutcheon, *Critics Not Caretakers: Redescribing the Public Study of Religion* (Albany: State University of New York Press, 2001), 172–73.

CONCLUSION

1. Immanuel Kant, *Religion within the Bounds of Bare Reason*, trans. Werner S. Pluhar (Indianapolis: Hackett Publishing Company, 2009), 127.
2. Frithjof Schuon, *Logic and Transcendence: A New Translation with Selected Letters*, trans. Mark Perry, Jean-Pierre Lafouge, and James S. Cutsinger, ed. James S. Cutsinger (Bloomington, IN: World Wisdom, 2009), 28.
3. Jacques Derrida, *Margins of Philosophy*, trans. Alan Bass (Chicago: Chicago University Press, 1982), 213.
4. Grace M. Jantzen, *Power, Gender, and Christian Mysticism* (Cambridge: Cambridge University Press, 1995), 344.
5. Grace M. Jantzen, "Could There Be a Mystical Core of Religion?," *Religious Studies* 26, no. 1 (1990): 63.
6. While Schuonian Perennialism discursively appropriates various modes of intellectual mysticism found in Stoicism, Platonism, and Neoplatonism (including their Christian and Islamic variations) in which unitive knowledge of the divine, Intellect, or *Logos* is attainable through inward, direct "gnosis," Kantian rationalism decidedly rejects any notion that knowledge of the "noumenal" realm (i.e., the divine "as such") is attainable. Yet, as I will argue here, Kantian metaphysics draws heavily upon the intellectual mysticism of the Christian Platonic/Neoplatonic tradition that Schuonian Perennialism claims for itself. Moreover, the German Pietist tradition not only heavily informed Kant's understanding of religion but also served as an important basis of German Romanticism, which (as I noted in chapters 2 and 3) appears to have influenced Schuon. Pietism stressed a radical inward spirituality

that de-emphasized the place of ritual within Protestantism, which was already notable for its marginalization of ritualism from Catholicism. Regarding Kant's response to Pietism see Stephen Palmquist, *Kant's Critical Religion* (Aldershot: Ashgate, 2000), 140. Regarding the debt that German Romanticism has to Pietism see Richard Littlejohns, "Early Romanticism," in *The Literature of German Romanticism*, ed. Dennis F. Mahone (Rochester, NY: Camden House, 2004), 63. Regarding Pietistic de-emphasis of ritual, see F. Ernest Stoeffler, "Pietism," *Encyclopedia of Religion*, 2nd ed., vol. 10 (Detroit: Macmillan Reference USA, 2005), 7143.

7. George Lakoff and Mark Johnson, *Metaphors We Live By* (Chicago: University of Chicago Press, 1980), 193. As Lakoff and Johnson state: "Our ordinary *conceptual system*, in terms of which we both think and act, *is fundamentally metaphorical in nature*." Ibid., 3 (emphasis mine).
8. Schuon referred to Kantian thought as "suicidal rationalism" and modern rationalist philosophy in general as "rationalist Luciferianism." See Schuon, *Logic and Transcendence*, 31; and Frithjof Schuon, *From the Divine to the Human: A New Translation with Selected Letters*, trans. Mark Perry and Jean-Pierre Lafouge, ed. Patrick Laude (Bloomington, IN: World Wisdom, 2013), 5, 152.
9. Ramón Grosfoguel and Eric Mielants, "The Long-Durée Entanglement between Islamophobia and Racism in the Modern/Colonial Capitalist/Patriarchal World-System: An Introduction," *Human Architecture: Journal of the Sociology of Self-Knowledge* 5, no. 1 (2006): 8. As Grosfoguel and Mielants note, 1492 was formative for modern categories of knowledge in that it marked the fall of Granada and the Spanish reconquest of Andalusia along with the expulsion of Jews and Arabs from Iberia, and the simultaneous "discovery" of the Americas along with the colonization of its indigenous peoples. Through these events, "Jews and Arabs became the subaltern internal 'Others' within Europe, while indigenous people became the external 'Others' of Europe" (ibid., 2).
10. Santiago Castro-Gómez, "(Post)Coloniality for Dummies: Latin American Perspectives on Modernity, Coloniality, and the Geopolitics of Knowledge," in *Coloniality at Large: Latin America and the Postcolonial Debate*, ed. Mabel Moraña, Enrique Dussel, and Carlos A. Jáurequi (Durham, NC: Duke University Press, 2008), 278.
11. C. R. P. Rogers quoted in *Zero Degrees: Geographies of the Prime Meridian*, by Charles W. J. Withers (Cambridge, MA: Harvard University Press, 2017), 5 (emphasis mine).
12. As Robert Young trenchantly notes, "It was with a supremely knowing gesture towards the future that in 1884, the division of the newly homogenized temporal world into East and West was placed not in Jerusalem or Constantinople but in a South London suburb." Robert J. C. Young, *Colonial Desire: Hybridity in Theory, Culture and Race* (London: Routledge, 1995), 1.
13. Castro-Gómez, "(Post)Coloniality for Dummies," 278 (emphasis mine).
14. Ibid.

15. Slavoj Žižek, "Multiculturalism, Or, the Cultural Logic of Multinational Capitalism," *New Left Review* 225 (1997): 44 (emphasis original).
16. Walter D. Mignolo, "Preface to the 2012 Edition," in *Local Histories/Global Designs Coloniality, Subaltern Knowledges, and Border Thinking* (Princeton, NJ: Princeton University Press, 2012), xiii.
17. Kant famously distinguishes "transcendental" from "transcendent." While the transcendent is beyond the boundaries of cognition and experience, the transcendental "refers to the type of cognition concerned not with objects but with our a priori concepts of objects." Helmut Holzhey and Vilem Mudroch, *Historical Dictionary of Kant and Kantianism* (Lanham, MD: Scarecrow Press, 2005), 268.
18. David S. Pacini, *Through Narcissus' Glass Darkly: The Modern Religion of Conscience* (New York: Fordham University Press, 2008), 10.
19. In the preface to the second edition of the *Critique of Pure Reason*, Kant compares his subjective turn to Copernicus: "Let us once try whether we do not get farther with the problems of metaphysics by assuming that the objects must conform to our cognition. . . . This would be just like the first thoughts of Copernicus." Immanuel Kant, *Critique of Pure Reason*, trans. and ed. Paul Guyer and Allen W. Wood (Cambridge: Cambridge University Press, 1998), 110; and Guyer and Wood, introduction to *Critique of Pure Reason*, 2–6. See also Stephen Palmquist, *Kant's Critical Religion* (Aldershot: Ashgate, 2000), 45.
20. See pp. 97–98.
21. Schuon, *Logic and Transcendence*, 4.
22. Castro-Gómez, "(Post)Coloniality for Dummies," 279.
23. Walter Mignolo, *The Darker Side of the Renaissance: Literacy, Territoriality, and Colonization* (Ann Arbor: University of Michigan Press, 2003), 256–57.
24. Castro-Gómez, "(Post)Coloniality for Dummies," 279.
25. Sixteenth-century imperialism marks the beginning of a shift from premodern religious exclusivity and the inferiorization of different religions to modern racism and the inferiorization of the human beings who practice them. It is here where race arises "as one of the central conceptual inventions of modernity." David Theo Goldberg, *Racist Culture: Philosophy and the Politics of Meaning* (Oxford: Blackwell, 1993), 3. See also Grosfoguel and Mielants, "The Long-Durée," 4.
26. Goldberg, *Racist Culture*, 53.
27. James M. Byrne, *Religion and the Enlightenment: From Descartes to Kant* (Louisville, KY: Westminster John Knox Press, 1997), 67 (emphasis mine).
28. Susan Meld Shell argues that the Cartesian mind–body problem "stands at the heart" of Kant's early philosophical concerns and thus was formative for "his later, critical insistence on the dependence of the transcendental unity of consciousness on outer sense." Susan Meld Shell, *The Embodiment of Reason: Kant on Spirit, Generation, and Community* (Chicago: University of Chicago Press, 1996), 10, 306.
29. Pacini, *Through Narcissus' Glass*, 172.

30. Thus, for Kant, the autonomous "I that thinks is not part of that world, not subject to causal categories but rather responsible for causal structuring." Christina Howells, "Conclusion: Sartre and the Deconstruction of the Subject," in *The Cambridge Companion to Sartre* (Cambridge: Cambridge University Press, 1992), 322.
31. Immanuel Kant, *Critique of Practical Reason*, trans. Mary Gregor (Cambridge: Cambridge University Press, 2015), 38.
32. Kant, *Religion within the Bounds*, 7. Indeed, in the Preface to the first edition, Kant envisions *Religion* as required reading in an advanced class for theologians and finally suggests that the biblical and philosophical theologian could be imagined to be "united." Ibid., 9.
33. Ian Hunter, "Kant's Regional Cosmopolitanism," *Journal of the History of International Law* 12, no. 2 (2010): 173. Although it is often referred to as Christian Neoplatonism, this tradition as most influentially known through the writings of St. Augustine (d. 430) also sought theological inspiration in the older Platonism. See Janet Coleman, "The Christian Platonism of St Augustine," in *Platonism and the English Imagination*, ed. Anna Baldwin and Sarah Hutton (New York: Cambridge University Press, 1994), 27–37.
34. Coleman, "The Christian Platonism," 30–31.
35. Hunter, "Kant's Regional Cosmopolitanism," 173.
36. Stephen R. Palmquist, *Comprehensive Commentary on Kant's Religion within the Bounds of Bare Reason* (Chichester: John Wiley & Sons, 2016), 8.
37. Kant, *Religion within the Bounds*, 66–67.
38. Ibid., 67. Chris Firestone and Nathan Jacobs argue that Kant's language here constitutes "a transcendentally chastened form of Platonic idealism, which is rooted in practical reason." Chris L. Firestone and Nathan Jacobs, *In Defense of Kant's Religion* (Bloomington: Indiana University Press, 2008), 155. For a detailed discussion of Kant's use of Platonic idealism see their following section "The Prototype of Perfect Humanity" (ibid., 155–70).
39. Hunter, "Kant's Regional Cosmopolitanism," 173.
40. Ibid., 173–74.
41. Yirmiahu Yovel, *Kant and the Philosophy of History* (Princeton, NJ: Princeton University Press, 1980), 4, 7.
42. Kant, *Religion within the Bounds*, 135, 139–51.
43. Ibid., 135 (emphasis mine).
44. Kant also calls this moral predisposition the "pure *moral* legislation whereby the will of God is originally inscribed in our hearts." Kant, *Religion within the Bounds*, 114 (emphasis original).
45. Ibid., 136 (emphasis mine).
46. Ibid., 154.
47. Palmquist, *Kant's Critical Religion*, 190.

48. Kant, *Religion within the Bounds*, 154.
49. Ibid., 155 (emphasis mine).
50. Ibid., 155n446 (emphasis original). See also Palmquist, *Comprehensive Commentary*, 360.
51. Kant, *Religion within the Bounds*, 155n446. See also Palmquist, *Comprehensive Commentary*, 360.
52. Kant, *Religion within the Bounds*, 141 (emphasis mine).
53. Ibid., 90 (emphasis mine).
54. Ibid., 141–42.
55. For example, Stephen Palmquist, who has perhaps written most widely (and often insightfully) on Kant's ideas on religion states: "The fact that the Jews are first and foremost an *ethnic* group that established itself as a community on the basis of 'merely statutory laws,' and that their 'national structure' was set up explicitly to give the people political power in competition with other secular states, does suggest (on Kant's terms) that 'Judaism is actually not a religion at all.'" Palmquist, *Comprehensive Commentary*, 330 (emphasis original).
56. Kant, *Religion within the Bounds*, 139 (emphasis mine).
57. This is not necessarily the case, however. As Simcha Raphael observes, there are "scant traces of the notion of immortality throughout the Bible." Simcha Paull Raphael, *Jewish Views of the Afterlife*, 2nd ed. (Lanham, MD: Rowman & Littlefield Publishers, 2009), 75. Raphael further notes that while "the Hebrew Bible is certainly not a definitive source" for the later traditions on the afterlife, "certain Jewish notions of life after death are seeded in biblical times." Thus, "notions of the hereafter developed in biblical times remained as the foundation for all future Jewish conceptions of the afterlife experience" (ibid., 4, 75).
58. Kant, *Religion within the Bounds*, 139 (emphasis mine).
59. Ibid.
60. Ibid., 172 (emphasis mine).
61. Ibid., 138.
62. Yovel, *Kant and the Philosophy*, 207 (emphasis mine).
63. Kant, *Religion within the Bounds*, 172 (emphasis mine).
64. Ibid., 139.
65. Ibid., 173.
66. Ibid., 173.
67. Ibid. (emphasis mine).
68. Ibid., 141 (emphasis mine).
69. Ibid. (emphasis mine).
70. Ibid., 185 (emphasis original).
71. Ibid., 113. As Palmquist notes: "the crucial clothing metaphor Kant presents in the Preface and employs throughout the book, whereby rational religion is a 'bare'

(*bloß-*) body that is inevitably clothed by some historical faith." Indeed, the term *bloßen* has been traditionally mistranslated as "alone" or "mere," thus missing the entire implication of Kant's nuanced metaphor. See Stephen R. Palmquist, introduction to *Religion within the Bounds of Bare Reason*, by Immanuel Kant, trans. Werner S. Pluhar (Indianapolis: Hackett Publishing, 2009), xv n1.

72. Kant, *Religion within the Bounds*, 173.
73. Ibid., 135 (emphasis mine).
74. 1 Corinthians 13: "When I was a child, I spoke like a child, I thought like a child, I reasoned like a child; when I became an adult, I put an end to childish ways." Michael D. Coogan, ed., *The New Oxford Annotated Bible: New Revised Standard Version with the Apocrypha* (New York: Oxford University Press, 2010), 2018. For example, see Kant, *Religion within the Bounds*, 135n318; and Palmquist, *Comprehensive Commentary*, 320n173.
75. Galatians 4:1–11. Coogan, ed., *The New Oxford Annotated Bible*, 2047–48 (emphasis mine).
76. Coogan, ed., *The New Oxford Annotated Bible*, 2048n4.10.
77. Ursula Goldenbaum, "Understanding the Argument through Then-Current Public Debates or My Detective Method of History of Philosophy," in *Philosophy and Its History: Aims and Methods in the Study of Early Modern Philosophy*, ed. Mogens Lærke, Justin E.H. Smith, and Eric Schliesser (New York: Oxford University Press, 2013), 80.
78. Immanuel Kant, "An Answer to the Question: 'What Is Enlightenment?'," in *Kant: Political Writings*, trans. H. B. Nisbet, ed. H. S. Reiss (Cambridge: Cambridge University Press, 1991), 54 (emphasis original).
79. Susanne Lachenicht, "Early Modern German States and the Settlement of Jews: Brandenburg—Prussia and the Palatinate, Sixteenth to Nineteenth Centuries," *Jewish Historical Studies* 42 (2009): 11.
80. That is, the "Revised General Privilege for the Jewry in the Kingdom of Prussia" (*Revidierte General-Privilegium und Reglement vor die Judenschaft im Königreiche Preussen*). Lachenicht, "Early Modern German States," 11.
81. Goldenbaum, "Understanding the Argument," 85.
82. Ibid., 81 (emphasis mine).
83. Ibid., 82 (emphasis mine).
84. Ibid., 84, 86 (emphasis mine).
85. Ibid., 86. Although Goldenbaum here mentions *Religion* in passing as confirming her suspicions regarding "An Answer to the Question," I am not aware of any scholarship that has looked closely at Kant's *Religion* in relation to Paul's anti-Judaic stance found in Galatians.
86. Kant, *Critique of Practical Reason*, 38.
87. For example, Palmquist, introduction to *Religion*, xxi.

88. Immanuel Kant, *Religion within the Boundaries of Mere Reason and Other Writings*, trans. and ed. Allen Wood and George Di Giovanni (Cambridge: Cambridge University Press, 1998), 127.
89. Kant, *Religion within the Bounds*, 135 (emphasis original).
90. Susan Meld Shell, *Kant and the Limits of Autonomy* (Cambridge, MA: Harvard University Press, 2009), 2 (emphasis mine).
91. Mario Perniola, "Between Clothing and Nudity," in *Fragments for a History of the Human Body: Part Two*, ed. Michel Feher (New York: Zone, 1990), 239.
92. For Schuon's connection to Lutheranism see p. 85.
93. As Perniola notes, in the Hebraic tradition, the connection "between clothing and the service of God, is rooted in the fact that God Himself 'clothed' the earth in the process of Creation and that He manifests Himself 'clothed' with honor and majesty, / who coverest thyself with light as with a garment' (Psalm 104.1–2)." Perniola, "Between Clothing and Nudity," 238.
94. Ibid., 237, 238.
95. Ibid., 238–39 (emphasis original).
96. Ibid.
97. Coogan, ed., *The New Oxford Annotated Bible*, 2071 (emphasis mine).
98. Kant employs this metaphor of nudity throughout *Religion*. For example, see Kant, *Religion within the Bounds*, 38, 67, 87.
99. Ibid., 89 (emphasis original).
100. Michael Mack, *German Idealism and the Jew: The Inner Anti-Semitism of Philosophy and German Jewish Responses* (Chicago: University of Chicago Press, 2003), 3.
101. Ibid., 39.
102. Immanuel Kant, *The Conflict of the Faculties: Der Streit der Fakultäten*, trans. Mary J. Gregor (New York: Abaris Books, 1979), 93 (emphasis original).
103. Thus, while Kant ostensibly rejects "the old Christian dream of converting the Jews," as Paul Rose notes, "in its place he envisages something far more insidiously destructive of Judaism, namely moral and human purification. The first step to this is to reform Judaism into a rational and moral religion of human freedom." Paul Lawrence Rose, *Revolutionary Antisemitism in Germany from Kant to Wagner* (Princeton, NJ: Princeton University Press, 1990), 95.
104. Kant, *The Conflict*, 93 (emphasis mine).
105. Ibid., 95 (emphasis original). As Shell notes, "*Judaism, thus transformed, becomes one Christian sect among others.*" Shell, *Kant and the Limits*, 326 (emphasis mine).
106. Kant, *The Conflict*, 95 (emphasis mine). "The restoration of all things" refers to Origen's doctrine of *Apokatastasis* and the universal "restoration" of all souls to their pure spiritual state. See Robert Turcan, "Apocatastasis," *Encyclopedia of Religion*, vol. 1, 2nd ed., ed. Lindsay Jones (Detroit: Macmillan Reference USA, 2005), 422.
107. Shell, *Kant and the Limits*, 306. See also Rose, *Revolutionary Antisemitism in Germany*, 117–32; and Mack, *German Idealism*, 23–41.

108. Frithjof Schuon, "Excerpts from Letters of the Shaykh," in *Shari'ah 2* [Maryamiyya handbook] (privately circulated photocopied typescript, 1995), 2 (emphasis mine). See p. 137.
109. Schuon quoted in Oldmeadow, *Frithjof Schuon*, 190 (emphasis mine). See p. 137.
110. Schuon, "Excerpts from Letters," 1, 2.
111. Frithjof Schuon, *Islam and the Perennial Philosophy* (London: World of Islam Festival Publishing Company, 1976), 146 (emphasis mine).
112. As Roger Griffin notes, "The vision of rebirth, of palingenesis, of a new cycle of regeneration and renewal growing out of what appeared to be an irreversible linear process of decay, dissolution, or death, appears to be an archetype of human mythopoeia, manifesting itself, for example, as much in the Christian faith in the Resurrection of Christ and of all true believers as in the Hindu cosmology, which computes in mathematical detail the universe's infinite cycle of creation and destruction." Roger Griffin, "Fascism," in *New Dictionary of the History of Ideas*, vol. 2, ed. Maryanne Cline Horowitz (Detroit: Charles Scribner's Sons, 2005), 795.
113. See Howard Williams, "Metamorphosis or Palingenesis? Political Change in Kant," *Review of Politics* 63, no. 4 (2001): 693–722.
114. Shell, *Kant and the Limits*, 316.
115. Kant, *Religion within the Bounds*, 114 (emphasis original).
116. Ibid. (emphasis mine).
117. Ibid., 185.
118. Immanuel Kant, *To Perpetual Peace: A Philosophical Sketch*, trans. Ted Humphrey (Indianapolis: Hackett Publishing Company, 2003), 24 (emphasis original).
119. Talal Asad, "Reading a Modern Classic: W. C. Smith's 'The Meaning and End of Religion,'" *History of Religions* 40, no. 3 (2001): 216.
120. Ibid., 216–17 (emphasis mine).
121. Frithjof Schuon, *Sufism: Veil and Quintessence: A New Translation with Selected Letters*, trans. Mark Perry, Jean-Pierre Lafouge, and James S. Cutsinger, ed. James S. Cutsinger (Bloomington, IN: World Wisdom, 2006), 24 (emphasis mine).
122. Schuon similarly refers to such "relativity" as "the divinely foreseen divergences of the religions." Schuon, *Sufism*, 69–70.
123. Frithjof Schuon, *Gnosis: Divine Wisdom*, ed. James S. Cutsinger, trans. Mark Perry, Jean-Pierre Lafouge, and James Cutsinger (Bloomington, IN: World Wisdom, 2006), 18 (emphasis mine).
124. Ibid., 18 (emphasis mine).
125. Kant, *Religion within the Bounds*, 118 (emphasis original).
126. Ibid. (emphasis mine).
127. Ibid., 185 (emphasis mine). Kant refers to this in the *Critique of Practical Reason* as "the *autonomy* of pure reason." Kant, *Critique of Practical Reason*, 38.
128. Schuon, *Gnosis*, 20 (emphasis mine).
129. Ibid. (emphasis mine).
130. Ibid. (emphasis mine).

131. Kant, *Religion within the Bounds*, 142.
132. Schuon, *Sufism*, 21 (emphasis mine).
133. Schuon, *Islam and the Perennial*, 146.
134. See p. 134 and chap. 4, n. 146.
135. "Subjectivity," 3.b., *Oxford English Dictionary* (3rd Edition, June 2012) online version June 2017, accessed January 03, 2018, http://www.oed.com/view/Entry/192707.
136. As Kant states in *Critique of Pure Reason*, "in *a priori* cognition nothing can be ascribed to the objects except what the thinking subject takes out of itself." Kant, *Critique of Pure Reason*, 113.
137. Jill Vance Buroker, *Kant's Critique of Pure Reason: An Introduction* (Cambridge: Cambridge University Press, 2006), 62.
138. Indeed, in *Castes and Races*, Schuon asserts that because of the absence of the caste system in Semitic religions, there is an imposition of "a certain mental uniformity" on people of different spiritual capacities. Such a mode of "collectivity," notes Schuon, "represents a principle tending to increase density and complexity; *it is always ready to lend an absolute character to facts*, and this is the tendency for which religious dogmatism makes allowance from the outset." It is such Semitic dogmatism, Schuon continues to note, that ultimately creates "doctrinal simplification and *a need for external activities* which are *the very antipodes of intellection and contemplation*." Frithjof Schuon, *Castes and Races*, trans. Marco Pallis and Macleod Matheson (Bedfont: Perennial Books, 1982), 24 (emphasis mine).
139. Frithjof Schuon, *Echoes of Perennial Wisdom*, trans. Mark Perry and Jean-Pierre Lafouge (Bloomington, IN: World Wisdom), 60 (emphasis mine).
140. Frithjof Schuon, *Form and Substance in the Religions*, trans. Mark Perry and Jean-Pierre LaFouge (Bloomington, IN: World Wisdom, 2002), 24n19 (emphasis mine). See also p. 130.
141. Schuon, *Form and Substance*, 24 (emphasis mine). See also p. 129.
142. Schuon, *Logic and Transcendence*, 128 (emphasis mine). See also p. 134.
143. Here, Chamberlain quotes from Kant's *Religion* itself, asserting: "Kant pronounces of Jehovah that He 'is not that Being the conception of which is necessary for religion,' and so Judaism as a general proposition 'taken in its purity contains no religious faith.'" Chamberlain thus immediately comments: "In order to understand Kant here *we must therefore begin by once for all getting rid of the whole heavy burthen of inherited and indoctrinated Jewish conceptions*. Kant's doctrine of religion, however scientifically dry it may seem, is a true fountain of youth: *out of it we may emerge washed and purified from Semitic delusions after millenniums, able to adopt as our own that most modern form of primeval Aryan religiosity which is accurately fitted to the order of thought of the living present*, to the results of the only pure exact science, and to the social requirements of our time and of our future." Houston Stewart Chamberlain, *Immanuel Kant: A Study and a Comparison with*

Goethe, Leonardo Da Vinci, Bruno, Plato and Descartes, vol. 2, trans. Freeman-Mitford Redesdale (London: John Lane, 1914), 390 (emphasis mine). (Originally published as *Immanuel Kant. Die Persönlichkeit als Einführung in das Werk* [München: F. Bruckmann, 1905]). See also Mack, *German Idealism*, 103–4.

144. Houston Stewart Chamberlain, *Foundations of the Nineteenth Century*, vol. 1, trans. John Lees (New York: Howard Fertig, 1968), 422 (emphasis mine).
145. Mack, *German Idealism*, 39.
146. Schuon, *Form and Substance*, 24 (emphasis mine). See also p. 129.
147. See Kant, *Critique of Pure Reason*, 38.
148. Schuon, *Echoes of Perennial Wisdom*, 77 (emphasis mine).
149. Schuon, *Sufism*, 40n29. See also p. 132.
150. William C. Chittick, *Imaginal Worlds: Ibn al-ʿArabī and the Problem of Religious Diversity* (Albany: State University of New York Press, 1994), 173 (emphasis mine).
151. Hugh Nicholson, *Comparative Theology and the Problem of Religious Rivalry* (New York: Oxford University Press, 2011), 8.
152. Reza Shah-Kazemi, *Paths to Transcendence: According to Shankara, Ibn Arabi, and Meister Eckhart* (Bloomington, IN: World Wisdom, 2006), 251 (emphasis mine).
153. Reza Shah-Kazemi, *The Other in the Light of the One: The Universality of the Qur'ān and Interfaith Dialogue* (Cambridge: Islamic Texts Society, 2006). In his introduction, Shah-Kazemi notes that his book is based on the "particular point of view . . . [of] those most steeped in the spiritual and mystical tradition of Islam, Sufism" (xvi). Shah-Kazemi goes on to identify this view as the "vision of the inner unity of religions" (xvii), which in a footnote he further identifies as "what Frithjof Schuon referred to as the 'transcendent unity' of religions" (xvii n14). Finally, Shah-Kazemi asserts that "the metaphysical perspective elaborated here on universality . . . [is] based on the metaphysics of Ibn ʿArabī" (xxii).
154. Ibid., 192.
155. Ibid., xxv (emphasis mine).
156. Ibid., 162 (emphasis mine).
157. Ibid., 164.
158. Ibid., 162 (emphasis mine).
159. Ibid., 164.
160. As I discussed in the introduction, I use "strong misreading" in the Bloomian sense to denote an innovative "misreading" that has been seminal in establishing a (now) canonical Schuonian interpretation for understanding Ibn 'Arabi and his perspective on the religious Other. See p. 20 and intro., n. 137.
161. See discussion, pp. 15–16.
162. Shah-Kazemi, *The Other in the Light*, 191.
163. Ibid., 164–65 (emphasis mine).
164. Schuon, *Echoes of Perennial Wisdom*, 60–61 (emphasis mine).
165. Ibid., 157 (emphasis mine).

166. See discussion pp. 18–19, 124–25, 132, 134–135.
167. Schuon, *Sufism*, 41. See p. 148.
168. Wouter J. Hanegraaff, *New Age Religion and Western Culture: Esotericism in the Mirror of Secular Thought* (Leiden: E. J. Brill, 1996), 329.
169. Ibid.
170. Wendy Brown, *Regulating Aversion: Tolerance in the Age of Identity and Empire* (Princeton, NJ: Princeton University Press, 2006), 186.
171. Shah-Kazemi, *Paths to Transcendence*, 129 (emphasis mine).
172. Seyyed Hossein Nasr, *Knowledge and the Sacred* (Albany: State University of New York Press, 1989), 107.
173. James S. Cutsinger, introduction to *Frithjof Schuon, Splendor of the True: A Frithjof Schuon Reader*, ed. and trans. James S. Cutsinger (Albany: State University of New York Press, 2013), xxxv. See also p. 123.
174. James William Graham, "A Treatise on Sufiism, or Mahomedan Mysticism: Read 30th December 1811," in *Transactions of the Literary Society of Bombay with Engravings*, vol. 1 (1819; reprint, Bombay: Education Society's Press, 1877), 96 (emphasis mine).
175. Graham, "A Treatise on Sufiism," 96–97 (emphasis mine).
176. Ibid., 97.
177. Ibid., 101–2.
178. Ibid., 102 (emphasis mine).
179. Ibid. (emphasis mine).
180. Carl W. Ernst, *The Shambhala Guide to Sufism* (Boston: Shambhala Publications, 1997), 8–9.
181. Pacini, *Through Narcissus' Glass*, 6–7.
182. Ibid., 13.
183. "The power of a *Deus absconditus*," according to Castro-Gómez, "can see without being seen and can observe the world without having to prove to anybody . . . the legitimacy of that observation." Castro-Gómez, "(Post)Coloniality for Dummies," 282.
184. Kant, *Religion within the Bounds*, 135 (emphasis mine).
185. Brown, *Regulating Aversion*, 167.
186. Ibid., 171.
187. Russell T. McCutcheon, *Manufacturing Religion: The Discourse on Sui Generis Religion and the Politics of Nostalgia* (New York: Oxford University Press, 1997), 92.
188. Ibid., 93.
189. David Theo Goldberg, *The Racial State* (Malden, MA: Blackwell Publishers, 2002), 43, 46. Goldberg compares this type to "racial naturalism." Whereas such naturalism seeks difference in the restrictions of "nature" (i.e., biology), racial

historicism understands difference according to an immaturity due to the buildup of historical forces over time. Although Kant certainly held blacks to be inferior based on a naturalist conception, his view of the Jews is clearly more nuanced and historicist. Schuon's Othering of the "Semite" seems to lean the other way, however.

190. Ashwani Sharma, "Postcolonial Racism: White Paranoia and the Terrors of Multiculturalism," in *Racism Postcolonialism Europe*, ed. Graham Huggan and Ian Law (Liverpool: Liverpool University Press, 2009), 123 (emphasis mine).
191. See Emmanuel Levinas, *Totality and Infinity: An Essay on Exteriority*, trans. Alphonso Lingis (The Hague: Martinus Nijhoff Publishers, 1979), 44.
192. Robert J. C. Young, *White Mythologies: Writing History and the West*, 2nd ed. (London: Routledge, 2004), 45.
193. Gilles Deleuze and Félix Guattari, *A Thousand Plateaus: Capitalism and Schizophrenia*, trans. Brian Massumi (London: Athlone Press, 2005), 178.
194. Michael Mack, *German Idealism*, 19.
195. Ibid.
196. Brown, *Regulating Aversion*, 171.
197. As noted earlier, Kant recognized a "moral predisposition" of the human being where "the will of God is originally inscribed in our hearts." See n. 44 above.
198. On the *religio perennis* as a "religion," see pp. 19, 148, and chap. 4, n. 250.
199. Schuon, *Logic and Transcendence*, 101.
200. Rose, *Revolutionary Antisemitism in Germany*, 96.
201. Besides his anti-Semitism, Kant displayed an evident white supremacism. For example, Kant asserts that "Humanity exists in its greatest perfection in the white race." Kant quoted in Emmanuel Chukwudi Eze, "The Color of Reason: The Idea of 'Race' in Kant's Anthropology," in *Postcolonial African Philosophy: A Critical Reader*, ed. Emmanuel Chukwudi Eze (Cambridge: Blackwell Publishers, 1997), 118. Indeed, in similar ways to Schuon (as discussed in chapter 4), Kant understood race itself to be an ontological marker of rationality—exemplified in his remarks that an African man's blackness was "clear proof" of his purported stupidity. Ibid., 119.
202. Here, I define ideology as a concealed means to control or dominate a discursive domain. See Terry Eagleton, *Ideology: An Introduction* (London: Verso, 1991), 5, 11. Similarly, Russell McCutcheon defines ideology as a universalizing and homogenizing discourse deployed to authorize "representations whose trace, history, or context is obscured (whether intentionally or not)." McCutcheon, *Manufacturing Religion*, 29–30.
203. Nicholson, *Comparative Theology*, 10 (emphasis mine).
204. Hunter, "Kant's Regional Cosmopolitanism," 183 (emphasis mine).
205. See n. 201 above.
206. Eze, "The Color of Reason," 131.

207. Young, *White Mythologies*, 43.
208. As Prasenjit Duara notes, "The history of the world may, from one perspective, be seen as the recurrent capture and institutionalization of transcendent authority." Prasenjit Duara, *The Crisis of Global Modernity: Asian Traditions and a Sustainable Future* (Cambridge: Cambridge University Press, 2015), 6.

Index

ʿAbdul-Hādī. *See* Aguéli, Ivan
Abraham
  primordial religion of, 15–16, 47, 59, 174
abrogation (*naskh*). *See* Chittick, William; Dagli, Caner; al-Ghazālī, Abū Ḥamid; Ibn ʿArabi; People of the Book; Schuon, Frithjof; Shah-Kazemi, Reza
Adang, Camilla, 107
Addas, Claude, 12, 56, 62, 190n61, 204n125
Affifi, Abdul Ela, 28, 31, 34, 40–41, 211n18
Aguéli, Ivan (ʿAbdul-Hādī)
  and Guénon, 117, 131, 247n109
  interpretation of Ibn ʿArabi, 117–18, 131, 247n109, 252n198
al-ʿAlāwī, Aḥmad, 187n28, 238n5
Anquetil-Duperron. *See* Vedanta
Aristarchus of Samos, 227n96
Aristotelian law of noncontradiction (in theology), 93–94, 100–101, 115– 16, 144–45, 167
Arvidsson, Stefan, *Aryan Idols*, 249n146, 250n170
Aryanism, 241n33, 243nn52–53
  and Kant, 170, 179, 264n143
  and philology (nineteenth-century European), 126–28
  Romantic roots of, 126, 128, 191n75, 244n56, 250n170, 251n173
  and Schuon, 19, 22, 119, 121–38, 143, 145–47, 149–51, 166, 169–70, 246n87
  and universalism, 150, 179
  See also Chamberlain, William; Gobineau, Joseph Arthur de; Hitler, Adolf; Lassen, Christian; Orientalism; race and racialism; Renan, Ernest
Asad, Talal
  on belief, 26
  Genealogies of Religion, 96
  on "the missionary's standpoint," 167, 173, 175
  on religion and power, 96–97, 116
  on a universal definition of religion, xi
  on "the West," 187n24
Aslan, Adnan, 91
Augustine (Saint), 17, 60, 96, 259n33
Austin, R. W. J., 56
Aymard, Jean-Baptiste, 95, 237n4

Balibar, Etienne, 20
Ballard, Frank, 199n57

Balyānī, Awḥad al-Dīn, *Risālat al-aḥadiyya*, 247n107, 252n198
Baudrillard, Jean, 2
Beck, Ulrich, 3
belief
  conflated with religion, 8, 21, 25–32, 34, 48–51, 53–54, 81, 147–48
  divinity of, 7–8, 27–28, 34, 54, 147
  as reflecting God in Ibn ʿArabi, 25, 27, 30–31, 34, 43, 48, 54
Bernard of Clairvaux, 17
Blavatsky, H. P., 243n53
Bloom, Harold ("strong misreading"), 20, 54, 81, 140, 174, 195n137
Bonini's paradox, xiii
Brown, Norman O., 38, 103, 203n107
Brown, Wendy, 18, 176, 178, 180
Bruno, Giordano, 98, 228n98
Buddhism, 93, 118, 186n9
Burckhardt, Titus, 18–19, 213n33, 223n44

cartography
  and ethnocentrism/imperialism, 2–3, 13–14, 22, 83, 152–53, 155, 181
  as interpretive framework, xii–xiv, 2–4, 11–14, 20, 22, 151–55, 177, 181
  and metaphysics, 12
  prime meridian, 153
  Ptolemaic, 13, 154
  See also Copernican turn; Mignolo, Walter
Castelli, Elizabeth, 20
Castro-Gómez, Santiago, 153, 155, 178, 181
Catherine of Siena, 17
Cavanaugh, William, 60–61
Chamberlain, Houston Stewart
  as Aryanist, 126, 128, 130–31, 134
  Foundations of the Nineteenth Century, 130, 170, 245n72
  and Kant, 170, 264n143
  and Schuon, 130–31, 134, 145, 254n229
Chittick, William, xiv–xv, 90, 205n131–32, 207n157
  on abrogation (*naskh*) in Ibn ʿArabi, 57, 65–73, 77, 80–81, 88, 97–99, 101
  Faith and the Practice of Islam: Three Thirteenth Century Sufi Texts, 66, 68–69, 72, 88
  Imaginal Worlds: Ibn al-ʿArabi and the Problem of Religious Diversity, 57, 65, 68, 72, 88, 97, 104
  on law in Ibn ʿArabi, 8–9, 56–57, 175, 198n49
  on Muhammadan saints, 45–47
  "The Religion of Love Revisited," 42–43, 199n62
  and the Schuonian interpretive field, 8, 31, 87–90, 98, 116, 171, 223n32
  Science of the Cosmos, Science of the Soul, 88–89
  on scriptural corruption (*taḥrīf*) in Ibn ʿArabi, 104–5, 111
  universalist interpretation of Ibn ʿArabi, 8, 56–57, 65–73, 80, 89, 171, 175, 212n20
Chodkiewicz, Michel, 58, 107
  on law in Ibn ʿArabi, xiv–xv, 218n125
  on Muhammadan saints, 78, 190n63, 192n97
  on *religio perennis* and Ibn ʿArabi, 16
Christianity
  Ibn ʿArabi on, 8–11, 16, 21–22, 25, 35–36, 43–44, 55–57, 65, 73–75, 82, 87, 101, 110, 115–17, 189n55, 202n92, 230n142, 236n208, 252n202
  and Kant, 155–62, 164–65, 168, 180, 256n6, 262n103
  Protestantism and privatization of religion, 17, 60, 62, 85, 92, 256n6
  and Schuon, 81, 85, 87, 93, 130, 139–40, 145, 152, 165, 249n136

supersession of Judaism by, 3, 13, 64, 180
and universalism, 58, 118, 152, 155, 180, 194n122, 236n208
universalizing, xiii–xiv, 3, 14, 180, 186n9
See also Jesus; Paul (apostle); People of the Book (*ahl al-kitāb*); Protected People (*ahl al-dhimma*)
Cohen, Mark, 82, 210n8
colonialism, 4, 117, 153–55, 179
constructivism, 17
Coomaraswamy, Ananda K., 6, 89
Copernican turn, 153
Kantian, 22, 154–55, 157, 178, 258n19
Schuonian, 21–22, 91, 97, 118–19, 140, 155, 178
Corbin, Henry
and Aryanism, 191n75
esoteric interpretation of Ibn 'Arabi, 11, 29
and Izutsu, 29, 198n49
religion and belief, 29, 31, 34, 51
universalist/essentialist interpretation of Ibn 'Arabi, 31, 51, 191n73, 213n33, 224n57
Crusades, 10, 17, 62
Cutsinger, James
on Schuon, xiv, 121–23, 125, 177, 239n19

Dagli, Caner
on abrogation (*naskh*) in Ibn 'Arabi, 80–81
on Muhammadan saints, 206n147
on prophetic hierarchy in Ibn 'Arabi, 141
on translating *fuṣūṣ* as "ring stones," 190n68
on voluntarism according to Ibn 'Arabi, 249n133
Deism, 26. *See also* Herbert, Lord Edward, of Cherbury
Deleuze, Gilles, 180
dualism
Cartesian, 155, 258n28
essence/manifestation, 179
inward/outward, 51–52
See also nudity (metaphorics and metaphysics of)

Eckhart, Meister, 91, 222n31
Eliade, Mircea, xii, 124, 184n9, 224n57, 241n34
Enlightenment
European, 12, 17, 26, 61, 91, 147–48, 155, 191n75
Jewish, 161
Kantian, 92, 161–62
Enoch, 78, 201n86
Ernst, Carl, 52, 149, 178, 185n3
esoteric and esotericism. *See* Aguéli, Ivan; Corbin, Henry; Guénon, René; Schuon, Frithjof
essentialism, 102, 179–81, 213n33, 224n57
and interpretations of Ibn 'Arabi, 100, 167
Kantian, 173, 176
Schuonian, 137, 148, 150, 167, 175, 179, 181, 242n40
and Schuonian Perennialism, 21, 90, 92, 95, 148, 170
See also Schleiermacher, Friedrich; universalism
Eurocentrism, 11–13, 18, 20, 59, 121
Europe, 85
ethnocentrism, 1, 13, 18–19, 22, 178–80
imperialism, 2, 4
privatization of religion, 17, 26, 31–32, 60
racial exclusion in, 22, 122, 180
and universalism, 18–19, 36, 178–80

Eze, Emmanuel, 181
Ezra, 113, 141, 201n86, 234n189

Fabbri, Renaud, 139
Fascism, 241n34, 244n56
Fidus. *See* Höppner, Karl
Foucault, Michel, 194n120
Frederick the Great,
General-Privilegium, 161

Geoffroy, Éric, 28, 86
geography. *See* cartography
German idealism. *See* idealism
German nationalism, 165
German Romanticism. *See* Romanticism
al-Ghazālī, Abū Ḥāmid, 109, 201n83, 232n161
on abrogation, 64, 73
and Ibn 'Arabi, 34, 60, 108
on People of the Book, 210n11
Ghazālī, Aḥmad, 205n125
Gobineau, Arthur de, 126, 191n75
Essay on the Inequality of the Human Races (Essai sur l'inégalité des races humaines), 127, 250n149
and Schuon, 134, 145, 239n16, 254n229
on three races, 250n149
Goldberg, David Theo, 179, 254n224
Goldenbaum, Ursula, 161–62
Goldziher, Ignaz, 24–25, 231n147, 232n159
Gospel, 145, 233n177
Ibn 'Arabi on, 9, 51, 103, 105, 115
Ibn Ḥazm on, 113, 233n177
Schuon on, 145, 252n202
See also scriptural corruption (*taḥrīf*)
Graham, James William, "A Treatise on Sufism," 177–78
Guattari, Félix, 180
Guénon, René
and Aguéli, Ivan, 117, 131, 247n109
on gnosis, 84
on Hinduism, 126, 131, 247n105
on Ibn 'Arabi, 28, 131, 247nn107–9
on Islam, 131
and the occult (French), 117, 126
on orthodoxy, 221n9
as Palingénius, 84, 220n4
and Perennialism, 5–6, 28, 85, 117, 124
on Protestantism, 92
and race, 243n52
and Schuon, 5, 85–87, 118, 124, 126, 139, 221n22, 247n106
as Sufi, 131
and Traditionalism, 84–85, 118, 183n5, 242n36, 243n53

hadith of theophany (*ḥadīth al-tajallī*), as narrated by Abu Saʿid al-Khudrī, 34–35, 48
al-Ḥallāj, Manṣūr, 43, 52
Hammer, Olav, 19–20
Ḥanbalīs, 41, 204n122, 249n134
Hanegraaff, Wouter, 176, 187n22, 237n3
Hegel, Georg W. F., 157, 224n59, 255n246
Herbert, Lord Edward, of Cherbury, 26, 198n54
Hick, John, 90–91
Hinduism
Aryanist interpretations of, 122, 125–26, 128–31, 246n87
Guénon and, 131, 243n53, 247n105
Kant on, 158
Schuon and, 118–19, 121, 125–26, 128–29, 132–33, 135–39, 149, 247n106, 255n236, 256n250
Vedanta, 119, 121–22, 126, 128, 130–32, 135, 138–39, 149, 245n70
Hitler, Adolf, 244n53

Hodgson, Marshall
  Ibn 'Arabi and the spiritual caliphate, 14
  and Islamic studies and Sufism, 58–61, 212nn29, 31
  universalist interpretation of Ibn 'Arabi, 58–61
Höppner, Karl, 251n173
Horsley, Richard, 196n18, 197n19, 209n197, 220n158
Houman, Setareh, 194n129
Hunter, Ian, 156, 181
Huxley, Aldous, 237n3

Ibn 'Arabi (Muḥyī al-Dīn Ibn al-ʿArabī)
  on abrogation (*naskh*), 9, 16, 21, 34, 57–58, 63, 66–83, 90, 102, 106–10, 115–16, 174, 180
    and influence of Ibn Ḥazm, 106–11
    universalist interpretation of, 57, 63–73, 77, 80–81, 88, 97–101
  absolutism of, 17, 19, 21, 26, 53, 97, 118–19, 121, 171, 175, 177
  and Ashʿarīs, 34
  on associationism (*shirk*), 55–56, 75, 114, 202n92, 210n11
  audience of (contemporaneous), 108
  and belief
    divinity of, 7–8, 27–28, 34, 54, 147
    as reflecting God, 25, 27, 30–31, 34, 43, 48, 54
    religion (universalist interpretations of), 8, 21, 25–32, 34, 48–51, 53–54, 81, 147–48
  biography of, 190n61, 209n2
    Muhammadan Station, 14, 37–38, 46, 52, 65, 78, 102, 112
    spiritual journey, 10–12, 14
  celebrated verses of (*see* poetry)
  cosmology of, 9–10, 231n155
    celestial spheres, 78, 115
    heliocentric, 78–79, 97, 227n96
    hierarchical, 14–17, 53, 97, 115, 118, 140–41, 149
    Muhammad as central, 21, 26, 40, 54, 70, 77–79, 97
    Muhammadan Reality, 15–16, 40–41, 46
    pluralist interpretation of, 97–98, 115, 140–41
    and politics, 82
    seven heavens, 70–71, 78–79, 111, 115
  on divine attributes, 8–9, 41, 44, 54
  on the hadith of theophany (*ḥadīth al-tajallī*), 34–35, 43
  on Hell (as eventually blissful), 6–7, 9, 200n76
  and Ibn Ḥazm, 21, 106–11, 113, 116–17, 210n8, 230nn145–46, 232n159
  interpretations
    absolutist, 118, 121
    contemporary, 20, 117, 206n147
    esoteric, 118, 121, 132, 147–48, 174, 179
    Euro-American, 11–13, 17, 36, 97
    modern, 4
    non-hierarchical, 149
    non-supersessionist, 90
    post-9/11/2001, 68, 80, 87, 121, 222n31
    racist/racialist, 19, 22, 121–22, 143, 147, 149–50
    Schuonian Perennialist, 1, 5–6, 17–19, 28, 36–38, 49–50, 53, 86–87, 90, 97–99, 120–23, 149, 177, 179, 222n31
    Traditionalist, 131
    universalist, xi, xiv, 1–2, 8, 13, 15, 20–21, 24–26, 29–32, 46, 53, 56, 63, 65–68, 70, 73, 80–81, 89, 96, 98–100, 105, 115–16, 121, 140

Ibn ʿArabi (Muḥyī al-Dīn Ibn al-ʿArabī) (*cont.*)
interpreted by
Addas, Claude, 12, 56, 62
Affifi, Abdul Ela, 28, 31, 34, 40–41, 211n18
Aguéli, Ivan, 117–18, 131, 247n109, 252n198
Austin, R. W. J., 56
Chittick, William, xiv–xv, 8–9, 42–43, 45–47, 56–57, 65–73, 80, 89, 97–99, 101, 104–5, 111, 171, 175, 198n49, 212n20
Chodkiewicz, Michel, xiv–xv, 16, 78, 107, 218n125
Corbin, Henry, 11, 29
Dagli, Caner, 80–81, 141, 249n133
Geoffroy, Éric, 28
Goldziher, Ignaz, 24–25
Guénon, René, 28, 131, 247nn107–9
Hodgson, Marshall G. S., 14, 58–61
Izutsu, Toshihiko, 29–31, 34, 37, 49–50
al-Jazāʾirī, ʿAbd al-Qādir, 117
al-Jīlī, ʿAbd al-Karīm, 117
Keller, Carl-A., 57
Keller, Nuh Ha Mim, 68–70
Khalil, Mohammad, 6–8
Landau, Rom, 211n18
Lings, Martin, 131, 196n8
Lowney, Chris, 25
Morris, James, 106, 112, 204n112
Nasr, Seyyed Hossein, 6, 87, 90–92, 98, 119
Nicholson, Reynold A., 24–25, 27–28, 42–46, 49, 117
al-Qāshānī, ʿAbd al-Razzāq, 206n147
Rahman, Fazlur, 211n18
Rauf, Bulent, 1
Scattolin, Giuseppe, 57
Schimmel, Annemarie, 25, 31, 46, 51
Schuon, Frithjof, 1, 4–5, 19, 50, 86–88, 118–19, 121–22, 131–33, 138, 140, 142–43, 147–50, 171, 177, 211n18, 252n202
Schwartz, Stephen, 11–12
Sells, Michael, 25–26, 34, 36, 46–47
Shah-Kazemi, Reza, 6, 36–39, 50, 63–64, 80–81, 89, 98–104, 113, 116, 121, 172–75, 222n31, 265n153
Smith, Wilfred Cantwell, 13
Stoddart, William, 5
Zargar, Cyrus Ali, 41, 204n125, 208n178
The Interpreter of Desires (*Tarjumān al-ashwāq*), 21, 33, 38, 41, 51–52
heart as metaphor, 26, 47–48
and love, 20, 42, 200n78
religious universalism (interpreted as), 5–6, 24–26, 36, 48–49, 86, 89
on Jesus, 36–37, 74–75, 77, 82, 202n91, 207n156
on jihad, 108
and journey trope from Occident to Orient, 11–12
on Judaism, 8–9, 21, 43–44, 73, 109–10, 112, 115–16
Kaykāʾus I, ʿIzz al-Dīn, 10, 55–58, 82
on law (sharia), 9, 48, 55–56, 76, 81, 102, 105, 179
abrogation (*naskh*), 16, 34, 71, 74, 82, 101, 106–7, 111
relative (interpreted as), 100
and Ẓāhirīs, 106–7, 231nn147–48, 232nn156, 159
letter to Seljuk sultan of Anatolia (*see* Kaykāʾus I, ʿIzz al-Dīn)
and love
"religion of love" (*dīn al-ḥubb*), 5–6, 41–42, 44–47, 53, 86–87, 90

universalist interpretation of, 90, 92, 138
The Meccan Openings (*al-Futūḥāt al-makkiyya*), 10, 15–16, 27, 33, 35, 41, 43, 47, 54, 56, 58, 66–67, 69–72, 74, 76–77, 79–80, 82, 97–98, 101, 105–6, 108–9, 111–12, 114, 142
"attainment passage," 37–40, 44, 46, 102
metaphysics, 9, 39–41
hierarchical, 14, 53
political, 58, 62–63, 82–83, 89, 97
universal (interpreted as), xi–xii, 4, 6–7, 13, 66, 82
and Muhammad, 50, 78, 111, 117
as comprehensive, 38–41, 44–47, 53–54, 69, 79, 102, 105–6
as cosmic (solar) king, 58, 71, 77, 79, 82, 115, 140–41
as given "the comprehensive words" (*jawāmiʿ al-kalim*), 39–40, 44, 142
as God's beloved, 21, 26, 45, 53
as lawgiver, 15, 34, 71–72, 76–77, 80, 106
as *Logos*, 40–42, 46–47, 54, 80, 82, 138, 142
and Muhammadan Reality (*ḥaqīqa muḥammadiyya*), 15, 40–41, 76, 79, 102, 149, 175
as "Perfect Human Being" (*al-insān al-kāmil*), 15, 40–41, 44, 46, 53
as prophet "when Adam was between water and clay," 15, 40, 47, 71, 76, 79, 105, 142, 193n101
as "Seal of the Prophets" (*khātam al-nabiyyīn*), 40, 46–47, 52, 116, 142
supersessionary significance of, 6, 39, 42, 46, 74–75, 81–82, 106, 142, 174–75
and Muʿtazilīs, 34
and Niẓām, 42, 205n129
and People of the Book (*ahl al-kitāb*), 8, 35, 58, 236n208
and associationism (*shirk*), 55–56, 75, 114, 202n92, 210n11
and humiliation, 9, 72–73, 77, 82, 101, 115
and indemnity tax (*jizya*), 9, 21, 72–73, 75–77, 82, 101, 114–15, 174
as Protected People (*ahl al-dhimma*), 11, 22, 55–57, 73, 82
qualified subjugation of, 56, 74, 76–77, 101, 114, 116
and scriptural corruption (*taḥrīf*), 9, 16, 21, 68, 104–6, 110–13, 115–17, 174
poetry (see *The Interpreter of Desires* [*Tarjumān al-ashwāq*])
political theology of, 13, 19, 62, 80
coercion and religion, 96, 116
religious freedom (interpreted as advocating), 65
and the Qur'an
as abrogating other scripture, 102–3, 105–11, 115, 171, 174
literal readings of, 106–7, 141
as Muhammad, 41, 44
"station of," 44
verse3:84 (interpretation of), 37–39, 44, 102
verse9:29 (interpretation of), 9, 16, 73, 82, 101, 115, 174, 209n3
verse9:30 (interpretation of), 35, 201n86, 234n189
on rational discourse as hazardous, 34
on religion (*dīn*), 71
as law, 34, 71, 81
as "obedience," 32–34, 116, 174
Revelations in Mosul (*al-Tanazzulāt al-mawṣiliyya*), 51–53

Ibn ʿArabi (Muḥyī al-Dīn Ibn al-ʿArabī) (*cont.*)
- *The Ring Stones of Wisdom / The Bezels of Wisdom* (*Fuṣūṣ al-ḥikam*), 11, 27–28, 30–33, 36, 40–41, 46–49, 52, 56, 78, 105, 131, 141–43, 147
- as "Seal of the Saints" (*khātam al-awliyāʾ*), 10, 14–15, 46, 50, 52, 78, 149, 207n156
- on salvation, 174
  - and punishment
  - through submission to prescribed law, 32, 82, 108, 114, 116
  - universally available (interpreted as), 5, 8–9, 174
- as "Semitic" (*see* Aryanism)
- *The Spirit of Holiness in the Counseling of the Soul* (*Rūḥ al-quds fī munāsaḥat al-nafs*), 10
- Sufism, as representative of, 131
- on supersession of Islam, 5, 9, 21, 58, 66, 69, 71, 76, 80, 97, 102, 107, 171, 174, 180
- theomonism of, 6, 30–33, 50, 52–53, 97
- *The Treasury of Lovers: A Commentary on the Interpreter of Desires* (*Dhakhāʾir al-aʿlāq: sharḥ tarjumān al-ashwāq*), 42–47
- on the Trinity, 36

Ibn ʿAṭāʾ Allāh, 249n131

Ibn Barrajān, 65, 110

Ibn Barthamlā, 74–75, 106, 218n125

Ibn Ḥazm, 233n172, 235n192
- and Ibn ʿArabi, 21, 106–11, 113, 116–17, 210n8, 230nn145–46, 232n159

idealism
- German, 22, 152
- Ibn ʿArabi (interpreted as idealist), 28
- Kantian, 91, 152, 154, 165, 170, 180, 259n38
- Platonic, 130, 152, 164, 259n38
  - and race, 179–80, 244n56
  - Schuonian, 179

Idrīs, 78

al-Idrīsī, Muḥammad, 13

ʿIllaysh, ʿAbd al-Raḥmān, 117, 131

imperialism
- European, 2, 22, 152–53, 155, 179, 181
- Islamic, 1, 4, 14
- and race, 153, 179, 258n25
- and religion, 96
- and universalism, 3, 155, 179, 181

indemnity tax (*jizya*). *See* People of the Book

Isrāʾīliyyāt literature, 109

Izutsu, Toshihiko
- on belief and religion in Ibn ʿArabi, 34, 49–50
- as translator of Ibn ʿArabi, 31, 49–50
- universalist interpretation of Ibn ʿArabi, 29–31, 34, 37

Jackson, Sherman, 17

Jantzen, Grace, 12–13, 17, 152

al-Jazāʾirī, ʿAbd al-Qādir, 117, 131, 236n208

Jesus
- Aryanist interpretation of, 130–31, 170
- Ibn ʿArabi's interpretation of, 36–37, 74–75, 77, 82, 202n91, 207n156
- Kantian interpretation of, 158–61, 165, 170
- Schuon's interpretation of, 129–31, 150, 169–70, 252n202
- Sufism (interpreted as Christian), 12

al-Jīlī, ʿAbd al-Karīm
- *al-Insān al-kāmil*, 117
- on scriptural corruption (*taḥrīf*), 117

Johnson, Mark, 152

Joseph II of Austria, 161

Judaism, 64, 161
- anti-Judaism, 11, 165, 180
- and Aryanism, 130, 134

and early Qur'an commentary, 65, 109
and Enlightenment, 161–62
European, 180
Ibn ʿArabi on, 8–9, 21, 43–44, 73, 109–10, 112, 115–16
and Kant, 153, 157–66, 169–70, 180
"legalism," 11, 191n75
and Mālikīs, 107–9
and Schuon, 19, 130–31, 166
superseded by Christianity, 180
superseded by Islam, 16, 35, 64–65, 73, 107
See also indemnity tax (*jizya*); Protected People (*ahl al-dhimma*); People of the Book (*ahl al-kitāb*); Torah
Judea, 130–31

Kant, Immanuel
and Aryanism, 170, 264n143
autonomy of religious subjectivity, 152, 154–56, 163, 169, 177–78
and Cartesian dualism, 155, 258n28
and Christianity, 156–62, 165, 180
The Conflict of the Faculties, 165
Copernican turn of, 157
Critique of Practical Reason, 162–63
on Enlightenment, 162
heteronomy and autonomy, 18, 101, 152, 154, 162–63, 165–66, 170–71, 176, 179–80
idealism, 22, 91, 154, 170, 179
and imperialism, 178–80
on Judaism, 153, 157–66, 169–70, 180
metaphysics, 152, 154, 156, 163–65, 177, 256n6
morality, 157, 162–63, 167
"noumenal" and "phenomenal," 152, 156–57, 256n6
and nudity (metaphorics and metaphysics of), 160, 164–65, 169, 178, 260n71
and Paul's Epistles, 160–62, 169
To Perpetual Peace, 167
and Pietism, 256n6
post-Kantian thought, 18, 178
and race, 180–81, 267n201
on rationality of religion, 152, 156–57, 159, 169, 173, 180
on relativity of religious form, 167–68, 170, 180
Religion within the Bounds of Bare Reason, 156–57, 159, 162–66, 168, 177
and Schuon, 152–55, 166–70, 176–81
and universalism, 18, 152, 157, 166, 168, 180
Kantorowicz, Ernst, 82
Kaykāʾus I, ʿIzz al-Dīn (Seljuk sultan of Anatolia), 10, 55–58, 75, 82, 108, 116, 212n20
Keller, Nuh Ha Mim, 68–70, 72, 216n95
Khalil, Mohammad Hassan
on Ibn ʿArabi, 6–8
universalism/damnationism binary, 6–7
Khiḍr, 74
Kidd, Colin, 144
King, Richard, 185n4
Kirmānī, Awḥad al-Dīn, 204n125
Korzybski, Alfred, xii–xiii, 2
Koslow, Mark (and Schuon scandal), 240n27

Laclau, Ernesto, xiii–xiv
Lakoff, George, 152
Landau, Rom, 211n18
Lassen, Christian, 126, 128, 134, 249n146
Laude, Patrick, 19, 94–95, 237n4
Leibniz, 237n3
Levinas, Emmanuel, 3, 179
Lewisohn, Leonard, 29
Lindbeck, George, 94

Lings, Martin, 131, 196n8, 221n9
as disciple of Schuon, 203n95
Lowney, Chris, *A Vanished World: Muslims, Christians, and Jews in Medieval Spain*, 25

Malamud, Margaret, 14
Mālikīs, 107–8. *See also* Ẓāhirīs
al-Manṣūr, Abū Yūsuf Yaʿqūb (Almohad caliph), 107
maps. *See* cartography
Mariña, Jacqueline, 95
Mary (Virgin), 117. *See also* Schuon, Frithjof
Masuzawa, Tomoko, 4
McAuliffe, Jane, 103
McCutcheon, Russell, 123–24, 150, 179, 267n202
Mendelssohn, Moses, *Jerusalem*, 161
Mignolo, Walter, 2, 4, 17–18, 153–55
misreading. *See* Bloom, Harold
modernity (Western), 3, 13, 20, 61, 91, 147, 149, 258n25
Morris, James, 4, 87–88, 106, 112, 203n104, 204n112
Moses
Ibn ʿArabi on, 15, 43, 46, 74, 112
Mosse, George, 127, 244n56, 251n173
Mostaganem (Algeria), 140, 187n28, 238n5
Mouffe, Chantal, 63
Muhammad (Prophet), 70
Ibn ʿArabi's interpretation of
as comprehensive, 38–41, 44–47, 53–54, 69, 79, 102, 105–6
as cosmic (solar) king, 58, 71, 77, 79, 82, 115, 140–41
as given "the comprehensive words" (*jawāmiʿ al-kalim*), 39–40, 44, 142
as God's beloved, 21, 26, 45, 53
as lawgiver, 15, 34, 71–72, 76–77, 80, 106
as *Logos*, 40–42, 46–47, 54, 80, 82, 138, 142
as "Perfect Human Being" (*al-insān al-kāmil*), 15, 40–41, 44, 46, 53
as prophet "when Adam was between water and clay," 15, 40, 47, 71, 76, 79, 105, 142
as Seal of the Prophets (*khātam al-nabiyyīn*), 15, 40, 46–47, 52, 116, 118, 142
Muhammadan Reality (*ḥaqīqa muḥammadiyya*), 15, 40–41, 76, 79, 102, 149, 175
Muhammadan Station, 14, 37–38, 65, 203n104
Schuon's interpretation of, 129–30, 140–41, 146, 150, 170
supersessionary significance of, 6, 39, 42, 46, 74–75, 81–82, 106, 142, 174–75
Muir, William, 209n8
Müller, Max
as Aryanist, 243n53
on henotheism, 146, 255n236
mysticism
as "authentic" religiosity, 11, 56, 58–62
Christian, 12, 17
depoliticized, 9, 13, 53, 58, 60
exclusionary, 17
as inclusive, 6, 25, 213n33
individual, 13, 17, 60–62
political, 13, 17–18, 54, 60–63, 82, 177, 181
and race, 122, 125, 128, 244n56
universalist understanding of, 5, 53, 58, 91, 140, 172, 177, 181, 256n6
See also esoteric and esotericism; Sufism; universalism

al-Nābigha al-Dhubyānī, 72–73, 76–79, 81–82, 217n109
al-Nābulusī, ʿAbd al- Ghanī, 235n196
Nasr, Seyyed Hossein
The Essential Writings of the Frithjof Schuon (introduction), xii–xiii, 98
on gnostic journey from Occident to Orient, 11
"Islam and the Encounter of Religions," 6, 89–90
Perennialist interpretation of Ibn 'Arabi, 6, 87, 90–92, 98, 119
and Schuon, 4, 50, 86–91, 93–94, 98, 123, 184n6, 222n25, 240n24
and study of religion, xii–xiii, 90, 240n23
Three Muslim Sages, 87
Neoplatonism. *See* Plato
Newby, Gordon, 109, 201n86
Nicholson, Hugh, 9, 63, 149–50, 171, 181, 194n122
Nicholson, Reynold A., 205nn131–32
interpretation of Ibn 'Arabi, 24–25, 27–28, 42–46, 49, 117
The Mystics of Islam, 25
religion as belief, 27–28
al-Niffarī, 248n131
Nongbri, Brent, 199n63, 200n79
nudity (metaphorics and metaphysics of), 41, 137, 145, 149, 160, 163–66, 169, 178, 260n71
Nyberg, H. S., 117, 236n210

Olender, Maurice, 129–30, 241n33
Orientalism, 11, 40–42, 59, 85, 126, 128, 178, 185n3, 191n75, 211n18, 213n33, 243n52. *See also* Corbin Henry; Goldziher, Ignaz; Nicholson, Reynold A.

Pacini, David, 154, 178
Pact/Stipulations of 'Umar, 55–57, 82, 209n8, 211n12
Palacios, Miguel Asín, 57, 116–17
Palingénius. *See* Guénon, René
Paul (apostle)
Epistle to the Colossians, 164
Epistle to the Galatians, 160–62, 169
First Epistle to the Corinthians, 160–61
and Kant, 160–61, 169
People of the Book (*ahl al-kitāb*), 35
and associationism (*shirk*), 55–56, 75, 114, 202n92, 210n11
humiliation, 9, 72–73, 77, 82, 101, 115
Ibn Ḥazm on, 21, 106–11, 113, 116–17, 210n8, 230nn145–46, 232n163, 233n172, 235n192
indemnity tax (*jizya*), 9, 16, 21, 72–73, 75–77, 82, 101, 114–15, 174
qualified subjugation of, 56, 74, 76– 77, 101, 114, 116
See also: Christianity; Ibn 'Arabi; indemnity tax (*jizya*); Judaism; Protected People (*ahl al-dhimma*); scriptural corruption (*taḥrīf*)
Perennialism, xiv
as essentialist, 21, 90, 92, 95, 148, 150, 170
as Eurocentric, 18–19, 178
and German idealism, 22, 166
and gnosis, xiv, 5, 91, 94–95, 101, 115, 225n61
as hegemonic, 4, 19–20, 123, 150
and Ibn 'Arabi, 1, 5–8, 15, 17–19, 28, 36–38, 49–50, 53, 86–87, 90, 97–99, 115, 120–23, 149, 177, 179, 222n31
and *philosophia perennis*, xiin 5, 120, 237n3

Perennialism (*cont.*)
and politics, 53, 123
and race/racialism, 22, 122–24, 128, 178
and relativity of religions, 99, 115
and religious studies, 90
and Sufism, 90
and universal validity, 88–91, 98–100, 115
See also Aguéli, Ivan; Aristotelian law of noncontradiction; Coomaraswamy, Ananda K.; essentialism; Guénon, René; Ibn 'Arabi; Laude, Patrick; Lings, Martin; Nasr, Seyyed Hossein; Schuon, Frithjof; Shah-Kazemi, Reza; universalism
Perniola, Mario, 164
Philolaus of Croton, 227n96
Plato
Aryanist interpretation of, 122, 130, 133
Christian Platonism, 156, 164, 256n6
idealism, 130, 164
interpreted by Schuon, 132–34, 152, 166
Neoplatonism, 91, 224n59, 256n6
and nudity (metaphorics and metaphysics of), 164
Platonic intellect, 185n23
poetry, 25, 29, 42, 73, 217n109
Ibn 'Arabi's "celebrated verses" (in *The Interpreter of Desires*), 6, 21, 24–26, 36–38, 42, 47, 51, 53, 86, 89, 205n132
Persian tradition of "infidelity" (*kufriyyāt*), 43
See also Rūmī, Jalāl al-Dīn
politics and the political
as metaphysical, 13, 17–18, 54, 58, 60–63, 82–83, 89, 97, 177, 181
"of nostalgia," 194n123
universalism and, 4, 13, 53, 123, 179
polytheism, 16, 29, 56, 255n236
post-Orientalism. *See* Orientalism
Protected People (*ahl al-dhimma*), 11, 22, 55–56, 58, 73, 77, 82, 209n3. *See also:* Ibn 'Arabi; indemnity tax (*jizya*); People of the Book (*ahl al-kitāb*); Christianity; Judaism
Ptolemy, 13, 84, 154, 227n96

al-Qāshānī, ʿAbd al-Razzāq, 200n78, 206n147, 252n202
Qūnawī, Naṣīr al-Dīn, 66–67
Qūnāwī, Ṣadr al-Dīn, 66–67, 204n125, 209n2, 215n84

race and racialism, 22
and imperialism, 153, 179, 258n25
and Judaism, 11, 130, 134, 165, 180
Kant on, 180–81, 267n201
and philology (nineteenth-century European), 126–28
racial historicism, 179–80, 266n189
racial spirituality/metaphysics, 121–22, 125–28, 143–44, 149–50, 253n219
Schuon and, 19, 22, 119, 121, 125–29, 134, 143–44, 147, 180–81, 241n34, 254n229
as universalist, 20, 122, 180–81
See also Aryanism; Chamberlain, Houston Stewart; Gobineau, Joseph Arthur de; Orientalism
Rauf, Bulent, 1
al-Rāzī, Fakhr al-Dīn, 210n11, 228n97
relativity (among religions). *See* universalism
religion, 1, 178
and power, 26, 61, 96, 196n18, 209n197
privatization of, 12–13, 26, 60–62, 92
sui generis ("as such," nonreductive), xii, 92, 95, 119, 154, 173, 175, 181, 220n158

as "a set of beliefs," 21, 25–27, 31–32, 49–50, 147–48
as universalizing, xiii, 2–3, 14, 175, 186n9
religious studies
conflation of religion with deity, 148–49
European, 10, 61–62
and Islam, 61
and maps, xii, 184n12
and Perennialism, xiv, 89–90, 122, 149
and politics, 12–13, 18, 62, 196n18
"religion," 1, 31, 92
as situated, 62
and Sufism, 59–61, 177–78
and universalism, 2, 4
Renan, Ernest, 126–31, 134
Romanticism, German, 85, 126, 128
and Kant, 152, 256n6
and Schuon, 85, 251n173
See also Schlegel, Friedrich
Rūmī, Jalāl al-Dīn, 11, 27, 87, 191n73

Safi, Omid, 62
Sanskrit, 126–27
Satan, 111–12, 234n187
Schelling, Friedrich, 226n80, 255n236
Schimmel, Annemarie, 25, 31, 46, 51
Schlegel, Friedrich, 126–28, 244n55
Schleiermacher, Friedrich
experiential-expressivism, 102
"historical religions," 92–93
intuition and feeling, 95, 152, 224n57, 225n61, 226n79
On Religion, 92, 95
and Schuonian Perennialism, 21, 92–96, 151–52, 224n59
symbolic relativity, 95–96
"true religion," 93, 255n246
Schmitt, Carl, 12, 63
"School of Passionate Love" (*madhhab-i ʿishq*), 41
Schuon, Frithjof
as absolutist, 119, 148, 150, 154, 180
and Aguéli, Ivan, 117, 252n198
and Aryanist discourse, 19, 22, 121–24, 126–30, 132–37, 143, 145, 149–50, 166, 169–70, 179, 181
on Ashʿarism, 132–33
biography, 85, 121, 124–25, 139–40, 187n28, 238n5, 240n27, 241n34, 244n56
Castes and Races, 125, 127–28, 134, 143–44, 169, 241n34, 264n138
and Christianity, 85, 130, 139–40
Copernican turn of, 154–55
cosmology, 98, 100, 128, 154
and Cutsinger, James, xiv, 121–23, 125
essentialism of, 137, 148, 150, 167, 170, 175, 179, 181, 242n40
on esotericism/"esoterism," 19, 90, 118, 121–22, 126, 131–39, 145, 147–49, 172, 179–80
and ethics, 123, 240n30
Eurocentrism, 4, 121, 178–80
Form and Substance in the Religions (Forme et substance dans les religions), 138
on gnosis (intuitive knowledge), xiv, 5, 91, 94–95, 101, 115, 123, 131, 133, 169, 225n61, 256n6
Gnosis: Divine Wisdom, 98, 143–46
and Guénon, René, 85–86, 131, 139
and henotheism, 146, 148, 255n236
on Hinduism, 118–19, 121, 125–26, 128–29, 132–33, 135–39, 149, 246n87, 247n106, 255n236, 256n250
as "human instrument for the manifestation of the *Religio perennis*," 136, 147, 150
on Ibn ʿArabi (de-Semitization of), 19, 50, 86–88, 118–19, 121–22, 131–33, 138, 140, 142–43, 147–50, 171, 177, 252n202

Schuon, Frithjof (*cont.*)
and abrogation, 97, 100
Schuon compared to Ibn 'Arabi, 120–21, 237n4
and idealism (German), 22, 179
influence of, 18, 81, 88–89, 121–23
on the Intellect, 123–26, 134, 169, 177
on Jesus, 129–31, 150, 169–70
and Kant, 152–55, 166–70, 176–81
Logic and Transcendence, 146
and Mary (Virgin), 139
ʿAlāwiyya Maryamiyya Sufi order, 85–86, 136, 187n28
as Aryanized/de-Semitized, 136
nudity as spiritual metaphor, 137, 145, 149
superiority of, 146–48, 150, 180
as supreme/universal *Shakti*, 136–38, 146, 149
as "virginal Mother of all the Prophets," 146
and metaphysics, 85, 88, 120, 124–26, 132–33, 139, 145, 149–50, 152, 154, 163
and Muhammad, 129–30, 140–41, 146, 150, 170
Muslim name (ʿĪsa Nūr al-Dīn Aḥmad al-Shādhilī al-ʿAlawī), 125, 187n28, 221n16
and Nasr, Seyyed Hossein, 4, 86–89, 93, 98, 123
and Nazism/Fascism, 130, 241n34
and noncontradiction (Aristotelian), 100
on nudity (metaphorics and metaphysics of), 137, 145, 149, 166, 169
and objectivity, 134, 149
and Orientalism, 126
as "paracletic spokesman of the *sophia perennis*," 139
and Perennialism, 4–5, 19–20, 85, 88, 183–84nn5–6
and Platonism, 133, 166
and pluralism, 85, 93–94, 98, 118, 154
principle of relativity, 86, 93–94, 96, 100, 125, 132, 135, 140–41, 148–49, 167–68, 170–72, 175, 177, 180
as prophet, 122–23, 147
prophetology (non-hierarchical), 140–41, 146
on Protestantism, 92
and racialism/racism, 19, 22, 119, 121–22, 125–29, 134, 144, 147, 180–81, 241n34, 254n229
on *religio formalis*/*religio perennis* binary, 135, 149, 166, 176
on the *religio perennis*, 2, 50, 92, 98, 124, 131, 136, 147–48, 150, 152, 173, 175, 180
and religious studies, 4, 90, 122, 148
and romanticism, 85, 251n173
and Schleiermacher, 92–96, 224n59
and Shah-Kazemi, Reza, 39, 89–90, 98–101, 104, 121, 172–77
on *sophia perennis*, 94, 124, 128, 138–39
as Sufi shaykh, 5, 85, 120, 125
on Sufism, 132–35
Sufism: Veil and Quintessence (Le Soufisme: voile et quintessence), 125, 132, 134, 147
"The Ternary Aspect of the Monotheistic Tradition" ("L'aspect ternaire de la tradition monothéiste" in *Le voile d'Isis*), 140
The Transcendent Unity of Religions (*De l'Unité transcendante des Religions*), 5, 86, 120, 124–25, 140
truth, absolute, 118, 124–25, 132, 138
truth, relative, 128

"Two Esotericisms," 132
on transcendent unity of religions, 8, 18, 28, 54, 85, 86, 88, 90, 92, 98, 104, 115–16, 118, 124–25, 140, 145, 148–49, 154, 167, 187n22
Understanding Islam (*Comprendre l'Islam*), 86
See also: Ibn 'Arabi; Perennialism; universalism
Schwartz, Stephen, 11–12
scriptural corruption (*taḥrīf*), 101, 103–5, 112–13, 115–17
corruption of the meaning (*taḥrīf al-ma'ānī*), 104–5, 110–11
corruption of the text (*taḥrīf al-naṣṣ*), 9, 104–5, 111, 117
secular-liberal tradition, 163, 171
Sedgwick, Mark, 117, 131, 139, 223n32
Sells, Michael, 45, 207n165
universalist interpretation of Ibn 'Arabi, 25–26, 34, 36, 46–47
Semler, Johann Salomo, 161–62
Seville, 10, 21, 65, 107, 110. *See also*: Ibn Ḥazm
Shādhiliyya-ʿAlāwiyya Sufi order, 117, 125, 131, 187n28
ʿAlāwiyya Maryamiyya Sufi order, 85, 136, 187n28, 243n47
Shah-Kazemi, Reza
on abrogation (*naskh*) in Ibn 'Arabi, 63–64, 80–81, 98–101
discourse of relativity, 99–101, 172–73, 175–77
and essentialism, 173, 175
The Other in the Light of the One: The Universality of the Qur'ān and Interfaith Dialogue, 172–73
Paths to Transcendence: According to Shankara, Ibn Arabi, and Meister Eckhart, 6, 36, 38, 50, 171
and Schuon/Schuonian interpretive field, 6, 39, 50, 89–90, 98–101, 104, 121, 171–77, 188nn37–38, 202n95, 265n153
on scriptural corruption (*taḥrīf*), 103–4, 113
The Spirit of Tolerance in Islam, 37
universalist interpretation of Ibn 'Arabi, 6, 36–39, 50, 89, 102, 116, 121, 172–75, 222n31, 265n153
al-Shahrastānī, Muḥammad ibn ʿAbd al-Karīm, *The Furthest Limits in the Knowledge of Theology (Nihāyat al-aqdām fi 'ilm al-kalām)*, 64–65, 76
sharia. *See* Ibn 'Arabi
Shell, Susan Meld, 163, 166, 258n28
Smith, Huston, 89, 105, 114, 122
Smith, Jonathan Z., "Map Is Not Territory," xii
Smith, Wilfred Cantwell, 13, 26, 61, 92, 149
Steuco, Agostino, *De perenni philosophia*, 184n5, 237n3
Stoddart, William, 5, 239n16
Stoicism, 133, 256n6
Sufism, 51
European interpretations of, 1, 11–13, 18–19, 24–25, 177–78
European order of, 5, 120
as mysticism, 4, 18–19, 59, 90, 227n91, 265n153
Perennialist interpretations of, 6, 18–19, 90, 118
and politics, 13, 14, 60–62
proto-Sufis, 109
racist interpretations of, 19, 118–19, 125, 178
and transcendence, 97
universalist interpretations of, 24, 67, 90, 132–33, 177

Sufism (*cont.*)
See also: Ibn 'Arabi; Schuon, Frithjof; Shādhiliyya-ʿAlāwiyya Sufi order
Suhrawardī, Shahābuddīn Yaḥyā, 60, 191n73
supersession of Islam, 3, 5, 9, 14, 64–65, 71, 76, 117. *See also* abrogation; Ibn 'Arabi; scriptural corruption

taḥrīf. *See* scriptural corruption
Talmud, 125
Taoism, 118
Taylor, Mark, 20
Teresa of Ávila, 17
theomonism. *See under* Ibn 'Arabi
theophany, 10, 29, 35, 51–52, 100, 184n9, 191n73
hadith of (*ḥadīth al-tajallī*), 48
Theosophical Society, 126, 243n53
Tillich, Paul, 29
Torah, 9, 43, 51, 64, 87, 105, 110–13, 115, 233n177, 252n202
according to al-Ṭabarī, 113, 234n189
See also Judaism; scriptural corruption (*taḥrīf*)
Traditionalism, 85–88, 126, 131. *See also* Guénon, René

ulama (as inheritors of the prophets), 11, 105–6, 117
ʿUmar ibn al-Khaṭṭāb (second caliph), 55, 74. *See also* Pact/Stipulations of 'Umar
"Unity of Being" (*waḥdat al-wujūd*), 4–5, 120, 133
universalism
and cartography, xiii–xiv, 12, 154–55
double bind of, xiii–xiv, 2–3, 20
essentialist, 102
exclusivist, xiii, 3, 16, 20, 153, 171–72, 176–78
hegemonic, 3, 22, 176
ideological, 149, 181
imperialist, 154–55, 179
and Kant, 18, 152, 157, 162, 166, 168, 180
and mysticism, 58
as particular, situated, xiv, 1, 12, 155, 177–81
and pluralism, 2–3, 7, 65, 99
and politics, 4, 13, 53, 179
and race, 20, 122, 178–80
and Schuon, Frithjof, 120–22, 125
and supersessionism, 23, 153
as transhistorical, 178–79
as universalizing religions, xiii–xiv, 2–3, 14
See also Affifi, Abdul Ela; Chittick, William; Corbin, Henry; Ibn 'Arabi; Izutsu, Toshihiko; Kant, Immanuel; Khalil, Mohammad; Perennialism; Schleiermacher, Friedrich; Schuon, Frithjof; Sells, Michael; Shah-Kazemi, Reza; Smith, Huston; Traditionalism
Upanishads, 125, 245n70, 249n131. *See also* Vedanta
Urban, Hugh, 240nn27, 30, 241n34

Vedanta
Advaita Vedānta, 119, 121, 128, 245n70
Anquetil-Duperron, 245n70
Schuon (Aryanist interpretation of), 119, 121–22, 126, 128, 130–32, 138–39, 149, 247n106, 256n250
See also *Upanishads*

Waardenburg, Jacques, 16, 116, 214n69
Wasserstrom, Steven, xii, 224n57
Weismann, Itzchak, 106, 236n208
"Western" and "the West," 187n24, 221n18, 223n32, 257n12

Eurocentric, 3, 12, 59, 151, 154–55, 178–79, 181, 212n31
and Ibn 'Arabi, 4–6, 23–24, 26, 57–58, 120, 177, 181
Islamic West, 10–12
on religion, 13–14, 17, 31–32, 59–62, 81, 83, 85, 91, 95, 102, 138, 149, 181, 196n18, 197n19, 199n63
White, Hayden, 11
Winkel, Eric, 212n27
Winter, Tim, 36, 202n91
witness play (*shāhid bāzī*), 41, 204n125
Wittgenstein, Ludwig, xi
Wright, Peter, xii, 184nn9, 11

Young, Robert, 179, 181, 186n15, 257n12
Yousef, Mohamed Haj, 227n96

Ẓāhirīs, 106–7, 231nn147–48, 232nn156, 159. *See also* Ibn Ḥazm
Zargar, Cyrus Ali, *Sufi Aesthetics*, 41, 204n125, 208n178
Žižek, Slavoj, 154–55